S0-DFJ-853

Analyzing E-Commerce
& Internet Law

ISBN 0-13-085898-6

9 780130 858986

90000

THE ADVANCED WEBSITE ARCHITECTURE SERIES

DESIGNING WEB INTERFACES
Michael Rees
Andrew White
Bebo White

SUPPORTING WEB SERVERS
Benay Dara-Abrams
Drew Dara-Abrams
Trevor Peace
Bebo White

ANALYZING E-COMMERCE & INTERNET LAW
J. Dianne Brinson
Benay Dara-Abrams
Drew Dara-Abrams
Jennifer Masek
Ruth McDunn
Bebo White

Analyzing E-Commerce & Internet Law

J. Dianne Brinson

Benay Dara-Abrams

Drew Dara-Abrams

Jennifer Masek

Ruth McDunn

Bebo White

Prentice Hall PTR
Upper Saddle River, NJ 07458
www.phptr.com

Library of Congress Cataloging-in-Publication Data

Analyzing e-commerce & internet law / J. Dianne Brinson ... [et al.].—1st ed.
   p. cm.—(Advanced website architecture series)
  Includes index.
  ISBN 0-13-085898-6
   1. Computer systems—Law and legislation—United States. 2. Internet—Law and
legislation—United States. 3. Internet. 4. Electronic commerce. I. Brinson, J. Dianne.
II. Series.
  KF390.5.C6 A95 2001
  343.7309'944—dc21
                                        00-069901

Editorial/production supervision: *Jessica Balch (Pine Tree Composition)*
Project coordination: *Anne Trowbridge*
Acquisitions editor: *Karen McLean*
Editorial assistant: *Richard Winkler*
Manufacturing manager: *Alexis R. Heydt*
Marketing manager: *Kate Hargett*
Cover design director: *Jerry Votta*
Interior designer: *Meryl Poweski*

© 2001 Prentice Hall PTR; © 2001 J. Dianne Brinson (ch 13–20)
Prentice-Hall, Inc.
Upper Saddle River, NJ 07458

Prentice Hall books are widely used by corporations and government agencies for
training, marketing, and resale.

The publisher offers discounts on this book when ordered in bulk quantities.
For more information, contact: Corporate Sales Department, Phone: 800-382-3419;
Fax: 201-236-7141; E-mail: corpsales@prenhall.com; or write: Prentice Hall PTR,
Corp. Sales Dept., One Lake Street, Upper Saddle River, NJ 07458.

All products or services mentioned in this book are the trademarks or service marks of their
respective companies or organizations.

All rights reserved. No part of this book may be reproduced, in any form or by any means,
without permission in writing from the publisher.

Printed in the United States of America
10 9 8 7 6 5 4 3 2 1

ISBN 0-13-085898-6

Prentice-Hall International (UK) Limited, *London*
Prentice-Hall of Australia Pty. Limited, *Sydney*
Prentice-Hall Canada Inc., *Toronto*
Prentice-Hall Hispanoamericana, S.A., *Mexico*
Prentice-Hall of India Private Limited, *New Delhi*
Prentice-Hall of Japan, Inc., *Tokyo*
Pearson Education Asia Pte. Ltd.
Editora Prentice-Hall do Brasil, Ltda., *Rio de Janeiro*

Thanks to my husband, Mark Radcliffe, for his help and patience.

—J.D.B.

Dedicated to my family who believed me when I said that the Internet and the Web would change how we communicate, how we do business, and how we teach and learn.

—B.D-A.

Dedicated to my family who have helped enable my dreams and who never tire of listening to my grand ideas.

—D.D-A.

Thanks go to my husband, Warren, for his infinite patience during this project.

—R.M.

Dedicated to my loving and supportive family—Nancy, Andrew, and Christopher—whose tolerance for patience is always severely tested whenever I take on a book project. We did it again!

—B.W.

CONTENTS

CHAPTER 3 Internet Usage   77

CHAPTER 6   Electronic Commerce Tools   **163**

CHAPTER 7   Getting Started Managing
Your Web Site   **193**

FROM THE EDITOR

As the Internet rapidly becomes the primary commerce and communications medium for virtually every company and organization operating today, a growing need exists for trained individuals to manage this medium. Aptly named *Webmasters*, these individuals will play leading roles in driving their organizations into the next millennium.

Working with the World Organization of Webmasters (WOW), Pearson PTR has developed two book series that are designed to train Webmasters to meet this challenge. These are *The Foundations of Website Architecture Series,* and *The Advanced Website Architecture Series.*

The Webmaster who masters the materials in these books will have working knowledge of Web site management, support, maintenance, organizational strategy, electronic commerce strategy and tools, as well as legal issues surrounding the Web. The Webmaster will be able to implement sound Web site design, navigation and HCI (Human-Computer Interaction) practices. Webmasters will also have a solid understanding of networking, Web servers, Web programming, and scripting, as well as supporting supplementary technologies.

The goal of *The Advanced Website Architecture Series* is to provide an advanced Webmaster training curriculum. *The Advanced Website Architecture Series* offers in-depth coverage of the content, business, and technical issues that challenge Webmasters.

Books in this series are:

> *Designing Web Interfaces*
> *Supporting Web Servers*
> *Analyzing E-Commerce & Internet Law*

The Foundations of Website Architecture Series is designed to introduce and explain the technical, business, and content management skills that are necessary to effectively train the new Webmaster.

Books in *The Foundations of Website Architecture Series* include:

> *Understanding Web Development*
>
> *Mastering Internet Protocols*
>
> *Administering Web Servers, Security, & Maintenance*
>
> *Exploring Web Marketing & Project Management*
>
> *Creating Web Graphics, Audio, & Video*

Thank you for your interest in *The Advanced Website Architecture Series,* and good luck in your career as a Webmaster!

Karen McLean
Senior Managing Editor
Pearson PTR Interactive

EXECUTIVE FOREWORD

Within the next few years, you will think about the Internet in the same way you think about electricity today. Just as you don't ask a friend to "use electricity to turn on a light," you will assume the omnipresence of the Web and the capabilities that it delivers. The Web is transforming the way we live, work, and play, just as electricity changed everything for previous generations.

Every indication suggests that the explosive growth of the Web will continue. The question we need to address is, "How can we deliver the most value with this ubiquitous resource?" Today, most of the world's Web sites were created and are maintained by self-taught Webmasters. Why? Because there were limited opportunities to receive formal standards-based education. Quality, accessible, affordable education will help provide the broad range of knowledge, skills, and abilities to meet the demands of the marketplace.

Over the last three years, the World Organization of Webmasters (WOW) has worked with colleges and universities, business and industry, and its own membership of aspiring and practicing Web professionals to develop the Certified Web Professional (CWP) program. Our three-part goal is to provide:

- Educational institutions with guidelines around which to develop curricula.
- An organized way to master technical skills, content development, business proficiency and personal workplace ability.
- An assessment standard for employers to measure candidates.

The Foundations of Website Architecture Series and *The Advanced Website Architecture Series* grew organically from the communities they will serve. Written by working professionals and academics currently teaching the material, and reviewed by leading faculty at major colleges and universities and the WOW Review Board of industry professionals, these books are designed to meet the increasingly urgent need for Web professionals with expertise in three areas: technical development, design and content development, and business.

There is a huge increase in demand for qualified Web professionals, with the number of Web sites projected to grow from about 5 million today to about 25 million by the year 2002. Web professionals with business, technical, design, and project management skills are, and will continue to be, the most in-demand and will receive the highest compensation.

On behalf of WOW and its members, we wish you the best of success and welcome you to this exciting field.

William B. Cullifer
Executive Director-Founder
World Organization of Webmasters
bill@joinwow.org

INTRODUCTION

WHAT YOU WILL NEED

A networked PC with access to the Internet. The faster the connection, the less time you spend on the "World Wide Wait."

A Web browser with as many plug-ins as you can support (to experience as much marketing media as possible) and an e-mail account. In your browser preferences, please enable cookies.

HOW THIS BOOK IS ORGANIZED

In this book, and the others in this series, you are presented with a series of interactive labs. Each lab begins with Learning Objectives that define what exercises (or tasks) are covered in that lab. This is followed by an overview of the concepts that will be further explored through the exercises, which are the heart of each lab.

Each exercise consists of either a series of steps that you will follow to perform a specific task or a presentation of a particular scenario. Questions that are designed to help you discover the important things on your own are then asked of you. The answers to these questions are given at the end of the exercises, along with more in-depth discussion of the concepts explored.

At the end of each lab is a series of multiple-choice Self-Review Questions, which are designed to bolster your learning experience by providing opportunities to check your absorbtion of important material. The answers to these questions appear in the Appendix. There are also additional Self-Review Questions at this book's companion Web site, found at http://www.phptr.com/phptrinteractive/.

Finally, at the end of each chapter you will find a Test Your Thinking section, which consists of a series of projects designed to solidify all of the skills you have learned in the chapter. If you have successfully completed all of the labs in the chapter, you should be able to tackle these projects with few problems. There are not always "answers" to these projects, but where appropriate, you will find guidance and/or solutions at the companion Web site.

The final element of this book actually doesn't appear in the book at all. It is the companion Web site, and it is located at http://www.phptr.com/phptrinteractive/.

This companion Web site is closely integrated with the content of this book, and we encourage you to visit often. It is designed to provide a unique interactive on-line experience that will enhance your education. As mentioned, you will find guidance and solutions that will help you complete the projects found in the Test Your Thinking section of each chapter.

You will also find additional Self-Review Questions for each chapter, which are meant to give you more opportunities to become familiar with terminology and concepts presented in the publications. In the Author's Corner, you will find additional information that we think will interest you, including updates to the information presented in these publications, and discussion about the constantly changing technology Webmasters must stay involved in.

Finally, you will find a Message Board, which you can think of as a virtual study lounge. Here, you can interact with other *Advanced Website Architecture Series* readers, and share and discuss your projects.

NOTES TO THE STUDENT

This publication and the others in *The Advanced Website Architecture Series* are endorsed by the World Organization of Webmasters. The series is a training curriculum designed to provide aspiring Webmasters with the skills they need to perform in the marketplace. The skill sets included in *The Advanced Website Architecture Series* were initially collected and defined by this international trade association to create a set of core competencies for students, professionals, trainers, and employers to utilize.

NOTES TO THE INSTRUCTOR

Chances are that you are a pioneer in the education field whether you want to be one or not. Due to the explosive nature of the Internet's growth, very few Webmaster training programs are currently in existence. But while you read this, many colleges, community colleges, technical institutes, and corporate and commercial training environments are introducing this material into curriculums worldwide.

Chances are, however, that you are teaching new material in a new program. But don't fret, this publication and series are designed as a comprehensive introductory curriculum in this field. Students successfully completing this program of study will be fully prepared to assume the responsibilities of a Webmaster in the field or to engage in further training and certification in the Internet communications field.

Each chapter in this book is broken down into labs. All questions and projects have the answers and discussions associated with them. The labs and question/

answer formats used in this book provide excellent opportunities for group discussions and dialogue between students and instructors. Many answers and their discussions are abbreviated in this publication for space reasons. Any comments, ideas, or suggestions to this text and series will be would be greatly appreciated.

ACKNOWLEDGMENTS

From Benay: My sincere appreciation to my supportive family, particularly my wonderful daughter Cassie, for encouraging me to develop, teach, and write about Web technology.

From Drew: My thanks to my family, who encouraged me to take on this project.

From Bebo: I am grateful to

- Robert Cailliau and Tim Berners-Lee, who let me share their visions a decade ago and have continued to support me;
- My book co-authors, who worked tirelessly to make this series the best that it could be;
- Bill Cullifer of WOW, for finding in Prentice Hall a publisher not interested in just another series about the Web, but a series which dares to address many of the Web management issues that have been previously overlooked or ignored;
- Karen McLean of Prentice Hall, for a patient, yet firm, hand which pushed this project to completion.

ABOUT THE AUTHORS

J. Dianne Brinson, an attorney, is the author of *Multimedia Law and Business Handbook, Internet Legal Forms for Business,* and *Internet Law and Business Handbook* (summer, 2000), available from Ladera Press, www.laderapress.com, (800-523-3721). She teaches Internet Law at the University of California–Berkeley Extension and San Jose State University's Internet Education Institute. A graduate of Yale Law School, she is a former law school professor and has also practiced law in Atlanta and Los Angeles.

Benay Dara-Abrams (http://www.dara-abrams.com/benay) is CEO of BrainJolt (http://www.brainjolt.com) and designer of the Web-based Online Adaptive Learning Environment™. Benay has been involved in the Internet since ARPANet days in 1970 and in Web development since 1993. She managed the development of the first WYSIWYG HTML editor and the first commercial Web-based intranet. She served as Curriculum Development Director for the Stanford University Western Institute of Computer Science. Benay has developed and taught intensive courses in Electronic Commerce and Web Business Management and in Networking Fundamentals for Webmasters at Stanford University and the University of Hong Kong. She was co-founder and Director of Engineering for Silicon Valley Public Access Link, a community network ISP. Benay has been involved in Electronic Commerce since 1980 when she managed public, packet-switched, network-based services for travel and home banking. She plans to complete her PhD in Computer Science and Educational Psychology in 2001.

Drew Dara-Abrams serves as CTO (Chief Technology Officer) for BrainJolt (http://www.brainjolt.com), an online learning technology start-up venture. He has designed and taught classes on Internet, Web design, programming, and advanced topics in computers to both adults and children. He has also served as Webmaster and Network and Systems Administrator for a number of high-tech start-ups, schools, and summer camps. He can be found on the Internet at drew@drewnet.net and http://drew.dara-abrams.com.

Jennifer Masek entered the field of Web development and design by way of SGML publishing for paper and electronic media. Jennifer has been working in Web design and management since the early days of the Web at the Stanford Linear Accelerator Center, home of the first Web site in the United States. As lead of SLAC's Publishing and New Media Group she was responsible for the development and management of a wide variety of sites, as well as developing training programs for the Web and Web-based collaboration projects. Jennifer has worked with a wide variety of nonprofit organizations and Bay Area firms as a user interface and restructuring consultant, helping organizations meet the demands of the constantly changing environment of the Web. Jennifer is currently the Content Director for Hotpaper.com, Inc., a San Francisco-based ASP specializing in document automation solutions for the Internet and wireless communities.

Ruth McDunn has been involved in creating and maintaining Web sites since the early days of the Web at Stanford Linear Accelerator Center. SLAC was an early participant in the Web, with the first Web server installed in December, 1991. Realizing the cross-platform advantages of Web sites, Ruth developed one of the first large Web sites at SLAC, for the Environment, Safety, and Health Division. Since then Ruth moved to the Technical Publications Department and has been involved in creating and maintaining many Web sites, from small to very large (take a look at the SLAC Virtual Visitor Center at http://www2.slac.stanford.edu/vvc/). She is now the Web Information Manager, responsible for managing Web space on the production Web servers (Unix and NT), teaching others to create and maintain Web sites, managing online resources for Web authors, analyzing the Web server log files, and creating Web site designs and organization schemes. Ruth also has a Master of Science degree from Vanderbilt University in Molecular Biology and a Bachelor of Arts degree from Gustavus Adolphus College. Ruth lives in San Jose, California, with her husband and two cats.

Bebo White is a member of the technical staff at the Stanford Linear Accelerator Center (SLAC), the high-energy physics laboratory operated by Stanford University. He also holds academic appointments at the University of California–Berkeley, the University of San Francisco, and Hong Kong University. He was fortunate enough to become involved with WWW development quite early while on sabbatical at CERN in 1989. Consequently, he was a part of the team instrumental in establishing the first non-European Web site at SLAC in December, 1991. Bebo has authored and co-authored multiple books and articles. He has lectured and spoken internationally to academic and commercial audiences and has been particularly involved with two major international conference series: the Computing in High Energy Physics (CHEP) Conference and the International World Wide Web Conference. He served as Co-Chair of the Sixth International World Wide Web Conference, co-hosted by SLAC and Stanford University. In 1996, Mr. White was added to the Micro Times 100 list of those making outstanding contributions to personal computing. He is a member of the IW3C2 (International World Wide Web Conference Committee), a fellow of the International World Wide Web Institute (IWWWI), and is cited by the World Wide Web Consortium.

C H A P T E R 1

INTRANETS

Web-based intranets provide the same ease of use and ready access to information as the external World Wide Web. The difference is that information on an intranet is shared within and across an organization.

In this chapter, we'll start by defining what an intranet is and how the intranet can be used by your organization. You have probably heard the term *intranet* used and may have used one in your own organization. Now, you are in a position to understand the options your organization has in the design and use of an internal network. Whether you are in a position to determine how the intranet is used throughout your company or in one part of the company, you need to understand various facets of intranets. You may be involved in a steering committee or you may be the one solely responsible for mapping out your organization's strategy for an intranet and for intra-company Web sites. Whatever your role, you should understand what intranets are, how they function, and what options should be considered when analyzing your organization's requirements and determining your organization's strategy for Web sites on the organizational intranet. Understanding the budgetary issues and costs involved in setting up and maintaining an organizational intranet will help you in your decision-making process. You can also see what other organizations are doing with their intranets. In order to illustrate the issues and concepts discussed in this section, we will use case studies based on an established computer company, which we'll refer to as A Corporation, and on a start-up Web company, BJ. These real-life examples will help you understand some of the trade-offs involved in the development and deployment of your organization's intranet.

In the lab exercises throughout this part of the book, you will be asked to answer questions regarding your organization. For these exercises, choose an organization with which you are familiar. This organization can be where you work or another organization to which you belong. Because the lab exercises build on each other, you will find them more meaningful if you base your answers on the same organization throughout the exercises. For the answers to the lab exercises, we will use the case studies of A Corporation and BJ with which you can then compare your answers to the exercises.

In order for you to understand the case studies, we'll first describe the companies and each one's business model. A Corporation is a computer company, which was founded in the 1970s in order to provide lower-cost computers with advanced technology while maintaining compatibility with IBM computers, which then dominated the market. By the 1990s, A Corporation was an established computer manufacturer, software systems developer, and service provider with an international market. Customer companies were generally other large, established companies in the insurance, financial services, health care, manufacturing, and service industries. A major problem that A Corporation faced was in maintaining communication between corporate headquarters and research and development, both based in California, and the field sales offices located throughout the world. In the following six chapters, we will explore the use of intranet, extranet, Internet, and electronic commerce technology and approaches to assist A Corporation in its communication challenges.

The case study of BJ differs from that of A Corporation. BJ is a new Web-based start-up in online education, with a virtual organization building and deploying the technology. The company primarily uses contractors and consultants rather than full-time employees. As a start-up, BJ does not face the legacy systems issues that A Corporation faces, but BJ does not have the resources to commit to expensive solutions. While technical people can implement their own in-house solutions since they understand the technology, their time is needed to develop the product technology. Therefore, BJ faces a different set of challenges from A Corporation, but both companies have benefited from a strategic approach to the implementation of intranet, extranet, Internet, and electronic commerce technology plans. We will discuss more of the approach that BJ, as a start-up, has found to be effective.

L A B   1 . 1

INTRANET BASICS

LAB OBJECTIVES

After this lab, you will be able to:

✔ Define and Describe an Intranet
✔ Understand the Facilities Provided by an Intranet

First let's define what we mean by the word *intranet*. The term was coined from the Latin "intra," which means "within," to mean an internal network. In a way this is a misnomer, because it's not really "within a network," it's logically "within an organization." The term "Internet" makes more sense, since the Latin word "inter" means "between" and the Internet is indeed a network of networks. The term intranet caught on because it's easier to say than internal network and it's related to the Internet by using Internet protocols. Also, people like a term that sounds like the Internet but indicates that the network uses an Internet-type of network as an intra-organization or internal network. We define an intranet to be a network employing standard Internet protocols, such as TCP/IP (transmission control protocol/Internet protocol) and HTTP (hypertext transfer protocol), to connect a set of clients within an organization or a group of associated clients supporting a community of interest. An intranet can also be defined as a network using IP (Internet protocol) connecting multiple nodes behind a firewall. A *firewall* is a hardware/software combination that provides security for the intranet by separating network nodes into those on the inside and those on the outside. An intranet may reside behind more than one firewall and may have nodes that are connected by secure networks. The secure networks may themselves be virtual private networks (VPNs). A *virtual private network* refers to a network that sends encrypted data across the public Internet. Encryption provides privacy across a public channel, thereby providing a network, which is "virtually" private rather than "physically" private.

Other definitions of the term *intranet* also exist. The CommerceNet industry consortium takes the approach that an intranet includes other technologies in use for in-house purposes. According to this approach, an intranet is defined as Internet technology services used on a LAN or within an organization. The term *intranet* may be used to encompass the complete information network of an organization. By this definition, an intranet is not limited to the use of Internet technologies; an intranet also includes client/server networks and data warehouse integration, as well as support for mobile communications and connectivity between PCs and mainframes.

An organizational intranet provides facilities to:

- Share information within the organization
- Transfer information between departments or other entities within the organization
- Make information accessible across geographic and organizational boundaries
- Collaborate with other people in the organization
- Automate internal operational processes
- Provide a single user interface to organizational information resources and tools
- Train and educate individuals within the organization

With these facilities, an intranet offers the opportunity for an organization to:

- Provide ready access to information needed to make informed decisions
- Increase awareness of other projects happening within the organization
- Support geographically dispersed individuals and departments
- Stay abreast of the latest advances in fields related to the organization's mission

An organization can use these capabilities to:

- Improve the quality of its decisions
- Expedite decision making
- Eliminate duplication of effort
- Improve communication throughout the organization
- Increase the cohesiveness of the organization
- Facilitate collaborative efforts

- Enhance competitive advantage
- Boost morale and increase employee retention
- Increase productivity

Now let's look at how the phrases *internal Web* and *corporate Web* are used. The term *Web* is used to mean an unstructured client/server network with HTTP as its transaction protocol. If we look at the public Internet and the World Wide Web, the HTTP nodes on the public Internet comprise the World Wide Web. An internal Web, on the other hand, is made up of all the network nodes on a private network connected via HTTP as the transaction protocol. A private network can be an organizational LAN (local-area network) or WAN (wide-area network). The phrase "corporate Web" indicates that the internal network is run by or for a corporation. Internal Webs are also referred to as intranets. It is important to understand that these networks or Webs are intra-organizational or internal to a company, organization, or community of interest in a logical sense. In a physical sense, the network nodes in an intranet may be spread around the world. Indeed, an intranet may be composed of many Web sites and network nodes, any or all of which may reside in different physical locations. In fact, geographically dispersed organizations benefit the most from intranets because individuals can share data via Web sites on the intranet, helping people and departments feel part of the overall organization despite their physical distance from corporate headquarters or other departments within a multinational corporation. We think of an intranet as serving a specific community of interest, which may be referred to as a COIN (community of interest network), rather than a specific physical location. An intranet can be very large and very dispersed. While the scale of the intranet needs to be taken into account for performance and availability, an intranet can, in reality, be as large as the community of interest that the intranet serves. An intranet may consist of just one Web server in a small organization, hundreds of departmental Web servers spread around the country, or even multiple thousands of Web servers in various corporate offices around the world.

With this flexible structure, intranets can provide facilities to share:

- Strategic plans
- Budgets and financial analyses
- Benefits information
- Product development documents
- Comments on collaborative projects
- Competitive analysis
- Data sheets
- Personnel data

Intranets are logically centralized and physically distributed. An intranet provides a common entry point for data collection and information dissemination. At the same time, the intranet distributes the processing of data onto various application servers connected via the intranet. This is an efficient and user-friendly way for the intranet to perform the operational tasks of the organization and allow for cost-effective sharing of resources throughout the organization. You can put security measures in place to protect confidential documents and the intranet can then be used as a repository for the increasingly valuable knowledge assets of the organization.

The intranet can thereby support intra-organizational efforts in the following areas:

- Internal communications
- Collaborative and cooperative projects
- Intellectual capital management
- Business process reengineering

LAB 1.1 EXERCISES

1.1.1 DEFINE AND DESCRIBE AN INTRANET

a) What is an intranet?

_____

_____

b) What does it mean for an intranet to be logically centralized and physically distributed?

_____

_____

1.1.2 UNDERSTAND THE FACILITIES PROVIDED BY AN INTRANET

a) What documents does your organization or could your organization share via an intranet?

_____

_____

b) How can your organization benefit from using an intranet?

LAB 1.1 EXERCISE ANSWERS

1.1.1 ANSWERS

a) What is an intranet?

Answer: We define an intranet to be a network employing standard Internet protocols, such as TCP/IP (transmission control protocol/Internet protocol) and HTTP (hypertext transfer protocol), to connect a set of clients within an organization or a group of associated clients supporting a community of interest. The intranet at A Corporation was the first commercial intranet to be based on the World Wide Web and to use the HTTP protocol. The intranet at BJ uses TCP/IP and HTTP to support a group of web browser clients located in geographically dispersed facilities.

b) What does it mean for an intranet to be logically centralized and physically distributed?

Answer: Servers and services can be located in various locations with the home page for the organization providing hyperlinks to the services and information. To the user, it appears that the services and information are centrally located but, in fact, the resources can be distributed on various servers, without requiring the user to know their physical location. The A Corporation intranet home page provides links to various lines of business and departments, including human resources, benefits, technical publications, engineering, professional services, software, and international field sales offices. While these organizations physically reside in various locations around the world, the home page for the corporate intranet provides a logical centralization point. The home page itself resides on a server located in the corporate Information Services facility in California, but the main point is that users see the corporate intranet home page as their logical central link to other resources. While the other resources are physically distributed, users do not need to know the address or location of the other resources since links are provided from the intranet home page. The BJ intranet provides a jumping-off point for project planning and software development efforts that are produced and stored on systems in various locations. Again, the user is not required to know the physical location of the resources as long as he or she knows the name of the intranet home page, which provides links to all the other resources.

1.1.2 ANSWERS

a) What documents does your organization or could your organization share via an intranet?

Answer: Any documents that are currently physically copied and distributed are candidates for dissemination on an intranet, including personnel policies, organization announcements, information about products and services, competitive analysis, and project plans. The A Corporation human resources department was an early adopter of the corporate intranet, providing information on health, dental, and life insurance plans and vacation and sick leave policies to employees. The corporate and marketing libraries adopted the intranet to provide facilities for checking the library catalogs and requesting marketing reports while the market analysis department set up searchable repositories on the intranet for competitive analysis. The PR (public relations) group decided to post announcements on the intranet and enhanced the announcements through the addition of audio and video clips of announcements by the president of the company. BJ provides contact information for all staff people via the intranet. A major use of the intranet by BJ involves sharing of project requirements and development plans.

b) How can your organization benefit from using an intranet?

Answer: Your organization can use an intranet to:

   Share information across departments and groups

   Support collaborative projects

   Add to the organizational knowledge base

BJ uses its intranet to support collaboration among developers on project teams, while A Corporation primarily uses the intranet to share information across various departments and lines of business within the corporation.

LAB 1.1 SELF-REVIEW QUESTIONS

In order to test your progress, you should be able to answer the following questions.

I) Intranets are differentiated by which of the following?

   a) _____ Physical location

   b) _____ Content

2) Intranets are _____ centralized and _____ distributed.

    a) _____ physically, logically
    b) _____ physically, physically
    c) _____ logically, logically
    d) _____ logically, physically

3) Intranets can be used to facilitate collaborative efforts.

    a) _____ True
    b) _____ False

4) Intranets usually are not used to share information within an organization.

    a) _____ True
    b) _____ False

Quiz answers appear in the Appendix, Section 1.1.

LAB 1.2

INTRANET MANAGEMENT

LAB OBJECTIVES

After this lab, you will be able to:

✔ Understand Management Issues Related to the Adoption of an Intranet Throughout Your Organization

✔ Engage Management in a Discussion of Organizational Issues Related to the Deployment of an Intranet in Your Organization

---

Let's consider some interesting statistics about corporate adoption and acceptance of intranets from major market research firms, including IDC, Forrester Research, and Zona Research.

- More than half of the larger corporations now have an intranet in place.

- The majority of corporations are considering implementing an intranet if they don't have one yet.

- By 1998, corporations were spending close to $11 billion on intranets.

- With intranet expenses accounting for approximately one-quarter of the money spent on Web initiatives by U.S. companies, the amount spent on intranets continues to rise.

In addition, intranets are in use in many nonprofit organizations, academic institutions, and government agencies. Many organizations realize the benefits of an intranet no matter how little, how much, or even whether they use the public Internet and the external World Wide Web.

Web technology has made the hardware and software for an intranet affordable and easy-to-use by organizations of all sizes and types. As organizations downsize and refashion themselves with flatter management structures, cross-functional teams, and collaborative projects with strategic partners, intranets become critical to the communication and effectiveness of the organization. Management consultants are encouraging a move toward virtual organizations for flexible deployment and use of resources. At the same time, management consultants are encouraging organizations to empower each individual in the organization. In the past, the old adage "knowledge is power" encouraged some people to hoard knowledge. Many organizations now realize the value of their intellectual assets, the knowledge base of the organization. Understanding that it is in their best interest to build the knowledge base of the entire organization, many organizations now encourage sharing and dissemination of information throughout the organization to increase the awareness and effectiveness of each individual in the organization. Intranets support empowerment by providing ready access to needed information and resources at each person's desktop. At the same time, many organizations are encouraging their people to follow the "keep it simple" principle. Intranets powered by Web servers, browsers, and WYSIWYG (what-you-see-is-what-you-get) publishing tools provide straightforward ways to disseminate and share information across departments and throughout organizations.

Your intranet may already be in place, thanks to your own initiative or that of one or a few people in your organization who understand its benefits. If this hasn't happened yet in your organization, you may become the "intranet evangelist" who can spread the word. Whether your organization's intranet is a grassroots effort or a project managed by the IS (Information Services) department, the intranet is a tool that supports decentralized decision making and control. Since an intranet is ideally a resource for everyone in the organization, it's a good idea to establish a World Wide Web Council or Intranet Steering Committee.

■ FOR EXAMPLE

When my team developed the corporate intranet for our company, we found that the formation of our World Wide Web Council was a key to the success of the deployment and acceptance of the intranet. Bringing together representatives of each major group, such as engineering, IS/MIS, manufacturing, marketing, corporate communications, human resources, legal counsel, or whatever comparable groups make up your organization, really pays off. If you want your intranet to be a tool to help your organization increase its effectiveness and communication, make sure that your World Wide Web Council is involved in the definition and planning of your organizational intranet.

LAB 1.2 EXERCISES

1.2.1 UNDERSTAND MANAGEMENT ISSUES RELATED TO THE ADOPTION OF AN INTRANET THROUGHOUT YOUR ORGANIZATION

a) What impact do you think an intranet might have on the knowledge capital of your organization?

_____

_____

1.2.2 ENGAGE MANAGEMENT IN A DISCUSSION OF ORGANIZATIONAL ISSUES RELATED TO THE DEPLOYMENT OF AN INTRANET IN YOUR ORGANIZATION

a) What impact do you think an intranet might have on the control of your organization?

_____

_____

LAB 1.2 ANSWERS

1.2.1 ANSWER

a) What impact do you think an intranet might have on the knowledge capital of your organization?

Answer: Sharing knowledge not only serves to increase the knowledge of individuals in the organization, it also fuels an increase in the overall knowledge base of the organization. This is a situation in which the whole is greater than the sum of its parts. We definitely experienced an increase in the understanding of competitive and marketing issues among the engineering teams as well as in the field sales offices when we made competitive analysis and market research data available via the A Corporation corporate intranet. The BJ engineering team has an increased understanding of strategic planning issues as well as of the cognitive psychology foundation of the online learning environment.

a) What impact do you think an intranet might have on the control of your organization?

Answer: An intranet is highly distributed and tends to support decentralized decision making and control. If your organization has a hierarchical management structure in place, an intranet can serve to break down some of the barriers between management levels, increasing communication and making people at each level more responsible for the success of the organization. Adoption of a corporate intranet facilitated A Corporation's move toward lines of business from a centrally controlled vertically integrated business model. With the information it needed to operate as separate profit and loss (P&L) centers, each line of business could make decisions on a local level, reporting results to corporate management. While BJ started as a decentralized effort, control can be shared more easily through communication via the corporate intranet.

LAB 1.2 SELF-REVIEW QUESTIONS

In order to test your progress, you should be able to answer the following questions.

1) Hardware and software for an intranet are affordable.

    a) _____ True
    b) _____ False

2) Intranets are best when

    a) _____ In wide use
    b) _____ Used only by select groups
    c) _____ Used only by engineers
    d) _____ Used only by human relations and marketing groups

3) It is best to

    a) _____ Make intranets complex
    b) _____ Keep intranets simple

Quiz answers appear in the Appendix, Section 1.2.

L A B   1 . 3

STRATEGIC INTRANETS

LAB OBJECTIVES

After this lab, you will be able to:

✔ Understand How an Intranet Supports Your
Organization's Mission
✔ Pose Questions in Order to Design an Intranet
for Your Organization

The first step in determining what your organization should do with an intranet
is to consider your organizational strategy. The strategy comes first, then tools to
implement the strategy come next.

Let's talk about your organizational strategy. If you don't have one, it's time for
people to sit down and determine the mission and function of the organization.
What is the mission of the organization? If you have a mission statement, ask
your World Wide Web Council or Intranet Steering Committee to review the mission statement and make sure that it reflects the overall goals of the organization.
If you don't have a mission statement, now is the time to develop one.

There's no use developing an intranet to help your organization carry out its mission unless you know what mission the organization is trying to accomplish.
What role does your organization play in the overall landscape? What internal
structure and facilities are needed to support the work that is being done within
the organization? Is the current organizational structure and strategy effective? If
so, you can design an intranet to support the current functioning of the organization. If not, this is a good opportunity for your organization to reassess the organizational structure and strategy and design a structure and strategy to help the
organization accomplish its intended mission. There are excellent resources and
guides for developing or refining your organizational mission statement and your
organizational strategy. For the purposes of our discussion, we will assume that you
now understand and can state the organization's mission and the organization's

strategy to accomplish its overall mission. With these two important pieces in hand, you are ready to formulate your strategy for your intranet.

Let's pose a number of questions for your organization to answer.

1. How does an intranet support your organizational mission?
2. How can an intranet assist your organization in information sharing?
3. What data processing functions are currently performed within the organization?
4. What additional data processing functions need to be performed within the organization?
5. Which of these functions can be performed on application servers on the intranet to distribute the load, improve the user interface, or make the data or application more accessible throughout the organization?
6. How can an intranet streamline your data processing operations?
7. What business processes can you reengineer by implementing them on the intranet?
8. What are your organizational requirements in the following areas?

    Collaborative and cooperative projects

    Sharing information

    Protecting information
9. What content do you want to make available on the intranet? What form is the content currently in?

    Strategic planning documents

    Budgets

    Sales data

    Beta test products

    Product specifications

    Technical reports

    Research results

    Reports

    Other organizational information
10. What existing internal databases do you want to make accessible via the intranet?
11. What internal publications do you want to put on the intranet?
12. What external databases and publications (for instance, competitive information) do you want to make available on the intranet? Do you have the appropriate licenses? Is the information

licensed for individual use or do you have a site license? If you have a license to share the information within one department or organizational entity, do you have a way to limit the use to people within that group? What information do you want to share throughout the organization and, according to the terms of your licensing agreement, what information can be shared freely throughout the organization?

13. What type of shared content do you want to make freely available on the intranet?

14. Will your intranet include employee-developed content?

15. What style of intranet fits your organization? Are there separate organizations within the overall organization that may have their own styles and information sharing requirements?

16. Do you want a corporate bulletin board with departmental Web sites?

17. Do you want your intranet to be an informal community kiosk on which everyone can post and share information? If so, who decides what is and isn't appropriate? Do you have a moderator for discussion groups? Who ascertains if certain content is offensive or inappropriate? What action is taken when some one posts offensive or inappropriate information?

18. Are the people in your organization capable of posting information on an internal Web site? Do they have the tools and expertise to make the information available on a Web site?

19. Do you have a style guide governing the format of internal Web sites?

20. What security measures do you currently have in place? Do you have a firewall (or multiple firewalls)? Do you require the use of difficult-to-guess passwords? Do you have a callback system? Is your information sensitive enough to require encryption? We will return to security questions when we discuss technical decisions in Lab 1.5.

LAB 1.3 EXERCISES

1.3.1 UNDERSTAND HOW AN INTRANET SUPPORTS YOUR ORGANIZATION'S MISSION

a) What is the mission of your organization?

_____

_____

b) How does an intranet support this mission?

_____

_____

**1.3.2 POSE QUESTIONS IN ORDER TO DESIGN
AN INTRANET FOR YOUR ORGANIZATION**

Take time to consider each of the questions posed in this lab.

a) Which of the questions posed in this lab can you answer for
your organization?

_____

_____

b) Which ones need answers from other people within the
organization?

_____

_____

LAB 1.3 EXERCISE ANSWERS

1.3.1 ANSWERS

a) What is the mission of your organization?

Answer: This needs to be defined by each organization. If you need help in defining a mission, there are consultants who work with organizations as well as books to read to assist in mission development. The A Corporation mission is to deliver innovative systems, software, consulting, services, and support for data centers. The BJ mission is to provide an educationally sound online adaptive learning environment, based on research in cognitive psychology, educational methodologies, and effective learning strategies.

b) How does an intranet support this mission?

Answer: Intranets can support an organization's mission by facilitating communication, enhancing cooperation, and promoting collaboration. Examples of ways in which an intranet can support an organization's mission include:

Providing competitive analysis to marketing so that the company can fulfill its mission of remaining the market leader in a particular product arena.

Supporting the sharing of information and case loads in an organization with a mission to offer low-cost community legal services to those in need of legal aid.

Facilitating technology transfer from a research and development group to a number of product divisions in a large corporation.

For A Corporation, the intranet supports the corporate mission by providing new product information to the field sales offices so that the sales force can offer the latest technology solutions to customers whether they are located in Australia, Ireland, or in the United States. For BJ, the intranet provides information on current research in cognitive psychology, educational methodologies, and effective learning strategies to support development work in online adaptive learning.

1.3.2 ANSWERS

a) Which of the questions posed in this lab can you answer for your organization?

Answer: Even if you can answer all the questions, take time to meet with others and discuss these questions and their answers. Input from various constituencies in your organization will pay off in realizing the benefits of an intranet designed to fulfill the objectives of your organization.

We discussed how the intranet supports the mission of both A Corporation and BJ and how the intranet supports information sharing among lines of business in A Corporation and across development teams in BJ. At A Corporation, we found that while our web engineering team needed to address each of the questions in this lab, members of the World Wide Web Council needed to provide input on each of the questions since various departments had their own specific concerns. In addition, each department was able to contribute by addressing different questions raised in this lab. At BJ, which is operating in start-up mode, the answers to these questions come primarily from the founders, though input has been solicited from others in the organization to make sure that the intranet satisfies the needs of all members of the team. Since the intranet is such an important communication vehicle for BJ, it is important that the design and contents reflect the requirements and wishes of everyone in the organization.

b) Which ones need answers from other people within the organization?

Answer: Create or use an existing task force to form a World Wide Web Council or Intranet Steering Committee. This group, with representatives from each major group in the organization, can help you determine the answers to these questions. Participation from this group is critical to the success of an intranet.

The A Corporation World Wide Web Council provided information on data processing functions currently performed within the organization, which additional data processing functions needed to be but weren't being performed within the organization, and which functions could be performed on application servers on the intranet. This led to a cooperative effort between the web engineering team and the corporate Information Services department. At BJ, various team members provided input to questions of interest to that particular team member. It is helpful to solicit input no matter how large or how small your organization is, so that the intranet will support the mission, strategy, objectives, and operation of your organization.

LAB 1.3 SELF-REVIEW QUESTIONS

In order to test your progress, you should be able to answer the following questions.

1) What should be done first?

a) _____ Identify and purchase tools
b) _____ Create a strategy for an intranet

2) Information in "legacy" (old and outdated) databases can be integrated into a new intranet.

a) _____ True
b) _____ False

3) An intranet should be centered around your organization's mission.

a) _____ True
b) _____ False

Quiz answers appear in the Appendix, Section 1.3.

L A B 1 . 4

INTRANET COMPONENTS

LAB OBJECTIVES

After this lab, you will be able to:

✔ Understand the Components of an Intranet
✔ Compare the Internet and an Intranet

Let's map out the components that may be part of your intranet. Your intranet may be as simple as individual browsers on people's desktop machines, connecting to one organizational Web server. Or your intranet may be much more complex, including multiple Web servers and multiple application servers, each performing a specific function, such as time card processing, benefits tracking, and other intra-organizational tracking and planning tasks. In addition, your intranet may use CGI (common gateway interface) to accept data through forms and pass the data along to a back-end relational database server. Alternatively, your intranet may incorporate servers, hosting applications that have been developed within your organization; these servers may communicate via custom APIs (application program interfaces). In this way, organizations can protect their investment in software developed for applications strategic to the organization's mission or critical to day-to-day operations. If an application is performing its function well, there may be no need to replace it with an entirely new application, incurring development, training, and data filtering expenses. People in your organization can use their browsers as the common interface and access these proprietary applications via CGI scripts, JDBC (Java Database Connectivity™) drivers, or, if necessary, proprietary APIs. JDBC is an industry standard for database-independent connectivity between the Java platform and a wide range of databases. CGI scripts and JDBC drivers allow people in your organization to access and manipulate data in organizational database management systems via their browsers.

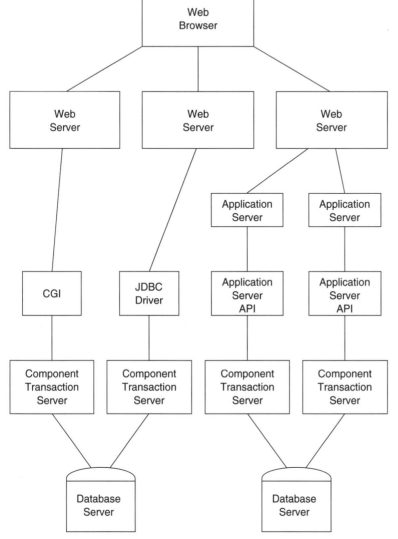

**LAB
1.4**

Figure 1.1 ■ Logical View of an Intranet

To better understand this view of an intranet, we can map out a rough correspondence between the components of an intranet and the architecture of a multi-tier
client/server system (Fig. 1.1).

> *Top Tier*—Browser corresponds to the client layer.
>
> *Second Tier*—Web server and optional application server(s) are part of
> the business logic tier.

> *Third Tier*—Middleware layer, which most commonly contains CGI scripts. The middleware layer may also include JDBC drivers as well as specific application server APIs, most often developed in-house to connect to operational applications.
>
> *Fourth Tier*—Transaction manager layer, which may consist of a component transaction server. Component transaction servers function as an interface to the back-end database servers.

Database servers are often connected into the intranet via transaction servers. Therefore, the lowest tier constitutes the back-end data stores or, in intranet parlance, the database servers.

Search and retrieval tools developed for the Internet can be used on the intranet to locate specific pieces of data. One of the important advantages of using Internet technology for your intranet is that you can use the same tools you use to access information outside your organization when you're accessing information within and across your organization.

LAB 1.4 EXERCISES

1.4.1 UNDERSTAND THE COMPONENTS OF AN INTRANET

a) Which components are found in most intranets?

_____

_____

b) What components are optional?

_____

_____

c) What components (if any) does your organization have in place?

_____

_____

1.4.2 COMPARE THE INTERNET AND AN INTRANET

a) How are the Internet and an intranet the same?

_____

_____

b) How does an intranet differ from the Internet?

_____

_____

LAB 1.4 EXERCISE ANSWERS

1.4.1 ANSWERS

a) Which components are found in most intranets?

Answer: An intranet usually contains at least one Web browser and at least one Web server.

b) What components are optional?

Answer: Additional Web servers, application servers, CGI scripts, JDBC drivers, application server APIs, component transaction servers, and database servers are all optional. They add power and flexibility to the intranet, but some of these components may not be appropriate to your organization's intranet configuration.

c) What components (if any) does your organization have in place?

Answer: This answer depends on the status of the intranet in your organization. Many organizations have at least one Web server in place but may not have connected database servers to the back-end. Many organizations have not extended their intranet throughout the organization and therefore have not yet realized the true benefits of an organizational intranet.

At A Corporation, the first components implemented in the intranet were the Web browsers and servers, along with CGI scripts and component transaction servers. These were connected to corporate database servers. Application servers were developed for specific applications once the intranet was up and running. BJ, with its Java development environment, implements Web browsers, Web servers, CGI scripts, and JDBC drivers on the intranet.

1.4.2 ANSWERS

a) How are the Internet and an intranet the same?

Answer: The Internet and the intranet use the same protocol, IP (Internet Protocol).

At A Corporation, the public Web site on the Internet is supported on a different system from the internal Web site on the intranet. The Web servers are set up the same but support different contents and different application processes. The intranet communicates with non-IP-based mainframes via CGI scripts and application servers. BJ's communication and systems are entirely IP-based.

b) How does an intranet differ from the Internet?

Answer: An intranet serves an organization or a community of interest and restricts access to members of the organization or community. The Internet is the public network of networks and servers connected via IP (Internet Protocol) around the world.

At A Corporation, the intranet supports application processing while the Internet public site provides information on the corporation and products. At BJ, the intranet provides confidential information on product development plans and allows access to code under development, while the Internet provides access to information released to the public.

LAB 1.4 SELF-REVIEW QUESTIONS

In order to test your progress, you should be able to answer the following questions.

1) When creating an intranet, all servers, databases, and so on should be updated or else they will not be able to be a part of the intranet.

 a) _____ True
 b) _____ False

2) Web browsers connect directly to application servers.

 a) _____ True
 b) _____ False

3) Many Internet technologies can also be used in an intranet environment.

 a) _____ True
 b) _____ False

**LAB
1.4**

4) CGI can be used to interface between _____ and _____.

    a) _____ Web browsers, Web servers
    b) _____ Databases, proprietary applications
    c) _____ Web browsers, proprietary applications
    d) _____ Web servers, databases

Quiz answers appear in the Appendix, Section 1.4.

LAB 1.5

INTRANET TECHNICAL DECISIONS

LAB OBJECTIVES

After this lab, you will be able to:

✔ Pose the Technical Questions That Need to Be Answered to Formulate Your Intranet Strategy
✔ Make Technical Decisions Within Your Organization Regarding Your Intranet Strategy and Security Requirements

---

There are a number of technical decisions to make when you formulate your intranet strategy.

Let's look first at existing applications and information systems.

1. What components of an intranet are currently in place in the organization?
2. Do all members have Web browsers on their desktop systems?
3. Is connectivity in place for all members of the organization to access all Web sites on the intranet?
4. Does your organization have existing internal Web sites? Can existing Web servers accommodate additional Web sites? Can existing Web sites accommodate additional content?
5. What hardware is available for use within the intranet?
6. What software is available for use within the intranet?
7. Which existing applications and legacy systems are worth maintaining?
8. Which of these can be easily connected to the intranet?

9. What interface is required to connect each existing application/system?

10. What technical expertise and resources exist to develop and deploy the intranet?

11. What technical expertise and resources exist to maintain, update, and enhance the content of the intranet?

12. What technical expertise and resources exist to enhance the capabilities of the intranet?

13. What security measures are in place and what additional security measures are required to effectively protect any sensitive information on the intranet?

Now that you've considered the technical issues that need to be addressed, let's focus on the security requirements of your organization. Unfortunately, the accessibility of data on the intranet increases the risk of unauthorized changes to data, unauthorized distribution of information, corruption of data through viruses brought into and passed around the organization, and actual stealing of data by those who gain access to the intranet. Part of developing an intranet development strategy is to assess the risks and costs associated with protecting the organization's data. There are four aspects to a comprehensive security plan:

- Deterrence
- Protection
- Detection
- Response

**LAB
1.5**

Volume 2 in this series, *Supporting Web Servers, Networks, and Emerging Technologies*, describes security technologies that can be used to address each of these four aspects of your organization's plan to protect its valuable information assets.

In order to develop a specific set of security policies and procedures for your organization, consider the following questions for your organization:

1. Does your organization have in-house expertise to design, implement, and manage your security policies and security technologies?

2. What software, documentation, data, and resources does your organization rely on? These are the resources that need protection.

3. Which group(s) of people pose the greatest threat to your organization's resources: people internal to the organization, those who are external but are in established relationships with the organization, or external parties? Determine how much risk each group poses and how you would like to protect your resources from each of these groups threatening the integrity of your resources.

4.   Who has access to passwords and network documentation? It is important to put security measures in place to safeguard and severely limit access to passwords, which serve as the "keys to the kingdom." These include root passwords on servers, router passwords, database passwords, and other passwords that allow people to change configurations, access data anywhere on the network, or act as a "super user."

5.   How much would it cost for you to secure your valuable resources? If you don't know enough about security technologies, you can refer to Volume 2 in this series, *Supporting Web Servers, Networks, and Emerging Technologies*, which provides information on security technologies. Once you understand the options available, look at the costs and make sure that the value of the resources that need to be protected justifies the cost of the security technologies and procedures. That is, do risk assessment. The financial services industry balances the risk of losing financial assets against the costs associated with protecting them. In the same way, organizations need to evaluate the risk of losing information assets and other resources on the intranet and balance the costs of securing them against the risks associated with losing them.

6.   Who develops your information security policies and procedures? Your organization needs a person or a small group to develop, disseminate, and monitor information security policies.

7.   Once you've developed security policies and procedures, which members of the organization will have responsibility for enforcing and monitoring them? Organizations often keep logs to show who accesses what, but no one has the time to review the logs and identify intruders. Make sure that you budget for the means and the personnel to monitor security exposures and breaches.

LAB 1.5 EXERCISES

1.5.1 POSE THE TECHNICAL QUESTIONS THAT NEED TO BE ANSWERED TO FORMULATE YOUR INTRANET STRATEGY

Consider the list of questions posed in this lab.

a) Which of these questions need to be addressed in your organization?

_____

_____

b) Which of these questions can you answer today? Which ones do you need help answering?

_____

_____

1.5.2 MAKE TECHNICAL DECISIONS WITHIN YOUR ORGANIZATION REGARDING YOUR INTRANET STRATEGY AND SECURITY REQUIREMENTS

a) What is the difference between deterrence and protection?

_____

_____

b) What problem might you encounter if you implemented deterrence and protection mechanisms without implementing detection procedures?

_____

_____

**LAB
1.5**

c) What problem might occur if your organization decides to encrypt all data that is transmitted?

_____

_____

LAB 1.5 EXERCISE ANSWERS

1.5.1 ANSWERS

a) Which of these questions need to be addressed in your organization?

Answer: This will differ within each organization. Even if all the technical decisions have been made in your organization, take time to review them with members of your World Wide Web Council. Those questions that relate to security policies and technologies need to be addressed by your task force so that you are in agreement on which security technologies will be implemented and supported.

b) Which of these questions can you answer today? Which ones do you need help answering?

Answer: Again, look to members of your World Wide Web Council to assist in answering these questions. They need to be involved in the technical decisions, particularly those that relate to information security.

1.5.2 ANSWERS

a) What is the difference between deterrence and protection?

Answer: Deterrence involves trying to keep people out. In the same way as a double bolt lock on your front door deters unwanted intruders, firewalls, routers, and filters make it more difficult for network intruders to gain access to your intranet. Protection includes measures to ensure that the sender and receiver of data are who they say they are (authentication) and measures to safeguard the confidentiality of data if it is seen by other than the intended recipient (encryption). Authentication and encryption technologies can be used together to protect the integrity of the data, that is, to ensure that the data has not been altered.

At A Corporation, we used firewalls, routers, and filters to limit access to development servers, that is, for deterrence. While we used multiple levels of authentication for protection, we did not usually encrypt the data we were sending within the corporation. BJ, as a start-up, has more limited means, but in some ways more sensitive data. Therefore, we combine deterrence in the form of firewalls, routers, and filters with protection in the form of authentication and encryption to keep network intruders out and to safeguard the integrity of the data.

b) What problem might you encounter if you implemented deterrence and protection mechanisms without implementing detection procedures?

Answer: An intruder could get past your firewall, get authenticated using some one else's login and password, and not be noticed until something catastrophic, such as the destruction or disappearance of data, occurred.

Both the A Corporation and BJ network administration teams regularly scan the logs to see if any intruders have gained access to the gateway systems, which would allow them access to other systems. Without such detection procedures in place, data corruption could occur before the company was aware that there was a break-in.

c) What problem might occur if your organization decides to encrypt all data that is transmitted?

Answer: Since it takes time to encrypt data on the sending side and to decrypt data on the receiving end, performance may be degraded more than is acceptable to users.

**LAB
1.5**

Since SSL (secure sockets layer) encryption encrypts and decrypts each packet of data, it is important to weigh the potential loss or compromise of confidential data versus the adverse impact using SSL for all data would have on performance.

A Corporation chose not to encrypt all data being transmitted to avoid performance degradation. BJ uses encryption on a selective basis to avoid performance degradation as well.

LAB 1.5 SELF-REVIEW QUESTIONS

In order to test your progress, you should be able to answer the following questions.

1) Security is an issue with intranets.

   a) _____ True
   b) _____ False

2) Security policies are best when developed by the whole company.

   a) _____ True
   b) _____ False

3) Firewalls are an example of a protection.

   a) _____ True
   b) _____ False

4) Encryption is an example of a protection.

   a) _____ True
   b) _____ False

Quiz answers appear in the Appendix, Section 1.5.

**LAB
1.5**

LAB 1.6

INTRANET POLICIES

LAB OBJECTIVES

After this lab, you will be able to:

✔ Understand the Need for Policies Governing Your Intranet
✔ Develop Guidelines and Policies for Intranet Usage

Many organizations have policies in place to protect certain confidential documents. Markings on documents may indicate the level of confidentiality associated with a particular document. At times, people are specifically instructed to keep certain pieces of information confidential for a specified period of time. In certain circumstances, people are only allowed to share documents and information within the organization but not with people outside the organization. Some organizations have developed specific markings—such as confidential, proprietary, secret—each of which connotes a different level of protection and requires authorization and approval for dissemination. Some documents are restricted to viewing by only certain members of the organization. Yet another set of documents may be available for viewing but not for reproduction.

The organization may have an Acceptable Use Policy (AUP) already in place. The AUP defines how people are allowed to use certain documents and information. The AUP also defines the policies that control dissemination of the organization's knowledge assets. Organizations are increasingly aware of the value of their intellectual capital, the information and knowledge acquired and managed by members of the organization. Developing a sensible policy to protect and use these knowledge assets is a worthwhile exercise for the organization to undertake.

Some organizations also have developed policies and procedures to back up and maintain data stored on magnetic tapes, disk drives, and various other electronic media. Critical data may be available on mirrored sites with hot backup so that people can use the mirrored site if one site is not available. Other critical data may be stored on-site or off-site. Sometimes, tapes with critical data are stored in fireproof safes or at a geographically distant location in case of earthquakes or other natural disasters. In order to develop your intranet, you need to examine any organizational policies that have been developed for backing up, storing, and sharing data, whether the data's in print or on electronic media. If your organization has no policies in place, it's time to develop such policies in keeping with your organizational strategy. Your organization's information, documents, and data are valuable knowledge assets. Categorize the documents, information, and data that your organization generates, develops, distributes, maintains, and/or owns. Determine which of your current data and document protection policies should be applied when the data moves to the intranet.

■ FOR EXAMPLE

At our company, we placed a red "internal use only" mark on each page of company-confidential documents on an internal Web site. This indicated that the data should not be shared with anyone outside the corporation. We also marked certain documents "not for distribution" since we had licensed this information and our licensing agreement precluded sharing the data with customers and others who were not employees of the corporation. In addition, we had a password-protected internal Web site for corporate strategy documents that were under development. This site had restricted access; only members of the strategic planning and corporate management teams were allowed access to this site. The group decided that these documents should not be reproduced while they were under development. Therefore, the documents were marked with the words "Do not reproduce" on the Web pages. In these cases, the policies that were used for hard-copy documents were applied directly to the documents when they resided on the intranet.

LAB 1.6

LAB 1.6 EXERCISES

1.6.1 UNDERSTAND THE NEED FOR POLICIES GOVERNING YOUR INTRANET

a) What is an AUP?

_____

_____

b) Does your organization have an AUP? If so, describe it. If not, what do you think your organization's AUP should cover?

_____

_____

1.6.2 DEVELOP GUIDELINES AND POLICIES FOR INTRANET USAGE

a) Does your organization have policies regarding confidentiality or use of documents? If so, what are they? If not, what do you think they should be?

_____

_____

b) Do you think the same policies that apply to your hard-copy documents should govern the use of the intranet? Why or why not?

_____

_____

LAB 1.6 EXERCISE ANSWERS

1.6.1 ANSWERS

a) What is an AUP?

Answer: AUP is the acronym for Acceptable Use Policy. This policy describes what is allowed and not allowed by your organization regarding the use and dissemination of information and documents. It is important to develop such a policy regarding the use and dissemination of information and documents for your organization's intranet.

At A Corporation, there were licensed marketing databases, which could not be shared with people outside the company. It was important to include a notice in the AUP for the intranet that this information was for internal use only. Since BJ is a start-up venture, the AUP for the intranet provides guidelines for protecting software and project plans that are under development and not ready for release yet.

b) Does your organization have an AUP? If so, describe it. If not, what do you think your organization's AUP should cover?

Answer: This answer depends on the state of your organization's policies. If your organization has one, review it with your World Wide Web Council and make sure that it covers use and dissemination of information and documents on the intranet. Your organization's current AUP may only cover hard-copy documents and may need to be updated to cover the intranet. Or, your organization's AUP may cover Internet usage but not intranet usage.

It is important to cover:

Confidentiality issues

Distribution of documents and materials developed by the organization

Dissemination of documents and materials that were not developed by the organization

Markings on documents to indicate appropriate usage and distribution

The A Corporation AUP was extended to include information on the policies regarding site licenses for marketing databases, to cover in-process strategic planning documents that were only shared within the strategic planning group, and to define markings on internal use web pages. At A Corporation, the Internet AUP statement was extended to cover corporate intranet guidelines, whereas at BJ, the AUP was developed to cover Internet and intranet usage from the start.

1.6.2 ANSWERS

a) Does your organization have policies regarding confidentiality or use of documents? If so, what are they? If not, what do you think they should be?

Answer: Check on confidentiality policies and make sure that they apply to documents that are available on your organization's intranet. Develop or update confidentiality policies with members of your World Wide Web Council so that each group understands the ramifications of making documents available on your organization's intranet.

A Corporation and BJ both developed policies for confidentiality and for internal use of documents that were posted to the intranet. A Corporation modeled its intranet policies after its hard-copy document policies, while BJ developed its document policy along with its intranet and Internet policies when the company was started.

b) Do you think the same policies that apply to your hard-copy documents should govern the use of the intranet? Why or why not?

Answer: In some cases, you can apply the same policies to hard-copy documents as to intranet documents. Sometimes, merely marking a document "Internal Use Only" is sufficient. Sometimes, password protection is required to control access to confidential documents. It is important to review license agreements for information and documents that have been purchased from external sources. Your organization may be required to limit access according to the terms of the license agreement, or you may need to renegotiate the terms of the agreement if you want to offer wider distribution of such materials within your organization.

At A Corporation, the document policies were translated from hard-copy to web-accessible documents. The corporation decided not to make all documents available on the intranet. However, at BJ, all documents are available on the web and can be printed on an as-needed basis. The same confidentiality and distribution requirements pertain whether the document is online or on paper.

LAB 1.6 SELF-REVIEW QUESTIONS

In order to test your progress, you should be able to answer the following questions.

1) Acceptable Use Policies (select all that apply)

    a) _____ are vital for companies that have intranets.
    b) _____ set access and reproduction guidelines for company content.
    c) _____ deter hackers from breaking into company servers.
    d) _____ none of the above

2) AUPs can include guidelines on marking documents to show appropriate usage and distribution.

    a) _____ True
    b) _____ False

3) It is possible to mark electronic documents confidential.

    a) _____ True
    b) _____ False

Quiz answers appear in the Appendix, Section 1.6.

**LAB
1.6**

LAB 1.7

INTRANET BUDGETS

LAB OBJECTIVES

After this lab, you will be able to:

✔ Understand the Cost Factors Involved in the Development, Deployment, and Maintenance of an Intranet

---

Experience within different organizations has demonstrated that Web site costs can vary by at least a factor of 10. These costs vary widely due to major differences in the functionality desired for different Web sites. An internal Web site can serve as the portal to your organization's intranet. However, this internal Web site is only one of the line items in the budget for your organization's intranet.

Intranet costs include the following items:

- Technology—hardware and software
- Management
- Network security
- Training
- Learning curve
- Maintenance and update
- DBMS and legacy systems integration
- Human resources—headcount and expertise

**LAB
1.7**

Many organizations budget for the hardware and software but fail to take into account the other items on this list. One item that has caused major headaches in organizations is the human resources area. Often the organization does not budget for the people who need to maintain the intranet. Another area that is often ignored is search facilities. If your organization's intranet contains lots of information, but there is no way to locate what's needed, the intranet will not serve its purpose. A search engine should be included in the technology line item.

Consider the cost of training and the time involved in everyone's learning how to use the intranet. Working with members of your organization's World Wide Web Council, you can determine who needs training to publish information on the intranet. If someone in your organization can develop templates, a style guide, and/or a set of publishing guidelines, there will be a more consistent appearance. These guidelines can give the new "publishers" a jump-start for making their information available via the intranet. Budget for some one to develop "online help" to assist the new "publishers" in your organization. Your "online help" facilities can and should be part of your intranet so that new people can take on these "publishing" tasks in the future.

Table 1.1 outlines the costs involved in developing and deploying an intranet for your organization. These amounts reflect costs as of the publication of this book. Over time, personnel costs are apt to rise and technology prices are apt to fall.

Table 1.1 ■ Projected Costs for Year 1 of Intranet

Component	Low	Medium
Web Server	$5,000	$50,000
Firewall	$5,000	$50,000
Router	$5,000	$25,000
Internet Connection	$10,000	$120,000
Content Development	$25,000	$500,000
Licensed Content	none	$120,000
Creative Design	$10,000	$150,000
Update and Maintenance	$25,000	$250,000
Intranet Management	$50,000	$150,000
Technical Management	$50,000	$150,000
Customization	$10,000	$250,000
Legacy Systems Integration	$50,000	$1,000,000
Training	$10,000	$100,000
Total Year 1	$255,000	$2,915,000

In examining the amounts listed in this table, you may feel that some of the amounts are too high or too low for your organization. You may be able to combine the function of Intranet Manager and Technical Manager. You may decide not to do any programming for your initial rollout of the intranet. Or, you may be in a large organization that has decided to deploy an intranet that integrates the organization's ERP (enterprise resource planning) and accounting systems. This may require significant programming effort. Use this table as a planning tool to determine what the budget for your organization's intranet should be. Whether the total figure is lower or higher, it is important to decide what resources you are budgeting for each task and each line item.

LAB 1.7 EXERCISES

1.7 UNDERSTAND THE COST FACTORS INVOLVED IN THE DEVELOPMENT, DEPLOYMENT, AND MAINTENANCE OF AN INTRANET

a) What item is the most often forgotten in an intranet budget?

_____

_____

b) What does the item "learning curve" entail?

_____

_____

LAB 1.7 EXERCISE ANSWERS

LAB
1.7

1.7 ANSWERS

a) What item is the most often forgotten in an intranet budget?

Answer: Maintenance and update are areas that are often ignored. It is important to budget for people to maintain and update the intranet and for software enhancements and hardware upgrades as your intranet grows.

This was a real problem in transferring the market analysis intranet application from the development team to an Information Services group at A Corporation. Though we developed the intranet to minimize needed maintenance, it still needed someone to keep up with upgrades and enhancements. After the intranet gained acceptance and more people were using it in their daily work, money was budgeted for maintenance and upgrade. That is the reason that pilot projects help in gaining acceptance and in realistically budgeting for ongoing use.

b) What does the item "learning curve" entail?

Answer: This budgetary item includes time and resources for people to become familiar with the use of the intranet for disseminating information. It may not take very long for people to learn to locate personnel policies, reserve conference rooms, or file expense reports on the intranet, but it does generally take some time for people to change the way they do these day-to-day tasks. It will also take time for people to learn to "publish" their information on the intranet.

"Learning curve" items, including training and becoming comfortable with moving applications and practices to the web, were critical to realistically moving processes and information to the intranet at A Corporation. At BJ, everything was started on the intranet from scratch and everyone in the organization is comfortable using the web. This is a major difference between moving to an intranet in a large, mature organization and implementing an intranet in a start-up at the beginning.

LAB 1.7 SELF-REVIEW QUESTIONS

In order to test your progress, you should be able to answer the following questions.

1) It is not necessary to allocate money to maintain a new intranet.

a) _____ True
b) _____ False

2) What are necessary costs in setting up an intranet (select all that apply)?

a) _____ search facilities
b) _____ training
c) _____ security
d) _____ hardware
e) _____ software

3) Intranet content publishers can figure the tools out on their own.

a) _____ True
b) _____ False

4) Not much programming is needed to create an intranet.

a) _____ True
b) _____ False

Quiz answers appear in the Appendix, Section 1.7.

LAB 1.8

INTRANET PILOT

LAB OBJECTIVES

After this lab, you will be able to:

✔ Understand a Pilot Intranet Deployment
✔ Understand the Reasons for a Pilot Project

In 1993, our company needed a way to share competitive analysis information with people in sales, marketing, and engineering. At that point, information came into one location in corporate headquarters and there was no effective way of sharing the information. If an individual salesperson in the field requested competitive information, email or fax communication could be used, but then the information was forwarded to only one specific individual. A marketing library in corporate headquarters was available to people in the area but sales and marketing people were located in field sales offices all over the world. An additional problem resulted from the sales force's urgent need for information. In the middle of developing a sales proposal or bid for a major account, field sales offices had little time to search for information. At that time, a competitive analyst found out about our World Wide Web project and asked me if I could help disseminate the competitive and marketing information. After discussion with the marketing library, vendors of market research purchased by the company, marketing management, and engineering management, we decided to develop a pilot intranet application, which we named the Marketing Information Repository (MIR). The steps that we took are overviewed in the following sections.

**LAB
1.8**

DEVELOP A PROJECT PLAN

Our first step was to develop a project plan. We mapped out the steps involved in defining, developing, testing, training, and deploying our intranet pilot. We decided that in order to be successful, we needed to understand both the needs of the users and the information providers.

ASSEMBLE A TASK FORCE OF INFORMATION PROVIDERS, USERS, AND INTRANET DEVELOPERS

We assembled a task force consisting of representatives from the intended user group of field sales and marketing staff and from the group of information providers, including the marketing library, competitive and marketing analysts, and corporate marketing staff. Our task force included the lead software engineer responsible for the development of the intranet marketing application. After successfully overseeing the development of this initial intranet marketing application, the task force formed the core group for our World Wide Web Council. Over time the World Wide Web Council oversaw the deployment of the intranet throughout the corporation's international locations. In addition, we used the corporate World Wide Web Council to move the public corporate Web site from an engineering project to a corporate resource.

WORK OUT VENDOR RELATIONSHIPS AND LICENSING AGREEMENTS

The next step involved talking to the vendors of market research information. Since we wanted to make this information available on our intranet, we needed to modify our licensing agreements. In addition, at that point, the information arrived in different forms—via fax, e-mail, and hard copy. We worked out agreements for each vendor to send us updates electronically and we determined the format of the information by asking each vendor's technical staff.

AUTOMATE CONVERSION AND POSTING OF INFORMATION

At that point, none of the market research vendors had moved to the Web, so my group developed an HTML converter to take the information from each vendor and convert it to HTML to post. We automated all the processes so that they were performed automatically during the night. We determined that 2 AM, 3 AM, and 4 AM were good times for the automated processes to occur. Thus, the information was received from each vendor and converted to HTML, indexed for the search engine, and posted to the appropriate Web pages. In the morning when people came into work, they found that the repositories were populated with updated market research and competitive information. From the beginning, we developed an automated system that required minimal maintenance or support.

FROM DEMONSTRATION TO PROTOTYPE TO PILOT IMPLEMENTATION

Since people in the organization were not familiar with intranets or the World Wide Web at that point, we developed a demonstration to illustrate what we were developing. Whenever we presented our plan, we allowed them to use the demonstration system. From user feedback, we realized that we needed to provide powerful search capabilities along with repositories of information that were structured for easy browsing. Once we had a prototype working, we presented our prototype system to small groups and encouraged each person to search for a particular piece of information or to browse through a repository of interest. We incorporated their feedback into the pilot implementation. As soon as our pilot was available, we offered training sessions so that people could become familiar with the application. At this point, since we had presented our demonstration and prototype, we already had support in other parts of the corporation. The phased development effort allowed us to incorporate valuable user feedback into our implementation and to gradually build acceptance by both users and management.

We found that implementing our intranet pilot in this way provided the corporation with a strong foundation on which to build other components of the intranet. By the end of the project, we had:

- A representative task force in place that served as the basis of the World Wide Web Council
- A working pilot implementation with automated tools that required minimal technical support
- A growing group of active users, providing regular feedback
- A trained group of information providers
- A group of evangelists who understood the intranet and wanted to extend its use throughout the corporation

LAB 1.8 EXERCISES

1.8.1 UNDERSTAND A PILOT INTRANET DEPLOYMENT

a) What do you think is the most important component of intranet pilot development?

_____

_____

1.8.2 UNDERSTAND THE REASONS FOR PILOT PROJECT

a) With so many people excited about intranets today, why is it important to develop a pilot?

_____

_____

LAB 1.8 EXERCISE ANSWERS

1.8.1 ANSWER

a) What do you think is the most important component of intranet pilot development?

Answer: Involving users and information providers from the beginning of the planning process is the best way to ensure that your system meets the needs of both the users and the information providers.

For A Corporation, it was critical to engage members of various departments in the development of an intranet pilot. The BJ community is much more comfortable using intranet applications and the main pilot project is the development of the online learning software for internal and external deployment. Once again, the needs of the user community are the most important factor to consider in developing a pilot intranet project.

1.8.2 ANSWER

a) With so many people excited about intranets today, why is it important to develop a pilot?

Answer: Pilot implementations allow organizations to:

Build user and management acceptance

Incorporate feedback into their plans and development

Understand costs and resources required to maintain and manage an intranet

Establish and support a group of trained users and information providers over time

Excitement is contagious and can get people to use the intranet, but a pilot implementation allows the organization to test out its assumptions and plans. With A Corporation, we had to prove the capabilities and usefulness of the intranet, but at BJ, a pilot

**LAB
1.8**

implementation served as a testing ground for a new approach to online learning. Thus, whether you're involved in an established organization that may be uncomfortable moving to an intranet or a new organization that includes an intranet in its initial network facilities, there is a need for a pilot implementation of the intranet. The pilot implementations at A Corporation and BJ have been used to test assumptions, figure out appropriate policies and procedures, plan and check out budget figures, and try new applications before deployment to a larger group.

LAB 1.8 SELF-REVIEW QUESTIONS

In order to test your progress, you should be able to answer the following questions.

1) For an intranet to succeed it must be accepted by the users and corporate management.

    a) _____ True
    b) _____ False

2) User feedback is useless.

    a) _____ True
    b) _____ False

3) Intranets do not change over the course of their lifespans.

    a) _____ True
    b) _____ False

Quiz answers appear in the Appendix, Section 1.8.

**LAB
1.8**

CHAPTER 1

TEST YOUR THINKING

Outline a plan for an intranet pilot of a fictitious organization. Remember that all aspects of the pilot must center on the organization's mission.

1) Does the organization already have a World Wide Web Council?
2) What is the goal of the intranet?
3) What facilities are already available in the organization? Which of these facilities would work better when coupled with the intranet? Should certain existing systems be replaced or upgraded?
4) What facilities will be available on the intranet? To whom?
5) What content is currently available in the corporation? Is the existing content going to be integrated into the intranet?
6) Will the deployment of the intranet alter the management practices of the organization?
7) What type of monitoring and approval mechanisms will be necessary?
8) Will individuals and groups create content for the intranet? Do they need tools to do this? What tools?
9) Will there be style guidelines for sites within the intranet?
10) What security measures are already in place within the organization? What security measures need to be added?
11) What software and hardware is needed for the intranet? What will be developed in-house? Will servers be located in-house or co-located at an ISP?

C H A P T E R 2

EXTRANETS

An extranet extends the power of an intranet to an organization's network of partners and suppliers. An extranet supports communication and relationships between the organization and allied organizations or between multiple organizations within a community of interest. In this way, an extranet connects organizations within a larger community.

In this chapter, we'll start by defining what an extranet is and how it can be used by your organization. You've probably heard the term *extranet* used and may have even used one. You'll find out how to move existing relationships between your organization and allied organizations and individuals to an extranet. In addition, you'll learn about setting up secure boundaries between the various extranet communities with which your organization interacts.

LAB 2.1

EXTRANET BASICS

LAB OBJECTIVES

After this lab, you will be able to:

✔ Differentiate Between Extranets and Intranets
✔ Differentiate Between Extranets and Traditional EDI

First let's define what we mean by the word *extranet*. In 1996, the word *extranet* was coined by Bob Metcalfe, inventor of the Ethernet and founder of 3Com Corporation. By then, organizations were using intranets and realizing the benefits of Internet-based technology for internal communications within their organizations. Some of these organizations then decided to extend their intranets to partners outside the organization. However, they wanted to differentiate between their three constituencies:

- Those inside the organization using their intranet
- Trusted partners working with the organization that reside outside the organization
- The general public on the external Internet

People began to see the need for an Internet-based approach to business and organizational relationships and communication, coupled with appropriate access control and security technology to safeguard communication between trusted partners. The prefix *extra*, the Latin word for "outside," is used to indicate that the network operates outside the organization's boundaries, since these networks extend beyond the boundaries of a single organization to include external partners.

The approach to defining an extranet taken by the electronic commerce industry consortium CommerceNet is to emphasize the business relationships that constitute the reason for establishing an extranet. Based on this approach, an extranet can be defined as a network using Internet, Web, and network security technologies and protocols to provide connectivity, support business relationships, and protect confidentiality for a group of organizations that interact via trading and business relationships. Extranets are established and controlled by the community of trading partners using the facilities to conduct their business. Extranets operate as Virtual Private Networks (VPNs), protecting the community from the general public on the Internet and at the same time offering connectivity via the Internet and the Web.

Key components of an extranet include:

- IP (Internet Protocol)-based technology
- Relationships with known and trusted partners
- Access to an organization's internal resources by external parties
- Security and controlled access

Therefore, we can define an extranet to be an IP-based network with controlled access to an organization's internal resources by trusted external partners. Extranet security facilities close off access to the network so that an extranet forms a network that appears to be private but is physically shared. The network is thus considered to be a VPN. Security measures are established to delineate and enforce boundaries and provide protection for trusted partners cooperating with but operating outside the organization hosting the extranet. Since the boundaries and security measures are accepted by both the organization and its trusted partners, we talk about an extranet providing bilateral security.

To better understand the evolution of the extranet, let's look at the first type of electronic commerce, EDI (Electronic Data [or Document] Interchange). Many large companies have used EDI to connect to other companies in their supply chain. EDI was developed in the 1970s to automate the exchange of information to manage ordering of parts and supplies for manufacturing, inventory control, warehouse management, and shipment of goods along the supply chain. Since the Internet was restricted to research and military use at the time, time-sharing companies established VANs (Value-Added Networks) to transmit EDI information from a company to its suppliers and partners. Companies adopted EDI to connect with their partners to achieve an integration of their supply chain. These organizations thought that supply chain integration via EDI would increase their operational efficiency, reduce their costs, and allow them to retain their competitive position in the marketplace. Although EDI did assist companies in its early years, over time, the highly structured nature of the electronic forms and the requirements of the private network for transmitting the simple electronic forms limited EDI transactions to known static relationships. While EDI was helpful in the 1970s and the 1980s, by the late 1980s and early 1990s, the manufacturing environment had become even more competitive and just-in-time manufacturing required more responsive tools to automate the process. In addition, companies began working with multiple partners in more of a "supply web" than a supply chain, with increased fluidity in business relationships and ordering, manufacturing, and warehousing processes. Traditional EDI, with its highly structured format, became a stumbling block to these new dynamic relationships between companies. With the advent of Internet technology and security technology, forward-thinking companies realized that they could automate their supply webs by implementing extranets. An extranet combines the automation and security mechanisms that companies found useful in EDI, with Internet open standards and collaboration tools to support dynamic business relationships and just-in-time processes.

The companies that were served best by EDI were the manufacturing companies, and these are the companies that are finding extranets to be very useful in coordinating design and manufacturing processes as well as in production and shipment scheduling. The personal computer market has become a price-sensitive commodity market and extranet technology has been useful to some vendors in obtaining the best prices on parts, in scheduling delivery based on availability, and in closely managing their inventories. Extranets can also be extended to support vertical markets. Many members of the personal computer supply chain along with government agencies (who are large customers of personal computer companies) are cooperating to develop a multi-organizational extranet with standard tools and protocols. This industry is thought of as the IT (information technology) industry. The cooperative effort has been named RosettaNet, based on the story of the rosetta stone. For those who are unfamiliar with the rosetta stone, it is a rock with an inscription that became the key to deciphering Egyptian hieroglyphics. Since the inscription is in three scripts: hieroglyphic, demotic, and Greek, scholars were able to figure out the hieroglyphic and demotic versions by comparing them with the Greek. RosettaNet was founded to define open and common processes to align the business interfaces between IT supply chain partners. Their extranet is an industry consortium extranet, supporting the community of interest in the IT supply chain.

Manufacturing companies can use their extranets to include their production and design partners in collaborative efforts employing Internet technology and inter-enterprise computing. Extranets let companies coordinate design, manufacturing, scheduling, and delivery across the supply chain.

Other industries also benefit from extranets. The financial services area was one of the first to automate business transactions with its proprietary financial networks. This was also one of the first industries to automate customer interaction with ATMs (Automatic Teller Machines) and home banking. (Note: ATM is used as an acronym for both Automatic Teller Machines in the financial industry and Asynchronous Transfer Mode, an advanced implementation of packet switching, in the telecommunications industry). Now extranets can replace proprietary financial networks, thereby reducing the cost of processing financial transactions. In both the high-tech world and the banking industry, extranets provide services and support to customers. In the software and publishing sectors, which increasingly rely on collaboration between various groups and individuals, extranets can provide access to geographically dispersed contributors to facilitate teamwork and cooperation.

LAB 2.1 EXERCISES

2.1.1 DIFFERENTIATE BETWEEN EXTRANETS AND INTRANETS

a) How does an extranet differ from an intranet and how would the difference benefit your organization?

_____

_____

2.1.2 DIFFERENTIATE BETWEEN EXTRANETS AND TRADITIONAL EDI

a) How does an extranet differ from traditional EDI and how would the difference benefit your organization?

_____

_____

LAB 2.1 EXERCISE ANSWERS

2.1.1 ANSWER

a) How does an extranet differ from an intranet and how would the difference benefit your organization?

Answer: An extranet extends some of the facilities of an intranet to selected members of an organization's community of suppliers, customers, partners, and allied organizations. The organization determines which members of its extended community are allowed access to which parts of the organization's extranet.

A Corporation accounting wanted an extranet to handle parts ordering from trusted partners. The manufacturing organization in A Corporation's mainframe division wanted to share printed circuit board designs with contractors via the extranet. BJ is establishing strategic partnerships with consulting companies, which will access software and services via an extranet.

2.1.2 ANSWER

a) How does an extranet differ from traditional EDI and how would the difference benefit your organization?

Answer: Extranets are built with standard Internet protocols and web technology. Traditional EDI networks are built on top of VANs (Value Added Networks) using proprietary protocols and network technology.

A Corporation used traditional EDI and wanted to move to an extranet to take advantage of the Internet infrastructure that was already in place. With traditional EDI, only partners with access to that VAN can work with a company online. With an extranet, A Corporation could extend its online support for strategic partners without the added costs associated with traditional EDI. BJ established an extranet from the beginning, using standard protocols unlike traditional EDI, which is built on a proprietary network infrastructure.

LAB 2.1 SELF-REVIEW QUESTIONS

In order to test your progress, you should be able to answer the following questions.

1) Extranets are normally open to the public.

    a) _____ True
    b) _____ False

2) Extranets run on IP-based technology.

    a) _____ True
    b) _____ False

3) An extranet extends some of the facilities of an intranet to selected groups of people and organizations outside of the corporation.

    a) _____ True
    b) _____ False

Quiz answers appear in the Appendix, Section 2.1.

LAB 2.2

EXTRANET BUSINESS STRATEGY

LAB OBJECTIVES

After this lab, you will be able to:

✔ Make the Transition from Intranet to Extranet
✔ Understand Collaboration Benefits of an Extranet

Businesses and organizations are moving to extranets for the same reasons that some adopted EDI earlier. Implementing an extranet, these organizations hope to:

- Decrease operational costs
- Increase speed of processing requests and handling day-to-day business operations
- Enhance information flow between organizations and individuals
- Increase quality of service
- Enhance quality of collaborative efforts
- Improve quality of products developed by partner organizations working together

An extranet provides support for:

- Information dissemination and sharing
- Distributed access to a shared knowledge base
- Collaborative projects

Let's consider your organizational requirements in each of these areas.

INFORMATION DISSEMINATION

- What information is shared with external partners?
- Which groups and individuals need access to the information?
- Who in the organization and among the trusted partners is allowed to disseminate the information?
- How often is the information updated?

KNOWLEDGE BASE

- Where are the people located who need access to the knowledge base?
- Are different levels of access control required for selective access for individual partners?
- Who maintains the knowledge base?
- Will trusted partners contribute to the knowledge base or will they just access the host organization's knowledge base?
- Are there highly confidential parts of the knowledge base?

COLLABORATION

- Is your organization involved in collaborative projects? If so, with whom are you collaborating and how do you carry out your present form of collaboration?
- What is the output from each partner?
- Is there a shared repository and, if so, who maintains the repository and where is it located?
- How do partners bring together the results of their individual efforts?
- Do these projects involve joint development of software? If so, how is the code checked in, modified, and tested?
- How is a software build done? Who is responsible for code check-in and build processes?

OPERATIONAL USE OF AN EXTRANET

Let's look at some of the ways that your organization may want to use an extranet. Shared business processes can lead to an increase in personnel efficiency. Remote partners, contractors, and employees can use the extranet to access shared systems and resources. The success of these efforts on the extranet depend on safeguarding the integrity of the data. Sharing business processes can reduce data re-entry since forms and information can be passed from one organization to another in an electronic form that each of the organizations can process. This is an important area to consider for your extranet. Are there business processes that are or could be shared between your organization and external partners?

Extranets are designed to assist organizations in their day-to-day operations. Some other areas to look for potential extranet applications include the following:

- Inventory control
- Collections and cash flow
- Reconciliation of accounts
- Ordering and delivery of office supplies
- Shipment of needed parts and supplies for product development and production

Customer service and support have been greatly enhanced by providing extranet facilities to key customers and major accounts. A tighter, more responsive relationship can ensue, leading to greater customer satisfaction. The benefits are great and the cost is lower than with traditional phone-based customer service. Customer service is the area that has moved most readily to an extranet since organizations can see a clear benefit in terms of cost reductions, ease of transition, and increased satisfaction on the part of both the customer and the customer service personnel.

Now, take some time to consider the day-to-day operations of your organization. Convene a meeting of your World Wide Web Council and discuss extranet applications that would benefit your organization. Start with the intranet applications that are working well in your organization and see if there are some that should be extended to your partners. Also start from your existing relationships with outside partners and see what processes or transactions can be moved to an extranet.

MAKING THE TRANSITION TO AN EXTRANET

Considering the obvious benefits of an extranet, your organization may be excited about implementing an extranet, but are you ready to make the transition?

- Most consultants advise organizations to implement their intranets first.
- Has your organization resolved network connectivity and bandwidth issues with your intranet?
- Is your intranet functional and are people in the organization using it comfortably?
- Have you resolved distributed and remote access issues, such as who gets access to what information and resources and how is security provided?
- Is your intranet reliable?
- Do you have people and processes in place to maintain your intranet?
- Take time to address these questions with your World Wide Web Council so that you are ready to take the next step in planning and implementing your extranet.

Your extranet plan should address the following questions:

- What information will be shared? What types of information are static? What parts are updated or modified? How often? Is there a regular update schedule?
- What resources or services will be made available on the extranet?
- Which trusted partners will have access to your extranet?
- What provisions will you make for security? We will discuss security measures in Lab 2.4.

Answering these questions will help your organization plan the implementation of extranet facilities.

LAB 2.2 EXERCISES

2.2.1 MAKE THE TRANSITION FROM INTRANET TO EXTRANET

a) Why is it advisable to have a good working intranet before your organization implements an extranet and how does it impact your organization?

_____

_____

2.2.2 UNDERSTAND COLLABORATION BENEFITS OF AN EXTRANET

a) How can an extranet support collaboration within your organization?

_____

_____

LAB 2.2 EXERCISE ANSWERS

2.2.1 ANSWER

a) Why is it advisable to have a good working intranet before your organization implements an extranet and how does it impact your organization?

Answer: *Implementing the intranet forces your organization to address such issues as network connectivity, information dissemination, access control, and network security. Once your organization knows how people within the organization can work together via an intranet, it will be better able to plan how the organization can work with partners and trusted external parties via an extranet.*

At A Corporation, it was critical that the organization gain experience first with an intranet pilot implementation and then full implementation of a corporate intranet before an extranet was added. Developing the intranet infrastructure allowed the company to work out the bugs and to determine how the organization would use the facilities with groups inside the organization. Then the extranet could be used in a similar way to the intranet but with trusted partners outside the organization. BJ needed to define working relationships within the organization via the intranet before adding the complexity of working relationships outside the organization supported by an extranet.

2.2.2 ANSWER

a) How can an extranet support collaboration within your organization?

Answer: *An extranet can provide a shared code repository for the development of software by virtual teams. The extranet can provide a shared space for project plans, status reports, updates, and FAQs (frequently asked questions) for collaborating parties. In addition, an extranet can host shared software applications, which may be used in project management and product development.*

This is the approach that BJ follows in shared code development by people working together on collaborative projects. A Corporation manufacturing wanted to share specifications for printed circuit boards to collaborate with contract design firms on the design of the boards for computers.

LAB 2.2 SELF-REVIEW QUESTIONS

In order to test your progress, you should be able to answer the following questions.

1) Extranets provide support for

    a) _____ collaborative projects.
    b) _____ distributed access to a shared knowledge base.
    c) _____ information dissemination and sharing.
    d) _____ all of the above.

2) Extranets cannot include support for customer service and support.

   a) _____ True
   b) _____ False

3) It is best to have a good working intranet before implementing an extranet.

   a) _____ True
   b) _____ False

Quiz answers appear in the Appendix, Section 2.2.

L A B   2 . 3

EXTRANET ARCHITECTURE AND COMPONENTS

LAB OBJECTIVES

After this lab, you will be able to:

✔ Understand the Components of an Extranet
✔ Understand the Types of Extranets

Extranets are very similar to intranets in terms of their components. The key components include:

- IP (Internet Protocol)-based network connectivity
- Hardware, usually including at least one Web server and at least one firewall
- Software including network facilities, Web server (HTTPD—HTTP daemon), and business application software to be used by an organization and its partners and that can be used through their firewalls
- Network security facilities and defined measures

The network connection uses Internet Protocol and can be provided via various types of connection:

- Dial-up line
- Leased or private line
- Secure tunnel on the Internet, providing end-to-end encryption

The hardware includes at least one Web server and at least one firewall, both of which may run on standard PCs with off-the-shelf components. The software includes shared applications that can be used on the extranet. Extranet server software is available to handle access control, security, and transaction and site management. Applications must be compatible between partners to allow for shared use.

The simplest form of security is browser-based encryption, which can be provided by an SSL (Secure Sockets Layer) enabled Web commerce server. Specific pages that are highly confidential or all pages can be transmitted using SSL. However, for shared use of applications, browser-based encryption is not sufficient. Shared applications require a VPN (Virtual Private Network) or tunnel. We will discuss security issues further in the next section.

**LAB
2.3**

There are two basic forms of extranets:

- Hub extranets
- Mutual extranets

A hub extranet is hosted by one organization offering access to trusted external partners. Hub Extranets are used to support an organization and its suppliers, key customers, or collaborative partners.

A mutual extranet allows multiple organizations to access designated areas on each other's intranets. Mutual extranets are used to support virtual communities and vertical industries.

LAB 2.3 EXERCISES

2.3.1 UNDERSTAND THE COMPONENTS OF AN EXTRANET

a) What are the key components of your organization's extranet?

_____

_____

2.3.2 UNDERSTAND THE TYPES OF EXTRANETS

b) What is the difference between a hub extranet and a mutual extranet? Which is right for your organization?

_____

_____

LAB 2.3 EXERCISE ANSWERS

2.3.1 ANSWER

a) What are the key components of your organization's extranet?

Answer: IP-based network connectivity, hardware including at least one Web server and at least one firewall, software including network facilities and shared business application server, and network security facilities and policies.

The components found in our case studies include a Web server, two firewalls (one allowing access to the extranet, the other providing a gateway from the extranet to the intranet), network facilities on the gateway systems, shared business applications running on the Web server, and network security policies and facilities running on the firewall systems.

2.3.2 ANSWER

a) What is the difference between a hub extranet and a mutual extranet? Which is right for your organization?

Answer: A hub extranet is hosted by a single organization whereas a mutual extranet is hosted by multiple organizations, each offering access to designated areas on their respective intranets.

Both A Corporation and BJ decided to host extranets, thereby providing hub extranets. Neither organization wanted to allow outside access to the company intranet facilities.

LAB 2.3 SELF-REVIEW QUESTIONS

In order to test your progress, you should be able to answer the following questions.

1) Extranets require firewalls.

    a) _____ True
    b) _____ False

2) A _____ extranet allows multiple organizations to access designated areas on each other's intranets.

    a) _____ hub
    b) _____ mutual

Quiz answers appear in the Appendix, Section 2.3.

LAB 2.4

EXTRANET SECURITY

LAB OBJECTIVES

After this lab, you will be able to:

✔ Understand the Demilitarized Zone (DMZ)
✔ Understand Systemic Security

When information is shared or transmitted, security questions include the following:

- How do I know where the information came from?
- Did the information arrive exactly as it was sent?
- Can the sender deny sending it?
- Can the receiver deny receiving it?
- Can anyone else read the data?
- How is tracking of the transmission handled?

Security requirements of organizations sharing information on an extranet include the following measures:

- Authentication
- Integrity
- Nonrepudiation—origin and receipt
- Confidentiality

Other management issues involved in extranet management include:

- Provision for system maintenance and mirrored sites to allow for availability 24 hours/day, 7 days/week (indicated as 24×7)

- File and storage management, including back-up and recovery facilities
- System monitoring with automated alerts when certain events occur
- Overall management of the network, with regular network maintenance and upgrades

Extranets raise the issue of management of access control and boundaries between the organization and its partners. Access control needs to be implemented to safeguard information and resources and allow access only to those within the appropriate group. An intranet may allow access to product development plans and code on a company-internal basis only. Consultants and people working with the company operate outside the internal company but are often given access to many of the documents and resources via an extranet. Suppliers and other trusted partners form another group. Major accounts and customers may have access to certain extranet facilities, some of which may be different from those provided to suppliers and trusted partners. The external public can be seen as the farthest group outside the internal boundary, accessing content on the public Web site. It is important to define the type of relationship the organization has with each of these constituencies and to determine the level of trust between the organization and each of these groups. The organization must decide which business processes are appropriate to share with each group and then determine appropriate levels of access for members of each group.

One of the security issues arises from the use of extranet applications, which may be CGI (Common Gateway Interface) scripts or Java applets communicating with back-end application servers. To control access through a single gateway allows your organization to more easily monitor, audit, and control who has access to what information and applications. However, it is advisable to not allow even your trusted partners access through your firewall into your intranet. The current approach is to establish a "demilitarized zone" (also known as a "DMZ"). Placing extranet servers outside the firewall allows trusted partners to access the organization's resources but still stay on the other side of the firewall. An improvement on this concept is to provide two firewalls, one that allows trusted partners to connect from the Internet to the extranet servers on the DMZ and the other serving as a gateway to the organization's intranet from the DMZ. The DMZ approach establishes specific Web and application servers as extranet servers with appropriate access control privileges for each extranet partner. Monitoring and tracking facilities allow these servers to provide intrusion detection mechanisms if people outside the organization attempt to break into the organization's intranet.

As we discussed in Chapter 1, it is important for the security of your organizational intranet to have a well-thought-out security policy. This policy should include a schedule for regular security audits. For extranets, it is critical to define access privileges for each trusted partner who has access to the extranet. Not only should there be firewalls in place but also there is a need for access logs and for information security staff to monitor and analyze the access logs. The security policy should address extranet issues including:

- How extranet users will access the organization's systems
- Which information resources and application resources will be made accessible to extranet users
- What procedures will be used for user authentication
- Requirements for encryption of data
- Intrusion detection plans
- Schedules for monitoring access logs
- Procedures for auditing and updating security mechanisms and policies

Firewalls may range from simple packet filtering software running on routers to application-level firewalls with intelligent security mechanisms and proxy servers. For extranets, networked applications should tunnel through existing protocols, such as HTTP and FTP. This provides more security than allowing direct access to networked applications.

Most security approaches have focused on protecting specific resources, each on an individual basis. However, some people have begun proposing the notion of systemic security to address a way to provide for the combination and interaction of system components. With systemic approaches, it is possible to provide system configuration and security monitoring, resulting in more secure and easier-to-maintain extranets.

LAB 2.4 EXERCISES

2.4.1 UNDERSTAND THE DEMILITARIZED ZONE (DMZ)

a) What is a DMZ and how would it be used in your extranet?

_____

_____

2.4.2 UNDERSTAND SYSTEMIC SECURITY

a) What is systemic security and how will it help your organization with your extranet?

_____

_____

LAB 2.4 EXERCISE ANSWERS

2.4.1 ANSWER

a) What is a DMZ and how would it be used in your extranet?

Answer: DMZ is the acronym for demilitarized zone as used in military parlance. The idea is that the DMZ is an area protected from enemy fire. In network security circles, DMZ is used to mean the area outside the firewall where your organization can place its extranet servers. This allows trusted partners access to the organization's extranet while protecting the organization's intranet from unwanted intrusion. The most effective approach to extranets with a DMZ is to provide a firewall on either side of the extranet servers, one allowing access from the Internet to the extranet and the other allowing access to the intranet from the DMZ.

The DMZ approach is implemented in both our case studies as a way to provide added protection for the organizational intranets. This approach is highly recommended by network security specialists.

LAB
2.4

2.4.2 ANSWER

a) What is systemic security and how will it help your organization with your extranet?

Answer: Systemic security addresses the interaction between the system components and allows for automated monitoring of system components. Automating the configuration of system components can also lead to easier-to-configure and easier-to-administer extranets.

In our case studies, both organizations have network administrators who are responsible for developing plans to address systemic security. Early Web server software was enhanced at A Corporation to offer easy-to-administer server configurations. Linux software has been used at BJ to provide for automated monitoring of system components.

LAB 2.4 SELF-REVIEW QUESTIONS

In order to test your progress, you should be able to answer the following questions.

1) Security issues arise from the use of intranet applications.

a) _____ True
b) _____ False

2) It is not necessary to keep and analyze log files.

a) _____ True
b) _____ False

Quiz answers appear in the Appendix, Section 2.4.

LAB 2.5

EXTRANET BUSINESS RELATIONSHIPS

LAB OBJECTIVES

After this lab, you will be able to:

✔ Describe Different Business Relationships That Your Organization Has
✔ Determine How an Extranet Can Support These Business Relationships

---

Before you can move your business relationships to an extranet, it is important to perform an inventory of existing relationships and determine the interaction in each relationship. Understanding each relationship will allow you to determine the type of electronic relationship that is required. However, you don't want to be limited to current thinking. An extranet may allow your organization to expand its relationships with trusted external partners in ways that have not been contemplated yet. A smoothly running extranet will support flexible working relationships so that organizations can collaborate in areas where they have previously drawn distinct boundaries between their operations.

Business partners can be divided into various categories. Your organization may be working with the following types of business partners:

- Key customers
- Suppliers and contractors
- Sales personnel, including sales representatives, dealers, distributors, and subsidiaries

- Customer and technical support, including repair and maintenance staff
- Joint venture partners
- Members of industry consortia
- Fellow members of community of interest

Your organization may also be cooperating in a joint venture with partner organizations. An extranet hosted by your organization or your joint venture partner can serve to support the strategic alliance. In addition, an extranet can be formed to support a vertical industry community, such as financial services, PC manufacturing and distribution, or real estate. Residential real estate communities can be effectively supported by an extranet since these services are dispersed and often include several smaller operations, which must cooperate to consummate a property sale. If forms can be transmitted electronically, the process will involve less human intervention and can be accomplished more expeditiously.

LAB 2.5 EXERCISES

2.5.1 DESCRIBE DIFFERENT BUSINESS RELATIONSHIPS THAT YOUR ORGANIZATION HAS

a) Perform an inventory of existing trusted partners and describe their relationships to your organization.

_____

_____

2.5.2 DETERMINE HOW AN EXTRANET CAN SUPPORT THESE BUSINESS RELATIONSHIPS

a) Which existing relationships can be supported best by an extranet?

_____

_____

LAB 2.5 EXERCISE ANSWERS

2.5.1 ANSWER

a) Perform an inventory of existing trusted partners and describe their relationships to your organization.

Answer: You will probably find it most useful to categorize your partners as:

Key customers

Suppliers and contractors

Sales personnel

Customer and technical support

Partners in joint ventures

Industry consortium members

Virtual community members

At A Corporation, the list of trusted partners includes major accounts, suppliers and contractors, members of the field sales force, customer service, technical support, and employees of other subsidiary companies. BJ is developing relationships with trusted partners, but as a start-up, the focus is on relationships with contractors and consultants. A Corporation's relationships with each of its trusted partners can be described in terms of the documents that are exchanged, the authorization and approval process, and the work flow process that occurs in the interaction between A Corporation and a trusted partner. Describing the relationship in these terms starts the process of specifying the processes and documents to be supported by the extranet.

2.5.2 ANSWER

a) Which existing relationships can be supported best by an extranet?

Answer: Look for relationships that include:

Geographic dispersion of parties

Frequent communication

Technology-ready partners

Shared business processes

For A Corporation and BJ, extranets can best support relationships with trusted partners who work with these organizations on an ongoing basis following clear procedures for the exchange of documents and information.

LAB 2.5 SELF-REVIEW QUESTIONS

In order to test your progress, you should be able to answer the following questions.

1) With extranets, we talk about trusted partners because (check all that apply):

   a) _____ Users of your company's extranet will be given access to some of your company's resources.

   b) _____ Extranets are used to support existing business relationships.

   c) _____ Extranets support confidential business transactions.

   d) _____ Your company's extranet may cause problems with another company's internal network.

2) It is useful to categorize business relationships for using an extranet because (check all that apply):

   a) _____ Your extranet may provide different levels of access privileges based on the various types of business relationships your company has.

   b) _____ This will help you decide which operating system to use for your Web server.

   c) _____ Understanding your company's business relationships can help in planning the services that your extranet will provide.

   d) _____ Extranets are complicated to install and support.

Quiz answers appear in the Appendix, Section 2.5.

**LAB
2.5**

L A B   2 . 6

EXTRANET BUDGET

LAB OBJECTIVES

After this lab, you will be able to:

✔ Project Extranet Expenses

Table 2.1 outlines the costs involved in developing and deploying an extranet for your organization. All amounts are listed in thousands of dollars.

Table 2.1 ■ Extranet Costs for First Year

Component	Low	Medium
Web Server	$5,000	$25,000
Firewall	$5,000	$50,000
Security Software	$5,000	$50,000
Extranet Software	$10,000	$75,000
Network Applications	$15,000	$100,000
Design	$10,000	$50,000
Information Security Staff	$50,000	$200,000
Technical Staff	$50,000	$250,000
Customization	$10,000	$50,000
Application Development/Integration	none	$100,000
Training	$25,000	$100,000
Total Year 1	$185,000	$1,050,000

Make sure that you have budgeted for adequate protection for your organization's and your partners' needs. Examine your budget to make sure that you have adequately planned for ongoing audit and monitoring by your Information Security team (which may consist of one or more people). It is important to routinely examine access logs for sensitive documents and applications that are critical to the operation of your organization. It is critical to know who has access to such information and processes and to track usage by external partners. Organizations often under budget for ongoing maintenance and upkeep of their extranets, particularly in the area of monitoring access logs.

LAB 2.6 EXERCISES

2.6.1 PROJECT EXTRANET EXPENSES

a) What single item do you think most contributes to budget shortfalls?

_____

_____

b) Do you think that extranet expenses will decrease in the coming years?

_____

_____

LAB 2.6

LAB 2.6 EXERCISE ANSWERS

2.6.1 ANSWER

a) What single item do you think most contributes to budget shortfalls?

Answer: Personnel expense for ongoing maintenance is the most often overlooked line item on the budget for an extranet. Either it is omitted altogether or it is severely underbudgeted.

At A Corporation, there was much discussion of which organization would provide personnel to support ongoing maintenance. In a start-up like BJ, it is difficult but necessary to budget for ongoing maintenance. With development efforts requiring the majority of funds, it is easy to underbudget for necessary maintenance work.

b) Do you think that extranet expenses will decrease in the coming years?

Answer: Based on historical trends, technology costs will continue to decline, making extranet technology affordable to a wide range of organizations. However, personnel expenses will most likely continue to increase. If vendors continue to develop easier-to-use system administration tools, the level of training and expertise required to administer and maintain extranets can be reduced to a certain degree.

Over the last few years, extranet software has become available, which makes it easier to administer extranet facilities. This reduces the expense over early projects that we did at A Corporation in the mid-1990s when we had to develop and maintain our own network administration tools. Off-the-shelf system administration tools are generally less expensive than in-house developed ones.

LAB 2.6 SELF-REVIEW QUESTIONS

In order to test your progress, you should be able to answer the following questions.

1) Hardware is often the _____ expensive component of an extranet.

    a) _____ Least
    b) _____ Most

2) _____ expenses are usually underbudgeted for _____ tasks (select the most appropriate combination).

    a) _____ Hardware, difficult
    b) _____ Personnel, maintenance
    c) _____ Administrative, normal

Quiz answers appear in the Appendix, Section 2.6.

**LAB
2.6**

LAB 2.7

EXTRANET COMMUNITIES

LAB OBJECTIVES

After this lab, you will be able to:

✔ Describe the Different Communities with Which Your Organization Interacts
✔ Determine Levels of Access Within Your Organizational Communities

---

Let's consider what happens when your organizational interaction spans different communities. In an Internet company, Sholink Corporation, there were four levels of access to content and applications. The company established a virtual organization with team members working in Massachusetts, New Jersey, and California. In California, team members worked from home and in the office. The network was set up to provide extranet facilities to partners who worked closely with the team. Levels of access differentiated the different communities and the different working relationships among team members. Members of product development teams required secure repositories for shared code under development. In addition, teams needed shared space for project plans to support collaborative product development efforts. Since engineers were geographically dispersed, they used a secure level of access to the development tools and to their development repository. Single-use challenge passwords were implemented for access to the systems from the outside. Packet filtering on the firewall provided another level of security. Members of the virtual organization also needed to work together to develop business, sales, and product plans. Planning documents were stored in an area with access limited to a specific set of users identified by user ID and password. Using UNIX (Linux) file and group permissions, some documents and code were protected from change by anyone other than the owner or, in some cases, a small group of people who were allowed to update or modify the contents or code.

Partners and other members of the virtual communities hosted by the company were served by extranet servers in the DMZ. Implementing a DMZ, servers hosting these extranets resided outside the firewall. The DMZ included two firewalls, one

**LAB
2.7**

that allowed partners and community members access from the Internet to the extranet servers and the second that served as a gateway from the DMZ to the company intranet. Individual PCs and development systems resided behind a proxy server on what is referred to as a masquerading subnet. Therefore, security measures effectively drew boundaries between the different communities and the resources of each community were protected from inappropriate access or use by outside parties.

LAB 2.7 EXERCISES

2.7.1 DESCRIBE THE DIFFERENT COMMUNITIES WITH WHICH YOUR ORGANIZATION INTERACTS

Consider the list of trusted partners you created in Lab 2.5.

a) Determine the levels of access to resources that are required by your organization's partners.

_____

_____

2.7.2 DETERMINE LEVELS OF ACCESS WITHIN YOUR ORGANIZATIONAL COMMUNITIES

a) Does your organization require different levels of access to internal resources? If so, how can these levels be implemented?

_____

_____

LAB 2.7 EXERCISE ANSWERS

2.7.1 ANSWER

a) Determine the levels of access to resources that are required by your organization's partners.

Answer: Divide information and application resources into categories based on which groups use them. Define the various communities in which people operate and interact with the organization. Consider which individuals and groups work together in communities of interest.

At A Corporation and BJ, lists of resources were developed along with lists of partners. A chart detailing the resources needed by each partner offers a guide to implementing the levels of access to resources required by the organization's partners.

2.7.2 ANSWER

a) Does your organization require different levels of access to internal resources? If so, how can these levels be implemented?

Answer: Security measures can be implemented, including a DMZ where servers for extranet use reside outside the firewall or, better yet, between two firewalls. Extranet software should be used to provide various levels of access privileges.

Both mature organizations like A Corporation and start-up ventures like BJ have a need for differing levels of access to internal resources. An organization may be small like BJ, but there is a need to differentiate between access privileges granted to software developers versus those granted to marketing and sales people who don't need access to source code under development. With a wide range of complex business relationships, A Corporation needs to provide varying levels of access privileges for online support of these different business relationships. With extranet software, access privileges can be provided that fit the nature of the business relationship.

LAB 2.7 SELF-REVIEW QUESTIONS

In order to test your progress, you should be able to answer the following questions.

LAB
2.7

1) Single-use passwords can be used on an extranet.

a) _____ True
b) _____ False

2) DMZ can be used _____ firewalls.

a) _____ Without
b) _____ Between
c) _____ Inside

Quiz answers appear in the Appendix, Section 2.7.

C H A P T E R   2

TEST YOUR THINKING

Outline a plan for a corporate extranet for the fictitious organization from Test Your Thinking in the previous chapter.

1) What are the goals of the extranet?
2) Who is the extranet for? How will it be used?
3) What facilities are going to be provided by the extranet?
4) How is the extranet going to tie into the existing intranet?
5) Will the extranet connect to existing legacy systems that are not connected to the intranet? Do these systems need to be updated?
6) What security is needed to protect data on the extranet? By connecting the extranet to the intranet, will you be opening new security holes?
7) What guidelines are needed for both internal and external uses of the extranet? Are there existing guidelines for dealing with disclosing information to outside sources?
8) What software and hardware is needed for the intranet? What will be developed in-house? Are servers going to be located in-house?

C H A P T E R 3

INTERNET USAGE

The Internet has many purposes. Originally used for email and file transfer, with the addition of the World Wide Web, the Internet provides an excellent vehicle for information dissemination. An organization of any size can promote its products and services on a public Web site.

In this chapter, we'll consider the development and use of Web sites available on the public Internet. We'll start by considering your organization's plan and then work on the development of a business strategy for your organization's use of the Internet. By now, people are comfortable accessing Web sites on the public Internet, but many organizations have yet to develop systematic plans for their use of the Internet. This chapter will assist you in developing an organizational plan and business strategy for Web sites available on the Internet and for your organization's presence thereon.

LAB 3.1

INTERNET
ORGANIZATIONAL PLAN

LAB OBJECTIVES

After this lab, you will be able to:

✔ Lead a Planning Session with Your World Wide Web Council
✔ Plan Your Web Site Organization

There are two major aspects to your organization's planned use of the Internet:

- Accessing content and using services on the Internet
- Providing content and services on the Internet

In the first scenario, your organization operates as a client, accessing content and using services. In this case, people in your organization may perform research; participate in discussion groups; locate products and materials; purchase parts, products, and services; make payments for such products and services; and track shipments. Your organization may have Internet access through modems on PCs and just use Web browsers for client access. Or your organization may plan for higher-speed access to the Internet using an ISDN (Integrated Services Digital Network) line, wireless connection, DSL (Digital Subscriber Line), or T-1 (T-Carrier) line, depending on the amount of access your organization expects. If you need more information on your connectivity options, please see Chapter 5, "Connectivity," in Volume 2 of this series, *Supporting Web Servers, Networks, and Emerging Technologies*.

In the second scenario, your organization has or is ready to have a Web site on the Internet. This server may be co-located at your ISP (Internet Service Provider), or your Web site may reside on a shared Web server hosted and maintained by another organization. If you have the systems and network administration personnel to maintain an Internet presence for your organization, you may just get your connection from your in-house server(s) to the Internet backbone through your ISP. In this case, your organization needs to take into account the quality of service (QOS) it plans to provide to visitors to your organization's presence on the Internet.

Let's consider the issues your organization needs to address in order to access content and services on the Internet. Then we'll consider the issues your organization needs to address in order to provide content and services. As with your planning for your organizational intranet and extranet, convening a meeting with your World Wide Web Council will help you plan your Internet strategy.

In order to access content, each person needs a browser on his or her desktop. It helps if your organization has a standard browser used by everyone in the organization. It also helps if someone is assigned the task of maintaining browser software so that browser software is updated regularly and everyone in the organization is using the same version of browser software. Most likely, your desktop systems will be connected via a LAN (local area network). With Internet connections, a good network configuration uses network cards in each PC, Ethernet hubs to connect multiple systems to the Ethernet LAN, and then a router to connect to the Internet. Your organization needs a network/systems administration person or group to maintain the local area network and Internet connectivity. This responsibility should include regular checks to make sure that throughput is sufficient to meet the needs of members of the organization and to make sure that all network connections are working reliably. Sometimes it is difficult for novice network users to differentiate between slow connections, slow servers on the other end, and network difficulties. A trained network administrator needs to troubleshoot such problems on a regular basis.

Now that your organization provides access to the Internet, are you ready to serve content on a Web server? Are you planning to serve static Web pages with organizational information or do you plan to provide transaction capabilities? Do you plan to provide 24 hours/day, 7 days/week (24×7) service through your Web sites? In this case, you need to provide mirrored sites and plan for hot backup. Again, this is a discussion that should be conducted with members of your World Wide Web Council. It's time to bring out your organizational mission statement and strategy documents that were helpful in designing your intranet and extranet plans. Now it's time to consider your organization's communication with the general public, which includes potential customers, interested parties, potential as well as current partners, and competitors. For the development of your organizational plan for the Internet, take a look at what information your organization makes publicly available via brochures, advertisements, direct mailings, videotapes, and other media. Any information that your organization currently distributes to the public has a place on your Web site. Take a look at information that is currently available on a toll-free telephone number. Do you have an automated telephone answering system that provides directions to your location, operating hours, or current training classes or events that are open to the public? Public announcements that are available when people call or that are distributed via newspapers are also appropriate content for your public Web site.

A well-designed public Web site is organized in a meaningful way. Does your organization provide one type of service or product? Does your organization serve one major community? If you are considering only one type of service or product and one audience, focus on how best to communicate your organizational mission and message to your intended audience. If you're working with a PR (public relations) or advertising firm, work with its personnel to develop your message and your approach to delivering this message in an appropriate way to reach your intended audience. Your plan for your public Web site becomes more complicated if you have more than one type of service or product, if your organization serves more than one community, or if your organization itself consists of multiple organizations. If you're in a multinational corporation with multiple divisions, as I was when I planned one of the first commercial Web sites in 1993, you need to decide whether it makes more sense to organize and present your information by product category or by division. This is definitely an important topic to discuss with your World Wide Web Council, since marketing and corporate communications will want to make sure that the Web site organization reflects the corporate image it wants to portray. Another important question to discuss is how best to search the site for specific pieces of information. The better organized your site is and the better the search capabilities, the more likely it will be that visitors will find what they came for when they decided to access your site.

Another decision to make is whether your organization will provide customer and/or technical support via your Web site. As we discussed in the extranet chapter, customer service is an area that lends itself very well to delivery via the Web. Certain components of your customer service can be delivered on your public Web site to all users. You can allow users to view data sheets, specifications for products, parts catalogs, and frequently asked questions (FAQs). Your organization may be ready to sell products via the Internet. We will discuss this process in further detail in chapter 5.

For now, let's look at your plan for the Internet and categorize your organizational efforts in the following ways:

- Access content only
- Access and serve content
- Serve static Web pages only
- Provide transaction services, which may include ordering and catalog facilities
- Provide business-to-consumer electronic commerce facilities, including secure payment

- Provide business-to-business electronic commerce facilities, including exchange and tracking of such instruments as requests-for-proposals (RFPs), purchase orders, requisitions, shipping manifestos, and letters of credit for international trade

We will address your Internet business strategy in the next lab of this chapter.

As we discussed in the first chapter on intranets, it is important to develop an Acceptable Use Policy (AUP) for the use of the Internet in your organization. The Internet AUP needs to be considered in light of such human resource policies as sexual harassment. One company specified in its Internet AUP that sexual harassment includes such acts as an employee viewing sexually explicit photographs on the Web if a co-worker sees the photographs and is offended. The AUP needs to address the content that is accessed and the services that are used as well as the content and services that are provided on publicly accessible Web sites. Are employees allowed to use the Internet as much as they want for personal use? Downloading large files, listening to music via streaming audio, or looking at movies via streaming video may impact the network bandwidth available for others. Who has the authority to approve content for the external Web sites? Who decides when the pages need to be updated and when they are ready for release? Who is responsible for maintaining the site(s)? These are questions that need to be addressed with your World Wide Web Council in order to develop a concrete plan for developing and deploying your external Web presence.

LAB 3.1 EXERCISES

3.1.1 LEAD A PLANNING SESSION WITH YOUR WORLD WIDE WEB COUNCIL

a) Consider the mission of your organization. Based on your mission, what type of Internet presence makes the most sense for your organization?

3.1.2 PLAN YOUR WEB SITE ORGANIZATION

a) Do you think it is best to organize a Web site by product/service category or by operating division?

LAB 3.1 EXERCISE ANSWERS

3.1.1 ANSWER

a) Consider the mission of your organization. Based on your mission, what type of Internet presence makes the most sense for your organization?

Answer: Think in terms of the types of content your organization already provides to the outside world. Also consider the types of business operations your organization currently conducts that are conducive to moving online, such as catalog searches and ordering.

Let's return to the mission statements of our case study organizations, A Corporation and BJ. A Corporation's mission is to deliver innovative systems, software, consulting, services, and support for data centers. The BJ mission is to provide an educationally sound online adaptive learning environment, based on research in cognitive psychology, educational methodologies, and effective learning strategies.

Based on these mission statements, both organizations provide information on their products and services that are appropriate for their public Internet presence.

3.1.2 ANSWER

a) Do you think it is best to organize a Web site by product/service category or by operating division?

Answer: This depends on how people are likely to look for information. In most cases, people will search for particular products or services and are not interested in the internal organizational structure of the company.

For A Corporation, public information was originally organized by operating division (coming out of the organization of the World Wide Web Council), which often made it difficult to locate product and service offerings. The Web site was reorganized into product and service categories, which made more sense in terms of providing information to customers and to the public. Financial news and corporate announcements continued to be available from corporate headquarters, but new product/service announcements could be found under the appropriate product or service category. For BJ as a start-up, the focus of the Web site is to announce product and service offerings and build the company's reputation; therefore, the Web site is organized in terms of publicly accessible information on products and services.

LAB 3.1 SELF-REVIEW QUESTIONS

In order to test your progress, you should be able to answer the following questions.

1) Your organization needs to take into account the quality of service it plans to provide visitors to your organization's presence on the Internet if in-house servers are to be used.

   a) _____ True
   b) _____ False

2) Networks do not require regular maintenance.

   a) _____ True
   b) _____ False

3) Any information that your organization currently distributes to the public has a place on your Web site.

   a) _____ True
   b) _____ False

4) Large corporations that are involved in many different areas should organize their Web site by

   a) _____ Product/service category
   b) _____ Operating division

   Quiz answers appear in the Appendix, Section, 3.1.

LAB 3.2

INTERNET BUSINESS STRATEGY

LAB OBJECTIVES

After this lab, you will be able to:

✔ Align Your Online Initiative with Your Sales
and Distribution Channels
✔ Explore New Approaches to Conducting Your
Organization's Business

Now that we've looked at your overall organizational plan for Internet usage, we are ready to consider your Internet business strategy. As with other strategic business initiatives, your organization's move to the Internet should be approached as an important business move. If you're just putting up an Internet presence because your competition has one or because you think it's the thing to do, you probably won't experience the results that you'd like to see. Let's take a strategic planning approach to implementing your move to the Internet.

It is important with any strategic planning initiative to first develop a set of measurable objectives and a set of measurable criteria to judge the success of the initiative. With the Internet and other new technologies, it is best to use a phased approach to development. A phased development cycle includes feedback loops in the design, implementation, and testing stages. Successive refinements of the design and implementation are based on feedback from testing and use by beta customers. Beta customers are those who are given early access so that they can give feedback to the developers before general release. These may be people in the organization or trusted outside parties, who are selected to try out a new Web site or new parts of the Web site and give feedback for improvements before the

Web site goes live. Since you devised measurable objectives at the front end of your planning process, you should make sure that you analyze the results after you have implemented your Internet strategy.

As with any development process, the entire strategic planning process for your Internet presence needs to have a feedback loop from the analysis of the results back to a further refinement of the design and implementation. In addition, your business objectives should be questioned and refined based on your experience with the Internet. Rather than limiting your organization to "tried-and-true" approaches, look at the Internet as a new way to approach your customers, a new way to satisfy your customers' needs, perhaps allowing your organization to expand in different directions. Also look at the Internet as a new way to work with other organizations. This may change the way your organization views its business as well. Perhaps it makes more sense to hand off some of your business operations to a partner and focus on the areas in which your organization has particular expertise. On the other hand, it may make sense to license software or parts from another company and incorporate their products into an overall offering that your organization markets and delivers. Using the Internet, you may be able to offer customers a seamless way to interact with your company along with some suppliers or partners so that customers can purchase an integrated package. This "package deal" approach may allow you to reach a new set of customers or expand your customer base.

Consider the Internet as a strategic tool that allows your organization to reexamine the way things have been done in the past. Brainstorm with strategic planners in your organization and use the addition of the Internet as a tool in your organization's toolbox to focus on customer problems that your organization is currently solving and those that your organization is now capable of solving. Examine your core competencies to see which ones are enhanced with your addition of the Internet. In planning the overall architecture of your organization's Web site, consider how people will locate the information. How will they find your Web site? What will attract people to your site? What will keep them there? One of the biggest problems is how to keep people on your site long enough to do business. Another issue is how to get people to return to your site. For your Web site to have an impact on your business, you need people to view your site— these people are sometimes referred to as "eyeballs." In addition, you need these eyeballs to stay for a while and take a look around your site. You also need these eyeballs to come back again and again. Consider what will attract eyeballs in the first place and what will keep them coming back. What will make your site interesting and dynamic enough to continue to attract new eyeballs? If you don't have promotions or marketing communications staff, you may find it helpful to work with a PR or advertising firm to determine how to attract eyeballs. Look at the paths a person will take to your site from various search engines, through links from other sites, and from referrals via email or off-line. In the process of reviewing the organization's mission with your World Wide Web Council, take time to reexamine your core competencies. Try using the Internet as part of your

LAB 3.2

solution to business problems and see if you can devise new approaches to old and existing problems.

View the Internet as not only part of your new marketing strategy but also as part of a new approach to solving your customers' problems. Now, look at your Internet-based approach and determine the value proposition for your existing customers. Does your Internet-based approach allow you to reach a new set of customers? Does your Internet-based approach allow you to reach current customers in a more cost-effective or more responsive way? In reaching these customers, does the Internet-based approach conflict with any of your existing sales or distribution channels? If so, is there incentive for your current channels to work with you via the Internet? Some people view the Internet as cutting out the middleman, with Web sites providing self-service and therefore bringing about a form of "disintermediation." Others see a changing need for middlemen and view the Internet as bringing about "re-intermediation" in a marketplace where some customers serve themselves and others rely on new kinds of brokers who aggregate information and assist users in finding what they want. Review your distribution strategy in light of your intended use of the Internet. Are there services or brokers who can help direct business to your site or are you relying on customers finding your site by themselves? The Internet has introduced new business models with advertising-based sites, offering free services, and with open source software, providing free software, while charging for support. Does the incorporation of the Internet into your business operations change your business model?

Once you are able to attract eyeballs to your Web site, you not only want to keep them there, you would like to profit from their stay. Take a look at what you are offering your customers and see if there are holes in your offering that partners can fill. Can you pull in partners to keep these customers with you long enough to profit from their visit? As you can see, developing an Internet business strategy means examining your current business model, modifying your marketing strategy, expanding or realigning your distribution channels, reviewing your profit model, and developing a strategic plan for your organization's use of the Internet.

LAB 3.2 EXERCISES

3.2.1 ALIGN YOUR ONLINE INITIATIVE WITH YOUR SALES AND DISTRIBUTION CHANNELS

a) Should you stop using the Internet for selling if you have a channel conflict?

3.2.2 EXPLORE NEW APPROACHES TO CONDUCTING YOUR ORGANIZATION'S BUSINESS

a) How can the Internet bring about a new form of "intermediation," sometimes referred to as "re-intermediation"?

_____

_____

LAB 3.2 EXERCISE ANSWERS

3.1.2 ANSWER

a) Should you stop using the Internet for selling if you have a channel conflict?

Answer: No, but you should consider how to work with the existing channel so that your use of the Internet and your use of the existing channel can complement each other rather than conflict with each other.

A Corporation's marketing and field sales engaged in serious discussion and planning before determining how to use the Internet in order to avoid channel conflict. Both A Corporation and BJ provide information but do not complete a sale online. However, other companies, such as a developer of low-end and high-end software packages and services for consumer electronics, offer their low-end products online and their high-end products through their direct sales force. In addition, this company offers private-labeled software packaged with another vendor's consumer electronic product, while the same software is offered online with the company's label. Thus, the provider of software for consumer electronic products avoids channel conflict via bundling its software with consumer electronic products to sell through the dealer channel.

3.2.2 ANSWER

a) How can the Internet bring about a new form of "intermediation," sometimes referred to as "re-intermediation"?

Answer: Information brokers can provide valuable services in aggregating information. Web services can provide "one-stop shopping" by integrating a number of related service offerings. In this way, a customer may find it useful to deal with a middleman.

Both A Corporation and BJ offer their own products rather than aggregating information on others, although A Corporation acts as a systems integrator through its professional services organization. Internally, A Corporation marketing offers re-intermediation by

aggregating information from various market research firms. There are online compa-
nies that specialize in providing services that aggregate information, such as online auc-
tion sites and travel sites. Some sites offer reviews and comparison information on
various products and services to help a consumer make choices.

LAB 3.2 SELF-REVIEW QUESTIONS

In order to test your progress, you should be able to answer the following questions.

1) With the Internet and other new technologies, it is best to use a _____ approach to development.

    a) _____ single-step
    b) _____ phased
    c) _____ quick
    d) _____ any of the above

2) Feedback is a necessary component of development.

    a) _____ True
    b) _____ False

3) It is best to

    a) _____ Limit your organization to tried-and-true approaches.
    b) _____ Look at the Internet as a new way to approach your customers.

4) Internet users, by default, will stay on your Web site long enough for you to do business with them.

    a) _____ True
    b) _____ False

5) The incorporation of the Internet into business operations can change an organization's business model.

    a) _____ True
    b) _____ False

Quiz answers appear in the Appendix, Section 3.2.

L A B   3 . 3

INTERNET BUDGET

> ## LAB OBJECTIVES
>
> After this lab, you will be able to:
>
> ✔ Understand Promotional vs. Content Web Sites
> ✔ Understand Transactional Web Site Expenses

According to industry estimates, the cost for building and maintaining a Web site for a year vary by at least a factor of 10, depending on the site's functionality. Web sites can be categorized into the following types:

- Promotional sites—These sites provide information and advertising on an organization's products and services. Often, these are hosted by a service the company uses.

- Content sites—These sites provide updated information, which may be news, weather, entertainment, stock quotes, or other business information.

- Transactional sites—These sites provide interactive online experiences for Web visitors, including such activities as shopping, banking, travel and accommodation reservations, and customer service and support.

Tables 3.1, 3.2, and 3.3 provide ranges of costs for the launch and first year of operation of promotional sites, content sites, and transactional sites. The line items and costs provide you with guidelines to consider when developing a budget for your own organization. As with other business decisions, your costs may vary. It is important to consider each line item in your budget when you make your plans for moving your organization to the Internet.

Table 3.1 ■ Promotional Web Site Line Item Costs for First Year

Component/Service	Launch and Year 1 Costs
Hosting	$6,000–$36,000
Content Development	$20,000–$150,000
Management	$50,000–$150,000
Sales and Marketing	$25,000–$100,000
Adverting and PR	$5,000–$200,000
Total Costs Year 1	$106,000–$636,000

**LAB
3.3**

Table 3.2 ■ Content Web Site Line Item Costs for First Year

Component/Service	Launch and Year 1 Costs
Hardware	$5,000–$100,000
Software	$5,000–$150,000
Network Connectivity	$7,000–$42,000
Content Development	$25,000–$200,000
Management and Staff	$50,000–$150,000
Sales and Marketing	$25,000–$100,000
Advertising and PR	$20,000–$250,000
Total Costs Year 1	$137,000–$992,000

LAB 3.3 EXERCISES

3.3.1 UNDERSTAND PROMOTIONAL VS. CONTENT WEB SITES

a) Why do you think a promotional Web site is less expensive to develop and maintain than a content Web site?

Table 3.3 ■ Transactional Web Site Line Item Costs for First Year

Component/Service	Launch and Year 1 Costs
Hardware	$50,000–$150,000
Software	$25,000–$250,000
Network Connectivity	$15,000–$65,000
Content Development	$50,000–$750,000
Management and Staff	$100,000–$250,000
Sales and Marketing	$100,000–$200,000
Advertising and PR	$75,000–$500,000
Technical Development	$50,000–$500,000
Total Costs Year 1	$465,000–$2,665,000

3.3.2 Understand Transactional Web Site Expenses

a) What line item do you think is critical to the success of a transactional site?

_____

_____

LAB 3.3 EXERCISE ANSWERS

3.3.1 Answer

a) Why do you think a promotional Web site is less expensive to develop and maintain than a content Web site?

Answer: Content Web sites need to be updated more frequently. Also, according to the definition in this section, a content Web site provides additional content beyond one company's product and corporate materials.

A Corporation and BJ both began by offering promotional Web sites to provide information on the companies and their products and services. Some companies offer newsletters to upgrade their promotional Web sites to content Web sites, hoping that people will visit their site to read the newsletter.

3.3.2 ANSWER

a) What line item do you think is critical to the success of a transactional site?

Answer:The line designated as Connections. Reliable network connections are critical to the success of a transaction site.When a site is providing transaction capability, customers expect reliability and availability 24 hours/day, 7 days/week.

A Corporation operates its computer centers with round-the-clock service and back-up systems in different locations in case of natural disasters, so it was not hard for the corporate IS department to understand how to support transactional capabilities on the Web.A Corporation used the acronym RAS for reliability, availability, and serviceability. These are good terms to keep in mind to support transactional sites.

LAB
3.3

LAB 3.3 SELF-REVIEW QUESTIONS

In order to test your progress, you should be able to answer the following questions.

1) Promotional Web sites are updated more often than content Web sites.

a) _____ True
b) _____ False

2) Put the following in order based on cost (least expensive to most expensive).

a) _____ Content sites
b) _____ Transactional sites
c) _____ Promotional sites

3) _____ sites provide interactive online experiences for Web visitors.

a) _____ Promotional
b) _____ Content
c) _____ Transactional

Quiz answers appear in the Appendix, Section 3.3.

L A B   3 . 4

MOVING TO THE WEB

LAB OBJECTIVES

After this lab, you will be able to:

✔ Recognize Difficulties Associated with Moving to the Web
✔ Establish a Presence on the Internet

In this section, we'll present a case study of the A Corporation's move to the Web. The A Corporation is an established high-tech multinational company.

CORPORATE WEB SITE RELEASE 1.0— ENGINEERING PROTOTYPE SITE

The first step in the process was the development of a site designed and hosted by the engineering team, which was the only group in the company with technical expertise in Web technology at that time. In order to launch this site on the public Internet, permission had to be obtained from the Information Security group. The Information Security team reviewed each document that would be put on the Web site and approved only those documents for the initial release. The initial Web site that was deployed included maps and directions to the research and development campus along with announcements for engineering meetings (SIGs—special interest groups) that were open to the public. This site was used primarily by the engineering group in the UNIX systems division.

CORPORATE WEB SITE RELEASE 2.0—CORPORATE PRESENCE ON THE INTERNET

The second release of the Web site included corporate information with the corporate logo. After review by the graphics department, it was determined that the logo was not exactly the right size or look. The logo was pulled from the site and redesigned based on promotional literature and corporate guidelines that had been produced by the graphics department. Not having the logo exactly right according to the specifications caused a great deal of concern about the presentation of the right corporate image. This was the reasoning behind my insistence on full participation in the World Wide Web Council, with representation by each major group. I wanted to make sure that our engineering team could gather input from all involved parties to be able to design and develop a site that would project the right corporate image. Once we were holding regular meetings of our World Wide Web Council, we were able to resolve such issues and get the right people involved to help make the site conform to corporate guidelines.

CORPORATE WEB SITE RELEASE 3.0—AUTOMATED SCRIPTS FOR HTML CONVERSION

After the site had been up and running for several months and many departments had provided content, it was time to work on handing off responsibility for the site to the corporate IS group. By this time, we had trained other engineers to maintain the Web server and the Web site. In addition, we had developed a WYSIWYG HTML editor for use by a marketing communications person who was experienced in the design of promotional materials. She was very excited about putting content on the Web site as soon as she had tools that she could use. We also developed scripts to automate conversion to HTML for regular input from the human resources and corporate communications departments. Since press releases came in a predictable format, they could be converted to HTML and posted on the site in reverse chronological order using one of our scripts. A corporate communications person was alerted via email and took responsibility for reviewing the accuracy of all postings. It was her responsibility to give the go-ahead before any new content regarding press announcements moved from the Web site staging area to the production Web site. Human resources (HR) also distributed postings for job openings in a predictable format and their postings were automatically converted to HTML and posted to the site after review and approval in the staging area by an HR staff person.

CORPORATE WEB SITE RELEASE 4.0—TRANSITION FROM ENGINEERING TO CORPORATE IS

The first problem that occurred with the move to corporate IS was that the graphics design staff decided to redesign the look of the site. Based on their experience with print media, they designed very colorful complex graphics that loaded extremely slowly as images on the Web site. The engineers who had developed the original site had been reluctant to turn over "their" site (which they viewed as "their baby") to corporate IS. Now they felt that their reluctance was fully justified. During a meeting of the World Wide Web Council, we scheduled a training session in which the engineer responsible for the initial graphics design could train the graphics designers in techniques for designing attractive yet compact graphics images. As expected, the involvement of all major groups in the World Wide Web Council and training were the two most important factors in making the transition from engineering to corporate IS successful. This transition was necessary for the Web site to be accepted, used, and fully supported as a corporate tool.

CORPORATE WEB SITE RELEASE 5.0—REORGANIZATION BY LIBRARIANS

From this point on, we had the systems in place to continue to expand the content on the Web site. We then needed to overhaul the site and reorganize the content, since organizing the content by division had made specific product information difficult to locate. The corporate and marketing library staff were instrumental in reorganizing the content in such a way that outside users could locate needed information. The librarians brought a sense of order to the proliferation of Web pages. The redesigned Web site was easy to maintain, update, and expand. The new organization not only improved the usability of the Web site but also it allowed the Web site to be updated by a highly distributed team of contributors.

LAB 3.4

LAB 3.4 EXERCISES

3.4.1 RECOGNIZE DIFFICULTIES ASSOCIATED WITH MOVING TO THE WEB

a) What should you do if your organization wants to move to the Web and has no one with Web expertise?

_____

_____

3.4.2 ESTABLISH A PRESENCE ON THE INTERNET

a) Your organization decides to establish its presence on the Internet but doesn't know what information should be made available or how it should be presented. What should you do?

_____

_____

LAB 3.4 EXERCISE ANSWERS

3.4.1 ANSWER

a) What should you do if your organization wants to move to the Web and has no one with Web expertise?

Answer: Not having people with the experience or expertise to develop or support a Web site is a common situation. There are organizations and people who can develop a Web site on contract. Another option, if your organization does not have in-house resources, is to outsource both the development and the ongoing hosting of the Web site.

3.4.2 ANSWER

a) Your organization decides to establish its presence on the Internet but doesn't know what information should be made available or how it should be presented. What should you do?

Answer: The first step in planning your organization's Web presence is to establish a World Wide Web Council. The World Wide Web Council brings representatives of each major group in the organization together to provide input to the design, organization, and deployment of the organizational Web site. This group provides valuable guidance so that the organizational Web site accurately reflects the image the organization wants to project and so that the Web site is used in a way that supports the mission of the organization. Including representatives of each major group helps ensure that groups will work together to build a site that truly supports the organization's mission.

LAB 3.4

LAB 3.4 SELF-REVIEW QUESTIONS

In order to test your progress, you should be able to answer the following questions.

1) World Wide Web Councils can help resolve issues such as a corporate Web site conforming to corporate guidelines.

    a) _____ True
    b) _____ False

2) Scripts can be used to automate content updates.

    a) _____ True
    b) _____ False

Quiz answers appear in the Appendix, Section 3.4.

CHAPTER 3

TEST YOUR THINKING

Outline a plan for a public Web site for a fictitious corporation.

1) What are the goals of the public Web site?

2) What services and facilities will the public Web site provide? To whom?

3) What are the reasons for users to want to visit the Web site? What keeps them at the Web site?

4) Will the Web site make changes in the business practices of the organization necessary? Will any existing channels conflict with the Web site? If so, how do you plan to deal with channel conflicts?

5) What costs are involved in developing, deploying, and maintaining the Web site?

C H A P T E R 4

LEGACY SYSTEMS INTEGRATION

Your organization's investment in legacy systems is worth considering. You may have spent a great deal of money and human resources developing the systems that are now in place in your organization. Integration between Web frontends and legacy systems can provide the best of both worlds: protection of your organization's legacy systems and easy-to-use standard Web interfaces.

In this chapter, we'll discuss integration at the presentation layer, the business logic layer, and the data access layer. Each point of entry for integration between the legacy system and the Web has advantages and disadvantages, which we'll explore in this chapter. Armed with this knowledge, you will be able to evaluate the legacy systems in your organization and determine how best to integrate them with the Web.

L A B   4 . 1

EVALUATING LEGACY SYSTEMS

LAB OBJECTIVES

After this lab, you will be able to:

✔ Understand Why Your Organization May Want to Integrate Its Legacy Systems with the Web

✔ Conduct an Inventory Process to Consider Which Legacy Systems Are in Place and Perform an Evaluation of Each One

---

The day-to-day operations of most organizations are maintained and supported on what are thought of as legacy systems, whereas most Internet-based systems reside on a new Internet server. Organizational data is stored and maintained in database management systems. For optimal support of the organization's operations, this data and the applications that process the data need to be available via an Internet (intranet/extranet) server. Unfortunately, the most common approach to integration is to have redundant applications and data processing with data entry or file transfers to load the same data into the Internet-based application that was processed by the legacy system application. If this is your organization's current form of legacy systems integration, your organization is not alone. However, there are other approaches to integration of legacy systems that do not introduce errors and that do not involve costly manual data entry or slow file transfers. In order for Internet-based technology (including intranets and extranets) to become organizational tools, these Internet-based applications must connect to and integrate with backend database management systems in a seamless, reliable, and secure manner. The security developed for your organizational intranet needs to encompass the legacy systems that are in use in your organization. This means that the legacy systems must be fully integrated into your organizational intranet to take advantage of the intranet's security mechanisms. In addition, backend database management systems need to allow the various levels of access and permission we discussed in the extranet and intranet chapters.

Your organization has many applications and systems in place, some of them working smoothly, others in need of upgrade or overhaul. When you're adding the Web to your arsenal of tools, you have the opportunity to reevaluate existing systems and applications and determine which ones are worth retaining, which ones need to be upgraded, and which ones should be replaced. Once again, we return to your organization's mission and operational business plan. Do the systems that are in place support carrying out your current mission? Take a look at your organization's operational business plan. If your organization doesn't have a plan for day-to-day business operations, it's important to draft one. This plan can be made available throughout the organization via the organization's intranet. If your mission statement or operational plan needs updating, review it with management and make sure it reflects today's assumptions and plans.

The next step is to perform an inventory of your existing systems and applications. It is useful to put together a chart listing the systems and applications and their functions, along with a checklist that can be used to evaluate the state of each of the applications. Make sure that you inventory both systems and applications. You can use this checklist to determine which systems and applications are worth retaining, which need to be upgraded, and which need to be replaced.

Existing applications and systems within your organization that are not Web-based or integrated with the Web yet are referred to as *legacy systems*. Legacy systems and applications may reflect the way the organization operated in the past, deserving the name legacy systems. However, some legacy systems may be working just fine, but may simply lack integration with your organization's Web-based intranet. As with other stages in technology evolution, some people assume that they need to replace all systems when they deploy the Web in their organization. However, this is not necessary. Most organizations have invested a great deal of time and money in their existing systems and applications, and many applications are performing the functions they need to perform. It is important to understand what systems and applications are currently in place in your organization to be able to protect the organization's investment in application development. At the same time, if you are moving to a Web-based information architecture for your organization, you will want to ensure a smooth transition by incorporating the integration of useful legacy systems into your plans.

Let's consider how you can determine which legacy systems are worth retaining. First, let's consider the systems (hardware and operating system) that are in place and then let's survey the applications running on those systems. It may be worth retaining the systems and revamping or replacing the applications, or, alternately, the systems may be too costly to maintain and it may be time to overhaul the organization's network and systems architecture. Do not feel that the introduction of the Web necessitates a complete overhaul of the organization's information systems. Legacy system integration with the Web is, in many cases, less costly and more beneficial than initially thought.

Consider the functions that need to be performed. Are these systems performing necessary functions for the organization? What is the level of effort required for systems administration of these systems? Are the systems reliable? Are you able to maintain these systems at a reasonable cost? Are the systems usable in their present form? Are the systems available wherever and whenever they need to be? Are applications automating repetitive tasks efficiently? Is there additional functionality required? Can these applications be upgraded and enhanced on the current systems? Would they benefit from integration with other applications on your organization's intranet? Would they benefit from a Web GUI frontend? Would the applications benefit from the distributed nature of the Web? Will it cost more to upgrade the applications than to replace them? Once the applications are upgraded, will they be maintainable? Are the applications useful in their present form? Do they require a significant amount of training to use and if so, are there trained personnel in place?

It is important to decide which systems and applications are basically performing their intended functions and are worth integrating into the Web and which level of integration is the most appropriate for each application.

During your inventory, make sure that you fully understand how each application is being used. Sometimes, an application serves a somewhat different purpose from its intended one, or, at other times, one group is using an application that has been abandoned by its original owner group. That's why it is important to review your findings with your World Wide Web Council to make sure that you don't forget some of the smaller or lesser-known applications. There may be surprising dependencies between applications that people forget to mention until you do your inventory and review of findings.

There are three basic levels of integration that may work with your legacy applications:

- Frontend integration whereby a Web GUI frontend provides the presentation layer for the legacy application
- Business logic integration whereby the business logic of the application is integrated with the Web
- Data access layer integration whereby the backend data access is integrated with the Web

For the exercises, it will help to make a chart of legacy applications and systems. Some example applications for the A Corporation are listed in the chart below to illustrate the way that you can inventory the legacy applications in your organization. We'll consider each of these approaches in the next three labs of this chapter.

Table 4.1 ■ Inventory of Legacy Applications for the A Corporation

Application	Function	Platform	Retain, Upgrade, Replace?	Web Integration
Vacation scheduler	Keep track of each employee's vacation	Mainframe	*Retain*—Works fine but needs better interface	Front-end integration
Payroll processor	Payroll processing for salaried and hourly employees as well as contractors	UNIX workstation	*Upgrade*—Need to allow for customization of reports and accessibility by others and need to tie in with other accounting software	CORBA interface available, business services integration
Benefits	Employee options on health, dental, vision, and life insurance, dependent care accounting	PC	*Replace*—Proprietary application processing, manual updates	Replace with interactive self-service Java app that works on intranet, JDBC interface to back-end databases
Library	Obtain market research materials from market research firms and from public sources	UNIX server	*Retain*—New Web application built for intranet	Already integrated with intranet

LAB 4.1 EXERCISES

4.1.1 UNDERSTAND WHY YOUR ORGANIZATION MAY WANT TO INTEGRATE ITS LEGACY SYSTEMS WITH THE WEB

a) The development team at A Corporation considered replacing all the legacy mainframe-based applications with Web-based ones but decided against this strategy. What type of strategy do you think they should adopt and why?

_____

_____

4.1.2 CONDUCT AN INVENTORY PROCESS TO CONSIDER WHICH LEGACY SYSTEMS ARE IN PLACE AND PERFORM AN EVALUATION OF EACH ONE

a) Conducting an inventory of legacy systems and applications is critical to developing a strategy for legacy systems integration. Carry out an inventory process of the legacy applications and systems in your organization. Develop a chart of legacy applications like the one provided. What types of problems do you think you might encounter with legacy applications?

_____

_____

LAB 4.1 EXERCISE ANSWERS

4.1.1 ANSWER

a) The development team at A Corporation considered replacing all the legacy mainframe-based applications with Web-based ones but decided against this strategy. What type of strategy do you think they decided to adopt and why?

Answer: Replacing all legacy mainframe-based applications would be an expensive and time-consuming approach. The Web and the development of the intranet allowed the organization to enhance support for its business operations without losing all of its investment in application development. Once the team implemented a Web frontend to a legacy application and had demonstrated that it was doable to integrate legacy applications with the Web, the IS and development teams concurred in a plan to replace far fewer of the legacy applications than originally proposed. After a thorough inventory of existing systems and applications, you may find that it is easier and less costly to integrate legacy applications with the Web instead of replacing them.

4.1.2 ANSWER

a) Conducting an inventory of legacy systems and applications is critical to developing a strategy for legacy systems integration. Carry out an inventory process of the legacy applications and systems in your organization. Develop a chart of legacy applications like the one provided. What problem do you think you might encounter if you decide to replace existing legacy applications?

Answer: At A Corporation, there were two types of unexpected problems. There were useful applications that were dependent on other applications that people were ready to discard until they realized that they were necessary to provide data to the useful applications. Some applications were used infrequently or were invoked automatically, resulting in their being forgotten. People may forget to mention the application that collects some needed data, processes one particular type of data, or produces a specific report. The other problem that occurred was that some legacy applications were still being used but no one was responsible for maintenance and no one was knowledgeable about the applications. In those cases, it may make sense to replace the applications rather than invest in upgrading or integrating with the Web. In some cases, there is redundant functionality between applications. In a large established organization, there may be many "hidden" applications that bear examination and discussion before deciding whether to retain, replace, or upgrade them and, if appropriate, how to integrate them with the Web. It is therefore important to remember to do a systematic and thorough inventory and review your findings with your World Wide Web Council.

LAB 4.1 SELF-REVIEW QUESTIONS

In order to test your progress, you should be able to answer the following questions.

1) In order for Internet-based technology to become organizational tools, the Internet-based applications must connect to and integrate with backend database management systems in a seamless, reliable, and secure manner.

a) _____ True
b) _____ False

2) When developing a new Web-based solution, corporations are given the opportunity to reevaluate their existing systems and applications.

a) _____ True
b) _____ False

3) It is necessary to replace all legacy systems when developing a new Web-based solution.

a) _____ True

b) _____ False

Quiz answers appear in the Appendix, Section 4.1.

LAB 4.2

FRONTEND INTEGRATION

LAB OBJECTIVES

After this lab, you will be able to:

✔ Understand Integration Between a Web GUI Frontend
and a Legacy System Application
✔ Determine Which Applications Should Be Integrated
on the Presentation Layer

The most obvious integration point is the frontend of the application. The look and feel of Web-enabled applications used through the browser present a desirable approach for improving usability. The frontend is called the *presentation layer* in networking terms.

Frontend integration provides the loosest form of coupling between a legacy application and the Web. The easiest way to integrate an application with the Web is to provide data entry facilities through a forms-based Web frontend. The frontend application is a CGI (Common Gateway Interface) script usually written in PERL (popular interpreted programming language). The script provides data capture and data cleansing through error and limits checking. After data is entered into a form presented via the Web browser, it is captured, checked, and then sent on to an application running on a legacy system. The frontend does not do any processing of the data; its function is to provide a data entry form and pass the data through to the legacy application for processing. The output data is then passed back and displayed in HTML through the Web browser.

There are distinct advantages to this approach. CGI scripts, especially PERL scripts, are quick and easy to develop. CGI scripts can be tested interactively and do not require any infrastructure components beyond a Web server. Of the three types of integration presented in this chapter, frontend integration is the fastest and least expensive to implement. The Web browser provides a standard easy-to-use graphical user interface. Forms can be easily developed for the Web and provide a simple type of data entry. Allowing data to be entered via the Web can provide time-and-space independence. In addition, it is easy to check errors and make sure data is in the right form and falls within the right limits through your frontend script. Thus, the data that is passed on to the legacy application can be "cleansed" before processing.

There are limitations to this approach, however. CGI scripts increase network traffic since data is passed through to the legacy application directly. This means that each client request is transmitted to the server and each response from the server is transmitted back to the client. An implementation that involves some processing on the client side or that batches requests to the server would reduce network traffic. With a CGI script, processing is handled by the Web server, which can increase the load on the Web server itself. Another limitation is in the presentation, since the frontend requires that any output be presented in HTML via the browser.

LAB 4.2 EXERCISES

4.2.1 UNDERSTAND INTEGRATION BETWEEN A WEB GUI FRONTEND AND A LEGACY SYSTEM APPLICATION

a) What are some benefits of front-end integration with legacy applications?

_____

_____

b) How would the A Corporation vacation scheduler application use a Web GUI frontend?

_____

_____

4.2.2 DETERMINE WHICH APPLICATIONS SHOULD BE INTEGRATED ON THE PRESENTATION LAYER

a) Why do you think the A Corporation decided to do frontend integration for the vacation scheduler application?

_____

_____

LAB 4.2 EXERCISE ANSWERS

4.2.1 ANSWER

a) What are some benefits of front-end integration with legacy applications?

Answer: There are a number of benefits including the following:

> *Easy-to-use Web GUI frontend*
>
> *Simple forms input*
>
> *Data cleansing with error and limit checking*
>
> *Easy-to-implement CGI script for integration*

b) How would the A Corporation vacation scheduler application use a Web GUI frontend?

Answer: For the A Corporation, major benefits could be gained from integrating the vacation scheduler application through frontend or presentation layer integration. Data could be entered via a form provided on the intranet, and the data would then be checked and passed onto the vacation scheduler application running on the mainframe via an easy-to-implement CGI script.

4.2.2 ANSWER

a) Why do you think the A Corporation decided to do frontend integration for the vacation scheduler application?

Answer: The application was working fine but needed a better user interface. Data could be entered via an easy-to-use HTML form. Also the data could be checked and cleansed before its entry into the vacation scheduler application. In addition, the CGI script development was fast and easy, taking much less time, effort, and money than would be required to replace the application. Since this application did not need to be integrated with other applications, the presentation layer integration provided sufficient integration to satisfy the needs of the managers and human resources staff.

LAB 4.2 SELF-REVIEW QUESTIONS

In order to test your progress, you should be able to answer the following questions.

1) The easiest way to integrate an application with the Web is to provide data entry facilities through a forms-based Web frontend.

    a) _____ True
    b) _____ False

2) CGI scripts are _____ and _____ to develop.

    a) _____ quick, hard
    b) _____ slow, hard
    c) _____ quick, easy

**LAB
4.2**

3) CGI scripts increase network traffic since (select all that apply)

    a) _____ data is indirectly passed through to the legacy application
    b) _____ data is passed through to the legacy application directly
    c) _____ they run only on Windows-based servers
    d) _____ processing is handled by the Web server

Quiz answers appear in the Appendix, Section 4.2.

L A B   4 . 3

BUSINESS SERVICES INTEGRATION

LAB OBJECTIVES

After this lab, you will be able to:

✔ Understand How the Business Services Layer Can Provide an Integration Point with Legacy Systems

✔ Determine Whether It Is Appropriate to Integrate Some of Your Legacy Applications on the Business Services Layer

---

Integrating your legacy applications at the business services layer requires the use of another set of technologies. There are a number of technologies that can be used to integrate your legacy application at this level. Two of the most common ones are: RPCs (Remote Procedure Calls) and ORBs (Object Request Brokers).

INTEGRATION WITH REMOTE PROCEDURE CALLS (RPCs)

The RPC protocol is specified in the International Standards Organization (ISO) Remote Procedure Call Specification. RPC spans the transport layer and the application layer in the ISO Open Systems Interconnection (OSI) model of network communication. RPC makes it easier to develop an application that includes multiple programs distributed in a network. Several models and implementations of the RPC protocol are available. UNIX vendors provide support for RPCs built on top of the operating system network facilities.

RPC is a protocol used by a program to request a service from another program located on a separate computer on the network, without requiring knowledge of the network configuration. RPCs are commonly used in systems programming to interface programs on separate computers on a network. A procedure call can also be referred to as a function call or a subroutine call.

The RPC protocol is based on the client/server model. The requesting program serves as a client, and the program providing the service acts as the server. Regular, local, and remote procedure calls all function as synchronous operations. Therefore, the procedure is required to finish and to return its results to the requesting program before the requesting program can continue. However, lightweight processes or threads that share the same address space can be used to implement multiple RPCs that can be performed concurrently.

When program statements that use the RPC protocol are compiled into an executable program, a stub is included in the compiled code. This stub implements the mechanism for communicating with the body of the remote procedure. When the program is run on the client system and the procedure call is issued, the stub receives the request. The stub then forwards the request to a client runtime program on the local computer. The client runtime program knows how to address the remote computer and the server application. The client runtime program sends a message across the network requesting the remote procedure. Similarly, the server includes a runtime program and stub that interface with the remote procedure itself. Results are returned in the same way.

RPCs can be used to implement a business services interface between the Web and the legacy application. Another approach is to wrap RPCs around an existing business services layer. Many UNIX systems programmers are familiar with programming with RPCs and find it easy to use RPCs to integrate the Web with legacy applications. One limitation of the RPC approach is that RPCs operate on a process-to-process basis, in which both processes must be available for successful execution of the RPC. Thus, the RPC approach requires that both sides of the connection be up at the same time.

COMMON OBJECT REQUEST BROKER ARCHITECTURE (CORBA)

Common Object Request Broker Architecture (CORBA) is a reference implementation of object services by members of the multivendor consortium Object Management Group (OMG). In CORBA, an Object Request Broker (ORB) is the software that acts as a "broker" between a client request for a service from a distributed object or component and the fulfillment of that request. An ORB is more sophisticated and provides more capabilities than an RPC mechanism for accessing remote facilities. ORB support in a network means that a client program can request a service without having to know where the server is located in a distributed network or exactly what the interface to the server program looks like. Components can find out about each other and exchange interface information while they are running.

The requests and replies that originate in ORBs are expressed through the Internet Inter-ORB Protocol (IIOP) or other transport layer protocols. ORBs provide facilities to abstract the location of an object as well as the nature of its implementation through well-defined interfaces. An ORB provides a location broker function that allows a client to request a service or object of some type. The ORB then passes back a location to the client. ORBs provide an Interface Description Language (IDL) to describe their interfaces. Web browsers now include ORBs as part of the browser. The Netscape browser includes a CORBA ORB and the Microsoft Internet Explorer browser includes a Distributed Component Object Model (DCOM) ORB.

With the inclusion of the ORB in the browser, the components that are shipped to the client become part of the runtime distributed processing architecture. Using ORBs to implement legacy system integration with the Web allows developers to adopt an object-oriented approach. Object-oriented approaches to development result in a producer-consumer model or factory model of development. The user of the object is not interested in the implementation and therefore the developer hides the complexity of the implementation from the user. The user is sometimes referred to as a consumer and the developer is then referred to as a producer. The focus with ORBs is on specifying standard services to interface components without caring about the underlying implementation of these components. The object model provides standard services and encapsulates (or hides) their implementation. In this way, the consumer is able to deal with abstractions of implementation details such as data and object location, network programming, data structures, and algorithms.

Hiding (or encapsulating) an existing system behind an object interface is known as wrapping a legacy system. Wrapping provides an object interface for object-oriented applications, making it easier to develop and maintain future applications.

There are several object-oriented approaches for mapping client applications to legacy systems. Starting with the legacy side, you can develop a thin-wrapper approach. Starting with the client side, you can develop an object model. Each approach has its own advantages and disadvantages.

The first approach, the thin wrapper, has the disadvantage of exposing legacy systems in the interface. The thin-wrapper approach uses a one-to-one mapping that duplicates the legacy system, providing CORBA-accessible counterparts. This approach provides CORBA access to legacy systems, but the thin-wrapper approach does not build any objects. The second approach, a client-side object model, requires that each object have a copy of the code that provides access. To perform their functions, some objects will access more than one legacy system. These objects will require code to access each of the legacy systems they access to execute their functions.

Combining the thin-wrapper and client-side object model approaches results in the creation of dual wrappers. The client-side object model provides a view of the actual objects and unifies the individual legacy systems. The object model ties the legacy systems together through an object-oriented approach to their interoperation.

OMG developed the Internet Inter-Orb Protocol (IIOP) to allow heterogeneous ORBs to communicate with each other. Distributed object computing can be accomplished using IIOP as the mechanism, that provides context for data transmission in a heterogeneous environment. IIOP allows the integration of both Component Object Model (COM) and CORBA approaches. While this integration provides advantages in addressing both the desktop (where COM/DCOM are more advanced) and the server-side (where CORBA provides more services), scalability and performance can be adversely impacted.

The advantages of integrating through CORBA or COM/DCOM result from placing the development burden on the producer and freeing up the consumer to use the component building blocks to assemble their applications. If enough services are provided, legacy applications can be integrated into the Web by assembling predeveloped components. This approach can yield integrated business processes that are flexible and can be modified easily.

Alternative methods for client/server communication for legacy system integration include message queueing and IBM's advanced program-to-program communication (APPC).

LAB 4.3 EXERCISES

4.3.1 UNDERSTAND HOW THE BUSINESS SERVICES LAYER CAN PROVIDE AN INTEGRATION POINT WITH LEGACY SYSTEMS

    a) Why do you think the A Corporation decided to integrate the payroll processing application on the business services layer?

    _____

    _____

4.3.2 DETERMINE WHETHER IT IS APPROPRIATE TO INTEGRATE SOME OF YOUR LEGACY APPLICATIONS ON THE BUSINESS SERVICES LAYER

    a) What is a disadvantage of integrating DCOM and CORBA approaches in your legacy system integration? Why do you think the A Corporation decided not to integrate a DCOM approach?

    _____

    _____

LAB 4.3 EXERCISE ANSWERS

4.3.1 ANSWER

a) Why do you think the A Corporation decided to integrate the payroll processing application on the business services layer?

Answer: The payroll processor application was determined to work fine but needed to be upgraded to make reports accessible to others and to tie in with other accounting software. It was noted on the inventory that a CORBA interface was available, allowing for integration on the business services layer without a lot of in-house development work. If done correctly, business services layer integration provides a flexible solution that can be extended in the future, which is useful for integrating payroll processing into other accounting and planning software used by the A Corporation.

**LAB
4.3**

4.3.2 ANSWER

a) What is a disadvantage of integrating DCOM and CORBA approaches in your legacy system integration? Why do you think the A Corporation decided not to integrate a DCOM approach?

Answer: Integrating DCOM and CORBA approaches will most likely have a negative impact on performance and scalability. However, it does combine the desktop functionality of DCOM and the business services of CORBA. The A Corporation therefore decided to stick to a CORBA approach and not attempt to integrate the desktop functionality of DCOM.

LAB 4.3 SELF-REVIEW QUESTIONS

In order to test your progress, you should be able to answer the following questions.

1) Integrating your legacy applications at the business services layer requires the use of another set of technologies.

   a) _____ True
   b) _____ False

2) RPC is a protocol used by a program to request a service from a different part of itself located on the same computer.

   a) _____ True
   b) _____ False

3) If done correctly, business services layer integration provides a flexible solution that can be extended in the future.

    a) _____ True
    b) _____ False

4) Integrating DCOM and CORBA approaches will most likely not have a negative impact on performance and stability.

    a) _____ True
    b) _____ False

Quiz answers appear in the Appendix, Section 4.3.

**LAB
4.3**

L A B   4 . 4

BACKEND INTEGRATION

LAB OBJECTIVES

After this lab, you will be able to:

✔ Understand the Benefits and Problems of Integrating Your Legacy Systems into the Web on the Data Access Layer
✔ Develop Plans for Access to Standard Relational Database Management Systems (DBMSs) from the Web

**LAB
4.4**

Integrating legacy applications on the backend through the data access layer results in a tighter coupling between the application and the Web. For example, Sun's Java Data Base Connectivity™ (JDBC) provides a set of functions for database connectivity, data query, and data retrieval. These APIs (application program interfaces) can be used by developers to integrate legacy applications on a data access level.

JAVA LANGUAGE SUPPORT

The Java™ programming language was introduced by Sun Microsystems in 1995, adding interactive capabilities to the static pages of the Web. Java is a programming language designed specifically for use in the distributed environment of the Internet. Java is object-oriented and therefore supports the concept of inheritance in which similar objects can take advantage of belonging to the same class and inherit common code.

Java provides a C++-like language designed for portability. Java was designed to allow application programs to be built to run on any platform without the need for modification or recompilation. Virtual machine is a term used by Sun Microsystems to describe software that acts as an interface between compiled Java binary code (bytecode) and the hardware platform that actually performs the program's instructions. The Java virtual machine specification defines an abstract machine, specifying an instruction set, a set of registers, a stack, a heap, and a method area. The implementation of this abstract machine can be in other code that is recognized by the real processor. The implementation of the abstract machine can be built into the microchip processor itself. Once a Java virtual machine has been provided for a platform, any Java program can run on that platform. A Java virtual machine can either interpret the bytecode one instruction at a time (mapping it to a real microprocessor instruction) or the bytecode can be compiled further for the real microprocessor using what is called a just-in-time (JIT) compiler.

Java code is designed to be robust so that, unlike in C++, Java objects cannot contain references to data external to the objects themselves or other known objects. This ensures that an instruction will not contain the address of data storage in another application or in the operating system itself. In this way, program or operating system crashes can be avoided. In addition, the Java virtual machine performs checks on each object to ensure integrity (e.g., array bounds checking).

The major Web browsers include a Java virtual machine. Most operating system developers now offer Java compilers as part of their product offerings. Java can be used to create complete applications that may run on a single computer or be distributed among servers and clients in a network. It can also be used to build small application modules or applets for use as part of a Web page. An applet is a small application program. On the Web, using Java, an applet is a small program that can be sent along with a Web page to a user. Java applets can perform interactive animations, immediate calculations, or other simple tasks without having to send a user request back to the server. Applets make it possible for a Web page user to interact with the page. In addition to being executed at the client rather than the server, a Java applet has other characteristics designed to make it run fast.

JAVA DATABASE CONNECTIVITY™ (JDBC)

JDBC is an API specification for connecting programs written in Java to the data in industry-standard database management systems. The application program interface lets you encode access request statements in structured query language (SQL) that are then passed to the program that manages the database. It returns the results through a similar interface. JDBC is very similar to Microsoft's Open Database Connectivity (ODBC). Using a small "bridge" program, you can use the JDBC interface to access databases through Microsoft's ODBC interface.

JDBC actually has two levels of interface. In addition to the main interface, there is also an API from a JDBC "manager" that in turn communicates with individual database product "drivers," the JDBC-ODBC bridge if necessary, and a JDBC network driver when the Java program is running in a network environment (that is, accessing a remote database).

When accessing a remote database, JDBC takes advantage of the Internet's file addressing scheme and a file name looks very similar to a URL Web page address. JDBC specifies a set of object-oriented programming classes to be used in building SQL requests. An additional set of classes describes the JDBC driver API. The most common SQL data types are supported and are mapped to Java data types. The API provides for implementation-specific support for transactional requests. The JDBC API also includes the ability to commit or roll back to the beginning of a transaction.

The JDBC API defines Java classes, which provide access to databases. These classes can be used to represent connections to a relational database management system (RDBMS) as well to represent SQL statements and metadata identifying particular databases. JDBC APIs allow developers to write Java code for SQL queries and for processing the results of database queries. The JDBC API is implemented via a driver manager that can support multiple drivers connecting to different databases. JDBC drivers can either be entirely written in the Java programming language so that they can be downloaded as part of an applet, or they can be implemented using native methods to bridge to existing database access libraries.

**LAB
4.4**

JDBC DRIVERS

There are four different types of JDBC drivers:

- The JDBC-ODBC bridge
- A native-API partly Java technology-based driver
- A net-protocol all Java technology-based driver
- A native-protocol all Java technology-based driver

THE JDBC-ODBC BRIDGE

This driver provides JDBC access to databases via most ODBC drivers. With the JDBC-ODBC bridge, it may be necessary to load some ODBC binary code and some database client code onto each client system that uses the driver. Therefore, it is best to use the JDBC-ODBC driver on an intranet in which you have control over all the client desktop systems or for Java application server code in a three-tier architecture. A three-tier application includes a Web client, a database server, and a Java program.

A NATIVE-API PARTLY JAVA TECHNOLOGY-BASED DRIVER

This type of driver converts JDBC calls into calls on the client API for standard DBMSs, including Oracle, Sybase, Informix, and DB2. As with the first type of driver, it is necessary to load some binary code onto each client system that uses this driver.

A NET-PROTOCOL ALL JAVA TECHNOLOGY-BASED DRIVER

This type of driver provides translation facilities, that take JDBC calls and convert them into a DBMS-independent network protocol. The DBMS-independent network protocol is in turn translated into a DBMS protocol by a server. Java technology-based clients can be connected to many different databases using vendor-specific protocols and a middleware server solution. Middleware solutions vendors primarily support intranet implementations. However, this approach can also be used on an Internet solution if appropriate security facilities are provided and if access through firewalls and other such requirements for Internet access are supported. Database middleware products are being enhanced with the addition of these JDBC drivers. This type of driver provides the most flexibility since it allows connections to many different database management systems.

A NATIVE-PROTOCOL ALL JAVA TECHNOLOGY-BASED DRIVER

This driver converts JDBC calls into the network protocol used by the DBMSs themselves. With a native-protocol technology-based driver written in Java, you can implement a direct call from the client machine to the DBMS server. The direct call capability makes this approach useful for integration with an intranet. Some of the database vendors are in the process of developing their own drivers to handle their DBMS-specific protocols.

**LAB
4.4**

LAB 4.4 EXERCISES

4.4.1 UNDERSTAND THE BENEFITS AND PROBLEMS OF INTEGRATING YOUR LEGACY SYSTEMS INTO THE WEB ON THE DATA ACCESS LAYER

   a) How does JDBC provide integration of legacy systems? Why do you think the A Corporation decided to use a Java/JDBC approach for benefits processing?

4.4.2 DEVELOP PLANS FOR ACCESS TO STANDARD RELATIONAL DATABASE MANAGEMENT SYSTEMS (DBMSS) FROM THE WEB

a) What is the disadvantage of implementing a JDBC-ODBC bridge driver or a native-API partly Java technology-based driver? Why would the A Corporation decide not to use a JDBC-ODBC bridge driver or native-API partly Java technology-based driver approach?

LAB 4.4 EXERCISE ANSWERS

4.4.1 ANSWER

a) How does JDBC provide integration of legacy systems? Why do you think the A Corporation decided to use a Java/JDBC approach for benefits processing?

Answer: JDBC provides Java classes for access to databases. This allows integration of legacy applications on the backend via the data access layer. Replacing a manual process and a mainframe application with a Java application using JDBC to connect to back-end database servers would allow the A Corporation to integrate benefits processing with the human resources database.

4.4.2 ANSWER

a) What is the disadvantage of implementing a JDBC-ODBC bridge driver or a native-API partly Java technology-based driver? Why would the A Corporation decide not to use a JDBC-ODBC bridge driver or native-API partly Java technology-based driver approach?

Answer: Both of these drivers require some code to be installed on the client systems. This means that you have to make sure that each client system has the right code installed before using this approach. As a large corporation, the A Corporation decided to replace the benefits processing application with a pure Java/JDBC approach rather than implementing an approach that would require installing code on each client system.

LAB 4.4 SELF-REVIEW QUESTIONS

In order to test your progress, you should be able to answer the following questions.

1) Java was designed to allow application programs to be built to run on any platform without the need for modification or recompilation.

   a) _____ True
   b) _____ False

2) Java virtual machines are only included in a few Web browsers.

   a) _____ True
   b) _____ False

**LAB
4.4**

3) JDBC is used for connecting programs written in Java to the data in industry-standard database management systems.

   a) _____ True
   b) _____ False

4) Implementing a JDBC-ODBC bridge requires some code to be installed on the client systems.

   a) _____ True
   b) _____ False

Quiz answers appear in the Appendix, Section 4.4.

L A B   4 . 5

LEGACY APPLICATIONS

LAB OBJECTIVES

After this lab, you will be able to:

✔ Appreciate the Ease of Use Gained from the Marriage of a Web GUI Frontend to a Legacy Application

✔ Decide If Some of Your Legacy Applications Just Need a New Frontend to Be More Usable

When does it make sense to replace an old application that is difficult to use and when is it better to update the legacy application with a new Web GUI frontend? Let's look at a real-life situation in which a large computer manufacturer was about to embark on a six-month development effort involving six software engineers. The time card application used throughout the company was difficult to use and could only be used on the mainframe that most groups no longer used. In order to continue using the time card application, data had to be submitted to a central group, which then had to rekey the data into the system. Therefore, the corporate IS department had decided that it was time to replace the time card application with a new one that people throughout the corporation could access. The decision to move forward was discussed in a task force meeting. Fortunately, one of the members of the task force knew that a group in his division was developing Web applications. He advised the task force to hold off until he could discuss the time card application with the Web applications group.

He approached the manager of the Web applications group and asked if it would be possible to solve the time card application problems with a Web application. There were two problems that needed to be addressed: The user interface to the current time card application was difficult to use and administrative staff often introduced errors into the data. Further, users did not have access to the time card application from the systems they used on a day-to-day basis. Integration with the Web could solve both these problems. With a time card form to fill out, a standard Web browser could be used on anyone's desktop. The time card form could be made available on the corporate Intranet and the form-processing script could include error-checking capabilities to improve the accuracy of the data entering the system. A script was developed to accept the time card information through the form and pass it to the existing time card application at the backend. The CGI script that was developed included functionality to check for errors in the data, making sure that the data was of the correct type, making sure that the data was within bounds, and making sure that the data was complete. These error-checking facilities greatly improved the accuracy of the data entered into the time card system and reduced the need for clean-up efforts at the backend. The time card application continued to be used on the mainframe, but the interface to it was the CGI script instead of a human administrator.

Making the time card application available via the corporate Intranet meant that each person could access the application, enter his or her own data, and then the time card could be approved with a simple workflow application, which allowed the manager to approve the time card before it entered the system. The Web integration was completed and tested in one week by one engineer in the Web applications group, working with one engineer in the time card group as a resource person. Contrast the cost difference between the frontend integration involving one man-week of effort and the development of a new system, scheduled to involve three man-years of engineering effort. In addition, the group that reentered the data was freed up to do other tasks. An added benefit was that people were much more willing to use the Web GUI frontend than the difficult-to-use mainframe application. The corporate IS group, often maligned in the company as being dinosaurs, were considered heroes.

**LAB
4.5**

LAB 4.5 EXERCISES

4.5.1 APPRECIATE THE EASE OF USE GAINED FROM THE MARRIAGE OF A WEB GUI FRONTEND TO A LEGACY APPLICATION

a) Consider systems in your organization that might benefit from a "makeover." Are there some applications used by the A Corporation that would benefit from a makeover?

4.5.2 DECIDE IF SOME OF YOUR LEGACY APPLICATIONS JUST NEED A NEW FRONTEND TO BE MORE USABLE

a) Why do you think the A Corporation decided that some of the legacy applications needed more than a new frontend?

LAB 4.5 EXERCISE ANSWERS

4.5.1 ANSWER

a) Consider systems in your organization that might benefit from a "makeover." Are there some applications used by the A Corporation that would benefit from a makeover?

Answer: Look for applications that involve data entry that could be done in forms with error-checking facilities in a CGI script. This was the decision that the A Corporation made for the vacation scheduler application. With an easy-to-use Web GUI frontend, users were satisfied entering data into the vacation scheduler application and data could be checked and "cleansed" before being passed onto the mainframe for processing.

4.5.2 ANSWER

a) Why do you think the A Corporation decided that some of the legacy applications needed more than a new frontend?

Answer: The payroll processing application needed to be enhanced to provide customization of reports and accessibility by others. Also the payroll processing application needed to tie in with other accounting software. With these requirements for flexibility and integration with other accounting software, a makeover with a Web GUI frontend wouldn't suffice. With a CORBA interface available as an upgrade it made more sense to integrate on the business services layer, thereby providing tighter integration with other accounting software. For benefits processing, a primarily manual process working on a PC had no reasonable upgrade path. A makeover was definitely not sufficient to meet the needs of a large, geographically dispersed corporation. With Java-based benefits software available that provides a JDBC interface to backend databases, the A Corporation could tie in benefits processing with other human resources databases.

LAB
4.5

LAB 4.5 SELF-REVIEW QUESTIONS

In order to test your progress, you should be able to answer the following questions.

1) Web interfaces to backend databases can check for errors in data that will be inserted into the database.

   a) _____ True
   b) _____ False

2) Developing a web-based interface to a legacy system is often _____ than completely replacing the legacy system (select all that apply).

   a) _____ Faster to develop
   b) _____ More expansive
   c) _____ Cheaper
   d) _____ Slower to develop

Quiz answers appear in the Appendix, Section 4.5.

CHAPTER 4

TEST YOUR THINKING

A legacy system is under consideration to be connected to a new Web-based solution (intranet, extranet, public Web site, etc.). Determine the best course of actions in the following situations.

- Outdated payroll system running on old mainframe; timecard data is manually entered into system from hardcopy forms; hardcopy reports produced
- Brand new inventory system running on new set of physically dispersed servers; inventory data entered through proprietary network of terminals; limited access to terminals

Consider these questions in developing your plans for each situation.

1) What facilities do the legacy systems provide?
2) Who interacts with the system currently? If the system were integrated into a Web-based solution, who would interact with the system?
3) Which of these facilities should be part of a Web-based solution? What level of integration is the most appropriate for each legacy system?
4) Do any of the legacy systems require updating or replacing?
5) How should the system be connected to the Web-based solution on the business services layer?

CHAPTER 5

ELECTRONIC COMMERCE STRATEGY

The hype today is all about electronic commerce. Underneath all the hyperbole, electronic commerce can open new distribution channels for your organization. In addition to supporting your sales and distribution strategy, electronic commerce can assist you in working with your suppliers more efficiently. It is important to develop a strategy for your organization to incorporate electronic commerce into your plans.

In this chapter, we'll discuss the history and evolution of electronic commerce. We'll discuss both business-to-consumer and business-to-business approaches. We'll look at industry initiatives using electronic commerce to support and transform supply chain management. Then we'll discuss the development of your electronic commerce strategy.

L A B   5 . 1

ELECTRONIC COMMERCE BASICS

LAB OBJECTIVES

After this lab, you will be able to:

✔ Understand What Electronic Commerce Entails and What It Can Do for Your Organization
✔ Appreciate How Electronic Commerce Has Evolved and How It Is Currently Evolving

Electronic commerce is referred to in several abbreviated ways:

- E-commerce
- eCommerce
- eComm
- EC

In addition, some people now refer to Internet/Web-based electronic commerce as Icommerce.

Electronic commerce can be defined as the use of internetworked computers to support business operations in order to increase delivery speed and reduce operational costs. There are three basic types of electronic commerce: business-to-consumer, business-to-business, and intra-business.

In this chapter, we will discuss business-to-consumer electronic commerce and business-to-business electronic commerce. Intra-business electronic commerce concerns itself with the intranet as we discussed earlier in Chapter 1 of this book.

Electronic commerce introduces a new paradigm for conducting business, which includes facilities for:

- Buying and selling information on the Internet
- Buying and selling products and services via the Internet
- Transmitting documents and integrating business processes through extranets
- Transferring and sharing information within organizations through intranets

These electronic commerce operations are intended to:

1. Improve decision making
2. Eliminate duplication of effort
3. Reduce operational costs
4. Expand distribution channels and markets

Electronic commerce includes online transactions to carry out day-to-day business tasks. With business-to-business electronic commerce, organizations have the opportunity to sustain and improve existing relationships as well as to build new relationships with suppliers, customers, and partners. Alliances and partnerships can be established and supported via electronic commerce.

EARLY ELECTRONIC COMMERCE

While many people focus on the introduction of the World Wide Web as the beginning of electronic commerce, the earliest use of electronic commerce was really in the 1930s. At that time, American Airlines introduced its "Request and Reply" system, which included inventory control at a central point for telephoning in changes to inventory with replies to requests received via teletype. In 1946, American Airlines introduced the Availability Reservisor, an electrical/mechanical device to handle inventory control of airline seats. In 1952, the Magnetronic Reservisor, a random access memory drum with arithmetic capabilities, allowed agents to check seat availability and sell or cancel seats. A year later, American Airlines and IBM decided to work together and invest $40 million in the development of the SABRE system. SABRE stands for the Semi-Automated Business Research Environment. By 1964, the SABRE Telecommunications Network System was the largest real-time data processing system, operating across the entire United States as well as in Canada and Mexico.

ELECTRONIC DATA INTERCHANGE (EDI)

In the 1970s, Electronic Data Interchange (EDI) was introduced. EDI provided proprietary, closed systems with a hub and spoke structure. EDI systems were used for inventory control, particularly in manufacturing and catalog operations. JC Penney used EDI for catalog operations, with proprietary shipment tracking devices on board delivery trucks. The 1970s to early 1980s brought more advances in online airline reservation systems, such as the TWA PARS II system, which ran on the Tymnet public packet-switched network. This system provided international availability as well as integration with the back offices of travel agencies through an application called Fully Integrated Reservation System for Travel (FIRST).

EARLY HOME BANKING AND TRAVEL SERVICES

The precursor to Web-based online banking was developed in the early 1980s with a PC-based home banking pilot developed by Tymshare, Inc. for First Interstate Bank. In 1985, easySABRE was introduced for PC users, allowing people to make reservations for airlines, hotel accommodations, and rental cars. In the late 1980s to early 1990s, with the proliferation of PCs at home, PC-based home banking applications were made available to consumers. In addition, proprietary financial systems operated between financial institutions for their electronic funds transfer operations. In 1995, with the availability of the World Wide Web, SABRE developed Travelocity for individual travel reservations over the Web. By 1998, SABRE was handling 4,176 messages/second and bringing in more than $45 billion/year. In the financial world, PC-based online banking evolved to Web-based online banking with the introduction of Wells Fargo's first online banking Web site in 1995.

INTERNET-BASED ELECTRONIC COMMERCE

STAGE ONE

In the first stage of Internet-based electronic commerce, the major technologies were communication-oriented. These technologies required specific commands to be typed by users on a line-by-line basis. Requiring technical knowledge and appearing quite intimidating to non-technical users, these tools were used primarily by technical people. The most widely used technology was email. Other technologies involved file transfer and group communication. Librarians began using gopher, a text-based information organization utility, for organizing and retrieving book and periodical catalog information. These tools included email, FTP, gopher, telnet, and news.

STAGE TWO

The World Wide Web supported the second stage of Internet-based electronic commerce, which basically consisted of one-way marketing via graphical Web browsers. The most popular Web browser was Mosaic, originally available to "techies" by downloading the code from the Internet. Mosaic was public domain software developed by the National Center for Supercomputing Applications (NCSA). In addition, the first publicly available Web server was developed by CERN, the European Center for Particle Physics, where Tim Berners-Lee and Robert Cailliau developed and continued to enhance the World Wide Web infrastructure. With the basic WWW infrastructure and graphical Web browsers, companies could disseminate their corporate and product information. The Web and email provided the capabilities to support basic customer service with FAQs (frequently asked questions) and online help facilities provided via email. In this way, the first generation of Internet-based e-commerce has supported online versions of traditional business models, including storefronts, catalogs, malls, advertising, and credit cards.

STAGE THREE

Some Web sites have entered stage three of Internet electronic commerce, providing customer interaction, CGI scripts, secure protocols, forms, company–customer communication, simple transactions, and buying and selling.

STAGE FOUR

Other organizations have moved onto stage four of Internet e-commerce and are now using the Web for organization and process transformation, intranets within their organizations, extranets between their organization and other organizations, transforming supply chains into supply Webs, and Java and interactive applications.

The functionality of the Web supports electronic commerce and moves organizations through the stages as they are ready to implement new features. The Web is configurable, thereby supporting personalization and customization. The multimedia capabilities of the Web make it an excellent advertising channel. The ability to interact with customers on a Web site allows organizations to collect valuable information and conduct market research studies. The real-time nature of the Web offers a high level of engagement with customers. With standards for protocols and nomenclature in use or under development, interoperability among organizations can lead to the development of marketplaces.

Although some industry analysts see organizations moving through four stages of Internet-based electronic commerce so far, others tie all of these stages together and call them the first generation of Web-based e-commerce. The idea of first-generation e-commerce has been to reduce costs through internetworking, outsourcing, and customer self-service. According to this view of the industry, first generation technologies include Web and email, security and payment (SSL, SET), and search engines (e.g., Yahoo, Altavista, and many others).

However, these technologies are limited in their search, automation, and integration capabilities. With these technologies, Web sites as of early 2000 are able to publish information for people and to support first-generation e-markets or digital markets. Web sites are generally single vendor sites with known categories and partners. There are virtual superstores for books and groceries, such as Amazon.com and NetGrocer. Some Web sites serve as electronic storefronts for existing services, such as banking for Wells Fargo and catalog shopping for LL Bean. Bid/ask marketplaces are also supported with online auctions and classified ads offered by such companies as OnSale and Classified2000. Some electronic commerce sites constitute virtual order centers, offering travel services on Travelocity or cars through CarPoint. Electronic business communities have been established in the hardware and software arenas by Cisco and Dell. Virtual trading marketplaces have begun to sprout up in cyberspace, with FastParts and PartsNet providing online parts acquisition. In the biotechnology area, mouse DNA and other specific and hard-to-find components may be obtained online.

NEXT GENERATION WEB

The next generation Web will provide information and services for both computers and people. A key feature of the next generation Web is Extensible Markup Language (XML). XML is a meta-language for coding domain-specific protocols. XML can thus be used to describe content, transactions, and workflow. XML is vendor-neutral and supported by major industry players including Sun Microsystems and Microsoft Corporation. The XML specification has been approved by the the World Wide Web Consortium (W3C), and XML is now accepted as an industry standard. XML extends the power of a Web markup language beyond HTML so that computers can automatically process Web pages without the complexity of Standardized General Markup Language (SGML). SGML was developed and is used for document publishing but is too complex for general Web publishing.

The ability for XML-based components to deliver interactive functionality allows organizations to overcome the Web's limitations in the areas of search, automation, and integration. Armed with automated component-based e-commerce tools, the technology then enables new business models, including buyer-centric markets and virtual organizations.

Open, interoperable e-markets are supported and can flourish in busy marketplaces that support vertical industries, including the IT industry and financial services. Multihosting capabilities support marketplaces with multiple vendors offering interoperable catalogs and comparison shopping. Multihosted marketplaces require critical mass in cooperative markets. These marketplaces also require electronic business rules, referred to as e-business rules or e-rules, for working together. There is a need for open business rules of engagement and behavior among trading partners and members of any electronic marketplace. In addition, organizations need to agree on product definitions and classification along with policies regarding common business processes in order to work together effectively.

In the next generation of Internet-based e-commerce, we are seeing the development of component-based commerce. Component-based e-commerce, powered by XML and e-commerce building block technologies, such as the Electronic Commerce (eCo) framework, supports the evolution of the e-market. With component-based commerce, there is a focus on a specific process and the ability to integrate cooperative industries working together to accomplish that process. One example of a cooperative process is that of buying a house. Component-based e-commerce supports electronic appraisals and the MLS (multiple listing service used for real estate postings), with pooling and intermixing of processes and resources. In the foreseeable future, component-based e-commerce will support cooperation between open e-markets. Not only can groups cooperate with each other but also entire e-markets can cooperate, accepting e-business opportunities from other e-markets. In this way, the shipping industry can collectively bid on orders or the insurance industry can make its entire inventory available to online purchasers of automobiles.

LAB 5.1 EXERCISES

5.1.1 UNDERSTAND WHAT ELECTRONIC COMMERCE ENTAILS AND WHAT IT CAN DO FOR YOUR ORGANIZATION

a) Take a look at www.cheaptickets.com, a first-generation electronic commerce site and www.ehitex.com, a second-generation electronic commerce site. What is the major difference between the first generation of Internet-based electronic commerce and the second generation?

_____

_____

b) From our case studies in previous chapters, why do you think the A Corporation is satisfied with a first-generation electronic commerce site whereas BJ is developing a second-generation site?

_____

_____

c) Consider the requirements of your organization. Do you think a first-generation or a second-generation site will fulfill the requirements of your organization?

_____

_____

5.1.2 APPRECIATE HOW ELECTRONIC COMMERCE HAS EVOLVED AND HOW IT IS CURRENTLY EVOLVING

a) New types of electronic marketplaces offer comparison shopping and feedback from customers. Take a look at one electronic marketplace on the Web—www.bizrate.com. Review the capabilities of the BizRate.com site. What do you think such electronic marketplaces will require to be successful?

_____

_____

LAB 5.1 EXERCISE ANSWERS

5.1.1 ANSWERS

a) Take a look at www.cheaptickets.com, a first-generation electronic commerce site and www.ehitex.com, a second-generation electronic commerce site. What is the major difference between the first generation of Internet-based electronic commerce and the second generation?

Answer: The first generation of Internet-based electronic commerce supports traditional business models and publishes information for people. Cheap Tickets developed its on-line reservation and ticket-purchasing site in a way that is analogous to the toll-free customer telephone lines (which are usually busy). The site offers many travel services and highly competitive fares. Though the site is interactive, its facilities are automated in such a way as to support interaction with a person.

The automation and "componentizing" capabilities of the second generation of Web facilities support new business models, such as buyer-centric markets and virtual organizations, and provide information and services for both computers and people. The High-Tech Exchange, ehitex.com, was designed to automate as much of the procurement process as possible. The auction, RFQ (request-for-quote), bidding, and catalog processes are set up with automated tools, providing information for both computers and people. The High-Tech Exchange provides electronic catalog development tools as well as catalog hosting services so that companies can create online surplus catalogs and liquidate smaller lots of surplus inventory.

b) From our case studies in previous chapters, why do you think the A Corporation is satisfied with a first-generation electronic commerce site whereas BJ is developing a second-generation site?

The A Corporation sells large-scale solutions to major accounts, thus engaging in direct sales to medium-to-large organizations. The corporate Web site provides information in much the same way as a corporate brochure does. However, BJ offers online products and services and can reduce its costs if it automates as much of the processing on the Web site as possible.

c) Consider the requirements of your organization. Do you think a first-generation or a second-generation site will fulfill the requirements of your organization?

In order to answer this question, consider the objectives of your organization's Web site. Are you trying to attract strictly "eyeballs" or are you using the site to automate some of the business processes of the organization? Would your organization benefit from participating in a multihosted marketplace in which there are electronic rules for behavior and shared business processes. If a strictly eyeball site is appropriate for your organization, then a first-generation site will fulfill the requirements of your organization. If, on the other hand, your organization can benefit from automating services on the site and/or from participating in a multihosted marketplace, a second-generation site is in order for your organization.

5.1.2 ANSWER

a) New types of electronic marketplaces offer comparison shopping and feedback from customers. Take a look at one electronic marketplace on the Web— www.bizrate.com. Review the capabilities of the BizRate.com site. What do you think such electronic marketplaces will require to be successful?

Answer: The BizRate.com site offers what the company refers to as a C3 marketplace. C3 stands for:

Choice: Millions of products at thousands of stores.

Convenience: Comparison shop for quality and price.

Confidence: Guided by millions of customer ratings.

In order for such electronic marketplaces to succeed, they require:

Critical mass of cooperative organizations to participate (BizRate's Choice)

Electronic business rules on behavior and cooperation in the marketplace

Agreement on product definitions and classification and common business processes

As the marketplace host, BizRate.com has established the rules for cooperation and developed its own classification of products. These features allow for comparison shopping (BizRate's Convenience). In a multihosted marketplace, there would need to be electronic business rules and agreement on definitions, classification, and business processes among the hosts of the marketplace.

For any electronic shopping site to succeed, consumers must have confidence that they will receive what they purchase on the site (BizRate's Confidence).

LAB 5.1 SELF-REVIEW QUESTIONS

In order to test your progress, you should be able to answer the following questions.

1) Which of the following constitutes a type of electronic commerce? (select all that apply)

a) _____ Intra-business
b) _____ Business-to-consumer
c) _____ Business-to-business
d) _____ All of the above

2) Electronic commerce came about because of the World Wide Web.

a) _____ True
b) _____ False

3) The third generation of Internet-based e-commerce has supported online versions of traditional business models.

a) _____ True
b) _____ False

4) The Web is configurable, thereby supporting personalization and customization.

a) _____ True
b) _____ False

5) Electronic commerce is limited to traditional business models.

a) _____ True
b) _____ False

Quiz answers appear in the Appendix, Section 5.1.

L A B   5 . 2

BUSINESS-TO-CONSUMER ELECTRONIC COMMERCE

LAB OBJECTIVES

After this lab, you will be able to:

✔ Identify Stages of Business-to-Consumer Electronic Commerce
✔ Understand Web-Based Marketing Approaches
✔ Plan a Phased Introduction of Electronic Commerce in Your Organization

---

Business-to-consumer electronic commerce is referred to as B-to-C e-commerce or simply B-C EC. The first Web sites involved one-way marketing, providing brochures on corporate Web sites. With the introduction of secure payment protocols, purchasing and catalog shopping were added to Web sites. With the proliferation of Web sites, there was a need for aggregation, and virtual malls began sprouting up on the Web. Using the interactive capabilities of the Web, people began to introduce survey forms and to gather market research information through tracking and profiling customers. These interactive capabilities also made customization and personalization possible. People looked for ways to increase customer satisfaction and to not only attract customers but also to keep them as repeat customers. Relationship marketing is the current approach to supporting ongoing interaction between companies and their customers. Let's look at each of these trends in terms of the stages of electronic commerce they represent.

STAGES OF ELECTRONIC COMMERCE

PULL ADVERTISING

Stage 1 of business-to-consumer electronic commerce focused on pull advertising. In this stage, static Web pages provided company, product, and service information to "pull" customers in. Hewlett-Packard (HP) built a very large, complex Web site, organized to provide consumers with information on various products and services.

CUSTOMER SERVICE

The biggest draw, however, came in stage 2 when HP expanded its site to offer basic customer service facilities. Printer drivers are the most commonly requested customer service item. Making them available on the HP Web site has brought many people to the site. Providing online access to printer drivers on their Web site, HP has fulfilled many customer service requests with a significantly reduced cost structure. In addition, customers have expressed greater satisfaction with this self-service approach since they can obtain their drivers when they want, with no time wasted waiting for a CD or floppy that has been shipped to them.

WEB AS DISTRIBUTION CHANNEL

Stage 3 of business-to-consumer electronic commerce has involved an expansion of sales and distribution channels, with some companies using the Web as their sole distribution channel. Catalog marketing companies may provide online ordering but require that customers refer to their hard-copy catalog. Some companies have not wanted to invest the time and money to put their complete catalogs online. J Crew, a catalog marketing company, took the approach of offering online ordering using a hard-copy catalog. From the beginning, Internet Shopping Network (ISN) saw the Web as its primary channel, offering electronic catalog, ordering, service, and support facilities. With these facilities, ISN was able to quickly reach more than 50,000 customers/day representing more than 25,000 products from over 600 companies. The numbers continue to grow and make it clear why doing business-to-consumer electronic commerce makes sense financially.

RELATIONSHIP MARKETING

Business-to-consumer electronic commerce has entered stage 4 on some Web sites, offering relationship marketing and promoting customer loyalty. With greater sophistication of tools on the Web, traditional marketing of brand name loyalty can be promoted through such services as Firefly. With Firefly, consumers join a community to receive services. These services include design and development services, such as customization of CD inventory and product review facilities, offering customers the opportunity to hear snippets of songs and to read biographies of individual artists. Online purchasing allows customers to buy CDs over the Web and customer service facilities answer their frequently asked questions with FAQs lists and email responses to specific customer questions. In this way, customers are encouraged to become and remain members of a community, buying products on a regular basis through one online service.

There are a number of factors that affect the success of business-to-consumer Web sites. Through experience, businesses have found that the direct shopping experience on the Web requires appropriate products and services. As online shopping has gained acceptance, the number and type of products and services that are appropriate has expanded. People are looking for an easy and fun experience or else they would prefer to continue to do their shopping in person. Secure ordering and payment facilities are expected. Consumers are also looking for flexible purchasing and payment options to attract their business. While transacting business, consumers look for instant feedback to make sure their transactions were successful; they are not content to send off their order into the ether without knowing that the transmission was received. Various types of online support are now expected, including order acknowledgement, shipment tracking, and customer help facilities.

B-to-C payment methodologies include encrypted transmission via SSL (secure sockets layer) of credit cards online. Bundling SSL into the Netscape browser greatly contributed to its acceptance by companies and their customers. In addition to SSL, other security technologies have been introduced including: electronic cash, electronic checks, digital signature cryptography (in which the signature is computed to authenticate the owner), and smart cards (which have gained more acceptance in Europe and Asia than in the United States). However, various online payment methodologies have not received such widespread acceptance as credit card payment online using SSL, which is the easiest to use. We will investigate these secure payment technologies further in the next chapter.

LAB 5.2 EXERCISES

5.2.1 IDENTIFY STAGES OF BUSINESS-TO-CONSUMER ELECTRONIC COMMERCE

Take a look at the following sites. Identify the stage of business-to-consumer electronic commerce on each site. Describe the use of that stage of business-to-consumer electronic commerce.

a) www.aspfree.com

_____

_____

b) www.mamamedia.com

_____

_____

c) www.pamf.org

_____

_____

d) www.enroute.com

_____

_____

5.2.2 UNDERSTAND WEB-BASED MARKETING APPROACHES

Investigate the www.mypoints.com site.

a) What type of marketing approach does the company offer?

_____

_____

b) How does this differ from the marketing approach used on other Web sites?

_____

_____

5.2.3 PLAN A PHASED INTRODUCTION OF ELECTRONIC COMMERCE IN YOUR ORGANIZATION

a) How can you start introducing electronic commerce into your organization?

_____

_____

b) Is there one activity that you could support online that your organization's customers would find particularly useful?

_____

_____

LAB 5.2 EXERCISE ANSWERS

5.2.1 ANSWERS

Take a look at the following sites. Identify the stage of business-to-consumer electronic commerce on each site. Describe the use of that stage of business-to-consumer electronic commerce.

a) www.aspfree.com

The site for ASPs (Application Service Providers) offers stage 2 functionality, customer service, since it provides a number of customer service facilities, including demonstrations and tutorials as well as answers to questions and tutorials.

b) www.mamamedia.com

The MaMaMedia site, incorporates stage 4 relationship marketing, developing relationships with kids and their parents through a number of relationship marketing approaches on its Web site. Free electronic greeting cards are offered so that parents can send them to their children. Music accompanies the selection of a Web page. There are educational games for children on the site.

c) www.pamf.org

The Palo Alto Medical Foundation provides stage 1 functionality, pull advertising. The site provides extensive information and material on their physicians and medical services.

d) www.enroute.com

Enroute Imaging sells still imaging software for cameras on its Web site and therefore provides stage 3 functionality. The company has introduced immersive video technology, which it offers through direct sales channels. For the immersive video technology, the Enroute site provides information using stage 1 functionality.

5.2.2 ANSWERS

Investigate the www.mypoints.com site.

a) What type of marketing approach does the company offer?

Answer: An interesting case study of business-to-consumer electronic commerce involves a company named Cybergold. Cybergold patented a method for attention marketing and introduced a new form of advertising via the Internet through which companies pay for a customer's attention. Advertising is delivered in the form of "infotainment," combining information with entertainment on the Web. People register as members and provide information about themselves and their interests to indicate their willingness to view specific types of advertisements. In return, members are paid for their attention in the form of cash, airline miles, and even charitable donations made on behalf of members. Member profiles and interests are tracked for market research. Advertisers are charged only for the number of consumers who view and participate in their Web ads. This form of advertising is targeted to specific consumers who have expressed interest in that type of product or service and who are willing to view the ads for those products and services at that time.

b) How does this differ from the marketing approach used on other Web sites?

Answer: Many marketing professionals believe that attention marketing is more effective than banner ads that are automatically displayed on most Web sites. With attention marketing, people who view the ads are making a conscious decision to view these particular ads. With attention in short supply, rewarding potential customers for their attention may be the most effective way to gain their attention.

5.2.3 ANSWERS

a) How can you start introducing electronic commerce into your organization?

Answer: Now, we're ready to discuss your organization's strategy for implementing electronic commerce. It's time to convene your World Wide Web Council for a strategic planning session. Involve strategic planners or business planners in your organization to facilitate the discussion. Start by determining which of the three major electronic commerce areas you will be addressing:

Business-to-consumer transactions

Business-to-business activities

Intra-organizational operations

Next, list your objectives in implementing electronic commerce in that particular area. Determine your success criteria and decide on some measurable criteria to judge whether you've succeeded or to recognize the shortcomings of your implementation. Make a list of your current suppliers and partners. Also make a list of potential partners. Adopting electronic commerce can increase the feasibility of working with remote partners, so include possible partners with whom you could work if your organization had a presence on the Internet. List your current major customers as well as customer groups you would like to reach that you may not be able to reach with your current distribution channels. Consider whether an electronic commerce approach will allow you to reach new customers. Will geographic dispersion be addressed so that you can have an international customer base?

Plan a pilot implementation and a phased approach to electronic commerce.

b) Is there one activity that you could support online that your organization's customers would find particularly useful?

Answer: You can determine at which stage of B-to-C electronic commerce your company is functioning and advance to the next stage by adding next stage functionality. If your organization is new to electronic commerce, you can start with stage 1 of business-to-consumer electronic commerce—pull advertising—providing online information on your organization's products and services. You can develop a plan for office supply purchasing by your organization as an intra-organizational e-commerce initiative. This initiative could support an online catalog, accessible throughout the organization on your intranet, with items that can be ordered online if they're under a certain limit. If you sell directly to consumers, consider developing an online catalog with photographs to illustrate the items to purchase, moving to stage 3 of B-to-C electronic commerce.

LAB 5.2 SELF-REVIEW QUESTIONS

In order to test your progress, you should be able to answer the following questions.

1) Self-service customer support is an example of a stage ____ feature of a Web site.

a) _____ 1
b) _____ 2
c) _____ 5

2) Customer loyalty incentives can be implemented on the Web.

a) _____ True
b) _____ False

3) Credit card information is encrypted during its transfer over the Internet.

a) _____ True
b) _____ False

4) An in-house Web server is not required to support electronic commerce.

a) _____ True
b) _____ False

Quiz answers appear in the Appendix, Section 5.2.

LAB 5.3

BUSINESS-TO-BUSINESS ELECTRONIC COMMERCE

LAB OBJECTIVES

After this lab, you will be able to:

✔ Understand the Development of Business-to-Business Electronic Commerce

✔ Determine How to Incorporate Business-to-Business Electronic Commerce into Your Organization's Day-to-Day Operations

---

Business-to-business electronic commerce supports supply chain management (SCM), managing companies involved as suppliers, partners, and customers and their business processes for efficiency, productivity, and reduced costs. We'll discuss supply chain management in further detail in Lab 5.4 of this chapter. Web-based business-to-business electronic commerce is able to improve the management of:

- Supplier relationships, transforming them into partnerships

- Inventory, with inventory control always an important way to reduce costs

- Channels, providing support to distribution channels with improvements in the flow of information to and from those working in the channels

- Distribution methods and the distribution process, transmitting shipping documents and purchase orders

- Sales force, providing up-to-date information on production as well as supporting customer communication

- Payment and collection of funds, improving communication between the company and its suppliers and distributors
- Money, supporting currency exchange in international situations

The promise of business-to-business electronic commerce is to support end-to-end electronic commerce. At this point, business-to-business electronic commerce is point-to-point. In order to transform business-to-business electronic commerce into real end-to-end electronic commerce, it is necessary to automate the following steps:

1. Customer Inquires
2. Supplier Confirms Availability
3. Customer Purchases
4. Supplier Accepts Purchase
5. Supplier Confirms Purchase
6. Supplier Places Order

As the technology and electronic business relationships improve, supply chains are being transformed into supply Webs with various suppliers, partners, and companies working together in a cooperative business arrangement. In addition, business-to-business electronic commerce is supported by legacy systems integration to protect current investment in automated business processes, new ways of working with customers, willingness and ability of suppliers to work cooperatively, business process reengineering within and between organizations working together, investment and risk on the part of participating businesses, and integration with new technologies.

For business-to-business electronic commerce to be accepted, security measures need to be adopted. Such required security mechanisms include:

- Authentication—knowing sender's identity
- Integrity—data arrived exactly as sent
- Nonrepudiation
- Origin—sender can't deny sending
- Receipt—receiver can't deny receiving
- Confidentiality
- For "right eyes" only

In Chapter 6, we will discuss security mechanisms in further detail.

LAB 5.3 EXERCISES

5.3.1 UNDERSTAND THE DEVELOPMENT OF BUSINESS-TO-BUSINESS ELECTRONIC COMMERCE

A case study of business-to-business electronic commerce involves a leading wholesaler in the pharmaceutical industry, McKesson HBOC, Inc. After a merger between McKesson and HBOC, the combined company is now the world's largest pharmaceutical supply management and healthcare information technology company.

**LAB
5.3**

a) Take a look at the McKesson HBOC Web site (www.mckhboc.com). Find information on Econolink.

_____

_____

b) Who is the customer for Econolink?

_____

_____

c) How does Econolink provide business-to-business electronic commerce?

_____

_____

5.3.2 DETERMINE HOW TO INCORPORATE BUSINESS-TO-BUSINESS ELECTRONIC COMMERCE INTO YOUR ORGANIZATION'S DAY-TO-DAY OPERATIONS

a) Take a look at your organization's day-to-day business operations. What do you think can be done first to help your organization benefit from business-to-business electronic commerce?

_____

_____

LAB 5.3 EXERCISE ANSWERS

5.3.1 ANSWERS

A case study of business-to-business electronic commerce involves a leading wholesaler in the pharmaceutical industry, McKesson HBOC, Inc. After a merger between McKesson and HBOC, the combined company is now the world's largest pharmaceutical supply management and healthcare information technology company.

a) Take a look at the McKesson HBOC Web site (www.mckhboc.com). Find information on Econolink.

Answer: To find the Econolink project, do a search from the home page or from the Technologies and Services page. According to the description, Econolink provides order entry and asset management software to manage pharmacy resources and make better purchasing decisions.

b) Who is the customer for Econolink?

Answer: The customer for Econolink is a pharmacy wanting to automate its purchasing process for drugs and other necessary supplies.

c) How does Econolink provide business-to-business electronic commerce?

Answer: Econolink provides business-to-business electronic commerce by automating the purchasing process for pharmacies to obtain drugs and supplies from pharmaceutical wholesalers.

5.3.2 ANSWER

a) Take a look at your organization's day-to-day business operations. What do you think can be done first to help your organization benefit from business-to-business electronic commerce?

Answer: Business-to-business electronic commerce supports a company's distribution channels and sales force by keeping them up-to-date on production information, by staying in contact with people in the field, and by supporting communication with customers. Consider your organization's business partners, sales channels, and customers. Choose a major account or trusted partner and find out what business processes that organization has already automated. This may make a good first step in establishing business-to-business electronic commerce with a trusted partner. Another approach is to locate the "point of pain," that is, a business process that is costly to perform using the current approach or that is causing problems in carrying out business with this customer or partner.

LAB 5.3 SELF-REVIEW QUESTIONS

In order to test your progress, you should be able to answer the following questions.

1) Business-to-business electronic commerce supports supply chain management.

    a) _____ True
    b) _____ False

2) End-to-end electronic commerce requires automation of the following steps (select all that apply).

    a) _____ Customer purchases
    b) _____ Supplier confirms availability
    c) _____ Supplier places order

3) Business-to-business electronic commerce requires strong security measures to be adopted.

    a) _____ True
    b) _____ False

4) Electronic commerce always involves selling directly to consumers.

    a) _____ True
    b) _____ False

5) You can do business with other organizations through (select all that apply):

    a) _____ COINs
    b) _____ extranets
    c) _____ intranets
    d) _____ the Internet

Quiz answers appear in the Appendix, Section 5.3.

**LAB
5.3**

LAB 5.4

SUPPLY CHAIN MANAGEMENT

LAB OBJECTIVES

After this lab, you will be able to:

✔ Understand How Business-to-Business Electronic Commerce Can Address Supply Chain Management Issues

✔ Develop Better Ways to Work with Your Organization's Suppliers Through Electronic Commerce–Based Supply Chain Management

---

Electronic commerce holds the key to improving the management of the procurement process and the supply chain. With electronic commerce, a supply chain becomes a supply Web, supporting multiway relationships between different organizations. Two different initiatives are underway to improve supply chain management: RosettaNet to address the IT industry supply chain and SCOR to address supply chain management in manufacturing.

PROCUREMENT PROCESS

First, let's take a look at what the overall procurement process entails. We view the procurement process as all the tasks involved in obtaining material, transporting it, and moving it toward the production process. The procurement process is a balancing act, dependent on having accurate information about the company's needs for materials and services and the external suppliers providing those goods and services. Procurement in manufacturing or production-oriented organizations depends on obtaining the right parts at the right time and for the right price. Efficient, cost-effective procurement is critical to the success of a manufacturing or production-oriented company, particularly given the shrinking profit margins in that sector. In the service sector, effective procurement processes may mean the difference between being able or not being able to deliver promised services within budgetary constraints. In the printing and publishing industry, companies spend approximately 35 percent of their revenues on purchasing while in the petroleum industry, purchasing may spend up to 90 percent of the company's revenues. If procurement can obtain materials of the right quality, in the right quantity, at the right time, at the right place, from the right source, with delivery at the right place, it can have a strong positive impact on the bottom line and the success of the company.

Web-based electronic commerce technologies, such as electronic catalogs, email, search engines, electronic RFPs (requests for proposals, often used in government projects), and component-based architectures can bring about major improvements in the purchasing process and in the management of the supply chain.

PURCHASING

Purchasing is a major component of the procurement process. In purchasing, buyers identify and evaluate their requirements and locate sources to fill these needs. At the other end, potential sellers arrange to determine who their potential customers are and offer their goods to these customers. These buying and selling processes are dependent on knowing the right information about the buyer's product requirements along with product availability on the seller's end. In addition, the process involves negotiation of an agreement and writing a purchase order to purchase the goods. When the goods are purchased, the monitoring of the process continues to make sure that the right goods are received and that they are paid for.

Traditionally, procurement has focused on processing these transactions in an efficient manner. The current approach considers account planning, forecasting, and policy issues related to purchasing control, the management of internal and external relationships, and scheduling and logistics tasks. Supply chain management has become the industry name to describe the integral administration of goods and services from the supply side through the transformation process and through distribution channels all the way to the end consumer.

Procurement is based on the exchange of information and communication between participants. This group of participants includes the company, its existing and potential suppliers, and third-party service providers, such as banks, insurance companies, consultants, industry associations, and information service providers. Online services and electronic catalogs are provided for access to remotely stored information at any time and search engines can help find information about products and supplies. Electronic data interchange (EDI) systems can connect companies and their business partners, automating the exchange of structured data for order placement or shipping announcements.

PROCUREMENT AUTOMATION

The first applications of information technology in the procurement process automated existing processes, often providing a one-to-one correspondence between the electronic transaction and the paper-based communication. Web-based electronic commerce allows the procurement process to evolve into the establishment of virtual communities of geographically dispersed trading partners, supported by an environment in which many types of information can be exchanged and tracked. A key feature of this environment is an electronic catalog, which provides product and service information to potential customers. The first versions of electronic catalogs automated existing processes by providing a graphical user interface and multimedia display of each vendor's individual catalog. Evolving Web technologies support the integration of electronic catalogs into electronic malls offering one entry point to the catalogs of a variety of sellers, with the ability to search through multiple catalogs simultaneously and provide links to complementary goods and services. Interoperable catalogs require standard descriptions of content, but some sellers are reluctant to participate in standards development since interoperable catalogs make it easier for lesser-known sellers to compete with brand-name companies.

NEGOTIATION SUPPORT

Information technology can also be used to support the negotiation process. Web-based auctions such as Onsale, Inc. and Consumer Exchange Network (CXN) provide asynchronous participation by bidders in an English style of auction, in which bidders can view current bids and submit competitive bids. Web-based auctions bring together bidders electronically without the need to bring them together in one physical location. Onsale, Inc. brings together more than one million bidders. Such auctions are also expected to support buying and selling in the business-to-business arena, in such areas as the computer OEM market. In addition to auctions, there are other new electronic mechanisms for bargaining, such as interactive pricing, in which potential buyers are allowed to place an offer to buy supplies at a lower price than the one stated in the published price list.

PURCHASING CONSOLIDATION

Web-based e-commerce tools support the consolidation of ad hoc individual purchases to take advantage of quantity discounts and reduction in shipping charges, but the technology must be coupled with appropriate procurement processes and policies. CommerceNet's COIN (Community of Interest Network) supports virtual organizations, with participants working together electronically to complete cooperative tasks, such as the purchase of a complex product or service or the processing of a loan.

ELECTRONIC COMMERCE BUILDING BLOCKS

The evolution of electronic commerce to a building block model affords the opportunity to integrate electronic catalogs, email, Web-browser GUI frontends, EDI, and search engines with established inventory control and enterprise resource planning (ERP) systems at the backend. When the tools have evolved to support the rich set of features required for this digital market, it will be possible to disseminate and exchange structured, unstructured, synchronous, and asynchronous information throughout the purchasing process, including settlement, maintenance, and customer support.

ROSETTANET CONSORTIUM

RosettaNet is the initiative established to develop a set of industry-wide electronic business interoperability standards for the IT industry. We mentioned RosettaNet in Chapter 2 when we were discussing industry extranets. The founders of RosettaNet understood the need for an industry-wide partnership with representatives of companies along every step of the IT supply chain, including hardware manufacturers, software publishers, distributors, resellers, system integrators, end users, technology providers, financial institutions, and shippers. Two initial projects include: 1) the development of joint specifications for memory products, including memory chips and memory expansion boards for PCs, and 2) the development of industry-standard specifications and taxonomy for laptop computers, defining the technical attributes and values associated with these attributes. With agreed-on specifications and nomenclature, purchasing agents can specify their requirements for memory products or laptops and locate products that meet their requirements.

LAB 5.4

RosettaNet is working on the development of efficient business process interfaces among supply-chain trading partners to rectify costly inefficiencies affecting manufacturers, distributors, resellers, and end users. Current processes involve complex inventory management along the supply chain, with manufacturers forced to rely on inexact inventory numbers or inaccurate inventory location information resulting from a lack of agreement on parts numbering and query processing interfaces. The lack of a common taxonomy in product information from hundreds of manufacturers impacts the processes and costs involved in production planning, channel allocation, and returns. While the product information is changing rapidly through the introduction of new products and addition of new features, distributors need to support their resellers and in the process, they must contend with tens of thousands of SKUs (stockkeeping units), described in many different ways. Aggregating and disseminating this content is an expensive and inefficient process performed individually by each distributor in the channel. Resellers are forced to learn and maintain different ordering and return procedures, and system interfaces to each distributor and direct manufacturer with whom they trade. This process may cause them to spend as much as 50 percent of their time maintaining their back-office operations—time they would rather spend on sales.

The procurement process affects everyone along the supply chain, including end users, who lack standard templates to allow them to coordinate with government authorized schedules. The government procurement process, hampered by these inefficient processes, results in delays so significant that the people who requested PCs end up receiving old technology by the time their purchase requisitions are completed.

Electronic commerce is in the process of fundamentally changing the buying and selling of IT products and services. All along the supply chain, companies are using the Web to look for and find new ways to build and support their relationships with their customers, to determine and build new opportunities for revenues, and to increase efficiencies in their operations. With the development of common business interfaces, IT supply chain participants look forward to increasing their productivity and significantly lowering their distribution and procurement costs. To support electronic business processes, RosettaNet is developing a master dictionary, defining properties for products, partners, and business transactions. In addition, RosettaNet is developing an implementation framework of protocols for the exchange of information to support the interface between trading partners, what they refer to as the "Partner Interface Process" or PIP.

**LAB
5.4**

SUPPLY CHAIN OPERATIONS REFERENCE (SCOR) MODEL

The Supply Chain Operations Reference (SCOR) model was developed in 1996 and 1997 by a group of seventy companies from a cross section of industries. These companies formed the Supply Chain Council (SCC), led by Advanced Manufacturing Research (AMR) and Pattiglio Rabin Todd & McGrath (PRTM). In November, 1997, the SCC launched SCOR as a public domain standard for evaluating and improving supply-chain management (SCM). With the increased popularity of SCM and the virtual corporation, discrete manufacturers became concerned that there was no common ground for evaluating processes they used for interacting with suppliers, while manufacturers were becoming increasingly dependent on these. EDI standards addressed business data transfer but did not address the actual business process flow and its management. Manufacturers saw the need for a common, standardized business, which led to the development of the SCOR model.

SCOR is a multilevel business flow model that provides a "best practices" standard for defining, communicating, and evaluating the supply chain. The SCOR model enables businesses to increase their responsiveness to customer needs and to competitive challenges. The model also significantly reduces the time to complete supply chain projects.

The SCOR model is based on four core management processes:

- Planning—The process balancing aggregate demand and supply to develop a course of action that best meets established business rules.

- Sourcing—Processes that obtain goods and services to meet planned or actual demand.

- Making—Processes to transform goods and services into a finished state to fill planned or actual demand.

- Delivering—Processes that provide finished goods and services, including order management, transportation management, and distribution management.

The SCOR model provides a metamodel of these four functions with a four-level model addressing business areas, domains, functions, work, and activity flows.

- Level 1—This is the top planning level that defines process types: Plan, Source, Make, Deliver. At this level, a company defines the scope and content of its supply chain operations reference model to meet supply-chain competitive objectives.

- Level 2—This is the configuration level, where process categories are decided. Companies implement their operations strategy through the configuration of these categories.

- Level 3—This level is the detailed process drill-down from Level 2 into specific elements to determine net demand, check capacity, and check material. Operations strategy is fine-tuned on level 3.

- Level 4—Implementation level. This level is not detailed in the SCOR model since it is the link into the host business processes and applications. Companies implement their specific supply chain management practices at this level to achieve competitive advantage and adapt to changing business conditions.

With the shift from a "make-to-stock" buildup of inventory approach to a just-in-time "make-to-order" approach, the SCOR model is becoming a standard for communicating supply chain issues and resolving differences between trading partners. It is expected that the SCC and SCOR will have a significant impact on how supply chain software is developed, sold, and supported as well as how original design and business process re-engineering are done. SCOR certification is expected to appear on vendor evaluation checklists and, as is the case with such checklist items as ISO9000 and EC/EDI, in time it is expected to become a de facto industry requirement.

LAB 5.4 EXERCISES

5.4.1 UNDERSTAND HOW BUSINESS-TO-BUSINESS ELECTRONIC COMMERCE CAN ADDRESS SUPPLY CHAIN MANAGEMENT ISSUES

a) Take a look at the RosettaNet Web site—www.rosettanet.org. How do you think RosettaNet can improve supply chain management for IT industry resellers?

_____

_____

5.4.2 DEVELOP BETTER WAYS TO WORK WITH YOUR ORGANIZATION'S SUPPLIERS THROUGH ELECTRONIC COMMERCE–BASED SUPPLY CHAIN MANAGEMENT

a) Take a look at the following Web sites: www.bizrate.com, www.officemax.com, and www.buy.com. How do you think your organization can use these (or similar) sites to improve its procurement process?

_____

_____

LAB 5.4 EXERCISE ANSWERS

5.4.1 ANSWER

a) Take a look at the RosettaNet Web site—www.rosettanet.org. How do you think RosettaNet can improve supply chain management for IT industry resellers?

Answer: At this point, IT industry resellers are forced to learn and maintain different ordering and return procedures as well as different system interfaces to each distributor and direct manufacturer with whom they work. RosettaNet seeks to rectify this problem by developing ways to interact with distributors and manufacturers through standard interfaces and common electronic business processes.

5.4.2 ANSWER

a) Take a look at the following Web sites: www.bizrate.com, www.officemax.com, and www.buy.com. How do you think your organization can use these (or similar) sites to improve its procurement process?

Answer: These sites and similar sites can help decentralize the procurement process in your organization. Some organizations have established approved spending limits for each department, allowing departmental purchases within those spending limits. This allows individual departments to obtain their own office supplies, computers, and electronic products without having to involve the purchasing department in every purchase. The BizRate.com site supports the RFQ (request-for-quote) process that many organizations use. The online office supply stores offer order tracking as well as delivery services. These can all automate steps of the procurement process while minimizing the impact on your organization's personnel.

LAB 5.4 SELF-REVIEW QUESTIONS

In order to test your progress, you should be able to answer the following questions.

1) With electronic commerce, a supply chain becomes a supply web, supporting _____ relationships _____ organizations.

    a) _____ one-way, between different
    b) _____ multiway, inside
    c) _____ one-way, inside
    d) _____ multiway, between different

2) Efficient, cost-effective procurement is critical to the success of a manufacturing or production-oriented company.

    a) _____ True
    b) _____ False

3) Procurement is based on the exchange of information and communication between participants.

    a) _____ True
    b) _____ False

4) Web-based e-commerce tools support the consolidation of ad hoc individual purchases to take advantage of quantity discounts and reduction in shipping charges.

a) _____   True
b) _____   False

5) Electronic commerce is in the process of fundamentally changing the buying and selling of IT products and services.

a) _____   True
b) _____   False

Quiz answers appear in the Appendix, Section 5.4.

LAB 5.4

CHAPTER 5

TEST YOUR THINKING

Analyze an electronic commerce Web site. Pick either a business-to-consumer (e.g., www.cooking.com) or a business-to-business (e.g., www.gmtradexchange.com) site.

1) Who is the customer?
2) In what stage of electronic commerce development (Lab 5.1) is the site?
3) Does the site offer any customer loyalty incentives?
4) Would you visit the site? Why? Would you stay at the site after coming up with an initial reaction? Why?
5) Would you return to the site? Why?
6) Are any aspects of the supply chain visible? Can you see the interfaces between the different organizations involved in a transaction?

C H A P T E R 6

ELECTRONIC
COMMERCE TOOLS

Electronic commerce promises gains in productivity, efficiency, and communication. At the same time, processing costs are expected to decrease. These objectives are achievable but they require the right types of electronic tools to support the move to electronic business (eBusiness) operations. The introduction of the Web has transformed operations, and appropriate tools are under development to support these objectives.

In this chapter, we'll discuss the tools and technology that provide the foundation for the electronic commerce initiatives discussed in Chapter 5. Now that you have an understanding of business-to-business, business-to-consumer, and intra-business electronic commerce and have developed a strategy with your World Wide Web Council, it is time to turn to the technology that you may use to implement your strategy. We will discuss technologies to protect and secure your electronic business transactions. Then we'll investigate what's happening in the move to a component-based electronic commerce system architecture. Armed with these tools and technologies, you'll be able to understand how to develop your own electronic commerce solutions.

<u>L A B   6 . 1</u>

PUBLIC KEY INFRASTRUCTURE (PKI) AND CERTIFICATE AUTHORITIES (CAs)

LAB OBJECTIVES

After this lab, you will be able to:

✔ Understand the Use of Public Key Encryption
✔ Identify Methods to Protect Electronic Document Transmission

---

Electronic commerce is dependent on a number of components. First, there must be a willing buyer and a willing seller. There must be product, service, or information offerings. If payment is to occur, there must be payment mechanisms available for use. In order to transact business, security technology and procedures are expected. Trust is an often overlooked item on the list of requirements for electronic commerce, but it is an essential ingredient for electronic commerce to take place and to succeed.

TRUST

Different forms of trust exist in the physical world and in the electronic world. The physical world has drivers' licenses, passports, membership cards, and ATM cards with PINs (personal identification numbers). The Internet is a public network and as such, is not secure. When organizations engage in electronic commerce via the Internet, they need a way to secure their data, particularly financial transactions. The public key infrastructure (PKI) was developed to enable Web users to exchange data and money securely and privately. The public key infrastructure is based on the use of a pair of public and private cryptographic keys obtained and shared through a trusted authority. The public key infrastructure involves the use of digital certificates to identify individuals or organizations. A digital certificate is a form of trust on the Web that corresponds to the physical forms of trust we use on a daily basis for identification.

DIGITAL CERTIFICATES

A digital certificate is used to establish your credentials when transacting business on the Web. A digital certificate is a digital document, attesting to the binding of a public key of an individual or entity. The certificate verifies the authenticity of the public key and prevents impersonation by a person using a phony key. A Certification or Certificate Authority (CA) is responsible for issuing the digital certificates.

Digital certificates contain the following information:

1. Name of entity being certified
2. Public key
3. Name of certificate authority
4. Serial number
5. Expiration date
6. Optional additional information

A copy of the certificate holder's public key is used for encrypting and decrypting messages and digital signatures. The digital signature of the certificate-issuing authority confirms to a recipient that the certificate is real. Some digital certificates conform to the X.509 standard, but at this point there are nonstandard digital certificates in use as well. The public key infrastructure provides directory services for storing and revoking digital certificates, if necessary. Digital certificates can be kept in registries to allow authenticated users to look up other users' public keys.

Digital certificates play several roles. They validate identities, provide branding in relationships between parties, function as a server capability with SSL (which we'll discuss in the next section of this chapter), and provide security and authentication in the SET protocol (which we'll also discuss in the next section).

Digital certificates are currently used in the corporate world for many purposes, including remote access, intranets, email, human resources records, Internet and Web access, and access to organizational mainframe systems. Current users of digital certificates include organizations involved in Internet banking, Internet brokerage, Internet content publishing, software publishing, health care, and Secure Electronic Transactions (SETs).

Most people think there is basically one type of digital certificate. In actuality, several different types of digital certificates are available for use in business-to-consumer, business-to-business, and intra-business electronic commerce applications, including email certificates, browser certificates, server (SSL) certificates, software signing certificates, corporate empowerment certificates, SET certificates, and EDI certificates.

However, at the present time, a number of barriers exist that are slowing the acceptance of digital certificates. For one, they are not very portable across systems. In addition, there are liability issues to consider. Interoperability poses a problem with current digital certificates. Revocation procedures have not been fully defined or established. Reliance on a password scheme is seen as a disadvantage. Full market acceptance has not been achieved at this time.

Critical issues must be addressed in order to achieve acceptance and full use of digital certificates. The authentication process is somewhat complicated at this point and needs to be simplified for regular use. Secure request methods need to be available via email and the Web. Distribution of certificates should be handled via the Web or email as well. The revocation and renewal of digital certificates has not yet been adequately addressed. In addition, the support infrastructure has not been fully developed. Preparations need to be made to address situations in which certificates may be compromised.

PUBLIC KEY CRYPTOGRAPHY

The public key infrastructure depends on public key cryptography, which has become the accepted method on the Web for message encryption and decryption as well as for sender authentication. Earlier cryptographic schemes were called private key cryptography or symmetric cryptography. Private key cryptography involves the creation and sharing of a secret key for the encryption and decryption of messages. Private key cryptographic schemes can be compromised if the key is discovered or intercepted during transmission. With the private key, messages can be easily decrypted. Public key cryptography is also known as asymmetric cryptography since there is one public key that is known and a private key that is protected.

Let's look at how public key cryptography works in practice. In public key cryptography, a public and a private key are created simultaneously using the same algorithm. A Certificate or Certification Authority (CA) is responsible for the creation of the pair of keys. The CA then gives the private key to the requestor and provides a digital certificate with the public key in it. The public key is stored in a publicly accessible directory. The private key is protected and not shared with anyone else or transmitted across the Internet. The private key is used to decrypt text that has been encrypted with your public key by another person who retrieves your public key from the directory. If you want to send an encrypted message to someone, you can contact a central administrator to determine his or her public key. Then you can encrypt the message using this public key. On the other end, in order to decrypt the message, the recipient uses his or her private key. Public key cryptography ensures privacy by encrypting messages and provides authentication of the sender. If you want to make sure that the recipient knows that it is you who really transmitted a message, you can use your private key to encrypt a digital certificate. The recipient uses your public key to decrypt the digital certificate and thereby authenticate the sender's identity.

Examples of public key cryptographic schemes are RSA, Diffie-Hellman, and El-Gamal. These schemes support the distribution of public keys and the use of digital signatures. However, public key cryptography is slow. Another disadvantage of public key encryption is that keys must be distributed or made readily available. User experience has demonstrated that public key encryption is too slow to be useful in handling large documents. One way to reduce the impact on performance is to combine public key encryption with a symmetric algorithm. In this combined scheme, a secret or session key is generated. The message is encrypted using the symmetric algorithm and the session key. The session key is encrypted using the recipient's public key, which becomes a "digital envelope." Then the encrypted message and the digital envelope are sent to the recipient. When the message is received, the recipient uses his or her private key to decrypt the session key. In turn, the recipient uses the session key to decrypt the message itself.

PUBLIC KEY INFRASTRUCTURE (PKI)

Let's consider now what the entire public key infrastructure consists of. The basic elements of PKI are as follows:

- A certificate authority (CA) responsible for issuing and verifying digital certificates.
- A digital certificate including the public key or information about the public key.
- A registration authority (RA) to serve as the verifier for the certificate authority before a digital certificate is actually issued to the requestor.
- A directory where the digital certificates and their public keys are stored.
- A certificate management system.

A standard for PKI is currently under development by the Internet Engineering Task Force— (IETF). At the present time, a number of different vendor approaches and services are available for PKI implementation and support. Some of the PKI vendors are RSA, the developers of the most commonly used public key cryptographic algorithm; Verisign, a certificate authority that also sells software to enable an organization to create its own certificate authorities; GTE CyberTrust, a provider of consulting services and a PKI implementation methodology; Check-Point, a security technology company with a certificate management product, VPN-1 Certificate Manager, based on the Netscape Directory Server; Xcert, with a product, Web Sentry, that checks the revocation status of certificates on a server using the Online Certificate Status Protocol (OCSP); Netscape (now part of AOL), offering the LDAP (Lightweight Distributed Access Protocol), which currently supports 50 million objects and processes 5,000 queries a second; Secure E-Commerce, providing management of digital certificates; and Meta-Directory, providing security management by connecting corporate directories into a single directory.

CERTIFICATE AUTHORITIES

A certificate authority is a trusted authority, an organization, that takes on the responsibility for issuing certificates. By issuing digital certificates containing public keys, the CA vouches for the identity of those to whom it issues the certificates. The CA's public key must be trustworthy. The CA issuance process consists of the following steps:

1. Generate public/private key pair.
2. Send public key to CA.
3. Prove identity to CA—verify.
4. CA signs and issues certificate.
5. CA emails certificate or Requestor retrieves certificate from secure Web site.
6. Requestor uses certificate to demonstrate legitimacy of his or her public key.

In order to act as Certificate Authorities, it is critical that these organizations inspire trust. The US Postal Service has entered the CA business with a technology partner, Cylink. Large established companies and start-ups are acting as certification authorities, including VeriSign, GTE CyberTrust, Entrust, IBM, CertCo, and USPS/Cylink.

Hierarchies exist in a chain of trusted authorities. A trusted chain or certificate chain is an ordered list of certificates containing an end-user certificate and its Certificate Authority certificates. A certificate chain may include the following elements: root certificate, subordinate CA certificates, registration authority certificates, and end-user certificates.

There may be multiple root certificates in the certificate chain. There are issues of delegation of authority. Issuance involves the physical process of signing the certificate. Authentication involves the determination of the identity and relationship of the public key and the signer of the certificate. There can be a segregation of roles into that of a Certification Authority (CA) and that of a Registration Authority (RA). The CA has the authority to issue certificates, whereas the RA is entrusted with the responsibility of registering other entities or authenticating those to whom certificates are issued.

LAB 6.1 EXERCISES

6.1.1 UNDERSTAND THE USE OF PUBLIC KEY ENCRYPTION

Use public key encryption to protect your email communication. Download and install a PGP (Pretty Good Privacy) package off the Internet (www.pgp.com and www.download.com).

a) Create a public and private key for yourself. Have a friend do the same. Swap public keys with each other (see software documentation for assistance).

_____

_____

b) Encrypt an email message with your friend's public key. Send him or her the message. Have your friend decode the message. Have your friend send you an encoded message. Decrypt it with your private key.

_____

_____

c) Can you have an encrypted email conversation with someone else on the Internet? Swap public keys. Sign your emails with your key so that he or she knows who you are.

_____

_____

6.1.2 IDENTIFY METHODS TO PROTECT ELECTRONIC DOCUMENT TRANSMISSION

Go to the United States Postal Service (USPS) site—www.usps.com. Take a look at what one service provider offers in terms of protection for electronic documents.

    a) Where are digital certificates currently used in the Post Electronic Courier Service (PosteCS)?

_____

_____

LAB 6.1 EXERCISE ANSWERS

6.1.1 ANSWERS

Use public key encryption to protect your email communication. Download and install a PGP (Pretty Good Privacy) package off the Internet (www.pgp.com and www.download.com).

    a) Create a public and private key for yourself. Have a friend do the same. Swap public keys with each other (see software documentation for assistance).

    b) Encrypt an email message with your friend's public key. Send him/her the message. Have your friend decode the message. Have your friend send you an encoded message. Decrypt it with your private key.

    c) Can you have an encrypted email conversation with someone else on the Internet? Swap public keys. Sign your emails with your key so that he/she knows who you are.

    Answer: In public key encryption, there is a public key and a private key pair. The steps involved in public key cryptographic transmission that you (as the sender) and your friend (as the receiver) followed were as follows:

        Create public and private keys (sender and receiver, that is, you and your friend).

        Sender transmits an encrypted message using the receiver's public key.

        Sender transmits an encrypted signature using the sender's private key.

        Receiver decrypts an encrypted message using the receiver's private key.

        Receiver uses the sender's public key to decrypt an encrypted signature and authenticate the sender.

6.1.2 ANSWER

Go to the United States Postal Service (USPS) site—www.usps.com. Take a look at what one service provider offers in terms of protection for electronic documents.

    a) Where are digital certificates currently used in the Post Electronic Courier Service (PosteCS)?

       Answer: Digital certificates are currently used for server authentication. According to the site, PosteCS service authenticates the secure postal server before uploading the document via a server digital certificate.

LAB 6.1 SELF-REVIEW QUESTIONS

In order to test your progress, you should be able to answer the following questions.

1) The Internet is a private network and, as such, is secure.

    a) _____ True
    b) _____ False

2) The public key infrastructure was developed to enable Web users to exchange data and money securely and privately.

    a) _____ True
    b) _____ False

3) No specific organization is responsible for issuing digital certificates.

    a) _____ True
    b) _____ False

4) Digital certificates are _____ portable across systems.

    a) _____ Very
    b) _____ Not very

5) Public key cryptography has become the accepted method on the Web for message encryption and decryption.

    a) _____ True
    b) _____ False

6) Put the following steps of public key cryptography in order (first to last numbered 1 through 4).

a) _____ Receiver uses the sender's public key to decrypt an encrypted signature and authenticate the sender

b) _____ Sender transmits an encrypted signature using the sender's private key

c) _____ Sender transmits an encrypted message using the receiver's public key

d) _____ Receiver decrypts an encrypted message using the receiver's private key

Quiz answers appear in the Appendix, Section 6.1.

LAB 6.2

SECURE SOCKETS LAYER (SSL) AND SECURE ELECTRONIC TRANSACTION (SET)

LAB OBJECTIVES

After this lab, you will be able to:

- ✔ Understand the Use of Secure Sockets Layer (SSL)
- ✔ Understand the Use of Secure Electronic Transaction (SET)

SECURE SOCKETS LAYER (SSL)

Secure Sockets Layer (SSL) is a general-purpose encryption system developed at Netscape Communications. Netscape released SSL version 2.0 in 1994 as a feature bundled into the Netscape Navigator browser. SSL is designed to secure the transmission of messages in a network. Netscape developers decided that it was a good idea to segregate the security software in a program layer between the Web browser or Web server and the Internet's TCP/IP layers. The software operates to safeguard the confidentiality of messages being transmitted. The "sockets" part of the term refers to the UNIX sockets method of passing data back and forth between a client and a server program in a network or between program layers in the same computer. Netscape's SSL uses the public key encryption algorithm from RSA, which also includes the use of a digital certificate.

Netscape includes the client part of SSL as part of any Netscape Web browser. If a Web site is on a Netscape server, SSL can be enabled, and specific Web pages can be identified as requiring SSL access. Other servers can be enabled with Netscape's SSL program library, which can be downloaded or licensed as appropriate for its use.

Netscape offered SSL to the World Wide Web Consortium (W3C) and the Internet Engineering Task Force (IETF) as a standard security protocol for Web browsers and servers. SSL version 3.0 was released in 1996 and has become an IETF specification.

Netscape SSL employs RSA public key cryptography, with optional certificates to identify the server and the browser. The Diffie-Helman key exchange is used for anonymous transactions. SSL operates at the TCP/IP Transport Layer, requiring a dedicated TCP/IP port (443). An SSL transaction is referenced via https:// rather than http://. In the layered SSL design, HTTP sits on top of SSL, which sits on top of TCP/IP. In an SSL transaction, a client opens a connection to the server and lists its capabilities (SSL version, cipher suites, compression method). The server then responds by telling the client which cipher suite and compression method it will use. In turn, the server sends the client a session ID. The next step is for the server to send its X.509v3 site certificate.

Next the client generates a "premaster secret" and encrypts it using the server's public key to create a "digital envelope." The client forwards this digital envelope to the server. After that, the server and client exchange "ChangeCipherSpec" messages to confirm. Both send "finished message" hashes of the entire conversation to that point. The client and server now use the session key to symmetrically encrypt subsequent messages.

There have been two well-publicized incidents in 1995 when SSL failed. The 40-bit secret key used in export versions is vulnerable to brute force attack. In fact, a single encrypted message is vulnerable to cracking in a few weeks using a network of workstations. Specialized hardware can crack a 40-bit secret key in a matter of minutes. Implementation problems were found with SSL. Since Navigator 2.0 used a predictable random number generator to generate secret keys, messages could be cracked in a few minutes on a Sun workstation.

SECURE ELECTRONIC TRANSACTION (SET)

SET, the acronym for Secure Electronic Transaction, was developed by the financial industry to ensure the security of financial transactions on the Web. It was supported initially by the major credit card vendors Mastercard and Visa, working with Web technology vendors Microsoft, Netscape, and others. With SET, a user is given a digital certificate or an electronic wallet. Then a transaction is conducted and verified using a combination of digital certificates and digital signatures among the purchaser, a merchant, and the purchaser's bank in a way that ensures privacy and confidentiality. SET uses security technology from SSL, Microsoft's Secure Transaction Technology (STT), and Terisa System's Secure Hypertext Transfer Protocol (S-HTTP). SET uses some but not all aspects of a public key infrastructure (PKI).

In order to use SET, the customer must have a SET-enabled browser such as Netscape or Microsoft's Internet Explorer, and the transaction provider, such as the bank, store, or vendor must also have a SET-enabled server.

The first step is for the customer to open a Mastercard or Visa bank account. Any issuer of a credit card is a bank of some form. The customer is then issued a digital certificate. The digital certificate functions as a credit card for online purchases or other electronic transactions. The digital certificate includes a public key with an expiration date. The certificate is digitally signed by the bank to ensure its validity. The bank also issues digital certificates to third-party merchants. A merchant's digital certificate includes the merchant's public key and the bank's public key. At this point, a customer places an order on the Web, by phone, fax, or some other means. The customer wants to know that the merchant is valid, which is confirmed by the merchant's certificate. With this confirmation, the browser transmits the order information. Payment information is encrypted with the bank's public key, which can't be read by the merchant. The transmitted information includes the message to order the merchandise, encrypted with the merchant's public key; any payment information, encrypted with the bank's public key; and information tying this payment to this particular order. The merchant verifies the customer by checking the digital signature on the customer's certificate. Verification may be accomplished by referring the certificate to the bank or to a third-party verifier. The merchant then forwards the order message to the bank. The order message includes the bank's public key, the customer's payment information, and the merchant's certificate. The customer's payment is transmitted encrypted in a form that the merchant can't decode. The bank verifies the merchant and the message. The bank uses the digital signature on the certificate with the message and verifies the payment part of the message. The last step in the process is for the bank to digitally sign and send authorization to the merchant. It is then up to the merchant to fill the order and complete the fulfillment process.

LAB 6.2 EXERCISES

6.2.1 UNDERSTAND THE USE OF SECURE SOCKETS LAYER (SSL)

Go to the amazon.com site. Place an item in your shopping cart. Go to the "checkout area" to fill in your credit card information. You do not need to enter any information. In your Web browser, open up the security information window (see software documentation for assistance).

a) Are you communicating with the server over an encrypted connection? If yes, what type of encryption are you using? If no, would you continue with your purchase?

_____

_____

b) To whom does the certificate belong?

_____

_____

c) Who issued the encryption certificate?

_____

_____

6.2.2 UNDERSTAND THE USE OF SECURE ELECTRONIC TRANSACTION (SET)

Go to the SET Secure Electronic Transaction LLC, (SETCo) site—http://www.setco.org/. Take a look at the documents on the site.

a) Why is it so important to have interoperability tests to get a SET mark?

_____

_____

LAB 6.2 EXERCISE ANSWERS

6.2.1 ANSWERS

Go to the amazon.com site. Place an item in your shopping cart. Go to the "checkout area" to fill in your credit card information. You do not need to enter any information. In your Web browser, open up the security information window (see software documentation for assistance).

a) Are you communicating with the server over an encrypted connection? If yes, what type of encryption are you using? If no, would you continue with your purchase?

Answer: Yes, we are communicating with the server over an encrypted connection. You can see the https in the URL to indicate that SSL is being used with a secure http server. You can also check the security information page (by selecting Communicator then Tools then Security Info using the Netscape Communicator browser).

b) To whom does the certificate belong?

Answer: The Security Info page lists the certificate as belonging to: www.amazon.com software, Amazon.com, Inc., Seattle, Washington, U.S.

c) Who issued the encryption certificate?

Answer: The encryption certificate was issued by Secure Server Certification Authority, RSA Data Security, Inc.

6.2.2 ANSWER

Go to the SET Secure Electronic Transaction LLC, (SETCo) site—http://www.setco.org/. Take a look at the documents on the site.

a) Why is it so important to have interoperability tests to get a SET mark?

Answer: Interoperability is required to allow the complete SET transaction process to work. The SET backgrounder describes the steps of the SET Transaction Process as follows:

The cardholder selects the "Payment with SET" option and then chooses the form of payment, e.g., Visa, Mastercard, etc.

The merchant "wakes up" the cardholder's SET wallet, which sends a message to the merchant indicating which payment card the consumer is using.

An exchange takes place between the merchant and cardholder, authenticating each party and encrypting the payment information. This encrypted data is then forwarded to the merchant, which sends it, still encrypted, to its bank for decryption and authorization.

The merchant bank (acquirer) authenticates all the parties in the transaction and processes the transaction with its normal authorization process.

If approved, the merchant ships the requested goods or provides the requested service and, in return, receives payment from its financial institution.

At any point in the process, the software that completes the next step needs to be able to accept data and pass it on for the next step of processing. If a software component isn't interoperable with the next, there will be a problem in accepting the data or passing it on to the next stage of processing. Interoperability tests allow for multivendor solutions instead of just single vendor solutions.

LAB 6.2 SELF-REVIEW QUESTIONS

In order to test your progress, you should be able to answer the following questions.

1) SSL uses public key cryptography.

   a) _____ True
   b) _____ False

2) With SET, a user is given a digital certificate or an electronic wallet.

   a) _____ True
   b) _____ False

3) Customers are issued a digital certificate at the time that they open a Mastercard or Visa bank account.

   a) _____ True
   b) _____ False

4) SET is fairly easy to set up and use.

   a) _____ True
   b) _____ False

Quiz answers appear in the Appendix, Section 6.2.

L A B   6 . 3

ELECTRONIC COMMERCE COMPONENT-BASED ARCHITECTURES

LAB OBJECTIVES

After this lab, you will be able to:

✔ Identify the Core Components of Electronic Commerce Solutions

✔ Understand Component-Based Architectures for Electronic Commerce Solutions

---

In this section, we will explore two views of component-based electronic commerce. Organizations are currently seeking end-to-end electronic commerce solutions. At the present time, primarily point-to-point electronic commerce solutions exist and there is a need to assemble components from various vendors to build a complete electronic commerce solution. Organizations are building their electronic commerce solutions through the selection of components that best meet their individual requirements. These components are often obtained from different sources.

CORE COMPONENTS

The core components in current electronic commerce solutions are:

- Catalog Management, which provides facilities to store, search, and retrieve product information. Product information is organized into predefined, structured categories. Electronic catalogs can be an electronic version of paper-based catalogs, but catalog management facilities need to include information search and retrieval capabilities. Relational database management systems are often used to store catalog information and provide sorting and searching technology.

- Content Management, to enhance product information available through catalog entries. With content management facilities, catalog descriptions are supplemented with marketing and technical materials, including data sheets, product reviews, magazine articles, and other types of marketing collateral and technical specifications.

- Transaction services, providing online purchasing mechanisms. These facilities may include online shopping carts and credit card authorization services. Other transaction services may support business-to-business electronic commerce with verification of purchase orders and support for procurement agreements.

- Personalization facilities, including user profiling and features to customize content delivery based on individual usage patterns and individual user preferences, background, and characteristics.

- Customer support and customer service, including facilities to handle customers' questions and requests for information. Real-time services may be offered to allow customers to get help when they're on a Web site and can't find what they need.

- Interfaces to internal business systems, including functions, APIs (application program interfaces), and development tools to connect Web-based electronic commerce solutions with in-house ERP (enterprise resource planning) systems and other applications performing day-to-day business operations. In addition, this component includes interfaces to organizational databases, including customer and employee databases.

By assembling these components, organizations can construct complete electronic commerce solutions and accomplish the objectives of their electronic commerce strategies.

BUSINESS-ORIENTED COMPONENT STRATEGIES

Most e-commerce server vendors are not offering business-oriented component strategies yet. However, vendors are offering network-available business services. There are transaction engines and catalog management applications. Using these business services allows companies to outsource transaction services by passing product information to the transaction engine. With these outsourced business services, individual organizations can take credit cards online, verify credit cards, authorize purchase orders, handle fulfillment, track product shipments and delivery, and even manage customer service without the need for investment in their own back-office services. Commerce Service Providers have sprung up to provide these business services and currently range from start-ups to established telecommunications service providers. The trend to outsource business component services is expected to continue, providing focused component services, such as content management, customer support, and personalization.

While an outsourcing approach requires far lower investment, there may be situations in which it is important for the information to reside under the control and ownership of the organization itself. Components of the electronic commerce solution or the information associated with the electronic commerce solution may be strategic to the objectives of the organization. In such circumstances, the organization should carefully consider the competitive advantages to be gained from developing/purchasing and owning the strategic component of their electronic commerce solution. With component services, organizations can successfully engage in electronic commerce without an end-to-end electronic commerce server application running in-house.

**LAB
6.3**

COMPONENT-BASED ARCHITECTURE

With a component-based architecture, electronic commerce solutions can be assembled for particular vertical industries to support digital marketplaces. The CommerceNet eCo System provides a component-based framework for business services. The eCo architecture has four layers from top to bottom:

- Vertical markets
- Business processes and applications
- Commerce services
- Network services

A key ingredient of the component-based architecture is XML (Extensible Markup Language). As we discussed in Chapter 5, XML is a meta-language for coding domain-specific protocols. XML can thus be used to describe content, transactions, and workflow. XML is vendor-neutral, supported by major industry players including Sun Microsystems and Microsoft Corporation. The XML specification has been approved by the W3C (the World Wide Web Consortium) and XML is now accepted as an industry standard. XML extends the power of a Web markup language beyond HTML so that computers can automatically process Web pages without the complexity of SGML (standardized general markup language).

COMMON BUSINESS LIBRARY

A common business library (CBL) is under development as part of the CommerceNet eCo framework. The library will include:

- APIs for businesses, markets, processes, applications, and services
- Common Business Objects for catalogs, product information, business forms, and companies

We can consider organizations as collections of internal and external services. Some examples of such services include proposal development, pricing, purchasing, invoicing, and inventory. When manufacturers work with their suppliers, these business services may also include ordering parts and components, authorizing payment, shipping, tracking order status and delivery, and confirming receipt.

Then we can view documents as the input and output to these business services. These documents are processed according to agreed-upon business rules. XML can be used to describe these documents and the common business library includes common business objects described in the form of XML DTDs (document type definitions). Some of these document types include:

- Profiles of customers and vendors
- Catalogs, data sheets, price lists
- Invoices
- Purchase orders (POs)
- Inventory reports
- Bill of materials
- Contracts
- Credit reports
- Reports on shipping, tracking, and order status
- Receipts

Other business documents can also be processed by these business services.

Facilitating the exchange of business documents via mutually agreed-on business rules, component-based electronic commerce supports the establishment of virtual organizations, electronic marketplaces, and trading communities. The interfaces in the component-based eCo architecture along with XML data description facilities allow new services and trading communities to be developed. Interfaces are defined in terms of business services and documents rather than APIs. Documents are self-describing and are composed of standardized metadata from the eCo framework

Common Business Library (CBL). CommerceNet has developed a registry of XML DTDs to be shared by organizations in particular vertical industries. The registry is available for use by other organizations so that they can make their XML DTDs available for use within their vertical industries or marketplaces.

LAB 6.3 EXERCISES

6.3.1 IDENTIFY THE CORE COMPONENTS OF ELECTRONIC COMMERCE SOLUTIONS

Take a look at the REI outlet electronic commerce site—www.rei-outlet.com.

a) Describe the use of each of the core components of an electronic commerce solution by the REI outlet site.

_____

_____

6.3.2 UNDERSTAND COMPONENT-BASED ARCHITECTURES FOR ELECTRONIC COMMERCE SOLUTIONS

Take a look at the www.commerceone.net site, an electronic commerce solution that has implemented an XML component-based architecture.

a) Why is CommerceOne conforming to UDDI Standards to describe business services of various vendors?

_____

_____

LAB 6.3 EXERCISE ANSWERS

6.3.1 ANSWER

Take a look at the REI outlet electronic commerce site—www.rei-outlet.com.

a) Describe the use of each of the core components of an electronic commerce solution on the site.

Answer: The core components that are incorporated into the electronic commerce solution at the online REI outlet store include catalog management, content management, transaction services, personalization, and customer support. It is not clear from the external site whether there are interfaces between the external site and internal business systems. Based on the inventory control management on the site, it appears that there is most likely an interface to internal business systems that manage inventory.

The catalog management component offers a searchable catalog with product information organized in predefined structured categories.

The content management component provides product information with photographs as well as advice on what to buy for specific needs.

The transaction services component supports online purchasing including a shopping basket and credit card authorization.

The personalization component offers a service called the Bargain Sleuth. Using the Bargain Sleuth, you can select categories of items and the Bargain Sleuth will notify you via email when such items are available.

The customer support and customer service component provides help determining appropriate sizes of clothing and outerware as well as help in ordering and returning items. Customer support is provided through FAQs (frequently asked questions) as well as email contact with the Customer Service department.

6.3.2 ANSWER

Take a look at the www.commerceone.net site, an electronic commerce solution that has implemented an XML component-based architecture.

a) Why is CommerceOne conforming to UDDI Standards to describe business services of various vendors?

Answer: UDDI stands for Universal Description, Discovery and Integration, an open initiative to create a standard to publish and find information on electronic commerce services. XML is a vendor and application neutral meta-language, which can be used for coding domain specific protocols for content, transactions, and business rules. Standards such as UDDI, coupled with XML, will enable the automated processing of requests for specific business services.

LAB 6.3 SELF-REVIEW QUESTIONS

In order to test your progress, you should be able to answer the following questions.

1) Organizations can construct complete electronic commerce solutions by assembling the core electronic commerce components.

   a) _____ True
   b) _____ False

2) With a component-based architecture, electronic commerce solutions can be assembled for particular vertical industries to support digital marketplaces.

   a) _____ True
   b) _____ False

**LAB
6.3**

3) XML is a key ingredient of the component-based architecture.

   a) _____ True
   b) _____ False

Quiz answers appear in the Appendix, Section 6.3.

LAB 6.4

ELECTRONIC COMMERCE SOLUTIONS

LAB OBJECTIVES

After this lab, you will be able to:

✔ Determine the Function, Customization, and Integration
Components of an Electronic Commerce Solution
✔ Design an Electronic Commerce Solution

When people consider an electronic commerce solution, they generally focus on the function of an off-the-shelf solution. At this point in the evolution of electronic commerce tools, it is more appropriate to think of an electronic commerce solution as the combination of three elements:

Electronic Commerce Solution = Function + Customization + Integration

FUNCTION

The electronic commerce solution function may consist of packaged off-the-shelf software. Off-the-shelf software may be enhanced in-house. Another alternative for organizations with appropriately trained IT staff is to develop the basic electronic commerce function in-house.

Whether the function is off-the-shelf, enhanced, or in-house, it will most likely require some customization. This customization is accomplished according to the organization's business model. Your World Wide Web Council should revisit the organization's operating business plan and examine the business model to understand what level of customization is appropriate for your electronic commerce solution. The next step is to perform an inventory of systems and applications that may be involved in the organization's electronic commerce operations, as we did in Chapter 3 when considering legacy systems integration. You can use this inventory to determine the applications and systems that need to be integrated into the organization's electronic commerce solution.

Another issue to consider is whether your electronic commerce solution is a business-to-consumer solution, a business-to-business solution, or an intra-business solution. Will your electronic commerce solution require one or more levels of access control? Will your electronic commerce solution invite anonymous users to engage in electronic commerce with your organization or will your electronic commerce solution involve registered users with permission to access specific operations? In general, if your organization is involved in business-to-consumer commerce, your electronic commerce solution will need to accept anonymous users. In many business-to-consumer Web applications, anonymous users may obtain information but users are required to register to transact business on the Web site. Most business-to-business electronic commerce solutions require access control for targeted usage of applications. Intra-business electronic commerce solutions also require access control on intranets. However, since we covered intranets in Chapter 1, we will focus this discussion on business-to-consumer and business-to-business electronic commerce solutions.

**LAB
6.4**

CUSTOMIZATION

Another option to consider is whether your electronic commerce solution should involve personalization according to the profile of the customer/user. Many business-to-consumer electronic commerce solutions increase their customer appeal by providing individual profiles for shopping. If your electronic commerce solution is oriented toward consumer purchases, you can use knowledge of individual users to personalize the content or the site for each individual's use. You do need to consider privacy issues and it is important to include a well-thought-out privacy statement if you are collecting personal information about your customers. Consumers want to know how you will use and whether you will distribute their data before they divulge their personal information. Gathering information on your customers when they are visiting your Web site provides you with valuable market research data and feedback on your overall electronic commerce solution.

If your electronic commerce solution is a business-to-consumer solution, you will need to provide facilities for product search. You may want to provide a searchable electronic catalog with multimedia representation of product information. If you can provide data on a range of products, you may be able to encourage up-selling (purchasing a higher-priced version of the product with more functionality). It is useful to provide information on related products as well so that you can encourage cross-selling (purchasing a related product that may not be the exact one the consumer requested). Cross-selling is particularly helpful if a requested product is out of stock or if your organization wants to push a different product. Consumers use electronic malls or electronic superstores particularly if they can engage in comparison shopping. Consider whether it makes sense for your organization to participate in an electronic mall, in which multiple vendors, usually in a related industry, offer their products and services. Also, consider whether your organization wants to run or participate in a superstore, representing products from multiple vendors across the same type of product category. Electronic catalogs facilitate upselling and cross-selling and interoperable electronic catalogs will enable comparison shopping when they are available.

In a business-to-consumer electronic commerce solution, your organization needs to determine the purchase and payment options that are appropriate to provide to customers. Some organizations have online order forms, but require that consumers print out the order form and fax, mail, or call in the order with a check or credit card number. This is not a full electronic commerce solution. A business-to-consumer electronic commerce solution should be available 24 hours/day, 7 days/week, (24×7) and should include secure payment technologies. Business-to-business electronic commerce solutions will offer the most benefits if they too are available 24 hours/day, 7 days/week. This allows your organization to operate internationally and not worry about time zones or workday schedules. Although most of your business-to-business transactions may occur within a certain time period, it makes sense to offer 24×7 availability (or 22×7 with a back-up time during a slow time of the day). Allowing transactions to come through at any time of the day provides a more flexible electronic commerce solution for geographically dispersed organizations and for those organizations where people work long hours or multiple shifts.

INTEGRATION

In designing your organization's electronic commerce solution, you need to consider the type of interaction that you want to see between a customer and the company. Do you want to provide frequently asked questions (FAQs) so that customers can help themselves? Do you want to do all your interactions online? Will you use email or toll-free telephone numbers to answer questions? It is important for customers to have a positive experience interacting with your organization so that they will come back again and again as repeat customers. Therefore, it is important to consider the total experience customers have when they decide to interact with your organization. Conduct a walk-through of your planned electronic commerce solution with your World Wide Web Council. Consider the types of people who may visit your electronic commerce-enabled Web site. For your walk-through, ask various council members to act as new users, repeat customers, customers needing to locate and purchase a specific product, casual shoppers looking and possibly buying, and other potential customers who may visit your electronic commerce enabled site.

If you are developing a business-to-business electronic commerce solution, you also need to consider the type of interaction that will occur within the business community in which your electronic commerce solution is operating. What type of interaction will occur between each individual organization and your organization?

Will the other organizations interact without your involvement at times? If so, is your organization the host and do you want to keep abreast of all interactions in the community? Although this type of electronic commerce is called "business-to-business," it can be called "organization-to-organization," with any types of organizations exchanging information that helps them carry out their missions. Your organization may interact with other organizations in multiple communities of interest (which are referred to as COINs). If so, consider your electronic commerce solution in terms of the interactions involved in each COIN. Each COIN may have its own requirements for interaction. Standard business process interfaces are under development through electronic commerce initiatives such as RosettaNet, as we discussed in Chapter 5. However, COINs may evolve with their own XML DTDs (document type definitions) to define the data types involved in communication within that COIN. If your organization is a member of a COIN, encourage your COIN to adopt standard rules for communication and transactions. Also encourage your COIN to adhere to industry standards such as XML and to develop or adopt standard XML DTDs for your marketplace. Adhering to industry standards will allow your COIN to communicate with other COINs and to participate in the development of interindustry communication and cross-industry digital marketplaces.

LAB 6.4

LAB 6.4 EXERCISES

6.4.1 DETERMINE THE FUNCTION, CUSTOMIZATION, AND INTEGRATION COMPONENTS OF AN ELECTRONIC COMMERCE SOLUTION

a) Look at the Staples electronic commerce solution—www.staples.com. Read about stapleslink at www.stapleslink.com/information.html. Determine the function, customization, and integration components of the stapleslink electronic solution.

6.4.2 DESIGN AN ELECTRONIC COMMERCE SOLUTION

a) Consider the case of a specialty food producer, offering long grain and wild rice, cooked cereals such as oatmeal and multi-grain, multiple types of granola, dried fruit, and homemade preserves. What do you think the function, customization, and integration components of an electronic commerce solution for such a company should be?

LAB 6.4 EXERCISE ANSWERS

6.4.1 ANSWER

a) Look at the Staples electronic commerce solution—<u>www.staples.com</u>. Read about stapleslink at <u>www.stapleslink.com/information.html</u>. Determine the function, customization, and integration components of the stapleslink electronic solution.

Answer: Electronic Commerce Solution = Function + Customization + Integration. Function provides the basic features of an off-the-shelf enhanced package or in-house developed solution. Customization provides the features in such a way that the solution meets the needs of your organization. Integration includes the organization's operational applications in the overall electronic commerce solution.

Staples provides a business-to-business electronic commerce solution, with the following components. The function appears to have been developed in-house. The basic function is that of ordering office products, including direct access to the Staples product catalog containing more than 30,000 products. The function of the electronic commerce solution also includes tracking, approval, status, inventory availability and analysis of orders. Customization is provided in two areas: 1) through custom shopping lists for customers' most frequent needs and 2) through custom contract prices. Integration is available with existing procurement systems.

6.4.2 ANSWER

a) Consider the case of a specialty food producer, offering long grain and wild rice, cooked cereals such as oatmeal and multi-grain, multiple types of granola, dried fruit, and homemade preserves. What do you think the function, customization, and integration components of an electronic commerce solution for such a company should be?

Answer: The function should consist of off-the-shelf software for shopping cart functionality (including order processing functionality). Customization should allow for repeat visits by regular customers, keeping track of a user profile with name, address, product preferences, credit card information, and shipping information. Another type of customization could be to keep track of special occasions such as birthdays of relatives and friends. Through this customization feature, the customer could receive a reminder about an upcoming birthday with a suggestion to send a certain food item or gift basket containing some of the foods. Integration on the backend with the specialty food producer's inventory management system and accounting system would be very helpful to the running of an efficient online operation.

LAB 6.4 SELF-REVIEW QUESTIONS

In order to test your progress, you should be able to answer the following questions.

1) At this point in the evolution of electronic commerce tools, it is not appropriate to think of an electronic commerce solution as a piece of off-the-shelf software.

   a) _____ True
   b) _____ False

2) Electronic commerce solutions can involve personalization according to the profile of the customer/user.

   a) _____ True
   b) _____ False

3) Business-to-consumer solutions do not need to contain search facilities.

   a) _____ True
   b) _____ False

4) When developing business-to-business electronic commerce solutions, the type of interaction that will occur within the business community in which your electronic commerce solution is operating must be considered.

   a) _____ True
   b) _____ False

   Quiz answers appear in the Appendix, Section 6.4.

LAB
6.4

CHAPTER 6

TEST YOUR THINKING

Think of an idea for a business-to-consumer or a business-to-business service that would be useful to offer online.

1) Describe the components of the electronic commerce solution in terms of its function, customization, and integration.

2) Consider the core components of catalog management, content management, transaction services, personalization facilities, customer support and customer service, and interfaces to internal business systems. Describe which of these core components your service would include and how they would be used.

3) Would your service offer secure transactions? If so, would your service use SSL or SET? Why?

GETTING STARTED MANAGING YOUR WEB SITE

We are now in the third stage of the industrial revolution. The first involved machines which extended human muscle; the second used machines to extend the human nervous system (radio, television, telephones); the third is now utilizing machines which extend the human mind—computers. About half of all service workers (43 percent of the labor force by 2000) will be involved in collecting, analyzing, synthesizing, structuring, storing, or retrieving information.... By 1995, 80 percent of all management will be "knowledge workers."

—Owen Davies

CHAPTER OBJECTIVES

In this chapter, you will learn about:

✔ Understanding Your Organization	Page 195
✔ Establishing a Web Site Mission	Page 204
✔ Evaluating Your Audience	Page 211

Welcome to the world of Web site management, maintenance, and support. In this part of the book, we will be using three fictitious case-study sites to demonstrate Web site management, support, and maintenance principles. With luck, one of these case studies may remind you of your own situation.

ABC Hardware: Our first case study is ABC Hardware, a large, warehouse-type home improvement center catering to do-it-yourselfers and trade professionals. ABC is a West-coast chain, typically located in the suburban mall environment and operating with extended hours. Its motto is "Service and Quality at Down

Home Prices." This chain is currently experiencing strong growth in its offline stores and, while they have established a Web presence, they have not yet moved fully into e-commerce, depending instead on the interface between their offline and online branches.

FANNC: Our second entity is the Flea Abatement Network of Northern California (FANNC). This group is a nonprofit, nongovernmental organization providing resources regarding fleas and flea control. Starting out as a primarily paper-based informational resource, this group has begun to expand into the service arena, building on its expertise in this field. FANNC has recognized the value of the Web in providing its information to a broader community and has placed static page equivalents of its offline brochures and manuals on the Web site along with an extensive list of useful links related to fleas.

SkaBoards: The third company is SkaBoards, a rapidly growing, high-tech snowboard boutique with a lot of cachet in the Boulder area. Tourists and locals alike come to the shop to hang out and swap stories about great conditions and gear. Providing top-of-the-line equipment and snowboard lore, it caters to an affluent and highly gadget-oriented clientele. SkaBoards already has a strong Web presence and is aggressively pursuing upgrades and fancier e-commerce and support solutions to take advantage of advances in Web technology. Its current goal is to have its Web site become as much of a "place to be" as its offline boutique on Valor Street.

One very important general tip we can provide from our experience is to find out who is in charge before you start managing any project. Spending days, weeks, or months creating, revising, or managing a Web site is lost if the person or people in charge are not in the loop from the beginning.

LAB 7.1

UNDERSTANDING YOUR ORGANIZATION

LAB OBJECTIVES

After this lab, you will be able to:

✔ Review a Mission Statement
✔ Perform Interviews to Determine Organizational Perspective
✔ Identify Keywords to Reflect Organizational Values

As the use of the Web expands into everyday life, institutions will find their Web site emerging more and more as a common point of the all-important first contact with potential customers, collaborators, investors, and the like. Unlike a front office or lobby receptionist, who may depend on his or her surroundings to help convey an organizational identity, a Web site must be able convey that message clearly and entirely on its own. While different institutions will have specific agendas and messages to convey, the most important messages are common to all: reliability, integrity, and authority within the domain of influence. This chapter examines management issues that affect organizational identity.

What are you representing with your Web site? The simple answer is the name of a company or an association; this site represents "The Albright Group," the "Athenaeum Society," or "Department of Human Resources." These answers, however, do not address the image, agenda, or "personality" of the institution that your Web site will represent. Web site management decisions must take into consideration not only the audience that the site must reach, but also reflect the personality of the institution that they represent.

THE MISSION STATEMENT

A mission statement is the formal declaration of what it is that an organization does. Find out if your organization has a mission statement, because it can provide a place to start building your profile. If you're lucky, your organization has actually managed to develop a Web site mission. Sometimes your institution's mission statement is actually clear enough and accurate enough to work with. Nonprofits have a really hard time with mission statements. They tend toward the grandiose and global; saving all the hungry puppies in the universe or finding the cure for despair. Be aware, though, that even if a mission statement is not silly, it may be out of date; written as the first paragraph in an initial venture capital proposal and never revisited. While a good place to start, the formal mission statement is only a partial help in the best of circumstances. Building a viable profile that will actually help you manage a Web site requires some further research and asking some questions that may seem a little odd.

BEYOND THE STATEMENT

To represent an institution accurately, you will need to go beyond the formal mission statement and probe the personality behind it. You will need to get a feel for how the institution sees itself as a whole, its "outward facing" personality, and how it wants itself to be known to the world. You will also need to know what it values internally. Does it place a higher value on reliability than on speed (the U.S. Post Office vs. overnight delivery service)? Does it place a higher value on nurturing care than on cutting-edge technology (Elder Care Haven vs. Nip 'n Tuck Laser Surgery)? How does it "see" itself in its own field: Is it a leader, a renegade, a solid citizen? A classic misrepresentation of an institution occurred at Stanford University during the mid 1990s. Their public site, one of the first in the country, was redesigned without considering a central aspect of the Stanford culture—its deep-seated rivalry with the University of California at Berkeley, whose school colors are blue and gold. The newly redesigned welcome page at Stanford featured clear California blue skies and golden buildings and gold text on a blue background; this caused an unprecedented and entirely unexpected uproar among students, faculty, alumni, and many other vocal parties.

■ *FOR EXAMPLE*

Regional feedback indicates that ABC Hardware's "physical" Garden Centers are enjoying strong sales and report regular repeat customers. The Garden Center pages of the Web site, however, are not providing the revenue that they would like to see and are, in fact, resulting in a significant number of complaints. Complaints seem to focus primarily on customers' inability to find merchandise that they know exists in the physical store. Usage analyses indicate that customers are using only the top 5 percent of the pages in the Garden Center site and are not using the search capabilities built into the site to locate the items they want to find. Sales figures indicate that the customers who do buy from the site are buy-ing the "bread and butter" items: flats of pansies, hoses, shears, and the like. They are not taking advantage of the site's exclusive offerings of organic seedlings, heirloom-quality tools, or exotic plants that go well beyond the hold-ings offered in the physical Garden Centers. Evidently, the experience of drop-in shopping in the physical Garden Centers far outshines that of shopping in the virtual Garden Centers. What makes the physical Garden Center so much more attractive than the online version? What are customers missing? Since the offer-ings of the virtual store are equal to and, in some cases, more extensive than their regional counterparts in the chain, it is clearly not a lack of goods. It is clearly time to take a closer look at the virtual Garden Center.

As a part of a larger institution, the Garden Center shares the ABC Hardware mis-sion statement with the rest of the company, "Service and Quality at Down Home Prices." Where else do you look to see what makes the Garden Center an attractive experience?

As a first step, try the people who work there, who manage it, and who shop there. Interviewing key individuals about an organization can give you a strong sense of "who" that organization really is. Ask them some questions that will give you a feel for what it is they do and what they think about their group. Ask questions that are designed to get past any "pat" or canned answers. For example:

- If you were to give the Garden Center a nickname, what would it be?
- What are you most proud of in the Garden Center? Why?
- What are the top five words you would associate with it as an institution?
- What are the top five words that you would associate with the field in which it operates (that you would associate with nursery services in general)?
- What misconceptions do you find most of your customers have?
- Recognizing you as an expert in the field, what questions do your competitors ask you?

LAB 7.1 EXERCISES

7.1.1 REVIEW A MISSION STATEMENT

Find the mission statement for your organization as a whole or of a group within your organization and read it carefully. If your organization or group does not have a mission statement, use the sample statement below.

Our mission is to provide unparalleled service by ethically and professionally assisting our clients to reach their fullest potential. We accomplish this by individualizing each assignment, helping clients establish and pursue personal goals, and creating the proper programs and strategies to produce measurable results. We pledge to provide a safe, nurturing environment where the individual's welfare comes before profitability and the corporate client always receives greater value than expected.

Check for the following:

- Does this statement provide a useful description of the organization's services and goals?
- Is the statement fresh or is it an aging or abandoned document?
- Do you need to ask someone in the organization to clarify the meaning of the statement?
- Can you use the information in it to inform your development?

a) Overall, how well does this mission statement assist in developing the organization's Web site?

_____

_____

7.1.2 PERFORM INTERVIEWS TO DETERMINE ORGANIZATIONAL PERSPECTIVE

Interview key individuals in the organization for their perspectives. Develop a list of questions designed to get beyond the easy answers. Try to ask questions that the individuals do not already know the answers to, but that will give you a feel for how the organization sees itself, its services, and its values.

a) Which individuals in your organization did you interview?

_____

_____

b) What questions, besides those discussed previously in this lab, did you come up with?

_____

_____

7.1.3 IDENTIFY KEYWORDS TO REFLECT ORGANIZATIONAL VALUES

a) To what degree would you associate each of the following words with your institution?

	1 never	2 not really	3 maybe	4 mostly	5 absolutely	Score
Formal						
Warm						
Inventive						
Dependable						
Speedy						
Deliberate						
Industrial						
Exciting						
Wealthy						
Nurturing						
Sober						
Unpredictable						
Sexy						
Thrifty						
Playful						
Stern						
Innovative						
Wise						
Other						

Add up the scores for each row and put the number in the final column. Circle the top five ranking adjectives. These are your preliminary keywords that your Web site should reflect. Circle the bottom five adjectives. Avoid additions, enhancements, tools, or anything else on your Web site that will suggest these items.

**LAB
7.1**

LAB 7.1 EXERCISE ANSWERS

7.1.1 ANSWERS

Find the mission statement for your organization as a whole or of a group within your organization and read it carefully. Check for the items outlined in the Exercise.

a) Overall, how well does this mission statement assist in developing the organization's Web site?

Answer: The answer depends on your site. However, you will probably find that few mission statements address Web site concerns, as such.

Most mission statements were written before the Web became such a prevalent method of communication and branding. Perhaps the most you could expect out of a mission statement is a summary of the business goals and a sense of the organization's overt values, perhaps as communicated in the style of the statement. For instance, do you get a sense that the organization puts a high value on sobriety and structure, or do they place an emphasis on exploration and innovation? Accurately reflecting these values in the Web site is a good idea.

7.1.2 ANSWERS

Interview key individuals in the organization for their perspectives. Develop a list of questions designed to get beyond the easy answers. Try to ask questions that the individuals do not already know the answers to but that will give you a feel for how the organization sees itself, its services, and its values.

a) Which individuals in your organization did you interview?

Answer: Your candidates, of course, will vary, but the following are some suggestions for folks you should seriously consider including when you do your interviews.

Key individuals to be interviewed in the organization would certainly include (depending on the size of the organization) departmental/project leads. It is a very good idea to expand your interview group to such stakeholders as a selection of individuals throughout the organizational structure and major clients.

b) What questions, besides those discussed previously in this Lab, did you come up with?

Answer: Again, you probably came up with different answers on your own. Some additional examples of questions that lead beyond pat answers could include:

- *If your organization were a radio station, what type of music would it play? Soft rock? Light classical? Techno-Pop? Bluegrass?*

- *What books, professional organizations, and magazines do you think are the best resources for anyone who wants to go into this field?*

- *Does your organization have a hero (either a person or another organization)?*

- *What are the top three words that you think your customers would use to describe you, your service style, and your human relationships?*

- *What questions are you repeatedly asked by customers?*

Asking questions that can't be answered with a simple yes or no will help you see beyond the formal mission statement and help you get a feel for the real organization. This will prove valuable when you are then able to reflect the real organization in the Web site.

7.1.3 ANSWERS

a) To what degree would you associate each of the following words with your institution?

Answer: Again, the answers to this will depend on the individual organization. For our friends at ABC Hardware, some possible scores might look like the chart on p. 202.

From the chart, it is clear that your Web site should be upbeat, inviting, and reliable. Services offered need to be useful to the customer and should provide innovative solutions without "stretching the envelope." Your Web site should not portray a stern or imposing presence or use technologies that might be intimidating to the casual net user. You should also try to avoid elements that would suggest frivolity or excess luxury. Note: Another useful exercise with charts of this kind would be to use them in your interviewing process. If a clear consensus is not achieved, perhaps another list of words might yield better results.

**LAB
7.1**

	1 never	2 not really	3 maybe	4 mostly	5 absolutely	Score
Formal		x				2
Warm					x	5
Inventive				x		4
Dependable					x	5
Speedy			x			3
Deliberate			x			3
Industrial		x				2
Exciting			x			3
Wealthy		x				2
Nurturing			x			3
Sober		x				2
Unpredictable	x					1
Sexy		x				2
Thrifty					x	5
Playful			x			3
Stern	x					1
Innovative				x		4
Wise			x			3

LAB 7.1 SELF-REVIEW QUESTIONS

In order to test your progress, you should be able to answer the following questions.

1) Your main competitor's advertising logo has bold colors in yellow and green. Which of the following statements is true?

a) _____ It would be good to use these colors on my Web site to confuse customers to think they are visiting my competitor's site.

b) _____ My advertising material features blues and purples. These colors should predominate in the design of my Web site.

c) _____ The color scheme on a Web site is not relevant. Any colors will work.

2) Your organization's formal mission statement will always provide vital information relevant to managing a Web site.

a) _____ True
b) _____ False

3) Which of the following are good questions to ask the CEO when interviewing to determine organizational values beyond the mission statement?

a) _____ What are your favorite colors?
b) _____ What brand of computer do you use?
c) _____ What are common questions asked by your customers?
d) _____ What browser do you use?

4) Why is it necessary to look at organizational values before embarking on a Web site management project? So the Web site:

a) _____ utilizes every new technology as it is released.
b) _____ is consistent with the values of the organization.
c) _____ uses the CEO's favorite colors even if they conflict with the logo art work.
d) _____ looks identical on every browser version and platform.

Quiz answers appear in the Appendix, Section 7.1.

LAB 7.2

ESTABLISHING A WEB SITE MISSION

LAB OBJECTIVES

After this lab, you will be able to:

✔ Review your Web Site Mission
✔ Evaluate a Web Site for its Primary Goals

Categories of Missions

A well-organized Web site relies on a clear understanding of both the audience and the Web site mission. Site missions may be divided into five categories:

1. Establishing mindshare (market identification)
2. Building community
3. Giving information to the user
4. Obtaining information from the user
5. Promoting a service

If you want users to look specifically for your site instead of searching for a type of site, then you need to establish market identification, or what we call *mindshare*. For example, if a user needs a printer driver for a Hewlett-Packard printer, they may know to go to www.hp.com because of mindshare. To build community, users need a way to talk to one another, identify themselves and others, and have a topic to discuss. Giving static information on the Web is easy. Giving information that is relied upon as valid and authentic requires reputation. Making the information easy to find requires planning and good Web site design. Providing information interactively requires some programming. Obtaining information from users can be straightforward—such as asking them to fill out a form—or obtained from a game or contest in which users participate. And, finally, promoting a service is a way to make money with your Web site. The most common service is selling your products.

Consider a typical corporate Web site. It will probably have three facets:

1. An outward-facing site to give information and sell the products or services.
2. An outward-facing site to sell the company to investors.
3. An inward site (intranet) to manage internal communication and services.

A typical nonprofit site could be similarly structured with:

1. An outward-facing site to provide information or promote services.
2. An outward-facing site to solicit funds from donors.

■ FOR EXAMPLE

Assume you are the Web manager for our ABC Hardware case study Web site. Let's evaluate this site for the common Web site missions, describe how they are implemented, and rank each in importance.

Mission	Implementation	Must Have	Can Wait	Don't Need
Establishing Mindshare	Recognizable logo	X		
	Easy-to-remember URL	X		
Building Community	Moderated public bulletin board for sharing tips and tricks		X	
	Chat room			X
Giving Information	Online catalog	X		
	Easy lookup for mail catalog items	X		
	Project plans		X	
Obtaining Information	Feedback surveys		X	
Promoting a Service	Online purchasing	X		
	Ask the expert		X	

It can be difficult to rank your mission, but it is worth considering. Objectives can change during the life of a Web site. Giving information is often the easiest goal to achieve. Obtaining information is more difficult (generally forms are needed, which require more advanced html) and actually offering an online service (such as product purchasing) requires advanced technology, programming, and secure server functions. Many sites that begin as sites designed to provide a service, later incorporate information-gathering elements as they discover that they need more information about their client base. Other sites, such as non-profit information sites, find that they have become so "expert" in their field of information that they expand into the service sector.

LAB 7.2 EXERCISES

7.2.1 REVIEW YOUR WEB SITE MISSION

a) Use the example from the main lab text and what you know about the FANNC organization (see p. 194) to evaluate its Web site mission.

_____

_____

Mission	How can this mission be implemented on the Web site?	Must Have	Can Wait	Don't Need
Establishing Mindshare				
Building Community				
Giving Information				
Obtaining Information				
Promoting a Service				

7.2.2 EVALUATE A WEB SITE FOR ITS PRIMARY GOALS

a) Match the following Web site features to the mission it could support. Each Web site feature could support more than one mission.

A. Establishing Mindshare
B. Building Community
C. Giving Information
D. Obtaining Information
E. Promoting a Service

_____ Logo
_____ Color coordination of graphic elements
_____ Common look and feel to all pages in the Web site
_____ Static Web pages
_____ Well-designed navigational tools
_____ JavaScript element showing today's date
_____ Search engine
_____ Real audio feed
_____ Cascading style sheets
_____ Animated logo
_____ Online ordering from online catalog
_____ PDF file of brochures
_____ Chatroom
_____ Multimedia elements, such as audio and video
_____ Public feedback form
_____ Customer survey
_____ Flash page for entry into site

LAB 7.2 EXERCISE ANSWERS

7.2.1 ANSWERS

a) Use the example from the main Lab text and what you know about the FANNC organization to evaluate its Web site mission.

Mission	How can this mission be implemented on the Web site?	Must Have	Can Wait	Don't Need
Establishing Mindshare	Professionally designed logo		X	
	Cute acronym ("fancy") in URL	X		
Building Community	Public bulletin board to share ideas		X	
	Chatroom			X
Giving Information	Static Web pages for most information	X		
	Site search engine	X		
	Links to other useful "flea" sites	X		
Obtaining Information	Public feedback form—rate our service		X	
	Solicit donations to keep nonprofit running	X		
Promoting a Service	Database link to find local services		X	

This evaluation of the Web site mission shows us that the initial needs of this site are fairly basic—a domain name with the FANNC acronym, searchable pages of static text, links to similar information elsewhere, and a page to ask for donations. This site would be easy to develop and could be managed by changing staff at a nonprofit agency. No fancy programming is needed. The site also reflects the organization—simple yet reliable and easy to use.

7.2.2 ANSWERS

a) Match the following Web site features to the mission it could support. Each Web site feature could support more than one mission.

   A. *Establishing Mindshare*
   B. *Building Community*
   C. *Giving Information*
   D. *Obtaining Information*
   E. *Promoting a Service*

A	*Logo*
A,C	*Color coordination of graphic elements*
A,C	*Common look and feel to all pages in the Web site*
C	*Static Web pages*
C	*Well-designed navigation tools*

B,C	*JavaScript element showing today's date*
C	*Search engine*
A	*Cascading style sheets*
A	*Animated logo*
E	*Online ordering from online catalog*
C	*PDF file of brochures*
B	*Chatroom*
C	*Multimedia elements, such as audio and video*
B, D	*Public feedback form*
D	*Customer survey*
A	*Flash page for entry into site*

Looking back at the FANNC mission statement evaluation, we see that giving informa-tion is the most important aspect for their site. In this case, static pages based on a clean, easy-to-read template with clear navigational tools and a search engine would serve FANNC well. Portable Document Format (PDF) versions of some of their brochures (especially those that are image intensive) or short audio or video multimedia elements demonstrating specific techniques would be good site enhancements.

LAB 7.2 SELF-REVIEW QUESTIONS

In order to test your progress, you should be able to answer the following questions.

1) Online descriptions of your products is an example of which type of Web site mission?

   a) _____ Establishing Mindshare
   b) _____ Building Community
   c) _____ Giving Information
   d) _____ Obtaining Information
   e) _____ Promoting a Service

2) An instant poll on the main page asking which product they like most is an exam-ple of which type of Web site mission?

   a) _____ Establishing Mindshare
   b) _____ Building Community
   c) _____ Giving Information
   d) _____ Obtaining Information
   e) _____ Promoting a Service

3) A discussion forum with answers provided by your technical support staff is an example of which type of Web site mission?

a) _____ Establishing Mindshare
b) _____ Building Community
c) _____ Giving Information
d) _____ Obtaining Information
e) _____ Promoting a Service

4) The mission of your Web site will remain the same throughout the life of the site.

a) _____ True
b) _____ False

Quiz answers appear in the Appendix, Section 7.2.

**LAB
7.2**

LAB 7.3

EVALUATING YOUR AUDIENCE

LAB OBJECTIVES

After this lab, you will be able to:

✔ Describe Your Audience
✔ Match Browser Features to Your Intended Audience
✔ Evaluate Features to Enhance Your Web Site

Simply speaking, your audience is whom you intend to use the site. The audience is defined not only by their intended use of the site, but also by their portal, the specific technology they will use to access the site, and their expected level of skill in Web navigation. For example, there are significant differences between the typical Web user at a large university and a home user on an AOL-type browser. It is important to know the expectations and abilities of the target audience.

In terms of managing a site, what does it matter if you know your audience? If you do, you can, for example:

- Effectively use your Web logs to show if you are reaching your target audience.
- Make informed decisions on the choice of tools to deliver content and provide navigation.
- Focus your site design to the width and breadth of your intended audience.

If your site is intended for use by anyone on the Web, your audience is very broad and your choice of tools will be limited to common browser technologies. A text-only version of the site might be necessary to make the site accessible to all users. If your site is intended for a narrow audience with advanced technologies, you may be able to use all the bells and whistles without restricting audience access.

DEFINING YOUR AUDIENCE

Demographics, as well as intangible aspects such as lifestyle, attitude, motivations, and purchasing habits define your audience. If you're lucky, your target audience will be determined for you by your marketing group (corporate) or expert group (educational). As a Web manager, you will probably not be responsible for determining exactly who your audience is, but being aware of your site audience may simplify some of your management decisions. Let's look at one of our case studies.

■ FOR EXAMPLE

Your marketing group says that you want to target customers who would normally shop at one of the large warehouse-type home improvement centers. The average customer is male, 28–45 years old, middle-income, middle education level, and does most of his shopping on Sundays. The goal is to figure out how to expand your market by attracting this buyer to your Web site at a time other than (and, with luck, in addition to) his typical Sunday shopping.

Let's consider why this person might shop at ABC Hardware. A major reason may be convenience. That is, the store has adequate parking, lots of checkout stands, long hours, and an adequate selection of reasonably priced products. Let's look at these factors and how they are expressed as Web site features:

Store Factor	Web Translation
Hassle-Free	No flashing ads or popping windows
No Crowds	Adequate server speed and bandwidth
	Optimized thumbnail graphics for quick download
	Optional full-size graphics, just a click away
Easy to Use	Larger typeface for middle-aged eyes
	Clear and consistent navigation
Enhancements	Search tool
	Online project plans with images of actual completed projects
	How-to tips
	Ask the expert
	Smart catalog
	Online ordering

LAB 7.3 EXERCISES

7.3.1 DESCRIBE YOUR AUDIENCE

a) Using a marketing analysis completed for your organization or your own best judgment, describe your Web site audience (circle your answers or fill in the description).

_____

_____

Gender	Male Female N/A
Age	Under 18 18–29 30–49 50–64 65+ All
Income	$50K+ $30–49K Under $30K All
Education	College Grad Some College HS Grad Less Than HS N/A
Net Use	Work Pleasure Education Mix
Net Savvy	Beginner Intermediate Advanced
Geographics	Will your Web site information/services be valid for a limited area, statewide, nationwide, or worldwide? Describe limitations.
Other	Consider audience lifestyle, attitude, and motivation. Could any of these factors affect your audience? Describe.

7.3.2 MATCH BROWSER FEATURES TO YOUR INTENDED AUDIENCE

For this exercise, your audience has been determined to be the home user working on a 28.8 K Baud modem with an AOL-type browser interface.

a) Which of the following do you think are appropriate features (based on current technology) for your Web site?

_____

_____

Feature	Yes	No
Dynamic HTML absolute positioning		
Cascading style sheets		
Full screen image map		
JavaScript form validation		
JavaScript mouseovers		
Java applets		
Text-only version		
Frames only		

LAB 7.3

7.3.3 EVALUATE FEATURES TO ENHANCE YOUR WEB SITE

Marketing has just told you that your tech-support site needs to be brought up to speed. Take a look the technical support page below.

a) What are your suggestions to enhance this Web page and the overall technical support features?

_____

_____

LAB 7.3 EXERCISE ANSWERS

7.3.1 ANSWERS

a) Using a marketing analysis completed for your organization or your own best judgment, describe your Web site audience (circle your answers or fill in the description).

Answer: The answer depends on your site. Let's examine the three case-study sites. You may want to flag this page, as we will be referring back to this data throughout the next five chapters.

When working on a Web site, understanding your target audience can simplify some management issues. For instance, using high-tech, bleeding-edge features on the FANNC site would be overkill and probably detrimental to reaching the target audience. On the other hand, those who demand high-tech, such as the SkaBoard customers, won't tolerate simple "boring" sites.

ABC Hardware

Gender	Primarily male. Features could be added to encourage female users.
Age	Primarily 30–49.
Income	At average or greater for the location. Income is very location-dependent (i.e., average household income greater in San Francisco bay area than Midwest).
Education	HS graduate, but not really applicable to this site.
Net Use	Pleasure (home).
Net Savvy	Beginning to advanced.
Geographics	Online catalog purchasing available nationwide, but with limited offerings. Full-service stores located only in the western United States.
Other	We want this site to appeal to those who are short on time and want their fingers to do the walking to find the home renovation/repair items they need.

Flea Abatement Network of Northern California (FANNC)

Gender	Primarily female.
Age	Over 18.
Income	Average income for the location.
Education	N/A
Net Use	Pleasure (home).
Net Savvy	Beginning to advanced.
Geographics	Tips and tricks could apply to anywhere. Specific services only available in northern California.
Other	Those who live in an urban area, animal owners, and people sensitive to environmental issues most likely will use this site.

SkaBoards

Gender	Primarily male.
Age	Under 30.
Income	Above average for the location.
Education	HS graduate.
Net Use	Education (available in school) and pleasure (home).
Net Savvy	Advanced.
Geographics	Shop located in Boulder, Colorado. Orders can be shipped nationwide.
Other	High-tech, high-speed, adventurous.

LAB 7.3

7.3.2 ANSWERS

For this exercise, your audience has been determined to be a home user working on a 28.8 K Baud modem with an AOL-type browser interface.

    a) Which of the following do you think are appropriate features (based on current technology) for your Web site?

Answer:The answers depend on the current state of technology, especially browser compatibility and average connection speed.The following are recommendations based on the time of writing.

Feature	Yes	No
Dynamic HTML absolute positioning		X

This feature is only available in modern browsers, version 4.0 or greater, and implementation differs in each of the top browsers. For these reasons, this feature is not recommended for those using AOL-type browsers.

Feature	Yes	No
Cascading style sheets	X	

This feature is only available in modern browsers, version 4.0 or greater, and implementation is different for the top browsers. However, they provide an easy way to maintain a consistent look and feel. Make sure, though, that the pages are at least readable in non-CSS compliant browsers.

Feature	Yes	No
Full screen image map		X

Download time would eliminate this feature from effective use on a 28.8K Baud modem.

Feature	Yes	No
JavaScript form validation		X

If you need validated forms, this is the easiest way to do it. However, users have the option of turning off JavaScript so you'll need a non-JavaScript version of the form or restrict use of the form for those with JavaScript enabled.

Feature	Yes	No
JavaScript mouseovers	X	

Mouseovers, if written well, work fine with or without JavaScript. However, keep the graphics small and maximized for quick loading. Also, provide text-only navigation for those who turn off graphics.

Feature	Yes	No
Java applets		X

Rendering across browsers and platforms is inconsistent and download speed can be a nightmare.

Feature	Yes	No
Text only version		X

If you want to hit every possible user, this is the only way to guarantee it. However, if you check your site on a text-only browser and it renders okay, don't bother keeping up the text-only version. It can be a maintenance nightmare.

Feature	Yes	No
Frames only		X

There are enough people who do not like frames and browsers that don't render frames that a frames-only site is never recommended.

Marketing has just told you that your tech-support site needs to be brought up to speed. Take a look the technical support page below.

LAB 7.3

a) What are your suggestions to enhance this Web page and the overall technical support features?

Answer: To answer this question, you may need to know something about snowboarding or at least look at other snowboarding sites to see what they offer that could add value to their site.

The Board Genie certainly adds value. The audience of this site would favor more features like this. Other interactive features could include systems that would:

- *Match binding patterns for your board/boot combination*

- *Match your boarding style with board design*

- *Match boarding conditions with wax type*

However, a helmet article from 1997 really dates the page. Updating the article or removing the date from the link would solve that problem. Daily updated snow conditions at boarding areas in Colorado would also be very useful. Because bandwidth is not really an issue for this level of net user, instructional video snippets could be offered on a variety of topics such as waxing techniques or building your own board. In some ways, updating a site like this is easy—you don't need to worry about the technology or skill level of the user. These folks are technologically advanced and not afraid to use the Web to its full advantage.

LAB 7.3 SELF-REVIEW QUESTIONS

In order to test your progress, you should be able to answer the following questions.

1) Your Web site audience is highly net savvy. You should:

a) _____ Be careful about using image maps.

b) _____ Not use JavaScript form validation or mouseover events.

c) _____ Feel free to use the latest Dynamic HTML features that render fairly well between browsers.

d) _____ Stick to static, plain text Web pages.

2) Your retail outlets are famous for their high level of customer service. Which of the following would not help to continue this trend?

a) _____ How-to tips and a FAQ

b) _____ Expert-led discussion forum

c) _____ Large images on each page

d) _____ Customer service email address, telephone, and fax number on every page

3) Features you add to your Web site are independent of the target audience and should be solely decided by the Webmaster.

a) _____ True

b) _____ False

Quiz answers appear in the Appendix, Section 7.3.

LAB
7.3

CHAPTER 7

TEST YOUR THINKING

In this chapter we learned the value of learning about the organization, the mission of the Web site, and the intended audience before taking on a Web site management project. Using a Web site you manage (or will manage) or one of the case study Web sites, complete the following assignments.

1) Describe the process you would take to understand your organization as it relates to its Web site. What information would you need and what tasks would you complete to accomplish this goal?

2) Develop a Web site mission for the site you evaluated in 1. List the Web features you think would be appropriate for the site.

3) Define the audience for this Web site and describe how this could impact the features you provide on the site.

CHAPTER 8

SITE MAINTENANCE

The Web currently changes so rapidly that a major redesign is needed at least once per year simply to avoid a completely outdated look and to accommodate changing user expectations. Additional maintenance is needed throughout the year to bring fresh content online, reorganize and revise old pages, and avoid linkrot.

—Jakob Nielsen, "Top Ten Mistakes of Web Management"

CHAPTER OBJECTIVES

In this chapter, you will learn about:

In this chapter, we'll learn about the importance of site maintenance, examine how tools can help with this process, and find out about the ins and outs of keeping site backups. Web sites are dynamic. Many sites change by the minute while others remain fairly static. However, even if your Web site is a set of static pages, if there are links to other Web sites, then broken links will happen. It's just a matter of time. And, few things can cause a site to lose credibility and perceived value more quickly than broken links.

L A B   8 . 1

SITE INTEGRITY AND LINKROT

LAB OBJECTIVES

After this lab, you will be able to:

✔ Evaluate the Potential Effect of Linkrot on Your Site
✔ Describe Ways to Reduce Linkrot
✔ Create a Custom "File Not Found" Message

Site integrity is reflected in comprehensive, correct, and up-to-date content and a site that is integrated into the Web as a whole. Links outside your Web site demonstrate confidence in your site. That is, you are not afraid that visitors will leave your site, never to return. Visitors may think you have something to hide if your site is isolated from the rest of the Web. Linkrot is the tendency of hypertext links from one page to another to become invalid as pages cease to exist or are moved during reorganization.

HOW BAD IS LINKROT?

Linkrot is a direct attack on the true strength of the Web and the reason behind its creation, that is, interconnectivity. Table 8.1 shows results from a 1999 "State of the Web Survey" (www.pantos.org/atw/35654.html), which showed that almost one of every four pages contained a bad link.

The amount of linkrot seems to correlate closely (and not surprisingly) with the passage of time. Links to the home pages of large Web sites, such as Microsoft, CNET, or CNN, appear to be the least likely to "rot." However, links to pages within companies often generate the dreaded "404 message":

```
404 Not Found
The requested URL /xxxxx.html was not found on this
server.
```

Table 8.1 ■ **State of the Web Survey**

	SOWS I (August 1997)	SOWS II (May 1998)	SOWS III (May 1999)
Pages Sampled	44 pages	213 pages	200 pages
Average Page Size	44 KB	61 KB	60 KB
Linkrot evidence	3%	5.9%	5.7%
Linkrot prevalence	18%	23%	28.5%

This message is often a result of site restructures or "old" material being removed. Links are broken as sites are updated and information is removed.

GOOD PRACTICES TO REDUCE LINKROT

While linkrot cannot be entirely prevented, using some or all of the following practices can minimize it.

- Check your links frequently. The frequency depends on the intricacy and size of your Web site.
- Don't move your own Web resources unless you really have to.
- If you have to move pages or sites, leave a redirect message to forward browsers to the new location.
- Plan, plan, and plan before putting materials on the Web in public areas.
- Plan subdirectories and expandable file structures to avoid the need to move online resources later.
- For resources that change regularly, consider using an alias or symbolic links to point a consistent URL to the desired resource.
- If you encounter a broken link, tell the owner of the referring page so it can be fixed.
- Separate development and production Web space and restrict indexing of development space.

Another way to reduce linkrot is to keep old content. In other words, once a page has been exposed to the Web, let it live forever. Old content still has value to site visitors. You may need to eliminate obsolete information, add a "not maintained" disclaimer, and/or add a link to recent or current information from these old pages. These methods will be well worth the efforts so a server "404" message does not turn users away. Adding a "created on" date to the pages will also put the content in time context. If the only date on the page is the date it is updated and the updating process is automated, the content may appear newer than it actually is. This can be very misleading.

CONSTRUCTIVE ERROR MESSAGES

If you want to know more, there are Web sites dedicated to abolishment of the cryptic 404 error messages (one such, the 404 Research Lab, is located at www.plinko.net/404). A somewhat tongue-in-cheek survey from this Web site offered the following question:

The Question: When you encounter a 404 do you:

     A.   Hit the back button and forget about it.
     B.   Try to get to the homepage to locate the missing page.
     C.   Write to the Webmaster.
     D.   Weep uncontrollably.

Results: There were 1937 responses as of July 1999:

     A.   49.56%
     B.   26.85%
     C.   4.65%
     D.   18.95%

So it seems that about half of visitors will just back up if they reach a 404 error. This could cause a lot of lost business for your Web site. This makes the time it takes to create redirects to minimize linkrot a valuable investment. Another way to help visitors is to create a customized 404 message that will assist visitors in finding what they wanted. Almost all Web servers allow some type of customized error messages.

LAB 8.1 EXERCISES

8.1.1 EVALUATE THE POTENTIAL EFFECT OF LINKROT ON YOUR SITE

As the manager of a Web site, you need to know how linkrot could affect your site. Consider how the following features affect the potential for your site to experience linkrot.

a) Site size (small, medium, large)

_____

_____

b) Links out of the Web site (none/few/many)

_____

_____

c) Links within the Web site (none/few/many)

_____

_____

d) Links into the Web site (none/few/many)

_____

_____

e) Script-generated vs. static pages

_____

_____

f) Content update frequency (daily/monthly/infrequently)

_____

_____

g) Content developers (one/few/many)

_____

_____

h) Consider the three case study Web sites (ABC Hardware, Ska-Boards, FANNC). Which site has the greatest potential to experience the side effects of linkrot? Explain.

_____

_____

i) Consider your Web site. How susceptible is your site to linkrot?

_____

_____

8.1.2 DESCRIBE WAYS TO REDUCE LINKROT

In this chapter we discussed several ways to reduce linkrot. For each of the methods described below, provide a sentence on how each could be implemented at your site.

a) Check your links frequently.

_____

_____

b) Don't move your own Web resources unless you really have to.

_____

_____

c) If pages or sites are moved, leave a redirect message to forward browsers to the new location.

_____

_____

d) Plan, plan, and plan before putting materials on the Web. Create subdirectories and expandable file structures to avoid the need to move online resources later.

_____

_____

e) For resources that change regularly, consider using aliases or symbolic links to point a consistent URL to the desired resource.

_____

_____

f) Let the owner of the referring page know that the link is broken.

_____

_____

g) Separate development and production Web space and restrict indexing in development space.

_____

_____

8.1.3 CREATE A CUSTOM "FILE NOT FOUND" MESSAGE

Almost all Web servers can be configured to provide a useful "not found" message in lieu of the cryptic default message. You may need to check with your server administrator to implement the customized message, but our task here is to create a useful message for our visitors. The following are some features we've found on "not found" messages.

I. Reasons why the error message was received.
The URL you requested could not be found on this server. The reason for this could be:

You typed in the wrong Web address. Please check the address and retype it, if necessary.

The site is under construction and should be up and running soon.

The page you are looking for has been removed or is now located elsewhere. Please check the address with the source you obtained it from and try again.

2. Things you can do to find what you need or to fix the link.

Mailto link to the Webmaster

A dead link report form with results sent to the Webmaster

Link(s) back to the home page, site search tool, or a general search tool

Search form for the Web site or a general search engine

Directions on how to get back to a valid page (click the browser back button)

3. A funny saying, quote, or graphic:

If you think you got this page in error, please let me know. The site is huge and we're not perfect (mailto link to Webmaster). Web haiku:

The Web site you see

cannot be located but

endless others exist.

a) Consider these features and others you may have seen and write a message you could use at your site.

_____

_____

LAB 8.1 EXERCISE ANSWERS

8.1.1 ANSWERS

Note: The answers to these questions depend upon your site. We will evaluate the three case study sites, ABC Hardware, SkaBoards, and FANNC.

a) Site size (small, medium, large)

Answer: Based entirely on size, SkaBoards would be most susceptible to linkrot. This is a large site with constantly updated information. However, the user of this site is the most Web savvy and may know some tricks to find the desired page.

b) Links out of the Web site (none/few/many)

Answer: Again, SkaBoards has numerous external links to other fast-moving sites. The more links out of the Web site, the greater the potential for broken links. If there are no external links, one would question if the Web is the right location for the material.

c) Links within the Web site (none/few/many)

Answer: Of course, the more links in a site the more potential for linkrot. The ABC Hardware Inc. site has the most internal links and is a relatively large, complex site.

d) Links into the Web site (none/few/many)

Answer: These links cannot be controlled, but the FANNC site is linked to from all its resources and the links may be to individual pages. Linking below the top level of a site is very useful for the user (who doesn't need to search for the page in question) but can be a serious source of linkrot.

e) Script-generated vs. static pages

Answer: Either type of page is a source of linkrot, especially if badly managed. Static pages may not be viewed and actively updated frequently but script-generated pages can propagate many bad links if there is a problem with a script. In addition, any automated system must be checked periodically. It's easy to let the automation take over and forget that things change. Of the three sites, SkaBoards and ABC Hardware use the most script-generated pages, while the FANNC Web is almost all static Web pages.

f) Content update frequency (daily/monthly/infrequently)

Answer: Content that is not updated very often but is highly linked internally and externally is the most susceptible to linkrot. This describes the FANNC site.

g) Content developers (one/few/many)

Answer: Content developers may make changes to their Web resources that unknowingly affect other resources in the same Web site. For this reason, there is always a balance between expeditious content development and centralized control and approval. Of the three case studies, the FANNC site is probably the most susceptible because the site is developed and maintained by a stream of volunteers, who may not know the overall Web site design. The SkaBoards site would also be susceptible because there are a number of "bleeding-edge" developers who may not always think through changes be-fore making them.

h) Consider the three case study Web sites (ABC Hardware, SkaBoards, FANNC). Which site had the greatest potential to experience side effects of linkrot? Explain.

Answer: We would consider the FANNC site most susceptible to linkrot. It is a small site, made of highly interconnected static pages maintained and updated as time permits. The site is maintained by a series of well-meaning but inexperienced Web developers who are not aware of the all the interconnections. In addition, the intended audience of this site is not very Web savvy and would not necessarily know how to find the information they want when faced with a "file not found" message.

i) Consider your Web site. How susceptible is your site to linkrot?

Answer: The answer depends on your Web site, but we have tried to provide enough analysis (above) to allow you to determine how linkrot may affect your Web site.

8.1.2 ANSWERS

Note: The answers to these questions depend upon your site. We will evaluate the three case study sites, ABC Hardware, SkaBoards, and FANNC.

a) Check your links frequently.

Answer: All Web sites need to have their internal links checked frequently. Even the most experienced Web authors make mistakes that can have impact on links. It is especially important to check the links after making updates to the Web site or deploying new parts to the site.

Adequate freeware tools are available that will do the checking for you (see the next section). Because of their size, complexity, and online sales, the ABC Hardware and Ska-Boards sites should be validated using an external tool at least weekly. If the number of bad links is large each time, increase the frequency until the number of broken links reaches a manageable level. The FANNC site could be checked every other week and immediately following significant updates.

b) Don't move your own Web resources unless you really have to.

Answer: This practice is difficult to implement for all sites because very few sites are de-signed in their entirety at conception. However, Web pages may be moved simply for convenience, and unless a redirect is left, this practice should be avoided. Multiple devel-opers or frequent developer turnover can also cause problems, with each developer structuring the site his or her own way. Again, as the manager of the Web site, you need to be aware of these potential problems.

Of the case study sites, we'd evaluate the SkaBoards site most susceptible to frequently moving Web resources as they tend toward bleeding-edge technology and multiple developers.

c) If pages or sites are moved, leave a redirect message to forward browsers to the new location.

Answer: Again, there is little reason not to provide this convenience. If you have access to the server administrator, redirects may be programmed at the server level.

For example, if your main page must be changed from index.html to index.shtml because server side includes are now used, the server administrator can redirect all index.html requests to index.shtml. On most Unix systems, symbolic links can be used to send the requestor to a new page on the Unix system. And, if all else fails, the Web author can create a page of HTML using a meta tag that redirects the visitor. The redirect can be timed so the visitor can read the redirect and be given the opportunity to notify the referring page owner or update his or her bookmark list, or the redirect can be essentially immediate. Unfortunately, all older browsers do not recognize this tag but a link to the new page within the redirect page solves this problem.

d) Plan, plan, and plan before putting materials on the Web. Create subdirectories and expandable file structures to avoid the need to move online resources later.

Answer: You may be taking over management of an existing site so preplanning will not be an option. And as we noted above, very few sites are designed in their entirety at conception. Sites that have been around since the early days are probably very convoluted because it was impossible to predict the Web explosion that occurred in the past few years.

With the FANNC site, the structure is fairly simple, but the original planner did not know the value of providing subdirectory structure to organize the site.

e) For resources that change regularly, consider using aliases or symbolic links to point a consistent URL to the desired resource.

Answer: This option is probably underused and a significant source of linkrot.

Consider a ABC Hardware Tips of the Week online newsletter, linked to from the home page. A first thought may be to rename the current newsletter each week and then replace the file named "current.html" with the new data. However, consider another method. Each week a file is created and named according to the calendar (such as 991210.html). When this newsletter is the feature, a symbolic link is created so those who request the link on the home page (current.html) will be redirected to

991210.html. Using this method, the URL for the newsletter doesn't change each week, just the symbolic link changes. This way the file, now exposed to the public, keeps a consistent URL.

f) Let someone where you got the URL from know that the link is broken.

Answer: Okay, it's not always easy to figure out who is responsible for the referring page, but when you can, report the problem link. It can be a tedious, but if we all do it linkrot will be easier to manage. Adding a mailto link to the Webmaster on your server "file not found" message can facilitate this process.

g) Separate development and production Web space and restrict indexing in development space.

Answer: Development space is, by definition, a moving target. If we don't have a place to do the development, we can't polish the site.

Adding a robots.txt (details about this file to eliminate indexing by most robots is at available at info.Webcrawler.com/mak/projects/robots/norobots.html) file to these areas to keep out indexing robots as well as maintaining separate test/development servers can keep bad links from propagating as a result of the development process.

8.1.3 ANSWERS

a) Consider these features and others you have seen and write a "File Not Found" message you could use at your site.

Answer: Following are some examples for such messages.

We're sorry, but the page you requested cannot be found on this server. You can:

- *Reload the page to make sure it wasn't a server problem or network fluke.*

- *Look for obvious typos in the URL, fix, and try again.*

- *Back up one level and try again.*

    For example, if you are at www.fannc.org/resources/net/contractors.html, erase everything after the last slash (leaving www.fannc.org/resources/net/) and try again. You can keep backing up until you are at the top of the domain.

- *Use this search box to search our site [single line form field].*

- *Go to our home page [link to main home page].*

- *Submit a report to our Webmaster:*

    [A small form that, if submitted, captures the referring page URL and sends it to the Webmaster.]

LAB 8.1 SELF-REVIEW QUESTIONS

In order to test your progress, you should be able to answer the following questions.

1) Of the following, which combination of factors provides the greatest potential for linkrot?

   a) _____ A small number of static pages with very few internal or external links.
   b) _____ A large number of static pages with many external links.
   c) _____ A large number of internally linked dynamically-generated pages.
   d) _____ Dynamically generated pages with frequent Webmaster turnover.

2) What are the potential effects of linkrot?

   a) _____ Lost visitor who gets the "file not found" message.
   b) _____ Improved credibility.
   c) _____ Strong customer loyalty.
   d) _____ No effect on my site.

3) Which of the following are methods to reduce linkrot?

   a) _____ Use the default "file not found" server message.
   b) _____ Frequently move top level files to accommodate growth.
   c) _____ Use a redirect (server or html) when a page has to be moved.
   d) _____ Encourage each new Webmaster to reorganize the Web site.

4) Which feature is most useful on a customized "file not found" sever message?

   a) _____ Funny animated graphic.
   b) _____ Nonlinked URL to your home page.
   c) _____ Names of common search engines.
   d) _____ Instructions for the visitor.

Quiz answers appear in the Appendix, Section 8.1.

LAB 8.2

SITE MANAGEMENT TOOLS

LAB OBJECTIVES

After this lab, you will be able to:

✔ Examine the Range of Site Management Tools
✔ Evaluate Features of Site Management Tools

Site integrity can be improved by effective use of site management tools. The trick is finding a tool that is cost effective for your site and has the features you need.

SITE MANAGEMENT TOOLS

New site management tools continue to become available every day, with increasing complexity and feature sets. Tools generally fall into three categories:

- Tools built into a development environment
- External tools for analysis, reporting, and correcting and performing specific functions
- Online services

DEVELOPMENT ENVIRONMENT TOOLS

Many tools used to create and deploy Web sites have built-in and extensive management tools. Many of these tools work during the development process or can be activated at various stages in the project. These tools can fail, however, once a Web site is moved to its final location. Sometimes links are broken and needed resources are no longer available in the new location. Periodically checking this Web site with an external tool is a good practice.

Development tools (such as FrontPage, CyberStudio, Dreamweaver, NetObjects, and ColdFusion) all include a set of analysis tools. These tools improve with each version and the current versions include features such as:

- Spell checking
- Find and replace
- Validating links, coding, and assisting in fixing problems
- Tag property inspection (to meet a specific version of HTML)
- Meta tag review
- Wizards to automate common tasks
- Site diagramming
- Script debugging
- Server-side source control for versioning
- Shared project management to keep track of all the files in a project
- One-step deployment to a remote server via FTP or HTTP
- Secure remote team development
- Content approval system
- Reports that list all files, images, unlinked files, linked files, slow pages, oldest files, newest files, hyperlinks (unverified, broken, external, internal)

EXTERNAL MANAGEMENT TOOLS

The variety of external management tools is extensive, with costs ranging from free to tens of thousands of dollars. These tools act outside of the development environment and test the Web site in its final public location. External management tools can be very function specific, such as to do a mass search and replace or meta tag management. The tools can also be fully featured and include Web site and log file analysis.

Most of the midrange commercial programs, with price tags less than $500, offer a wide variety of features. Finding a program that works on your platform and provides the tools you need may take a few attempts. Fortunately, most of these programs offer free limited-time downloads so you can test them before spending any money. A few examples of these programs include Astra Site Manager, Coast WebMaster, BluePrint, InContext WebAnalyzer, HTML Power Tools, and LinkBot Pro. These tools provide a variety of reports, canned or customizable, such as a site summary, download time based on modem speed, and a link summary showing files with broken links. Analysis can usually be customized to a specified scan depth (subdirectory level) and breadth (multiple servers), and offer exclusions based on URL, subdirectory, or file extension. These tools may also provide Web site deployment/publishing tools, site mapping, link repair, site-wide search and replace, scheduled site monitoring, site printing, and an image optimization tool. Some of these programs also have "pro" versions that include log file analysis tools.

There are many sitewide management tools that are integrated into the site development/server process and are a giant step above the midrange tools described above; they will provide much more than link checking and site validation. These tools, such as MKS Web Integrity and Net.Analysis, are sitewide tools used for large site maintenance and analysis. Some of these products also provide a method funnel for content approval before publication, archiving of content over time, versioning and history, and address security issues. These products can be very expensive, but if you have a large Web site or one that contributes significantly to the bottom line, these products may be cost effective.

ONLINE SERVICES

The number of online monitoring services increases every day. Some services are free (Dr. Watson, Dr. HTML, NetMechanic, Bobby) but have limits on the number of pages that can be validated. These services and others also offer a fairly inexpensive subscription to automatically check an entire Web site on a routine basis (Web Mechanic, Site Inspector). This does make the link checking process more likely to be completed. Some checkers also perform specific functions such as meta tag analysis and image optimization. The following is a partial list of features offered by these online services.

- Cascading style sheets analysis
- HTML syntax validation
- Accessibility
- Verify hyperlinks and image links
- Obtain word count
- Spell check
- Estimate download time
- Check for search engine compatibility
- Image analysis and optimization
- Online or emailed reports

LAB 8.2 EXERCISES

8.2.1 EXAMINE THE RANGE OF SITE MANAGEMENT TOOLS

As the manager of a Web site, you need to ensure that adequate tools are available to maintain the site.

a) How important is it to check the links on your Web site regularly?

_____

_____

b) Which type of management tool(s) would be best for your Web site (development environment, external midrange commercial, external online service)? Explain.

_____

_____

c) If you use a development tool, do you think there is value in using an external link-checking tool as well? Explain.

_____

_____

8.2.2 EVALUATE FEATURES OF SITE MANAGEMENT TOOLS

New site management tools become available daily and provide a wide range of features.

a) Review the feature lists above and list the top six features you need to adequately manage your site.

_____

_____

b) Review the feature lists above and list two features you do not need to manage your Web site.

LAB 8.2 EXERCISE ANSWERS

8.2.1 ANSWERS

Note: The answers to these questions depend upon your site. We will evaluate the three case study sites, ABC Hardware, SkaBoards, and FANNC.

a) How important is it to link check your Web site regularly?

Answer: There are few things that turn off site visitors more than bad links. With free tools available to identify bad links and inexpensive tools to assist in repairing bad links, there is no reason not to check links regularly.

b) Which type of management tool(s) would be best for your Web site (development environment, external midrange commercial, external online service)? Explain.

Answer: The FANNC site could use one of the free or inexpensive online services. Making the checks automatic will help correct problems caused by developer turnover.

ABC Hardware and SkaBoards sites are more than likely to use a development environment with built-in management tools. Periodic (weekly) external checks on the site would also be recommended.

c) If you use a development tool, do you think there is value in using an external link-checking tool as well? Explain.

Answer: One problem with development tools is that sometimes in the deployment or publishing process links are broken.

For instance, if the Web developer references a file or an image on their computer, the built-in management tool will show the link as valid. However, when the Web site is moved to the Web server, others who look at the pages won't be able to see the files that were not moved to the Web server with the Web pages. An external validator will catch these problems. Using an external validator immediately following "publishing" a site is a good practice.

8.2.2 ANSWERS

Note: The answers to these questions depend upon your site. We will evaluate the three case study sites, ABC Hardware, SkaBoards, and FANNC.

a) Review the features lists above and list the top six features you need to adequately manage your site.

Answer: These would be as follows:

Link checking with facilitated repair is vital.

Sitewide spell checking with facilitated repair and custom dictionary is essential.

Mass search and replace in the text and the html code is very useful to accommodate changes.

HTML syntax validation and accessibility is vital for making pages useful to the widest audience.

Scheduled monitoring is useful to ensure that the checking actually gets done. Making sure someone looks at and corrects problems is a managerial task.

Image optimization should be done before putting up the Web pages, but as with spell checking, it may not happen throughout the site.

b) Review the features lists above and list two features you do not need to manage your Web site.

Answer: These would be as follows:

Visual site mapping is interesting and fun, but for large sites it has proved to be of limited value.

Word counts are interesting statistics, but not vital for Web site management.

LAB 8.2 SELF-REVIEW QUESTIONS

In order to test your progress, you should be able to answer the following questions.

I) What is the most cost-effective site management tool for a small Web site (less than 20 pages and 20 external links) such as FANNC?

   a) _____ Sitewide development environment
   b) _____ Subscription online site validation
   c) _____ "Pro" level commercial program
   d) _____ Free online service with one-page limit

2) What is the most cost-effective site management tool for a high-tech bleeding-edge Web site such as SkaBoards?

a) _____ Sitewide development environment
b) _____ Subscription online site validation
c) _____ "Pro" level commercial program
d) _____ Free online service with one-page limit

3) Which set of tool features is essential for managing any Web site?

a) _____ Visual site mapping and online reports
b) _____ Word counts and estimated download time
c) _____ Facilitated link validation and spell checking
d) _____ Exclusion by URL and site printing

Quiz answers appear in the Appendix, Section 8.2.

LAB 8.3

BACKING UP

LAB OBJECTIVES

After this lab, you will be able to:

✔ Identify Backup Needs for Your Site
✔ Set up an Effective Backup Cycle

Your site is only as secure as its last restore (backups are only secure if you can restore from them). There is no getting around backing up, whether you are working with a site small enough to back up with a simple drag and drop to a floppy disk or a site that will require a fully automated secondary server or tape solution. When considering backup protection, you must not only consider the front end of your Web site (the pages that viewers will see), you must also take into consideration any back end services provided through those pages, such as databases and mail servers, which may not be residing on the same server as the Web pages and, therefore, may not be backed up in the same way or on the same schedule as the site is. While those backups may not fall within your area of responsibility (being part of a larger institutional backup program or a service provided by an ISP), you should be aware of that schedule and be familiar with their capabilities to make sure that the larger system can accommodate your needs and the needs of your client.

You must also consider how the backup is to be performed. While it may be theoretically possible to simply copy your site over to a removable disk, consider whether you or your operator will have the time to actually do that. Do you need an automated system? If so, when are you prepared to have a slowdown in services on the site to accommodate that backup?

Concern with backups is not limited to in-house Webmasters. Webmasters-for-hire must also watch their backs. Nothing can sour a new relationship in a contract design service than a backup failure. Picture this: You have completed a site for the Hazy River Chamber of Commerce, received full approvals, and moved the site from your development space onto their server. The check is in the mail and you have moved on to your next project. You receive a call late in the afternoon from a panicky representative from Hazy River, saying that there has been a power failure and the drive upon which your site was placed has failed to come back up. If you have backed up your final product and kept that backup, your response is soothing and serene, "No problem, I have a backup. Where would you like me to reinstall the site?" If not, you are faced with the ugly choice: "Do I rebuild at their expense or at mine and how much will either choice cost me in the long run?" Memory is cheap. Storage is cheap. Backups are a good investment.

The three key aspects to a solid backup program are:

1. Scheduling
2. Rotation
3. Distance

SCHEDULE

Establish a regular schedule for backing up your site. Whether this means you do this by setting up an automated backup schedule in a backup program such as Retrospect, or you download your site "by hand" to some form of removable data storage device every Wednesday night, you should set and maintain regularly scheduled backups. A regular schedule reduces the likelihood of backup failure. Most serious failures in backups are due to the failure to back up, rather than failures in hardware or software. Another benefit of regularly scheduled backups is that in the event of a catastrophic data loss, you can tell your clients the exact date and time to which they are backed up, saving both you and your clients the effort of tracking down that point to decide exactly what has been lost.

While regularly scheduled backups form the core of your protection, one should not hesitate to perform or call for a backup in the event that something "appears strange" with the site. If the hosting machine begins to behave badly, is about to undergo a major change (such as a system upgrade), or there has been a serious event (such as a power outage), and you are concerned about recent data, then a backup may be a wise idea, even if it isn't on the schedule.

ROTATION

Backups should be performed on rotating media. You should have a minimum of two, preferably three backup versions available at any time to safeguard against the event of a media failure. It does you no good to back up your site if you cannot restore the site because your backup disk has failed. A simple but effective system for backing up the pages of a moderate-sized Web site with relatively frequent updates involves the use of three 100Mb removable disks on a weekly schedule. Label the disks Web site X Backup 1, Web site X Backup 2, and Web site X Backup 3. Back up your site using the following schedule:

1st Wednesday night, back up site on to Web site X Backup 1

2nd Wednesday night, back up the site on to Web site X Backup 2

3rd Wednesday night, back up the site on to Web site X Backup 3

4th Wednesday night, back up the site on to Web site X Backup 1, overwriting the backup from the 1st Wednesday night

5th Wednesday night, back up the site on to Web site X Backup 2, overwriting the backup from the 2nd Wednesday night

And so on . . .

If your Web site is a fairly static site with few changes to the pages, this schedule could be altered to one in which the backups are done monthly, or after each change to the site, rather than on a weekly basis. The rotation, however, should stay intact. Never rely on just one backup.

DISTANCE

The third key element is distance. Be sure that your backups are removed from the area where the Web server is located. Do not store your backup in the drawer beneath the server hosting the files. In the event of fire, flood, theft, or other disaster, you want your backups to be in a safe location, far away from the damage. For small sites, this could mean taking the backup disks home with you after you run a backup. For larger sites, this could mean arranging for a remote backup to a server or tape drive that is not at the same physical location as the server hosting the site or arranging to have tapes transported to a remote location after backup. It is not uncommon for institutions to arrange to have their tapes transported to storage facilities in other states, just to be safe. The diligence you apply to this backup step should reflect the mission critical nature of your Web site.

When arranging for backups, remember to look at all of the components of your site, not just the HTML pages and the image files. If your site uses a database back end or special scripts, those will need to be backed up, preferably all on the same, predictable schedule. If the database is not under your direct control, you need to make arrangements to have it backed up in a way that is compatible with your needs.

Lab 8.3 Exercises

8.3.1 Identify Backup Needs for Your Site

Read the descriptions of the sites below and fill out the backup charts below them.

The FANNC site is comprised of approximately 150 HTML pages. Most of these pages are text with the FANNC logo at the top (a 2" × 3" GIF image). Approximately one-quarter of them have 2" × 2" JPEG images, showing fleas, larvae, and equipment. FANNC updates its site when new information becomes available through the monthly state and federal bulletins, from input from their own research teams' reports and write-ins, and from their loyal readers.

a) What would be an appropriate combination of media and transport for the FANNC's backup?

	Media for backup	Transport method
Front end		
Back end (Database, etc.)		

ABC Hardware is a "megasite," comprised of many standalone sites operated by ABC Hardware's central Web development team, by the development teams in individual departments (such as the Garden Center), or by the company's business partners (Pioneer Tools, for example, maintains its own site seamlessly connected to the greater site). The Garden Center, one department at ABC Hardware, has a large site with hundreds of pages, heavy use of images and PDF files, and an online catalog delivering pages from a back end database. They have not yet developed a "shopping cart" for this site but require customers to order via telephone or fax. The database is seeded several times a week with new items or updated pricing. As a draw, specials are featured on their top pages, with prices good for two weeks. The help pages for the Garden Center are updated seasonally.

b) What would be an appropriate combination of media and transport for the Garden Center's backup?

	Media for backup	Transport method
Front end		
Back end (Database, etc.)		

8.3.2 SET UP AN EFFECTIVE BACKUP CYCLE

Using the examples given in Exercise 8.3.1, describe an appropriate backup schedule for each of the sites:

a) FANNC

_____

_____

b) Garden Center of ABC Hardware

_____

_____

LAB 8.3 EXERCISE ANSWERS

8.3.1 ANSWERS

a) What would be an appropriate combination of media and transport for the FANNC's backup?

Answer: These two sites will have very different backup needs based both upon their differing size and that they have differing levels of interactivity. Possible backups solutions for this one might look like this:

	Media for backup	Transport method
Front end	Medium format removable storage media such as 100 Mb Zip Disk or 120Mb SuperDisk.	Simple transport offsite of removable storage device disks.
Back end (Database, etc.)	None. They have no back-end needs.	

FANNC will not require much space for backup. A site like this will probably use only about 3.5Mb of space so several (nonconsecutive) backups can be stored on the same disk. However, using more than one disk should make the possibility of disk failure less likely. While a tape backup could also be used for this site, it is not necessary and unless it is a part of the regular service for the site (offered by the ISP), would be too difficult to set up for this site only.

b) What would be an appropriate combination of media and transport for the Garden Center's backup?

Answer: Possible backup solutions for this one might look like this:

	Media for backup	Transport method
Front end	Automated backup to tape or remote server.	As per standard for the rest of the site.
Back end (Database, etc.)	Automated backup to tape or remote server.	As per standard for the rest of the site.

The Garden Center is not only a large site, it is part of a larger organization that it is likely to have a systemwide backup process already in place, which will most likely rely on a tape backup or transfer to a remote server. It makes sense to roll this site in with the existing infrastructure. It is, however, incumbent on the Webmaster to check to be sure that access for restores is compatible with the needs of the Web site.

a) FANNC

Answer: FANNC should be backed up approximately every two to three weeks, as follows:

1st Wednesday night of the month, back up site onto Backup 1

3rd Wednesday night of the month, back up the site onto Backup 2

1st Wednesday night of the (next) month, back up site onto Backup 3

3rd Wednesday night of the month, back up the site onto Backup 1, overwriting the backup from the 1st Wednesday night of the previous month

And so on….

We know from the description that the only regularly scheduled updates are those prompted by the monthly governmental bulletins, but we can probably assume that while the site does not have daily changes, other updates will happen between the monthly bulletins. Two- to three-week intervals should cover their needs.

b) The Garden Center of ABC Hardware, Inc.

Answer: At installation the entire site should be included in the organization's backup program, giving the site a full baseline backup to tape or server. For this site, incremental backups (in which new or changed files are added to the tape or remote server as they appear) should be performed a minimum of once every two weeks. The rotation of media is something that the company's IS group will have built into the process.

While most large organizations run incremental backups more frequently than at two-week intervals, two weeks is the minimum for this site as that is the most frequent interval at which the pages are updated regularly (in order to put up the new specials).

LAB 8.3 SELF-REVIEW QUESTIONS

In order to test your progress, you should be able to answer the following questions.

1) Web site managers are always responsible for performing all the backups necessary to maintain their site.

a) _____ True
b) _____ False

2) Which are the three basic elements of a solid backup plan?

   a) _____ Scheduling of backups
   b) _____ Number of pages in the site
   c) _____ Distance from the hosting server
   d) _____ Rotation of media for backup

3) What is the most common cause of serious backup failure?

   a) _____ Failure to back up
   b) _____ Tape drive failure
   c) _____ Network failure
   d) _____ Failure to choose the proper media

4) Which of the following should influence your choice of backup media?

   a) _____ Services provided by the hosting ISP
   b) _____ The number of pages and images in your site
   c) _____ Whether you have backend services
   d) _____ The schedule of the person assigned to do the backups

5) Backups should be stored near the server hosting the live copy for easy access.

   a) _____ True
   b) _____ False

6) Which of the following factors influence the backup schedule?

   a) _____ The frequency at which the pages are updated on the site
   b) _____ The size of the site
   c) _____ The number of users accessing the site
   d) _____ The condition of the hosting machine

7) Large sites may rely on incremental tape backups rather than a full backup every time.

   a) _____ True
   b) _____ False

Quiz answers appear in the Appendix, Section 8.3.

CHAPTER 8

TEST YOUR THINKING

1) Describe three methods you would implement on your Web site to preserve site integrity and reduce linkrot.
2) Based on your Web site needs, platform, and budget, which, if any, site management tools would you use?
3) Describe the backup scheme you'd establish for your Web site.

C H A P T E R 9

SITE TRAFFIC

 All things are difficult before they are easy.

—Thomas Fuller

If, as manager of a Web site, you need to know who is visiting your site, how they got there, where they went while in your site, and how long they spent on each page, then understanding your log files will prove useful. If you then want to increase visitors of a certain demographic, soliciting feedback from those visitors can help direct site improvements and customization. Detailed traffic information and feedback analysis can be used immediately after site launch or after a redesign. Once the site is in maintenance phase, a summary of site traffic and periodic feedback analysis may be adequate.

L A B   9 . 1

LOG FILE ANALYSIS

LAB OBJECTIVES

After this lab, you will be able to:

✔ Describe a Typical Entry in a Web Server Log
✔ Explain Hit, View, and Visit
✔ Evaluate Results from a Log File Analysis Tool

It is easy to fall into the "hits" trap. Hit counters have been around for some time now and hits are an easy statistic to quote. When managing a Web site, you don't need to know all the details of log files, but understanding what information is available to you and making your analysis consistent over time is important.

The type and depth of log file analysis you perform depends on the type of Web site you manage. If you are simply providing information, knowing who and how many are visiting your site is interesting information, but not vital to the company. If, however, your site is an e-commerce site with a significant impact on the bottom line, you may want to know how users are moving through the site, especially just before they decide to make a purchase.

INFORMATION IN SERVER LOGS

Web server logs are plain text (ASCII) files, independent of server platform. There are some differences between server software, but traditionally there are four types of server logs:

1. Transfer (access) log
2. Error log
3. Referer log
4. Agent log

The first two types of log files are standard. The referer and agent logs may or may not be "turned on" at the server or may be added to the transfer log file to create an "extended" log file format. Each HTTP protocol transaction, whether completed or not, is recorded in the logs, and some transactions are recorded in more than one log. For example, most (but not all) HTTP errors are recorded in the transfer log and the error log. Let's take a look at the type of information collected in an "extended format" transfer log file.

TRANSFER (ACCESS) LOG

The following is an example of a single line in a common transfer log. This typically displays as one long line of ASCII text, separated by tabs and spaces (useful for importing it into a spreadsheet program).

```
1Cust216.tnt1.santa-monica.ca.da.uu.net    -    -
[08/May/1999:12:13:03    -0700] GET
/gen/meeting/ssi/next/HTTP/1.0
200    9887 http://www.slac.stanford.edu/
Mozilla/3.01-C-MACOS8 (Macintosh; I; PPC)
GET /gen/meeting/ssi/next/    -    HTTP/1.0
```

IP ADDRESS OR DNS

```
1Cust216.tnt1.santa-monica.ca.da.uu.net
```

This is the address of the computer making the HTTP request. The server records the IP and then, if configured, will look up the Domain Name Server (DNS). However, with all the dynamically assigned IP addresses these days, you don't learn as much as you'd expect from the domain name. In this case, the visitor seems to be a customer of an ISP, which is located in Santa Monica, California.

RFC931 (OR IDENTIFICATION)

Rarely used, the field was designed to identify the requestor. If this information is not recorded, a hyphen (-) holds the column in the log.

AUTHUSER

List the authenticated user, if required for access. This authentication is sent via clear text, so it is not really intended for security. This field is usually filled by a hyphen (-).

TIME STAMP

```
[08/May/1999:12:13:03    -0700]
```

The date, time, and offset from Greenwich Mean Time (GMT × 100) are recorded for each hit. The date and time format is: DD/Mon/YYYY HH:MM:SS. The example above shows that the transaction was recorded at 12:13 pm on May 9, 1999 at a location 7 hours behind GMT.

By comparing time stamps between entries, we can also determine how long a visitor spent on a given page. From the following excerpts from the log, we see that the visitor spent about a minute on the page before moving to the detailed page.

```
[08/May/1999:12:20:53   -0700]   GET
/gen/meeting/ssi/next/index.html HTTP/1.0   200   9887
http://www.slac.stanford.edu/gen/meeting/ssi/

[08/May/1999:12:21:50   -0700]   GET
/ HTTP/1.0   200   13516
http://www.slac.stanford.edu/detailed.html
```

HTTP REQUEST

```
GET /gen/meeting/ssi/next/ HTTP/1.0
```

One of three types of HTTP requests is recorded in the log. GET is the standard request for a document or program. POST tells the server that data is following. HEAD is used by link checking programs, not browsers, and downloads just the information in the HEAD tag information. The specific level of HTTP protocol is also recorded.

STATUS CODE

```
200
```

There are four classes of codes:

1. Success (200 series)
2. Redirect (300 series)
3. Failure (400 series)
4. Server Error (500 series)

A status code of 200 means the transaction was successful. Common 300-series codes are 302, for a redirect from http://www.mydomain.com to http://www.mydomain.com/, and 304 for a conditional GET. This occurs when the server checks if the version of the file or graphic already in cache is still the current version and directs the browser to use the cached version. The most common failure codes are 401 (failed authentication), 403 (forbidden request to a restricted subdirectory), and the dreaded 404 (file not found) messages. Server errors are red flags for the server administrator.

TRANSFER VOLUME

```
9887
```

For GET HTTP transactions, the last field is the number of bytes transferred. For other commands this field will be a hyphen (-) or a zero (0).

The transfer volume statistic marks the end of the common log file. The remaining fields make up the referer and agent logs, added to the common log format to create the "extended" log file format. Let's look at these fields.

REFERER URL

```
http://www.slac.stanford.edu/
```

The referer URL indicates the page where the visitor was located when making the next request. The actual request is shown in the last field of the entry

```
GET /gen/meeting/ssi/next/   -   HTTP/1.0
```

and is duplicated from the HTTP Request, the fifth field in this log.

If you were looking at just the referer log, not integrated into the transfer log, it would be made up of just two fields. The left field is the starting URL and the right field is where the reader went from the URL. Transfers within your site would also show in the transfer log. For example, movement from one page to another within a Web site might show in the referer log as:

```
http://www.slac.stanford.edu/ -> /gen/meeting/ssi/next/
```

The visitor went from the top-level page to information about the next SSI conference through a link on the page.

USER AGENT

```
Mozilla/3.01-C-MACOS8 (Macintosh; I; PPC)
```

The user agent is information about the browser, version, and operating system of the reader. The general format is:

```
Browser name/version (operating system)
```

Confusion comes from the word "Mozilla," which is the original code name for Netscape. Now almost all browsers compatible with Netscape use the Mozilla code. The following are entries into a recent agent log:

> Mozilla/4.05 [en]C-PBI-NC404 (Win95; U)
>
> Mozilla/4.51 [en] (WinNT; I)
>
> W3C_Validator/1.22 libwww-perl/5.43
>
> Mozilla/4.0 (compatible; MSIE 5.0; Windows 95; DigExt)
>
> Mozilla/2.0 (compatible; MSIE 2.1; AOL 3.0; Mac_68K)
>
> Mozilla/4.0 (compatible; MSIE 4.01; AOL 4.0; Mac_PPC)
>
> Mozilla/4.0 (compatible; MSIE 4.01; Windows NT)
>
> Mozilla/4.06 [en]C-gatewaynet (Win98; I)

The one entry not identified by Mozilla is a robot used to test a specific page. Search engine robots are often similarly identified in the agent log. This is one way to find out who is indexing your site.

You can also find out how a reader is reaching your site from a referer log. The following is a typical entry from a user who entered your site from a category-based index, in this case Yahoo. From this information you can detect how your site is categorized.

```
http://dir.yahoo.com/Science/Physics/High_Energy_and_
Particle_Physics/Research/Accelerators/Stanford_Linear_
Accelerator_Center__SLAC_/ -> /
```

The following is an entry from a search engine, in this case Alta Vista. From this data you can see the key words used by the visitor to find your site.

```
http://www.altavista.com/cgi-
bin/query?pg=q&user=yahoo&q=computer
+programming+videos+&stq=20&c9k --> /comp/edu/classes.html
```

ERROR LOG

The following is a typical example of an error log transaction:

```
[Wed Aug 4 00:02:21 1999] HTTPd: send aborted for adsl-
209-233-19-101.dsl.snfc21.pacbell.net, URL:
/_vti_bin/_vti_aut/author.exe
```

Compared to the access log, the error log is designed for human eyes to decode. It starts with a time stamp, in an entirely different format than the access log, and is followed by a textual description of the error. The time stamp is in the following format:

[DAY MON DATE HR:MIN:SEC YEAR]

An entry is made to the error log when there are server startups and shutdowns, access failures (such as 404 error), lost connections, timeouts, and cancellations by the visitor. There is no information about the user.

HITS, VIEWS, AND VISITS

Hit counters continue to be popular features on Web pages, but they, in fact, have little value. First, most hit counters can be adjusted to start at any number. So the number you see in on a hit counter may be artificial. Second, just what is defined as a hit? In fact, requesting a single Web page can result in multiple hits to the server. First, if the requested URL does not have a following slash (such as http://www.mydomain.com), the server will first redirect to the URL with a slash (such as http://www.mydomain.com/). Then the page of html will show as a hit and each graphic on the page will also record as a hit in the log. So a page of html with six graphics in a navigation bar could record eight individual hits in the log. This set of eight hits is described as a view, that is, all the hits necessary to display a Web page. The next analysis is to look through the views to recreate the user's visit to the site—how that user got to your site, where he or she went in the site, and how long was spent there. Let's take a look at server logs and find out what they can tell us about our site visitors.

LOG FILE ANALYSIS TOOLS

There are a variety of log file analysis tools available today. There are even reasonably effective freeware, multi-platform tools, such as Analog (www.statslab. cam.ac.uk/~sret1/analog/). Midrange tools, such as WebTrends (www.Webtrends. com), provide customizable analysis and reporting, including collecting live data. High-end tools, such as Net.Analysis (www.netanalysis.com), can be set up to analyze network packets rather than log files. This can be particularly useful if your site has many Web servers distributed over a diverse network. Most of the log file analysis tools available today can be customized to meet your specific analysis needs.

For other tools, just enter "log analysis tools" into a search engine or take a look at Yahoo's list at (dir.yahoo.com/Business_and_Economy/Companies/Computers/ Software/Internet/World_Wide_Web/Log_Analysis_Tools/Titles/) to find one that suits your needs.

LAB 9.1 EXERCISES

9.1.1 DESCRIBE A TYPICAL ENTRY IN A WEB SERVER LOG

Take a look at the following excerpt from a real extended-format Web server log file.

```
Transaction #1
dejh.ipm.ac.ir - - [08/May/1999:00:47:07 -0700]
GET /spires/form/hepfnal.html HTTP/1.0 200 3529
http://www-spires.slac.stanford.edu/spires/forms.html
Mozilla/4.05 [en] (Win95; I)
GET /spires/form/hepfnal.html - HTTP/1.0
Transaction #2
202.41.102.153 - - [08/May/1999:02:11:25 -0700]
POST /cgi-bin/form-mail.pl HTTP/1.1 200 649
http://www.slac.stanford.edu/spires/find/hepnames/wwwupd?
ID=RCV&NODE=PBI.ERNET.IN
Mozilla/4.0 (compatible; MSIE 4.01; Windows 95)
POST /cgi-bin/form-mail.pl - HTTP/1.1
Transaction #3
oeias1-p2.telepac.pt - - [08/May/1999:03:16:08 -0700]
GET /BFROOT/Images/BABAR2.gif HTTP/1.1 404 360
http://www.slac.stanford.edu/BFROOT/old-www/Physics/Work-
shops/wkshp_home.html
Mozilla/4.0 (compatible; MSIE 4.01; Windows 95)
GET /BFROOT/Images/BABAR2.gif - HTTP/1.1
```

a) How many visitors are reflected in these Web transactions? Explain.

_____

_____

b) On what date did these transactions take place?

_____

_____

c) How many minutes passed between the first and last entry?

_____

_____

d) Were all three transactions successful? If not, explain.

_____

_____

e) Which transaction requested the largest file? What size was the file?

_____

_____

f) What browsers are being used to access these pages?

_____

_____

g) What platforms are being used to access these pages?

_____

_____

h) Can you determine the path the visitor from 202.41.102.153 took through the Web site?

_____

_____

9.1.2 EXPLAIN HIT, VIEW, AND VISIT

Take a look at the data below, extracted from real extended transfer log data from a single visitor to a Web site. This visit is made up of ninety records; all records have "GET" as the action code. After looking at the data, answer the following questions. As supplied, the entries are sorted by time stamp.

Time	Request	Referer
12:11:54	/	http://dir.yahoo.com/ Science/Physics/High_ Energy_and_Particle_ Physics/Research/ Accelerators/Stanford _Linear_Accelerator_ Center__SLAC_/
12:11:55	/welcome/images/blank.gif	http://www.slac. stanford.edu/
12:11:55	/welcome/images/new-welcome.gif	http://www.slac. stanford.edu/
12:11:55	/welcome/images/welcome-border.gif	http://www.slac. stanford.edu/
12:11:59	/welcome/images/wel-rp.gif	http://www.slac. stanford.edu/
12:12:01	/welcome/images/wel-si.gif	http://www.slac. stanford.edu/
12:12:02	/welcome/images/wel-comp.gif	http://www.slac. stanford.edu/
12:12:02	/welcome/images/wel-org.gif	http://www.slac. stanford.edu/
12:12:04	/welcome/rotate/slacwest.jpg	http://www.slac. stanford.edu/
12:12:05	/welcome/images/wel-was.gif	http://www.slac. stanford.edu/
12:12:09	/welcome/images/tent.gif	http://www.slac. stanford.edu/
12:12:09	/welcome/images/wel-detailed.gif	http://www.slac. stanford.edu/
12:12:12	/welcome/images/991-feature.jpg	http://www.slac. stanford.edu/
12:12:13	/welcome/images/welbutton-tours.gif	http://www.slac. stanford.edu/
12:12:15	/welcome/images/vvclogo.gif	http://www.slac. stanford.edu/
12:12:16	/welcome/images/welbutton-spires.gif	http://www.slac. stanford.edu/
12:12:19	/welcome/images/welbutton-education.gif	http://www.slac. stanford.edu/
12:12:20	/welcome/images/welbutton-aboutslac.gif	http://www.slac. stanford.edu/
12:12:20	/welcome/images/welbutton-employement.gif	http://www.slac. stanford.edu/
12:12:20	/welcome/images/welbutton-mission.gif	http://www.slac. stanford.edu/

```
12:12:21  /welcome/images/wel-        http://www.slac.
            beamline.gif              stanford.edu/
12:12:21  /welcome/images/welbutton-  http://www.slac.
            mediainfo.gif             stanford.edu/
12:12:21  /welcome/images/welbutton-  http://www.slac.
            reachus.gif               stanford.edu/
12:13:03  /gen/meeting/ssi/next/      http://www.slac.
                                      stanford.edu/
12:13:04  /gen/meeting/ssi/gif/       http://www.slac.
            blueball.gif              stanford.edu/gen/
                                      meeting/ssi/next/
12:13:04  /gen/meeting/ssi/gif/       http://www.slac.
            ssi99_newlogo.gif         stanford.edu/gen/
                                      meeting/ssi/next/
12:13:04  /icon/redball.gif           http://www.slac.
                                      stanford.edu/gen/
                                      meeting/ssi/next/
12:13:05  /gen/meeting/ssi/gif/new.gif http://www.slac.
                                      stanford.edu/gen/
                                      meeting/ssi/next/
12:14:59  /slac/sciinfo.shtml         http://www.slac.
                                      stanford.edu/
12:15:01  /icon/blank.gif             http://www.slac.
                                      stanford.edu/slac/
                                      sciinfo.shtml
12:15:01  /icon/border.gif            http://www.slac.
                                      stanford.edu/slac/
                                      sciinfo.shtml
12:15:01  /icon/slac2.gif             http://www.slac.
                                      stanford.edu/slac/
                                      sciinfo.shtml
12:15:04  /icon/nav-detail.gif        http://www.slac.
                                      stanford.edu/slac/
                                      sciinfo.shtml
12:15:04  /icon/nav-org.gif           http://www.slac.
                                      stanford.edu/slac/
                                      sciinfo.shtml
12:15:04  /icon/nav-rp.gif            http://www.slac.
                                      stanford.edu/slac/
                                      sciinfo.shtml
12:15:04  /icon/nav-was.gif           http://www.slac.
                                      stanford.edu/slac/
                                      sciinfo.shtml
12:15:05  /icon/nav-welcome.gif       http://www.slac.
                                      stanford.edu/slac/
                                      sciinfo.shtml
```

```
12:15:06  /icon/nav-comp.gif        http://www.slac.
                                     stanford.edu/slac/
                                     sciinfo.shtml

12:15:06  /icon/nav-feedback.gif     http://www.slac.
                                     stanford.edu/slac/
                                     sciinfo.shtml

12:15:06  /icon/nav-spires.gif       http://www.slac.
                                     stanford.edu/slac/
                                     sciinfo.shtml

12:15:07  /icon/nav-highlght.gif     http://www.slac.
                                     stanford.edu/slac/
                                     sciinfo.shtml

12:15:07  /icon/nav-hpt.gif          http://www.slac.
                                     stanford.edu/slac/
                                     sciinfo.shtml

12:15:07  /icon/nav-search.gif       http://www.slac.
                                     stanford.edu/slac/
                                     sciinfo.shtml

12:15:07  /icon/nav-si-g.gif         http://www.slac.
                                     stanford.edu/slac/
                                     sciinfo.shtml

12:15:09  /icon/nav-announ.gif       http://www.slac.
                                     stanford.edu/slac/
                                     sciinfo.shtml

12:15:19  /grp/pao/seminar.html      http://www.slac.
                                     stanford.edu/slac/
                                     sciinfo.shtml

12:15:20  /icon/slac3.gif            http://www.slac.
                                     stanford.edu/grp/pao/
                                     seminar.html

12:15:37  /grp/pao/semsearch.html    http://www.slac.
                                     stanford.edu/grp/pao/
                                     seminar.html

12:16:07  /spires/find/seminars/     http://www.slac.
          wwwsemfor?wwwtag=          stanford.edu/grp/pao/
          physacc&date=after+        semsearch.html
          yesterday

12:16:17  /spires/find/seminars/     http://www.slac.
          wwwsemfor?wwwtag=          stanford.edu/grp/pao/
          physstan&date=after+       semsearch.html
          yesterday

12:16:37  /spires/find/seminars/     http://www.slac.
          wwwsemfor?date=after+      stanford.edu/grp/pao/
          yesterday                  semsearch.html

12:17:39  /pubs/beamline/            http://www.slac.
                                     stanford.edu/slac/
                                     sciinfo.shtml
```

```
12:17:40   /pubs/beamline/images/          http://www.slac.
           bl-title.gif                    stanford.edu/pubs/
                                           beamline/

12:17:40   /pubs/beamline/images/          http://www.slac.
           welcome-border.gif              stanford.edu/pubs/
                                           beamline/

12:17:46   /pubs/beamline/images/          http://www.slac.
           99i.jpg                         stanford.edu/pubs/
                                           beamline/

12:17:49   /pubs/beamline/images/          http://www.slac.
           contrib.gif                     stanford.edu/pubs/
                                           beamline/

12:17:49   /pubs/beamline/images/          http://www.slac.
           editors.gif                     stanford.edu/pubs/
                                           beamline/

12:17:54   /pubs/beamline/images/          http://www.slac.
           pastissues.gif                  stanford.edu/pubs/
                                           beamline/

12:17:56   /pubs/beamline/images/          http://www.slac.
           line.gif                        stanford.edu/pubs/
                                           beamline/

12:17:56   /pubs/beamline/images/          http://www.slac.
           slacwelcome.gif                 stanford.edu/pubs/
                                           beamline/

12:18:01   /pubs/beamline/images/          http://www.slac.
           acroread.gif                    stanford.edu/pubs/
                                           beamline/

12:18:02   /pubs/beamline/images/          http://www.slac.
           lg_nlcta_people.jpg             stanford.edu/pubs/
                                           beamline/

12:18:03   /pubs/beamline/images/          http://www.slac.
           advsbrd.gif                     stanford.edu/pubs/
                                           beamline/

12:18:03   /pubs/beamline/images/          http://www.slac.
           comments.gif                    stanford.edu/pubs/
                                           beamline/

12:18:32   /slac/sciinfo.shtml             http://www.slac.
                                           stanford.edu/

12:19:01   /icon/nav-detail-g.gif          http://www.slac.
                                           stanford.edu/
                                           detailed.html

12:19:01   /icon/rdpin.gif                 http://www.slac.
                                           stanford.edu/
                                           detailed.html

12:19:02   /detailed.html                  http://www.slac.
                                           stanford.edu/
```

12:19:03	/icon/new.gif	http://www.slac.stanford.edu/detailed.html
12:19:41	/gen/meeting/ssi/	http://www.slac.stanford.edu/detailed.html
12:19:42	/gen/meeting/ssi/gif/updated.gif	http://www.slac.stanford.edu/gen/meeting/ssi/
12:19:55	/gen/meeting/ssi/gif/new_animated.gif	http://www.slac.stanford.edu/gen/meeting/ssi/
12:19:59	/gen/meeting/ssi/gif/ssi25image.jpg	http://www.slac.stanford.edu/gen/meeting/ssi/
12:20:53	/gen/meeting/ssi/next/index.html	http://www.slac.stanford.edu/gen/meeting/ssi/
12:21:50	/	http://www.slac.stanford.edu/detailed.html
12:21:54	/welcome/rotate/slacaerial.jpg	http://www.slac.stanford.edu/
12:22:06	/grp/pao/tour.html	http://www.slac.stanford.edu/
12:23:31	/spires/find/binlist/wwwg?record=78921	http://www.slac.stanford.edu/grp/pao/tour.html#evening
12:23:59	/	http://dir.yahoo.com/Science/Physics/High_Energy_and_Particle_Physics/Research/Accelerators/Stanford_Linear_Accelerator_Center_SLAC_/
12:24:25	/welcome/mission.html	http://www.slac.stanford.edu/
12:24:42	/gen/edu/education.html	http://www.slac.stanford.edu/
12:24:42	/gen/edu/sise/img/AWandJB.jpg	http://www.slac.stanford.edu/gen/edu/education.html
12:24:42	/images/border.gif	http://www.slac.stanford.edu/gen/edu/education.html

```
12:24:46  /gen/edu/sise/img/        http://www.slac.
          twogirls.jpg              stanford.edu/gen/edu/
                                    education.html
12:24:50  /gen/edu/sise/img/        http://www.slac.
          1998_Students.jpg         stanford.edu/gen/edu/
                                    education.html
12:24:59  /gen/edu/sise/img/        http://www.slac.
          RPTNandHK.jpg             stanford.edu/gen/edu/
                                    education.html
12:25:01  /gen/edu/sise/img/        http://www.slac.
          gogglegirlandman.jpg      stanford.edu/gen/edu/
                                    education.html
12:25:02  /gen/edu/sise/img/        http://www.slac.
          meterman.jpg              stanford.edu/gen/edu/
                                    education.html
12:25:04  /gen/edu/sise/img/        http://www.slac.
          SISEStaff.jpg             stanford.edu/gen/edu/
                                    education.html
12:25:12  /gen/edu/sise/img/        http://www.slac.
          boyandcopper.jpg          stanford.edu/gen/edu/
                                    education.html
```

a) How many hits could this visit record to a simple hit counter?

_____

_____

b) How many unique pages were viewed during the visit?

_____

_____

c) Were any pages viewed more than once?

_____

_____

d) How long did the visitor spend on the site during that single visit?

_____

_____

e) From this data can you easily track the path the visitor took through your site?

_____

_____

f) As the manager of a Web site, which of these bits of data is most useful to know?

_____

_____

9.1.3 EVALUATE RESULTS FROM A LOG FILE ANALYSIS TOOL

Large Web sites can have Web files with more than 100,000 daily transactions. Analyzing this data by hand is a difficult task. Consider the following data, collected using WebTrends Professional on one week of data from the Stanford Linear Accelerator Center's Unix Web server (the Web site contained over 420,000 pages in June 1999).

General Statistics (total activity)

Date & Time This Report Was Generated	Sunday August 15, 1999 – 15:45:49
Timeframe	05/02/99 00:30:34– 05/09/99 00:29:34
Number of Hits for Home Page	15,166
Number of Successful Hits for Entire Site	682,664
Number of Page Views (Impressions)	152,904
Number of User Sessions	51,399
User Sessions from United States	58.35%
International User Sessions	28.16%
User Sessions of Unknown Origin	13.47%
Average Number of Hits Per Day	97,523
Average Number of Page Views Per Day	21,843
Average Number of User Sessions Per Day	7,342
Average User Session Length	00:15:25

Summary of Activity for Report Period (excludes errors)

Average Number of Users per Day on Weekdays	8,870
Average Number of Hits per Day on Weekdays	119,419
Average Number of Users for the Entire Weekend	3,523
Average Number of Hits for the Entire Weekend	42,783
Most Active Day of the Week	Mon
Least Active Day of the Week	Sat
Most Active Day Ever	May 03, 1999
Number of Hits on Most Active Day	123,856
Least Active Day Ever	May 09, 1999
Number of Hits on Least Active Day	444

a) How many transactions (hits) were recorded for this site for the week? What is the daily range (low and high, excluding error)?

_____

_____

b) How many actual page views were reflected in these hits?

_____

_____

c) How many visits were reflected in these views?

_____

_____

d) How many views per day, on average?

_____

_____

e) How long does the average visit last?

_____

_____

f) If the server needs to be shut down for servicing, what would be the best day of the week to perform that work?

_____

_____

g) Does the number of hits on the least active day fit with the remaining statistics? Explain.

_____

_____

LAB 9.1 EXERCISE ANSWERS

9.1.1 ANSWERS

The following answers are based on the data found in Exercise 9.1.1.

a) How many visitors are reflected in these Web transactions? Explain.

Answer: Three visitors are reflected. Two are identified by DNS entry: dejh.ipm.ac.ir and oeias1-p2.telepac.pt. The third is identified by IP address 202.41.102.153.

b) On what date did these transactions take place?

Answer: All three transactions took place on May 8, 1999.

c) How much time passed between the first and last entry?

Answer: The first transaction took place at 12:47 am, the last at 3:16 am. There were 2 hours and 29 minutes spanned by these transactions.

d) Were all three transactions successful? If not, explain.

Answer: No. Transaction #3 shows a 404 status code. This is the "file not found" error message. Transactions #1 and #2 showed the okay code "200."

e) Which transaction requested the largest file? What size was the file?

Answer: Transaction #1 showed a transfer volume of 3529 bytes. The other two transactions show volumes of 649 and 360 bytes.

f) What browsers are being used to access these pages?

Answer: Netscape 4.05 and MS Internet Explorer 4.01.

g) What platforms are being used to access these pages?

Answer: All three transactions came through on machines identified as Windows 95.

h) Can you determine the path the visitor from 202.41.102.153 took through the Web site?

Answer: No, there is not enough data in individual transactions to determine the path of a visitor. A path could be determined by looking at all the transactions of a given visitor through a day of log files.

9.1.2 ANSWERS

The following answers are based on the data found Exercise 9.1.2.

a) How many hits could this visit record to a simple hit counter?

Answer: 90 hits were recorded.

b) How many unique pages were viewed during the visit?

Answer: 11 unique pages were viewed: /, /detailed.html, /gen/edu/education.html, /gen/meeting/ssi/, /gen/meeting/ssi/next/, /grp/pao/seminar.html, /grp/pao/semsearch.html, /grp/pao/tour.html, /pubs/beamline/, /slac/sciinfo.shtml, /welcome/mission.html.

c) Were any pages viewed more than once?

Answer: Yes, / was viewed three times, /gen/meeting/ssi/next/index.html was viewed twice (once just at /gen/meeting/ssi/next/), and /slac/sciinfo.shtml was viewed twice. This brings the total pages viewed to 15. There were also four records retrieved from SPIRES databases.

d) How long did the visitor spend on the site during that single visit?

Answer: 12 minutes, 48 seconds.

e) From this data can you easily track the path the visitor took through your site?

**LAB
9.1**

Answer: Easily, no. But by

1) *moving the transactions into a spreadsheet program,*
2) *deleting all the transactions that are not page views (gif and jpg download),*
3) *sorting by transaction time, and*
4) *doing a bit of time manipulation*

you can get a feel for the route the visitor made through the site and how much time was spent on each page.

```
Timestamp    Time       Page
12:11:54     0:01:09    /
12:13:03     0:01:56    /gen/meeting/ssi/next/
12:14:59     0:00:20    /slac/sciinfo.shtml
12:15:19     0:00:18    /grp/pao/seminar.html
12:15:37     0:00:30    /grp/pao/semsearch.html
12:16:07     0:00:10    /spires/find/seminars/wwwsemfor?
                        wwwtag=physacc&date=after+yesterday
12:16:17     0:00:20    /spires/find/seminars/wwwsemfor?
                        wwwtag=physstan&date
12:16:37     0:01:02    /spires/find/seminars/wwwsemfor?date=
                        after+yesterday
12:17:39     0:00:53    /pubs/beamline/
12:18:32     0:00:30    /slac/sciinfo.shtml
12:19:02     0:00:39    /detailed.html
12:19:41     0:01:12    /gen/meeting/ssi/
12:20:53     0:00:57    /gen/meeting/ssi/next/index.html
12:21:50     0:00:16    /
12:22:06     0:01:25    /grp/pao/tour.html
12:23:31     0:00:28    /spires/find/binlist/wwwg?record=
                        78921
12:23:59     0:00:26    /
12:24:25     0:00:17    /welcome/mission.html
12:24:42                /gen/edu/education.html
```

f) As the manager of a Web site, which of these bits of data is most useful to know?

Answer: This answer depends on your Web site. However, total hits is really only useful as a measurement of bandwidth requirements. The number of page views is more useful as a measure of site traffic. Seeing how a user works through a site can help determine if there are navigation problems.

9.1.3 ANSWERS

The following answers are based on the data found in Exercise 9.1.3.

a) How many successful transactions (hits) were recorded for this site for the week? What is the daily range (low and high, excluding error)?

Answer: There were 682,664 hits recorded for the week. The highest day had 123,856 hits, the least active day had 444 hits.

b) How many actual page views were reflected in these hits?

Answer: The data showed 152,904 page views for the week.

c) How many visits were reflected in these views?

Answer: The data showed 51,399 actual user sessions for the week.

d) How many views per day, on average?

Answer: The average number of views per day was 21,843, by 7,342 visitors.

e) How long does the average visit last?

Answer: About 15 minutes.

f) If the server needs to be shut down for servicing, what would be the best day of the week to perform that work?

Answer: The weekend seems to be the best time to perform a shutdown. There were, on average, 8,870 users per day on the weekdays and only 3,523 users for the entire weekend.

g) Does the number of hits on the least active day fit with the remaining statistics? Explain.

Answer: No. If you look at the time frame, there were only 29 minutes of data taken for the "Least Active Day" and that occurred just after midnight. Selecting the time frame from midnight to midnight would clear up this problem.

LAB 9.1 SELF-REVIEW QUESTIONS

In order to test your progress, you should be able to answer the following questions.

1) Site visitors are identified in which field of the Access Log?

    a) _____ Authuser
    b) _____ HTTP Request
    c) _____ IP Address or DNS
    d) _____ Status Code

2) Which of the following indicates a successful transaction in the Web log?

a) _____ 200
b) _____ 302
c) _____ 404
d) _____ 500

3) The referer URL shows?

a) _____ The browser, version, and operating system of the reader
b) _____ Number of bytes transferred
c) _____ Page where the visitor was located when making the next request
d) _____ Address of the computer making the HTTP request

4) Errors are recorded only in the error log.

a) _____ True
b) _____ False

5) Which of the following is probably a higher number?

a) _____ Hits
b) _____ Views
c) _____ Visits
d) _____ Hits = Views = Visits

6) Which of the following is the best description of a site visit?

a) _____ A list of all requests made to a Web server on a given date.
b) _____ All the pages and graphics needed to view a given page on the Web.
c) _____ The set of recorded transactions by a given IP address or DNS entry, from site entry to exit.
d) _____ Only the image downloads necessary to use a page effectively.

Quiz answers appear in the Appendix, Section 9.1.

LAB 9.2

OBTAINING FEEDBACK

LAB OBJECTIVES

After this Lab, you will be able to:

✔ Describe Various Methods of Obtaining Feedback
✔ Choose the Appropriate Methods of Obtaining Feedback

Communication is a two-way street. All forms of presentation are a form of communication and require dialog between the presenter and the recipient. Without that two-way flow of information, the presenter, performer, seller, or guru has no way to know if the communication is sufficient, well-received, or doing its job. For performance artists, feedback is immediate, the audience claps, hoots, or, worst of all, sits in deadly silence and the performer is made instantly aware of the success or failure of the performance. Authors and Web developers have to wait a bit longer and do more to get the feedback they need to evaluate their "performance." But, just like the stage performer, they need feedback to know whether they have reached their intended audience. To be truly effective, this feedback must be ongoing—mechanisms must exist to provide feedback on a site from its development stages throughout its entire lifetime.

Feedback on the Web can be divided into two broad categories: active and passive feedback. Active feedback requires active participation on the part of the "audience"—answering questions, or filling out a form. Passive feedback does not require that members of the audience make an active response. Observing and interpreting the behavior of the audience provides us with passive feedback. We will look at active and passive feedback separately.

ACTIVE FEEDBACK

Active feedback requires the audience, the users of a Web site, to respond in some manner, thus letting the owners of the site know how they feel about the site and its features.

Active feedback is, as any political organizer or special interest group can tell you, extremely difficult to solicit because it requires time and thought on the part of busy people who are unwilling to spend the time and thought on something that does not have an obvious reward. While site owners may need this feedback, site users are notoriously unwilling to supply it if it requires effort on their part. Let's look at some of the methods used to gather active feedback.

UNSOLICITED FEEDBACK

This is the form of feedback that is most beloved of Webmasters because it requires little effort on their part beyond setting up the initial access mechanism. Access mechanisms for unsolicited feedback include:

- A mailto link to the page owner or site's Webmaster on each page, allowing a simple e-mail contact.
- A "Contacts" page gives contact information for the site (may include contact info for sales, technical support for products, technical support for use of the site, investment opportunities). It's not a bad idea to provide some contact information on every page in the site, just to facilitate this contact.
- A "Comments" or feedback form for the site, generating e-mail to the site contact address.
- A "Guestbook" allowing people to comment on the site and, usually, have their comments or suggestions posted on the site.

These methods of communication provide feedback opportunities of the most basic kind. They provide a direct opportunity for the site's users to communicate with the site's presenters, if they so choose.

A mailto link and a contact page are absolutely critical to the success of a site, whether or not they prove to be a "popular" item. These tools offer an extremely important type of communication: immediate emergency contact if some form of interaction has gone wrong. Using an email link as the only way to contact a company, especially a service-oriented company, is a bad idea. Offering multiple methods for users to communicate with the company is a very good practice.

For extremely "deep" sites (those sites with relatively few "top level" pages and many lower level pages) the page owner or Webmaster link on all pages is extremely important because the "way back" may be somewhat obscure. While top level pages usually appear in navigation bars, in very deep sites, the lower level pages may not be represented in any structured way and finding one's way back up to a feedback form to report a broken link will be far beyond the altruistic tendencies of most visitors. Unfortunately, many commercial sites choose not to provide this form of contact, believing that by limiting this sort of contact, they are reducing costs. What they are doing is reducing their repeat business, instantly.

A general guideline for all of these modes of passive feedback is that each contact registered represents nine others who did not choose to follow through. If a Webmaster hears from one person indicating that a link or database query failed, that Webmaster can safely assume that nine others had the same experience, shrugged, and went back to the search engine to look for a site that "worked." A positive aspect of this "1 in 10" rule is that one message indicating that the site is "fantastic" means that a lot of other people are probably enjoying it, too.

A comment or feedback form or a guestbook requires a bit more work on the part of the reviewer. These methods are usually used by site visitors who really want to communicate something about the site in general. They are only used for the kind of emergency communication described above if there is no easier method supplied. They too, as unsolicited communication, fall under the "1 in 10" rule and their messages should be interpreted accordingly.

Many sites now offer a "feedback form" as the only on-line avenue of communication with the organization. A form is an attractive feedback mechanism for organizations because a form can structure the nature of the communication (via radio buttons, pull-down lists, and browser/platform detection scripts) in a way that the organization wants to receive it. This structured communication has been used a number of times by companies that have removed products from their line. To avoid the tide of complaints coming in, the freeform comments@software.com mailto link was replaced with a form that structured all communication (via pull-down lists) to address only the current product line. While this does reduce the "noise" (feedback regarding a decision already made), it can also result in some unforeseen problems. Allowing only carefully structured information to come in may also be eliminating valuable feedback that doesn't fit the structure of the communication system. A good example of difficulties introduced by systems such as this is the technical support site that offers a pull-down list of products based on the detected platform of the user. While it does seem like a good idea to only show technical support pertaining to the platform used, it can backfire for the user. Consider the user who is looking for support on a Windows version of a product but has had to borrow a friend's Macintosh to get Internet access because the Windows machine is no longer functioning. At the technical support site, based on a browser-detect script, only Macintosh-related support options are given, making it impossible to reach the needed information.

SWEETENING THE POT

Active feedback from users is very valuable information because it supplies the site owners with feedback that is intentionally given. Intentionally given feedback is "predigested" by those supplying the information and does not require as much interpretation as the various forms of passive feedback. Because site visitors may be reluctant to take the time to provide this kind of information, it is a good idea to come up with ways that make it more attractive for a visitor to take the time to provide the feedback. Various "incentive programs" may be applied including:

- Give something away in return for feedback. The word "Free" is a powerful motivator.
- If possible, provide a featured discount on merchandise or service for customers who fill out a form with their purchase.
- Enter the names of users who fill out a form in a monthly drawing. Commercial sites may provide merchandise discounts as the prize; nonprofits may provide prizes donated by site supporters or an opportunity to write a feature for the site. (Be careful here—the laws that cover sweepstakes and contests vary by region.)
- Provide an interactive game on the site that solicits the information you seek as part of the "forward motion" of the game. For each piece of information given, advance the player to another stage.
- Set up a chat room, forum, or bulletin board on the site and require users to provide the information that you want to see as part of their registration before they are allowed to post on your site. Employ a periodic update feature that requires them to update their information at specified intervals to make sure that your information stays current. (Note: For active sites, the interval may be more appropriately applied to number of posts rather than a time-lapsed interval.)
- Give users the opportunity to see their comments publicly posted. This is incentive for many and often provides more "reasoned" responses than an anonymous feedback form. Make it clear at the link to your feedback form that comments will be displayed on the site. This needs to be monitored, of course, for the occasional visitors who just want to see their profanity or vulgarity posted.

Note that chat rooms, forums, and bulletin boards, while more problematic to set up and run, can also bring in added value in that they encourage users to "hang around" the site more and can help to build a sense of community around the site. Again, moderating these activities may be essential.

OFFSTAGE FEEDBACK

In addition to the kind of feedback that can be obtained about a site from the site itself, good planning and management also require that site developers seek out direct "offstage feedback" from peers, key stakeholders, or target audience focus groups as part of the development process of a site. Prior to staging a site or a major revision, developers should ask for direct feedback on the site from a group that has not been deeply involved in that site's development. Fresh eyes looking at the site and trying it out from different points of view offer valuable feedback for the developers.

Focus groups can supply information regarding how potential users and target groups use and approach a site. Choose the members of these groups to match the target audience of your site. If, for example, you are working on a site selling motocross equipment, your focus group should contain a high percentage of males, ages 14 to 35, the main purchasers of this type of product.

Key stakeholder review involves input from those with specific interest in the site, from inside and outside the immediate organization. Members of this re-viewing group might include project managers, division managers, marketing or public relations people associated with the site, subject area experts, and touch-group personnel (those personnel who actually sell, repair, or deal with the items dealt with on the site).

Peer-to-peer feedback involves soliciting the opinions of other professionals in the Web-development field. One can solicit feedback from friends and colleagues or work through a larger arena, such as mailing lists (either those established as general development lists or those established for support and discussion on spe-cific development tools).

In soliciting this type of feedback, you may wish to impose some structure on the responses that you get. While peer-to-peer review may not require more than a "Take a look at this site and tell me what you think," supplying key stakeholders, or naïve reviewers in a focus group with a set of questions may yield more satis-factory results. In the latter stages of development, it is not particularly useful to hear that a reviewer does not like the font used in the site if that font is already established as part of the institution's "image" and is no longer up for discussion.

Some questions to supply general reviewers might include:

- Did the links on the top page lead you to where you thought you were going?
- How did the images used on the product pages render on your machine?
- How long did you have to wait for page X to load?
- Are we missing any critical links on the navigation panel?
- Is this the correct order of links in the navigation panel?

Some questions to supply subject experts or touch-group reviewers might include:

- Do you see anything misleading regarding content?
- Is there anything that is incorrect?
- Have we forgotten anything critical?

Particularly when one is dealing with stakeholders in an institution, one must be careful that an invitation to review a site before staging does not result in "feature creep" extending beyond the scope of the given round of development. Adding a question such as, "Does your review of this site give you ideas that should be included in a future revision?" can allow the reviewer to put in for additional features (good information) to be added at an appropriate time (good planning).

Another avenue of offstage feedback for a site can be found in the various departments of an institution. Webmasters should stay in touch with critical departments that can supply valuable feedback throughout the life of a site. If the organization has a technical support group, this group will likely be a prime supplier of information. Group members will have heard everything from ideas regarding what should be included in the site's technical support FAQs to reports about what users said they couldn't find on the site (most users with technical support needs will probably have visited the site before attempting to contact a person for help). If the organization is very small or does not have technical support, the first-contact group (reception, the phone operator, general sales, etc.) will be a good place to check for ongoing feedback regarding the site.

PASSIVE FEEDBACK

Passive feedback does not require active responses from the users. Passive feedback is information that is inferred from records of the behavior of visitors to the site. This information is retrievable by way of a site's log files. (Information regarding the reading of these log files is available in Lab 9.1, Log File Analysis.) The information from these log files can give you information about how people come to your site and what they do when they get there. You can use this feedback to adjust your site to the usage patterns of your clients.

Access information as reported in log files is particularly important to determine if you are reaching your target audience. Let's take a look at SkaBoards' information. An analysis of SkaBoards' log files in comparison with its purchase records indicates that the majority of dollars spent in its online sales come from visitors arriving from specialty sites, such as Boards Without Borders (a snowboard chat and forum site), rather than those coming from a generic search engine such as AltaVista. SkaBoards spends more of its advertising dollars on banners at special interest sites than it does on Yahoo's main boards because the passive feedback tells them where they get a greater return on their investment.

Another very useful feature available from the log files is the tracking of visitors' behavior once the get into the site. While the majority of "disappointed" users (those who do not find what they are looking for) simply leave a site without leaving a message for the Webmaster, their log file trail can alert a Webmaster that there is trouble in the navigation of the site. A persistent pattern of "long way around" paths to a sector in a Web site may indicate that the "direct link" to that area is either mislabeled (visitors do not recognize perhaps that a link labeled "Opportunities" leads to the employment opportunities of the organization) or improperly placed on the page. Webmasters should be alert for certain "trouble patterns" in the log. Sure signs of trouble are repeated Error 404, Missing file, and messages with the same search criteria showing in the error log. This indicates that search engines have outdated information regarding pages within the site and that measures should be taken to ensure clean access to existing information. At the server level, one can set up redirect pages or symlinks for pages that have moved as well as updating the information on the search engine registration.

LAB 9.2 EXERCISES

9.2.1 METHODS OF OBTAINING FEEDBACK

a) Various forms of feedback mechanisms are listed below. Complete the table placing an "X" to indicate whether each example represents an active or passive method of feedback.

Feedback Mechanism	Description	Passive Feedback	Active Feedback
Chat room	A chat room for a topic related to the hosting site.		
Mailto: link on a page	Link that provides contact via direct email message for a given page.		
Paper form	Form given to members in a focus group.		
Log file showing user's path into site	Log file data via an http reference that indicates the route by which a user entered the site.		
Interview with stakeholder	Interview conducted with a key stakeholder in a site to determine content validity.		

9.2.2 CHOOSING AN APPROPRIATE FEEDBACK MECHANISM

a) Which forms of feedback should be included in a site such as the FANNC site?

LAB 9.2 EXERCISE ANSWERS

9.2.1 ANSWERS

a) Various forms of feedback mechanisms are listed below. Complete the table placing an "X" to indicate whether each example represents an active or passive method of feedback.

Answer: Most of these require active feedback on the part of the user. See the table on p. 281 for specific details.

9.2.2 ANSWERS

a) Which forms of feedback should be included in a site such as the FANNC site?

Answer: FANNC, as a volunteer nonprofit organization, should make sure that its feedback mechanisms supply not only adequate access to the information of the site but also help to expand their sources of information and volunteer resources. In addition to the basic feedback mechanisms, a forum or bulletin board service might be an excellent idea. Allowing visitors to share their experiences in dealing with fleas might:

1. Expand the knowledge base of the network.
2. Give the organization a "trend-spotting source." (It may be that if the site is heavily used, that data regarding product effectiveness, variations in flea populations, etc. might be collected.)
3. Increase visitor "buy-in" to the organization that might result in a greater pool of volunteers or donations.
4. Generate a source of revenue for the site. Forums and bulletin boards with high volume are frequently good places to place advertisements—a flea-bomb manufacturer might spend a lot on ad space on a heavily used forum on fleas.

Feedback Mechanism	Description	Passive Feedback	Active Feedback
Chat room	A chat room for a topic related to the hosting site.		X (This requires that visitors post messages.)
Mailto: link on a page	Link that provides a contact via direct email message for a given page.		X (Visitors here must choose to click on the link and write an email message.)
Paper form	Form given to members in a focus group.		X (Focus group members must show up for the meeting and fill out the form.)
Log file showing user's path into site	Log file data via an http reference that indicates the route by which a user en-tered the site.	X (Visitors are tracked as they go about their exploration of the site. They are not required to do anything to reg-ister their presence.)	
Interview with stake-	Interview con-ducted with a key stakeholder in a site to determine content validity.		X (Stakeholder must make time for the meeting and respond to questions.)

LAB 9.2 SELF-REVIEW QUESTIONS

In order to test your progress, you should be able to answer the following questions.

1) A well-designed, well-tested site does not need to supply contact information.

   a) _____ True
   b) _____ False

2) The best information is obtained via active feedback mechanisms.

a) _____ True
b) _____ False

3) Which of the following methods of obtaining feedback are most likely to make users feel a "part of a community" in using them?

a) _____ a Web-based form
b) _____ a focus group
c) _____ a chat room
d) _____ a mailto: link

4) Feedback should be solicited from sources other than a site's users.

a) _____ True
b) _____ False

5) People are likely to provide unsolicited feedback.

a) _____ True
b) _____ False

6) Focus groups should contain

a) _____ a broad cross-section of the population.
b) _____ a mix of general population members and people who specifically match the target audience.
c) _____ a project manager associated with the site.
d) _____ only members of the target audience.

7) Deep sites with many sub-sites and referred pages require a different approach to providing feedback mechanisms.

a) _____ True
b) _____ False

8) Contact points in a Web site should be restricted to highly structured Web forms to filter input.

a) _____ True
b) _____ False

Quiz answers appear in the Appendix, Section 9.2.

CHAPTER 9

TEST YOUR THINKING

1) Given the opportunities for active and passive feedback you can obtain from those who use your Web site, describe three methods you would implement.

2) Describe what you could expect to learn from each feedback method and how it could impact your site.

GROWTH, REVISION, AND MIGRATION

The real problem is not whether machines think but whether men do.

—B. F. Skinner

CHAPTER OBJECTIVES

In this chapter, you will learn about:

- ✔ Accommodating Growth   Page 286
- ✔ When to Revise   Page 301
- ✔ Site Migration   Page 314

The Web is a dynamic place, changing and growing each minute. A healthy Web site is a changing Web site, and strategies for successful maintenance must address the needs for growth and change. For a successful site, revision will begin almost as soon as it is published and will continue for the life of a site. While everyone knows that it takes planning and resources to build a site, many forget that revising a site requires just as much thought and attention, if the site is to continue in a successful manner. Think of the release point of a Web site as 1.0, the immediate tweaking that comes with real-world operation as 1.1, and the first large adaptation to the market (usually in three to six months after launch) as 2.0. All of these releases and revisions should be done in a professional, planned way. Maintenance in a site's first year of operation (including revisions and additions) can cost from one-half to twice as much as the cost to build the site in the first place. Failure to properly maintain the site is to throw away the entire initial investment.

LAB 10.1

ACCOMMODATING GROWTH

LAB OBJECTIVES

After this lab, you will be able to:

✔ Identify Organizational Schemes
✔ Identify Organizational Structures
✔ Label Content
✔ Convert Labels to a Subdirectory Structure

A set of html pages does not a Web site make. A well-organized Web site is not necessarily recognized as such, but shows itself as a site that is easy to use and navigate. The person who is responsible for organizing the content is sometimes referred to as the "Information Architect," and this role may well fall to the Webmaster. Even if you are not directly involved in organizing the Web site content or you inherited an organization that can't be significantly altered, understanding schemes and structures can make future organizational decisions easier to make.

Web site content organization is often reflected in the navigational menus, page labels, and site indexing. Significant Web site growth, if not accounted for up front, may have negative effects on site navigation. Reorganizing all the pages in a Web site to accommodate new pages or subjects will no doubt cause broken links and probably annoy or alienate users. Planning for site growth is a stronger position to be in from the start.

ORGANIZATIONAL SCHEMES

We all organize information every day and use information others have organized for us, with various degrees of success. Consider the telephone books. If you are looking for a person's telephone number, opening up the white pages and looking up the last name is straightforward. This is an example of an *exact* organizational scheme. There is no question about how the information is listed—alphabetically by last name. Other exact schemes include chronological (assuming everyone agrees on the date) and geographical (when border disputes are not involved).

Now, when you go to the yellow pages to find a car repair shop, it is not as obvious. Do you look under repair, car, or automobile? It often takes several tries to figure out exactly where to look in the book or even in the index. The yellow pages are organized by function, using an *ambiguous* scheme. Although ambiguous schemes are more difficult to organize, they give users more opportunities to find what they are looking for, and sometimes much more. Just like browsing the Web, while looking for a car repair shop in the yellow pages, you may find an antique car dealer with the parts you need. Incidental learning is facilitated by ambiguous organizational schemes. And finding a car repair shop without a company name would be very difficult in the white pages. Other examples of ambiguous organizational schemes include task-oriented (like the dropdown menus on a word processor's main menu bar), audience-specific (public, media, investors), and metaphor-driven (departments in a shopping mall).

Hybrid organizational schemes, especially when evident on the top page of a Web site, can be very confusing to the user. Without looking, the user can't "intuit" what will appear when a link is selected. Hybrid schemes are probably not planned, but just happen as a result of not planning or not knowing about organizational schemes. For small or personal sites, having a detailed organizational plan is not an issue. But for large sites, preplanning an organizational scheme is essential to accommodate future growth.

ORGANIZATIONAL STRUCTURES

There are really only three organizational structures used in Web sites. We're all familiar with the *hierarchical* structure, common to organizational charts and computer file systems. This top down approach is a good place to start when organizing new information. The question is just how deep or how flat the structure should be to maximize usefulness for the user and still allow for site growth. Too many top levels may not fit well with the navigational model. People seem to do best with from five to nine list items. With more than nine elements, users search too hard to find what they need. However, trying to stay within the nine-item limit while forcing users to click down many layers to get to what they need will not work either.

The *database* structure is also familiar to us, but not well adapted for all types of Web content. There are segments of Web content that fit exceptionally well within the database model, such as personnel directory. The phone book could be offered as a database, using a search form to retrieve data. The phonebook could also, depending on the size of the staff, be provided as an alphabetical listing by last name or by department. These pages can be generated upon request from the database.

The last structure, *hypertext,* is the basis for the Web. This model relies on chunks of information and links between them. Hypertext is a valuable intermediary between the hierarchical and database structures, but a site based entirely on hypertext would be very difficult to navigate.

LABELING

Even the best organizational schemes and structures have limited value if the categories are mislabeled. Labels are used in page headings and subheadings and, especially important, in navigational systems. A label that adequately reflects the content is essential. If the user must click on the link to figure out what it leads to, the link is badly labeled. Keeping the label short is a real advantage if you are turning the label into a button, but it may not be the best way to convey information about the content. Keeping the content fairly narrow will facilitate accurate labeling, but this is not always feasible. Making consistent use of labels throughout a site, even to their format style, will increase usability.

One method for organizing links into categories and then labeling the categories was described by Jakob Nielsen (www.useit.com) and seems to work pretty well. We call it the "cards system." The process is fairly simple. First, create index cards with each link briefly described on a separate card. Find six to ten people who represent potential users of the site. These users should span from beginners to advanced Web users, and from those who know little about the topic to those who are familiar with it. Ask this test group to sort and group the cards into five to seven categories. Once sorted, each is asked to create a label for the category. With this small set of people, you'll be amazed at how much useful and creative information will be generated. One problem we have as Webmasters is that we are often very familiar with the material and we don't even look at the labels because we know where everything is located. This method of categorizing and labeling adds some distance to the process and will no doubt provide better, more intuitive, labels for the information in your site.

CONVERTING LABELS TO SUBDIRECTORY STRUCTURE

In addition to the root of your URL, the domain name, your site has an "extended address"—the paths leading to the rest of the pages on your site. Again, this is another area where you can make it easier for your users to get a feel for your site and navigate more surely through the pages. If you use the labels you identified above as your subdirectory names, users will have one more clue where

Table 10.1 ■ Examples of Skaboard's Page Names

Page Name	Page Contents
binding_prod.html	Descriptions of various bindings for snowboards.
binding_supt.html	Tips and tricks for use of different types of bindings. Links to contact information.
binding_price.html	Prices lists and in-stock status for various bindings.
binder_cables.html	Descriptions of various types of binder cables.
binder_cablesprice.html	Price lists and in-stock status of various types of binder cables.
clips_hints.html	Hints for using clips.
clips_prod.html	Descriptions of clip products.
jackets.html	Descriptions of jackets.
pants.html	Descriptions of pants.
wax_faq.html	FAQs on wax types and uses.
wax_prod.html	Descriptions of types of wax.
wax_table.html	Tables illustrating and comparing optimum usage conditions for various types of wax.
wax_supt.html	Support information regarding waxes, includes links to manufacturer spec sheets and contact information.

they are located by looking at the URL. Table 10.1 contains a list of pages and their contents in the SkaBoards site.

A user approaching the SkaBoards site for help using his new snowboard may be helped and reassured by an orderly structuring of the site's pages. Grouping the pages into directories that reflect their function can help identify for a user where he or she is in the site and can allow the use of shortcuts for navigating the site (Table 10.2).

These URLs clearly indicate to users when they are in a support area or a sales area of the site. They also allow the user to more easily "bounce" back to the top page of the specific area they're exploring, no matter how deeply into that region they've gone (a select-and-delete return in the URL window can be much quicker than clicking one's way back).

Table 10.2 ▪ Examples of SkaBoard's Subdirectory Structure

Directory	Contains	Results in a URL of
Products	index.html	http://www.skaboards.com/products/
	binding_prod.html	http://www.skaboards.com/products/binding_prod.html
	binder_cables.html	http://www.skaboards.com/products/binder_cables.html
	clips_prod.html	http://www.skaboards.com/products/clips_prod.html
	jackets.html	http://www.skaboards.com/products/jackets.html
	pants.html	http://www.skaboards.com/products/pants.html
	wax_prod.html	http://www.skaboards.com/products/wax_prod.html
Support	index.html	http://www.skaboards.com/support/
	binding_supt.html	http://www.skaboards.com/support/binding_supt.html
	clips_hints.html	http://www.skaboards.com/support/clips_hints.html
	wax_faq.html	http://www.skaboards.com/support/wax_faq.html
	wax_supt.html	http://www.skaboards.com/support/wax_supt.html

LAB 10.1 EXERCISES

10.1.1 IDENTIFY ORGANIZATIONAL SCHEMES

The following is a random list of links found at the top of the home page for a research institution. These links lead to pages of more links, presumably fitting the titles.

Announcements	Computing
Research Program	Search
Scientific Information	Phonebook
Working Here	Feedback
Organization	Home

a) How would you organize these links (exact, ambiguous, or hybrid)? Explain.

_____

_____

_____

_____

b) Does the content you expect to see at the other end of any of these links lend itself to an exact organizational scheme?

_____

_____

_____

c) Does the content you expect to see at the other end of any of these links lend itself to an ambiguous organizational scheme?

_____

_____

_____

_____

10.1.2 IDENTIFY ORGANIZATIONAL STRUCTURES

Consider the following set of Web pages for a small manufacturing company. The main pages are indicated in bold. These labels are used in the sitewide navigation tools.

Product List
Contact Us
Related Links
Online Security

Order Form
Product 1 Description
Product 1 Consumer Testimonials
Product 1 User's Guide
Product 1 Reviews
Who Are We
Product 2 Description
Product 2 Consumer Testimonials
Product 2 User's Guide
Product 2 Reviews
Search Our Web
National & Regional Retailers
Distributors
Local (by State) Retailers
E-commerce & Catalogs
Site Map
FAQ
Search the Knowledge Base
Retailer Testimonials
Investor Information
Ask the Experts
Test Your Knowledge

   a) Sort these pages such that they reflect a hierarchical subdirectory structure. Remember the 5–9 category rule.

   _____

   _____

   _____

   _____

   _____

   _____

b) Assume that the Local (by State) Retailers page contains a total of thirty retailers in ten states. Would you use a hierarchical or database structure to organize this information?

_____

_____

c) Would your answer to (b) change if there were 200 retailers located in 30 states?

_____

_____

10.1.3 LABEL CONTENT

Use the hierarchical structure you designed in Exercise 10.1.2a for this exercise.

a) You need to design a small navigational tool for this site. Create short labels for the main sections you identified to use on the bar.

_____

_____

b) You decided against the graphical navigation tool. You now decide to use a bullet list to access the subcategories. Create sentence fragments to label each section of the site.

_____

_____

c) Look at the two sets of labels you created. Which set of labels do you think the first-time user of your site would prefer? Explain.

_____

_____

10.1.4 CONVERT LABELS TO A SUBDIRECTORY STRUCTURE

a) How would you group the files from the FANNC site (Table 10.3) into directories that would give you good, clear URLs?

_____

_____

_____

_____

Table 10.3 ■ Examples of FANNC Page Names

Page Name	Page Contents
fleas.html	Pictures of fleas and descriptions of types and behaviors.
tapeworms.html	Pictures of tapeworms (often resulting from flea exposure) and descriptions of types and behaviors.
flealifecycle.html	Descriptions and charts of flea's lifecycle.
about_us.html	Mission and goals of FANNC.
contact.html	Contact information for the organization.
support.html	Donation and volunteer information.
sprays_house-yard.html	Reviews of products and links to external manufacturer and retail sites.
sprays_animal.html	Descriptions of various types of products to remove animal stains.
predators.html	Natural predators of fleas and how to promote them.
collars.html	Reviews of flea collars for animals.
dips.html	Reviews of flea shampoos and dips for animals.
otherlinks.html	Links to other related sites.
books.html	Recommended books on flea control.

LAB 10.1 EXERCISE ANSWERS

10.1.1 ANSWERS

There is no single "right" answer for these questions.

a) How would you organize these links (exact, ambiguous, or hybrid)? Explain.

Answer: Using an exact organizational scheme would lead to the following order:

Announcements

Computing

Feedback

Home

Organization

Phonebook

Research Program

Search

Scientific Information

Working Here

This might be okay if this is a relatively short page. However, some of the links seem like useful tools that the user might want on all pages in the site, such as Announcements, Feedback, Home, Phonebook, and Search. In a perfect world, the remaining links could then be organized exactly, such as:

Computing

Organization

Research Program

Scientific Information

Working Here

Now, this is where company politics plays a role. Since the research program is probably the real and perceived most important role at this facility, followed by scientific information, these two links will probably be at the very top of the page so they appear "above the fold" as it were. Ultimately this leads to a hybrid organizational structure. Unless content is very narrow, hybrid schemes may be a necessity.

b) Does the content you expect to see at the other end of any of these links lend itself to an exact organizational scheme?

Answer: The phonebook lends itself to an exact scheme, based on last name. There may be other "sorts" of the data, such as by department or by extension. The announcements could also be organized in an exact scheme by date.

c) Does the content you expect to see at the other end of any of these links lend itself to an ambiguous organizational scheme?

Answer: Most sections, except the phonebook and announcements, will be organized using an ambiguous scheme. For instance, the links under the Research Program may be organized by experiment or organizational unit. There is no one "obvious" way to sort the links, other than alphabetically, and that is not always useful. Sorting the links into groups that make sense to the organization will make the links easier to find, especially for those users who don't necessarily think linearly.

10.1.2 ANSWERS

There is no single "right" answer for these questions.

a) Create a hierarchical subdirectory structure to organize this information. Remember the 5–9 category rule.

Answer: It might look something like this:

Category 1

Product List
Product 1 Description
Product 1 Consumer Testimonials
Product 1 Reviews
Product 2 Description
Product 2 Consumer Testimonials
Product 2 Reviews

Category 2

Who Are We
Investor Information
FAQ
Related Links

Category 3

Retailer Testimonials

Distributors

E-commerce & Catalogs

Local (by State) Retailers

National & Regional Retailers

Order Form

Online Security

Category 4

Product 1 User's Guide

Product 2 User's Guide

Search the Knowledge Base

Test Your Knowledge

Category 5

Ask the Experts

Contact Us

Search Our Web

Site Map

b) Assume that the Local (by State) Retailers page contains a total of thirty retailers in ten states. Would you use a hierarchical or database structure to organize this information?

Answer: If there is easy access to a Web-enabled database, then put it in a database. However, for this fairly small set of numbers, a database could be overkill. The only reasonable search criterion is by state. Any finer granulation would produce a lot of "no results." Of course, each state would have access to the e-commerce, catalog, and online ordering. These could be the default response to a "no-result" database query. An alternative could be graphical—an image map of the United States with the states linked to lists of retailers in that state.

c) Would your answer to (b) change if there were 200 retailers located in 30 states?

Answer: Absolutely. With over 200 retailers in 30 states consumers would get frustrated scrolling through lists of retailers. A database would be a much better solution to handling this data.

10.1.3 ANSWERS

There is no single "right" answer for these questions.

a) You need to design a small navigational tool for this site. Create short labels for the main sections you identified to use on the bar.

*Answer: Products * Where to Buy * Support * Search * About Us*

b) You decided against the graphical navigation tool. You now decide to use a bullet list to access the subcategories. Create sentence fragments to label each section of the site.

Answer: Find Out About Our Products

Purchasing Online or at Your Local Retailer

User's Guide and Support

Contact Us, Ask Our Experts, or Search Our Site

Learn About Us and Investor Opportunities

c) Look at the two sets of labels you created. Which set of labels do you think the first time user of your site would prefer? Explain.

Answer: One distinct advantage to bullet lists is that the user can use the "find in this page" feature to look for specific words. With bullet lists there is a greater chance that descriptive words will be used. When confined to the artificial construct of graphical "buttons," mislabeling will have a more serious impact on usability. If the buttons are described and linked early in the site, then using the bullets as navigation will work better. There will always be a compromise between design and function. Labeling was much more difficult in the early days of the Web when using precise metaphors illustrated by icons was common. Developing icons that are universally recognized is an art form!

10.1.4 ANSWERS

a) How would you group the files from the FANNC site into directories that would give you good, clear URLs?

Answer: There is no one "right way" to group pages into a coherent site, but the grouping should follow related functions. One possible way is shown in Table 10.4. In this sample, the pages that deal with FANNC as an organization are left at the top level of the directory system, which would result in pages about the institution as a whole coming directly after the domain name (www.fannc.org/about_us.html). The pages dealing with products, remedy, flea facts, etc. are grouped into directories reflecting their overall content (www.fannc.org/resources/otherlinks.html).

Table 10.4 ■ FANNC Pages Grouped in Subdirectories

Top Level	fleas/	controls/	resources/
about_us.html	fleas.html	sprays_house-yard.html	otherlinks.html
contact.html	flealifecycle.html	sprays_animal.html	books.html
support.html	tapeworms.html	predators.html	
		collars.html	
		dips.html	

LAB 10.1 SELF-REVIEW QUESTIONS

In order to test your progress, you should be able to answer the following questions.

1) Web site organization and ease of navigation are not related.

   a) _____ True
   b) _____ False

2) Which of the following types of data lends itself to an exact organizational scheme?

   a) _____ Phonebook
   b) _____ Task list
   c) _____ Corporate structure
   d) _____ Library listing

3) The Web as a whole uses a(n) _____ organizational structure.

   a) _____ hierarchical
   b) _____ ambiguous
   c) _____ hypertext
   d) _____ database

4) A database would be the best solution for access to which of the following data on a Web page?

   a) _____ Your to-do list
   b) _____ Phonebook for a company with less than 20 employees
   c) _____ Hundreds of store locations across the country
   d) _____ Product description

Quiz answers appear in the Appendix, Section 10.1

LAB 10.2

WHEN TO REVISE

LAB OBJECTIVES

After this lab, you will be able to:

✔ Know What Constitutes a Revision
✔ Understand the Reasons for Revision
✔ Plan an Appropriate Revision Cycle

Revision is a vital part of the lifecycle of a Web site; it not only fixes what is wrong, but also adjusts the site to its audience with increasing accuracy and stimulates site traffic by providing visitors with a fresh experience. Revision is a process as integral to the business of the site as the changing of window-dressing is essential to the public image of a successful department store. Successful Web sites stay successful by being refreshed and revitalized on a regular basis. Fresh offerings in both content and presentation encourage visitors to come back and see what's new and to tell their friends about what they've seen. Periodic revision not only provides a stimulating experience for visitors, it is also a good opportunity to fine-tune the site to match the constantly changing demographics and trends of the Web.

IS IT REVISION OR MAINTENANCE?

A revision to a Web site is a change in the content or organization of the site that substantially affects the look and feel of the overall site or significantly alters the technology of the site. A revision is something more than the simple content changes that are a part of everyday maintenance on a site. For example, the FANNC site has a jump page linking out to individual descriptions and lifecycle pages for the fleas and ticks common to Northern California. If, in recent months, they discover that a large number of sightings of the Eastern Deer Flea (formerly thought to be common only to the Northeast) in the northwestern sector of the state, they might decide to add a new page, linked from the jump page to cover that flea. This is not a revision. It is an addition of similar content that will not alter the overall design of the site or significantly alter the navigation of the site. It does not add or subtract from the site's functionality. It is a simple content addition. If, however, FANNC decides to take all of its flea pages, move them into another area of the site, and link to them from another page (eliminating the jump page entirely), then they are changing how clients will find and navigate to those pages. This would be a revision to the site, not a simple content addition or deletion.

REASONS FOR REVISION

There are many reasons to revise a Web site, some related to the rapid change of technology, others to changes in site content, and yet others related to reactions from or changes to the site's audience. Among the major reasons for revision are:

- Changing site content
- Adapting to available technology
- Taking advantage of new resources
- Responding to the site's audience

CHANGING SITE CONTENT

By far the most common reason for revision of a Web site is a significant content change. Revisions to include new content or to update stale content are a critical part of maintaining the credibility of a Web site. A site with information that is out of date or content that never changes risks its credibility in the same way that a department store displaying dated, faded window dressings sends its customers the message that it is behind the times and perhaps on its way out.

Sites with product sales should update content regularly to feature a changing array of featured products and to keep their sales and other promotional devices fresh and interesting. These sites need to plan for regular revisions to certain areas of their Web site. Content in these sites should also include keeping the "press and reviews" area for the site (in which favorable product reviews are featured) current and well populated.

Information sites should include timely checks with content experts as part of their revision cycle to make sure that the site accurately reflects the latest information available in the topic area.

■ *FOR EXAMPLE*

FANNC would want to include periodic checks with state agencies and entomologists, as well as contacts with universities and pest-control industry experts to be sure that its site contains the most up-to-date information on flea control. Even if there are no breakthroughs requiring major changes in the site, a revision cycle could include an expansion of an existing topic to offer more depth or extended links to related sites. It is in FANNC's interest to use revision cycles to expand the depth as well as the breadth of its coverage of the topics.

ADAPTING TO AVAILABLE TECHNOLOGY

Web technology changes at an astonishing rate and it is very easy for a site to appear dated simply through a failure to adapt to current technology. Continuing to format your product price tables using the <PRE> tag is a sure way to date your site back to the dark ages of the Web, no matter how current your content may be. This is not to say that it is necessary to adopt every gizmo and whistle that comes along, just to look "cool." It is, however, in your best interest to be familiar with the available technology so that you can make the best decisions about what should or should not be used in your site (see Chapter 12, "Advanced Features and Accessibility," for more discussion on the choice of appropriate technologies).

Revisions in the technology arena may be as simple as keeping pace with the Web clients available or it may include revising your information delivery system to include an interactive database as your site's online business expands. A simple listing of forty products with stable pricing is an easy, hard-coded list to maintain. If, however, business is booming and the product line expands to include 300 items from varying manufacturers with fluctuating prices, your opportunities for misquotes and maintenance headaches increase dramatically. Under such circumstances, it would be wise to consider moving your price list from a hard-coded table to a database with dynamic page delivery.

TAKING ADVANTAGE OF NEW RESOURCES

As the Web grows, so do the opportunities to enrich your site by taking advantage of information or services available from other sites. A bed and breakfast site in Bermuda may find that it can enhance the attractiveness of its site and increase its traffic by linking to related sites such as airline flight status sites and the Chamber of Commerce site for the island. This allows it to form a one-stop nexus for travel to Bermuda without dramatically increasing its own maintenance costs. Keep a sharp eye out for sites that you can leverage to deepen the value of your site. Explore the possibilities of cross-linking or partnerships across sites. Just as small storefront businesses can benefit from critical mass proximity ("business districts" and "shopping districts" or malls), so it can benefit a Web site to form a virtual district by offering easy access to (and, with cooperation, easy return from) related or complementary services.

RESPONDING TO THE AUDIENCE

A site's audience may also be the driver for site revision, because of direct response to the site or from changing demographics in the target population.

■ FOR EXAMPLE

ABC Hardware's Web site contains a number of feedback mechanisms to solicit responses from its visitors (see Lab 9.2, "Obtaining Feedback," for more details on this topic), including a mailto link to the Webmaster. Through this link, the Webmaster receives a number of comments from visitors indicating that the site should offer more detailed information on the lawnmowers being sold, information like mileage, blade width, and cutting heights. In checking the site, the Webmaster realizes that such information is indeed available, but only on each individual mower's product description page. Revision of site content is indicated by these direct suggestions, as visitors are not finding the information that clearly exists. In this case, it's possible that what the site needs is a comparison chart showing the features of all of the lawnmowers in a single location.

You may also need to revise a Web site based upon external factors such as a change in demographics in the users of a site. A sleepy agricultural community that finds itself "discovered" as a tourist destination may need to rethink the structure of its community Web site when it realizes that the information in its pages is more geared toward the local community than the visitors they now want to cultivate.

REVISION CYCLES

Plan for revision. Include it as a part of the initial scope of the project and then establish a regular cycle for revision that will allow for proper consultation and feedback with all appropriate parties.

Regular revision cycles will not only make it easier to bring in proper consultants to the process, it will make it easier to control "feature creep"—the process of small, gradual accretions to a Web site that can turn a well-designed site into an unsightly, unusable mess. Very few Web designers/developers show their portfolio pieces by linking to the actual sites hosted on their clients' servers, preferring to provide these sites on CD or as hosted on their own server. This is because few clients plan adequately for maintenance up front, leaving the newly released site and its subsequent revisions to the mercy of someone in-house who can "do HTML." Within months these sites are subject to a variety of accretive elements; aggressive forces within the organization who seek higher prominence on the welcome page, great ideas from marketing, "just a little adjustment" from the page maintainer, and so on.

Rather than react to a constant series of small, potentially conflicting tweaks, establish a schedule under which you will revise the site. As suggestions and other feedback come in, keep track of them and assign them a place in the revision cycle where they can be considered in context. A revision cycle allows you to accumulate all of the suggestions, critiques, and statistics and evaluate them as a group, taking into consideration the planned directions for growth, the site's mission, and the technologies available at the time of the revision. This can allow you to spot potential conflicts and consult with the appropriate people to resolve those conflicts before they cost you large amounts of wasted effort and adversely affect your site.

■ FOR EXAMPLE

Consider the following fairly common happening. Judy, the Webmaster of Ska-Boards, is told that in addition to the phone numbers, e-mail addresses, and areas of expertise provided on the "Contact Us" page, she should add employee photographs so that customers can feel that they are getting in touch with a real person. She spends two weeks begging for suitable pictures of all of the customer service and tech support employees (photos in proper SkaBoard attire and attitude), scans and adjusts them for the Web, and puts them in place. One week later, the decision is made to eliminate individuals from the "Contact Us" and route everyone through a single, generic Customer Service phone number and e-mail address. Her work was wasted, the person who had the "personal touch" idea was disgruntled, and, what is worse, the rapid and contradictory changes that showed up on the site cannot help but communicate uncertainty and lack of clear planning to the site's regular customers. Had both suggestions been collected and held for "Web site v.3.5," the conflict would have become clear immediately and she would have been able to consult with the principals involved, saving time, feelings, and institutional image. She might even have been able to have the time to ask someone to do some research into contact patterns and their accuracy to indicate which way was in fact the best way to handle initial customer contacts.

A revision cycle should include scheduling for both major revisions (Web site v.1.0, 2.0, 3.0) that can change the character and overall experience of the site, and for minor revisions (v.1.5, 2.5) that adjust or fine-tune the site to its existing purpose.

SETTING UP A REVISION CYCLE

How frequently should you revise? The interval between revisions will depend on several factors, including

- The nature of the Web site's content: Does it change frequently? Is it a high-volume sales site that must pump up the excitement?

- The human and financial resources available for implementation: Does the developer have time? How frequently can the organization afford to put time and money into a revision? Are the necessary stakeholders available for consultation?

- External factors, including changes in technology and marketplace competition: Can you afford not to keep up with your competitors?

Most Web sites with changing content and active commercial interests consider three to four months to be standard for a revision cycle: frequent enough to pique the users' interest, not so frequent as to undermine the site's continuity.

 Some sites or subsites within an organization may not require frequent revision because their content is relatively static. The faculty roster of a university, for example, may not need updating or revising more than once each academic year, as the faculty is comprised of a relatively stable population. To reduce maintenance costs, one can build in a "news and updates" section to sites such as faculty rosters that would let you update a single page with flashy new looks and announcements regarding awards, appointments, and so on, without having to redo the entire site concept more than once a year.

Table 10.5 looks at some of the factors that may affect a Web site's revision cycle.

Table 10.5 ■ Correlation between Site Content and Revision Cycle

Content	Short Revision Cycle Interval (1 to 4 wks.)	Medium Revision Cycle Interval (2 to 4 mos.)	Long Revision Cycle Interval (6 mos. to 1 yr.)
Static content (e.g., list of flea types and their distribution)			No pressure, can set the schedule at will, to change looks or to accommodate new technology.
Sales-related content (product and pricing information, for example)	This could fall under either category, depending on the clientele. The shorter cycle would be for sites with a strong "hype" or "jazz" element that requires more novelty.		

(continued)

Table 10.5 ■ continued

Content	Short Revision Cycle Interval (1 to 4 wks.)	Medium Revision Cycle Interval (2 to 4 mos.)	Long Revision Cycle Interval (6 mos. to 1 yr.)
Event calendar content ("This Week in Santa Fe")		While the content will need very frequent updating, the site design should remain fairly consistent, so clients can find their way around easily.	
Designer content (Sites for design houses and studios)	This type of content has some of the fastest revision cycles in the industry. Staying competitive means showing off all the innovation you can.		
Content consisting of corporate/large institution information		Consistency is a plus here. Major revisions (the 1.0, 2.0, and 3.0) should come fairly infrequently. Intermediate revisions (1.5, 1.75, etc.) to subsites or features come at moderate intervals.	
Content for new and rapidly growing/ changing entities (businesses just establishing a Web presence, start-ups, etc.)		While the temptation is to put the revision cycle on fast forward, holding it to a moderate pace can reduce costly mistakes and help to establish the image of a new entity.	

LAB 10.2

One of the key factors in establishing a revision cycle is to make sure that the cycle is understood and agreed to by the site's entire major participants. This is particularly important to establish at the outset of a new site project. Establish clearly what features constitute Web sites 1.0 (initial public release), 1.1 (post-release adjustment to real-world circumstances), and 1.5 (initial refinement revision). All involved need to be in agreement on the time schedule for these critical early phases of the Web site so that approvers and content providers are available at the appropriate times and developers have a clear schedule under which they will implement changes. In addition to the critical early release and revision schedule, it is also a good idea to establish agreements regarding longer-term revision cycles early in the process to avoid conflicts and misunderstandings later on. This becomes vitally important if the project is done on a contract basis. Both clients and developers need to have a clear understanding of what the design team can be expected to do as part of the initial job and what constitutes work for a longer-term maintenance contract.

LAB 10.2 EXERCISES

10.2.1 KNOW WHAT CONSTITUTES REVISION

a) Look at the list below. Which of the following changes are revisions?

1) Eliminating a banner-style button bar in favor of a sidebar with listed links.

2) Adding the area code to all of the phone numbers listed on the site's contact pages.

3) Adding four new lawnmowers and their spec pages to those available for immediate purchase.

4) Adding explanatory rollovers to all of the organization's top-level links from the home page.

5) Eliminating tabular layout design on the top-level pages and moving to CSS formatting.

6) Adding database functionality to the sales section of the site.

7) Moving your site from a Netscape server to an Apache server.

10.2.2 UNDERSTAND THE REASONS FOR REVISION

a) What are three examples of revisions that ABC Hardware might make within the next six months in order to take advantage of new technology? (See page 194 for a basic description of ABC Hardware.)

_____

_____

10.2.3 PLAN AN APPROPRIATE REVISION CYCLE

At the end of January, Judy, the Webmaster of SkaBoards, completed the release cycle of the new site, taking it to v. 1.5. In the month following the close of the release cycle, Judy has received a list of suggestions for changes to the site. She looks at the SkaBoards revision schedule and sees that:

v. 1.75 is slated for the second week in March. It will involve the addition of two new specialty boutiques to the site: Trips, a monthly feature focusing on a new, off-the-path destinations for snowboarders; and School, a tips and tricks forum for young boarders.

v. 2.0 is slated for the end of May. It will involve a "refreshing" of the site to correspond with the move into the "off season." In addition to color changes and some new video clips, the revision will bring in Stay Strong, a partnership site focusing on conditioning and sports-related injuries sponsored by the local medical school.

v. 3.0 is slated for September and, in addition to a hot new look for the next year's season, it will include a comprehensive snow conditions feature using the USGS database as a feed and a live chat forum for boarders moderated and advised by champion performers.

a) Where would the following suggestions from Judy's list be placed on this revision schedule?

1) Incorporation of a new logo, optimized for online display.
2) Add the new Elastotek bindings to the product line, along with photo displays and pricing.

3) Automate on-line purchasing, adding shopping cart features and delivery memos.
4) Add a novelty feature, 101 Words for Snow, giving pronunciation guides and physical descriptions for the Umiak, Swedish, and Norwegian words for different types of snow.
5) Establish a "Reader's Rating" center for resort services where members of the online community rate the ski resorts and provide anecdotes.

LAB 10.2 EXERCISE ANSWERS

10.2.1 ANSWERS

a) Which of the following are revisions?
   1) Eliminating a banner-style button bar in favor of a sidebar with listed links.

Answer: This is a revision; it substantially changes the mode of navigation for the site and will have a significant effect on the design and presentation of the pages.

   2) Adding the area code to all of the phone numbers listed on the site's contact pages.

Answer: This is a minor content change and in most cases would not be considered a revision.

   3) Adding four new lawnmowers and their spec pages to those available for immediate purchase.

Answer: This is a content change, merely adding to the stock that is presented.

   4) Adding explanatory rollovers to all of the organization's top-level links from the home page.

Answer: This is a revision, changing the technology of the navigation in the site. Questions such as "What percentage of our users have JavaScript enabled?" are of critical importance when considering a revision of this kind.

   5) Eliminating tabular layout design on the top-level pages and moving to CSS formatting.

Answer: As is the case with the previous example, this changes the technology of the navigation and is a revision.

   6) Adding database functionality to the sales section of the site.

Answer: This is a revision.

   7) Moving your site from a Netscape server to an Apache server.

Answer: This is a revision. Major involvement of stakeholders will be needed to consider and implement such a change.

10.2.2 ANSWERS

a) What are three examples of revisions that ABC Hardware might make within the next six months in order to take advantage of technology they have not yet implemented?

Answer: There are many changes that ABC Hardware, a relatively low-technology site, could make within the next six months. Some possibilities include:

On a fairly modest level, ABC could provide a target page linked from each of its lawnmower pages providing an at-a-glance comparison of the various models as was discussed in the example in Exercise 10.1.1.

ABC could implement a reader service section with interactive capabilities such as an online garden diary for members (log on and record your planting and bloom notes on your own personalized garden site) or a project "notebook" for members to store their remodeling information (log on and record your expenses, quantities, construction notes etc. for home improvement projects).

In a more complex move, ABC Hardware could begin the move to true online commerce by providing the ability to actually purchase merchandise through the Web site as opposed to using it as an informational tool. A full e-commerce implementation for a store with as large and complex variety of products and services as ABC Hardware would most likely require more than four or five months to develop. The six-month limit in the question would most likely require limiting the development of this feature for a limited portion of the inventory: a single department or service group, perhaps.

10.2.3 ANSWERS

a) Where would the following suggestions from Judy's list be placed on this revision schedule?

Answer: The placement of any new item into the revision schedule will be determined by a wide variety of drivers, everything from who is available to implement to external considerations such as a competitor's most recent release. The answers below look only at the proposed change and the items already slated into the schedule. These "logical fit" answers may not always be appropriate in real-world situations that may be controlled by a wide range of factors.

    1) Incorporation of a new logo, optimized for online display. *This is a revision of look and representation of institutional identity. It would fit best in v. 2.0 or 3.0, revisions that will be specifically addressing the look and feel of the site.*

    2) Add the new Elastotek bindings to the product line, along with photo displays and pricing. *This is not a revision. It is an addition to an already existing content area and can be done by the site maintainer at any time.*

3) Automate online purchasing, adding shopping cart features and delivery memos. *This is a large technological revision that will change both how customers navigate the site and how they actually purchase merchandise. It would fit best in revision 3.0 for several reasons. First, revision 3.0 is already focusing on interactive technologies, so it is a good fit in terms of focus and team. In addition, revision 3.0 is scheduled to fall at the end of the "off season" a relatively slow time of year for the snow industries. There is a longer period to work on a more complex feature in a time when all stakeholders are more likely to be at liberty to collaborate in the process.*

4) Add a novelty feature, 101 Words for Snow, giving pronunciation guides and physical descriptions for the Umiak, Swedish, and Norwegian words for different types of snow. *This is a content revision and is a largely self-contained addition. It would fit in either v.1.75, a content-heavy revision, or in 2.0, as a novelty to spice up the action of the site in the off-season.*

5) Establish a "Reader's Rating" center for resort services where members of the on-line community rate the ski resorts and provide anecdotes. *Another interactive piece, this would fit the staffing and focus of v.3.0, but might also be a good feature to aim for summer release to encourage people to begin thinking about the coming season.*

LAB 10.2 SELF-REVIEW QUESTIONS

In order to test your progress, you should be able to answer the following questions.

1) What revision cycle would you expect for an informational site covering art history?

a) _____ 1 to 4 weeks
b) _____ 2 to 4 months
c) _____ 6 months to 1 year
d) _____ No revisions

2) Routine maintenance may impact site navigation.

a) _____ True
b) _____ False

3) What are some common reasons for revision?

a) _____ Adapting to new Web technology or browser features
b) _____ Moving to a new Web host site
c) _____ Log file analysis
d) _____ Comments from staff and users

4) Which of the following could be considered a major (2.0, 3.0) type revision?

    a) _____ Changing the Personnel Department to Human Resources
    b) _____ Adding an additional product line
    c) _____ Adding a new staff member to the sales staff
    d) _____ Updating the "What's New" page

Quiz answers appear in the Appendix, Section 10.2.

LAB 10.3

SITE MIGRATION

> ### LAB OBJECTIVES
>
> After this lab, you will be able to:
>
> ✔ Understand the Stages of Migration
> ✔ Set up a Migration Plan for Your Site

Migration describes the process of moving a site or pieces of a site into and out of use. Whether a new site is truly a brand new site or a revision of a previously existing site, it will likely be drafted and modified in one place and moved at least once into other space until it arrives at its live location and is linked into the Internet. Even modest revisions that include the addition or deletion of a just a few pages must go through this process. As sites age and grow, pages are moved out of service, replaced, or eliminated by the changes to the site. All of this is migration and it requires planning and structure or your site's visitors may find themselves lost in a tangle of dead ends and error messages.

STAGES OF MIGRATION

A NEW SITE

For a new site or a major revision, there are three main stages of migration: development, testing/approval, and "live." Each of these stages should take place in suitable space. It is not wise to develop a new site on a public server space unless you truly don't care that the whole world may be privy to your every spelling mistake and scripting blunder. In most circumstances, a site or a revision will often see its origins on someone's local drive or private sector of a shared space, long before it is moved to its final "live" location. In this early stage of development, pages are drafted and the basic structure and linking is established (either with actual links or placeholders for pages not yet in place), all in a local area. Backend development will be taking place, likely in a different local area. The next stage in the migration of the site is to move it to a development server (if it is not already there) for further development in a server environment. When the site is deemed ready for review, it will be moved and adapted to a test ground—a server environment that mirrors, as exactly as possible, the environment where the pages will eventually live, both in terms of software and available scripts, as well as server hardware, but is not public. It is extensively tested in this location. There are frequently a number of changes in the site that will become necessary at this stage in the site's development. Among them might be:

- Adaptation to a change in server platform, such as removing spaces from filenames for a site migrating from a Macintosh or PC development environment to hosting on a Unix server.
- Adaptation of CGI scripts to match the server software (all server software is not equal in how it relates to the world around it).
- Debugging database integration.

Once the site has been reviewed and approved in this test ground, it will be staged to its final location. It will be retested and debugged in this location until it is declared ready for its official launch and linked up. It is likely that a final round of approval might be needed at this stage as well.

MIGRATION ISSUES FOR REVISIONS AND ROUTINE MAINTENANCE

Many sites that began as pristine models of professionalism and state-of-the-art navigation have, over time, deteriorated into messy tangles that do not reflect well on their organizations and frustrate their users. Under these circumstances, loyal customers find that their bookmarked pages return Error 404s and new visitors may be put off by internal links arriving at outdated pages. Careful planning for migration takes into consideration that a site's pages will not "live" forever and will avoid the vast majority of these transitional woes. Through time, pages in a site will be retired from use or replaced by other pages. To avoid leading a site's users to dead ends and frustration, migration should follow two simple rules:

- Never leave a hole.
- Always provide a path from old to new.

■ FOR EXAMPLE

When SkaBoards first went on line, the "breaking news" section of their site was called *In the News* and the URL for the top page in that sector was www. skaboards.com/news.html. In their second major revision, SkaBoards replaced *In the News* with a trendier section called *Hot Stuff*, which contained service reviews, boarding tidbits, and industry gossip, all collected into a single directory /hot. The URL and top page path for the reconfigured news section was http://www.skaboards.com/hot/index.html. Recognizing that some of their customers may have bookmarked new.html (and that it would take a while for external links to their site to change), SkaBoards provided a path from the old destination to its replacement. The old page, news.html was renamed newsold.html. A new page, news.html was put in place announcing the change and redirecting the user from the news.html page to /hot/index.html.

SkaBoards' migration followed both of the rules. The retired page was not simply deleted, it was turned into a redirection page and the path to the new sector was established. This method not only redirects the user to the new page, it alerts the user that a change has taken place. If the goal is to make the change as unobtrusive as possible, then an alternative method of redirection, such as a symlink, is suggested. After renaming news.html to newsold.html, SkaBoards could have set a symlink in place redirecting the user from new.html to /hot/index.html.

A WORD ON ARCHIVING

Today historians can study artifacts of earlier forms of publishing, such as merchant records of thirteenth-century wool sales in Belgium or Depression-era news bills, and get a glimpse into the lives and customs of our ancestors. Stone tablets, parchment rolls, and paper have held their marks over time. This new form of publishing, the Web, is of a different nature, leaving far fewer traces of its evolution and the culture that surrounds it. While we can still look at ninth-century shopping lists, we are already hard-pressed to find any actual pages from the Web's "ancient history" in the early 1990s. There are many today that say that it is our responsibility to preserve the traces of our medium and provide for a systematic archiving of our records. As is the case with some models of database development, this translates to "never delete anything." Move it, hide it, but don't delete it. The SkaBoards example above illustrates a simple form of "archiving." The original news.html page was not deleted; it was renamed newsold.html before the news.html redirect page was placed into the directory. If a consistent renaming scheme is maintained throughout the site over time, it is relatively easy to search out the history of the site. Some examples of renaming schemes might include:

- Append "archive" or "old" to files and directories (page_archive.html, page-old.html, pageold1.html, pageold2.html, etc.)
- Append a retirement date to filenames (page_ret990903.html, page-r950423.html, etc.)
- Append a single-letter designation for retired or dead to a filename (page-r.html, page-d.html)

Another, more complex method of archiving old pages involves setting up a special directory on a site /archive to hold all pages moved out of use. If this method is used, the pages in the directory should be commented to indicate their original placement and function and their date of retirement, as well as any other information considered pertinent or interesting.

To be certain that old pages are not confused with those of the current site, pages that have been removed from active service should carry a clearly visible statement of their retired status. A statement such as, "This page was retired from active service on dd Month YYYY," or "This page is no longer maintained. Last update: dd Month YYYY," would be sufficient. A courtesy link to the top page of the site or a search engine may also be added.

While the need for archival awareness may be very clear in some sites, such as those of major research institutions, it is very hard to tell what may be historically significant before it actually becomes history.

Decisions on whether to follow a system of archival for a site should be made early, before it is too late to recover the pieces that may prove to be the most interesting. In addition to involving the appropriate organizational personnel in the archiving discussion, consider consulting an archivist as part of the process.

PLANNING FOR MIGRATION

Whether you are developing a new site or taking on an existing site, establish a migration plan and the structures that support it as early as possible. In a very large site that combines the work of many page authors, establishing the patterns of migration early will help to consolidate the site and minimize embarrassing exposures.

ESTABLISH PRODUCTION SPACE

Define the public production space of a site. This is the part of the site that is "open to the public" and should reflect only the most polished of your work. Declare it off-limits to tinkering and development. In the production space of a site, nothing that is not tested, debugged, and "ready for primetime" is permitted to appear.

ESTABLISH A TEST GROUND

Establish a behind-the-scenes test ground where all aspects of a site and its performance can be thoroughly tested before it is staged to the production space or server. The environment of this test space should mirror, as exactly as possible, the conditions of the production space where the site will eventually live. To minimize the possibility of activity in the testing space (new scripts, etc.) having a negative effect on the production server, this test space should be isolated from the production server.

ESTABLISH AN ARCHIVING POLICY AND RESOURCES TO SUPPORT IT

Decide what your archiving policy will be (none, rename older pages, move old pages to an archive directory, etc.). Make sure that all developers of the site are aware of the policy. Make sure that the resources exist to support it. If you have decided that an old page will be moved to an archiving space/directory, be sure that such a place exists and that the appropriate people have write permission to access it.

ESTABLISH A MIGRATION PATTERN

Establish at what level of development a site, subsite, or revision to a site is moved from development to test ground, from test ground to production space, and from production space to archival space. Be sure that everyone concerned is aware of those stages and is clear on the distinctions between the various stages.

LAB 10.3 EXERCISES

10.3.1 UNDERSTAND THE STAGES OF MIGRATION

a) Where should the following stages of revision be housed? Place the correct number in the blank.

   i) Development Space
  ii) Test Ground
  iii) Production Space
  iv) Archival Designation/Space

_____ Site with two or three pages complete, the remaining pages are merely placeholders

_____ A set of pages from one section of the site that were eliminated after a major revision

_____ New site, fully tested and approved by all the site's stakeholders

_____ Whole site; front-end page design is complete, database backend complete, front and back ends need to be synchronized

10.3.2 Set up a Migration Plan for Your Site

The upper image in the following figure illustrates the public pages in the current state of the art.com drawing and painting supplies sector. Marketing has advised that the distinction between pens and pencils be eliminated and that the production space be reconfigured to resemble the lower image in the diagram.

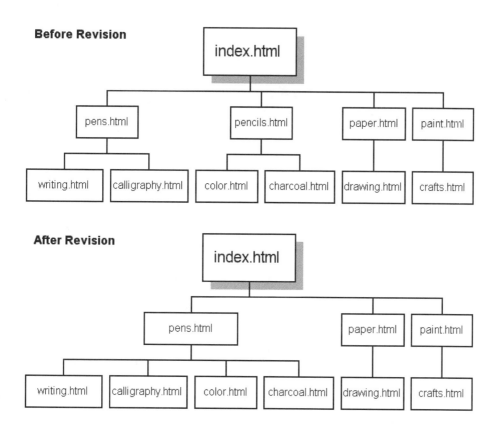

Before Revision

After Revision

a) Describe an appropriate migration process between the current site and the proposed site.

_____

_____

LAB 10.3 EXERCISE ANSWERS

10.3.1 ANSWERS

a) Where should the following stages of revision be housed? Place the correct number in the blank.

___i___ Site with two or three pages complete, the rest are merely placeholders

___iv___ A set of pages from one section of the site that were eliminated after a major revision

___iii___ New site, fully tested and approved by all the sites stakeholders

___ii___ Wholesite; front end page design is complete, database back end complete, front and back ends need to be synchronized

10.3.2 ANSWERS

a) Describe an appropriate migration process between the current site and the proposed site.

Answer: The revision to the art.com site involved the elimination of the pencil.html page and the movement of its contents to the pens.html page to form a page containing the information for both pens and pencils. To migrate to the new configuration, one possible solution would be:

- *Rename the pencils.html page as pencils_old.html to archive it and add a line or two to the page indicating that it is retired and giving the date of its retirement.*

- *Create a new pencils.html page containing a link to the newly revamped pens.html page, explaining the change (this can be combined with an automatic redirect with a timed delay to minimize user's inconvenience).*

In this solution, the first bullet takes care of the archiving issue in the simplest way (one could also migrate the page to a designated archival directory). The second bullet eliminates the hole left by the renamed page and provides a path to the new configuration.

LAB 10.3 SELF-REVIEW QUESTIONS

In order to test your progress, you should be able to answer the following questions.

1) Migration is a concern only for the movement of a new site into its public location.

a) _____ True

b) _____ False

2) For which of the following activities would you need to plan for migration?

a) _____ Updating the portrait images on the "who are we" page of the site
b) _____ Eliminating the support pages for a discontinued product
c) _____ Moving the new Web site for www.candles.com online
d) _____ Putting revision 3.0 of ABC Hardware's Lighting site online

3) What are the two most important rules of migration?

a) _____ Never leave a hole.
b) _____ Move the files.
c) _____ Provide a path from the old to the new.
d) _____ Track your changes.

4) Which of the following belong in production space?

a) _____ Testing of the integration between backend services and end user pages.
b) _____ Revision pages that have been thoroughly tested.
c) _____ A Web site or revision pages that have been tested and approved for full public release.
d) _____ A Web site that has been tested and linked on a local hard-drive.

5) Even a one-page revision should first be moved to a test ground before being placed in production space.

a) _____ True
b) _____ False

6) Archiving should be restricted to major research institutions.

a) _____ True
b) _____ False

7) The test ground for a site should be established in a region that cannot affect the production server.

a) _____ True
b) _____ False

8) Which of the following activities are appropriate for development space?

a) _____ Assembling a first draft of a site or a revision
b) _____ Preliminary link testing
c) _____ Client testing and review
d) _____ Testing backend functions with skeletal frontend placeholders

Quiz answers appear in the Appendix, Section 10.3.

CHAPTER 10

TEST YOUR THINKING

The Personnel Department at ABC Hardware changed its name to Human Resources. Their intranet Web site, located at /per/personnel.html, consists of a main page, a contacts/FAQ page, and a 20-chapter handbook. In addition to the name change, there have been many staff changes, the look and feel of the site is very dated, and the online version of the handbook hasn't been updated since 1998.

1) Develop a detailed revision plan.
2) Develop a detailed migration plan.
3) Describe who should be involved in each stage of revision and migration. (Consider the content providers, designers, Webmaster, testers, staff, computer department. . . .)
4) Would the subdirectory structure change? If so, how?

GETTING STARTED
ON THE WEB

URLs are the 800 numbers of the 1990s.

—Chris Clark

So, the powers that be have decided that a Web site will add value to your organization or promote your product. Your job is to get that Web site up and running—from domain name, hosting, development, and then promoting the site so others can find it. Not an easy task but not insurmountable either. In this chapter, we'll take a look at the steps involved in launching a Web site, from start to finish. Once the Web site is up and running, we'll look at what to do to make it noticed and keep it near the top of the search engines.

L A B 1 1 . 1

DOMAIN NAMES AND URLs

LAB OBJECTIVES

After this lab, you will be able to:

✔ Choose a Domain Name
✔ Establish a Domain Name

A URL (Universal Resource Locator, also referred to as a URI for Universal Resource Identifier) is the address you type into a Web browser to reach a specific Web site. The URL is really two parts—the protocol and the domain name. Lets look at the URL for the FANNC Web site: http://www.fannc.org/. The http://www part is the protocol and fannc.org is the domain name. Fortunately with today's browsers and servers, it is often unnecessary to type the protocol—the default protocol is assumed. As such, the domain name is increasingly important.

FUNCTION OF A DOMAIN NAME

Domain names are, in a way, like real estate—electronic real estate. It is the Web address of your site and it is unique, as no two parties can ever hold the same Web address simultaneously. Given these facts, it pays to make sure that your address is a positive reflection of your institution.

■ *FOR EXAMPLE*

Take a look at the list of street addresses below and pick out the "prestige addresses":

> 10 Park Place
> 15543 B Vermont Street
> 60 Wall Street

3698 San Jose Avenue

8 Rue de Rivoli

100034 197th Street

Chances are, you would pick the first, third, and fifth addresses as the higher-prestige addresses in the list. There are a number of factors contributing to the perception of higher prestige. The associations with the street names "Park Place" and "Wall Street" are obvious as a result of their place in cultural history; most people will recall Park Place from childhood Monopoly games and Wall Street is mentioned daily in the media as a source of power and influence. If you've ever been to Paris, Rue de Rivoli is probably a familiar street name. A more subtle distinction, however, is that the lower the street number, the more "established" an address sounds. Brick-and-mortar businesses are known for going to great lengths to situate their corporate addresses in a "prestige location" even to the extent of buying out adjacent buildings to relocate the front door to a more "valuable" street name.

WHAT'S IN A NAME

The most basic and important aspect of your Web address is the domain name. This is your "street-front address" and is what people will look for and try to remember. It will form their initial impression of your reliability and professionalism. The best names are ones that people can remember when they hear it, from a friend or over the radio, or see it on a passing truck. If the name needs to be written down, it is probably too long or not intuitive. A person looking for a reliable landscaping service is much more likely to be attracted to a site named www.hardyblooms.com than one named www.megalisters.com/users/corporate/small/hardyblooms/, which looks like it doesn't expect to be around long enough to invest in a real address that people can count on. (Something like buying your plants from the back of a truck in an empty lot—where do you go if they bloom the wrong color?)

CREATING A NAME

Make it as easy as possible for people to find you by choosing and investing in a domain name that reflects as closely as possible your institution's name or function. In some ways, this is easier than establishing a good street address in the brick-and-mortar world. You are not limited by existing street names and numbering systems. You are, however, limited by what has not already been taken. Domain name registration operates, essentially, on a first-come, first-serve basis. If you've missed the opportunity to register your actual company name, you may be forced to take an alternate route in naming your site. There have been recent court cases, though, where individuals who registered domain names with recognized trademarks have been forced to give up the name. (For a summary of this issue, see www.patents.com/pubs/comment.htm. See also Chapter 15, "Other Important Laws.") If your name isn't a trademark or you don't want to fight for the name, you may choose a less desirable name or attempt to persuade (financially or otherwise) the current holder to part with it. Many groups have found it worth their while to invest in a domain name long before they expect to establish a Web presence, just to make sure that the name is still available when they are ready to move onto the Web.

There are three top-level domains in the United States for general assignment:

- com—commercial
- org—organizations
- net—networks

There are three other specialty domains that you are not free to use, unless you fall into the specific category:

- edu—four-year, degree-granting colleges
- gov—agencies of the U.S. government
- mil—agencies of the U.S. Department of Defense

With deregulation of domain registration new domains, such as .tv, .us, and .cc, are becoming available every day. Just how widespread use of these domains will become is difficult to predict.

Sometimes your company name is too long and cumbersome to make into a clean, easily remembered name, so you need to look for an alternative. According to Network Solutions, domain names can be made up of letters, numbers, and hyphens. However, hyphens may not begin nor end the domain name. Spaces and special characters, such as exclamation points (!) and underscores (_), are not permitted. The domain name can be up to twenty-six characters long including the four characters used to identify the top-level domain (.com, .net, .org, or .edu) but excluding the protocol (http://www). The simplest method would be to use an acronym of your institution's name: ww.aip.org (American Institute of Physics), www.cbsh.com (Calloway, Barnett, Starndon, and Henley), www.atc.com (Acme Towing). Another possibility is to focus on function for your domain name, such as www.tow-u.com (Acme Towing) or www.fastfind. com (Anderson Detective Agency) or use the name of a product, such as www.snickers.com (Snickers Candy Bar).

It is fairly common practice to obtain the name in all domains. For example, when registering fannc.org, you may also want to register fannc.com and fannc.net if they are available.

What do you do with all these domain names? Hosting a single site can be costly enough; setting up three sites for each domain would be very expensive. Domain parking *is offered by many registrars and offers a place to keep the domain name so others can't register it. The service often comes with a "Coming Soon" page. As an alternative,* domain forwarding *(or domain aliasing) redirects the domains to another valid Web site. So, you can have three domains (.com, .org, and .net) redirected to the .com Web site. Some of these services offer* framed forwarding *so if you type fannc.com into the browser address, you'll be redirected to the fannc.org Web site, but fannc.com will remain in the browser address window. You can set up specific meta tags (see section 11.3) for each domain name. This service is fairly inexpensive and much easier than setting up your own name server.*

OBTAINING A DOMAIN NAME

Once you've decided on the name, there are two steps in obtaining a domain name: making sure it is available for registration, and completing and paying for the registration process.

SEARCH FOR AVAILABILITY

Once you have decided on a domain name, you need to make sure that it is available (that it hasn't been registered already by someone else). In the past, this was an easy process as InterNIC (see http://rs.internic.net/index.html), representing the Department of Commerce, held a monopoly on registering domain names. There was only one place to check. This, however, is no longer the case. There are now hundreds of domain name registrars. InterNIC provides a list of accredited registrars on its site. To check for availability, use the registrar's "whois" search service. All registrars offer a whois search, and it is a good idea to check with several registrars. Simply enter your proposed domain name (such as yourname.com) and hit Search. You will probably see one of two results: the identity of the person or company that has already registered that name or "No match for yourname.com" or "Domain is Available." If the domain is available after searching a few registrar sites, you may proceed to register that domain name.

There is one small hitch to this method: This search will only turn up a name that has actually been registered and paid for, and that process can take several weeks to complete. So if someone else is going for the same name just a bit before you, it may not show up as taken in the search, but you may not get your desired name.

REGISTER THE NAME

Registration of new domains is fairly easy—just fill out a form. But you need to have information ready before you start and it is much easier if this is all done correctly from the start. Making changes can sometimes be a challenge.

- Proposed domain name
- Registrant information (Address, City, State, Zip, Country)
- Contact information

    There are three contacts listed for each domain: Administrative, Technical, and Billing. For each type of contact you will need the name, organization, full address, phone number, fax number (optional), and email address. The first time you register as a contact you are assigned a NIC handle—your own Web ID number. This handle can be used when completing future forms.

    The Administrative and Billing email addresses are very important. In most cases these are the only people who can make changes to the registration. Make sure someone trustworthy and stable is assigned as the Administrative and Billing contact or you may find making changes to be a hassle. Generally (but not always), the Administrative contact is the Webmaster, the Technical contact is someone at the hosting location, and the Billing contact is the registrant or someone who works for the registrant.

- If the domain name will be hosted (where Web pages are actually put up) rather than just reserved (or parked), you will also need Primary and Secondary Server Hostnames and Net Addresses. The hostname is generally in the form of aaa.aaaaaaaaa.com and the netaddress is an IP, such as 111.11.111.1. These names and addresses are available from the company who will be providing the Web server.

Once the form is filled out with the registrar and submitted, you will get a confirming email. If all the information is correct (and please read it carefully), the message is usually forwarded to another email address to actually start the registration process. In the past this process was free—you didn't pay for the domain name until it cleared the registration process. Now, more and more registrars are requiring payment up front. The fee varies by registrar, but $70 for a two-year contract is fairly standard when setting up a new domain. (Domains can now be registered for up to ten years.) Fortunately, online payment is available in most cases.

If you use the NIC handle as a shortcut, please make sure it is correct. My handle is RM24396. When I completed a form, I accidentally typed RM4396. Now someone in Brazil is listed as the Administrative and Billing Contact for one of my domains. We are still trying to get this changed! Also, contact information is public so be prepared to receive unsolicited email.

Remember, if you don't want to do this yourself, the Web site hosting company may take care of all or part of the registration process, for a small fee. Or, they may recommend a registrar to use and lead you through the process. You can decide how much money your time is worth.

MAKING CHANGES TO A DOMAIN NAME REGISTRATION

As mentioned above, the usual way to make a change to information in a domain name registration is to fill out a form, similar to the one used when setting up the name, with the revised information. The form contents are then sent to the email account on record for the administrative contact. Once that person sends the mail back to the appropriate email address, the change will make its way through all the domain servers. This can take several weeks to process.

If you are changing the name of the administrative contact, the former contact needs to cooperate and return the mail from the email address listed on the form. If the administrative contact's email address is no longer valid, you have a registration problem that can't be handled through the automated email processes.

LAB 11.1 EXERCISES

11.1.1 CHOOSE A DOMAIN NAME

> **a)** What would be appropriate domain names for the following businesses?
>
> > i) Ace Aquatica Aquarium Products—Manufactures aquarium supplies such as scrapers, fake plants, nets, plastic figurines, etc. for the home aquarium market.

_____

_____

ii) Dame, Underhill, Maste, and Peel—Tax accounting firm
catering to the residential market.

_____

_____

iii) Party Time—Event coordinators specializing in social events
for civic and charitable groups.

_____

_____

iv) Chambers School for Boys—A preparatory school for
boys, specializing in college preparatory coursework and
competitive sports.

_____

_____

11.1.2 ESTABLISH A DOMAIN NAME

a) What are the steps for establishing a domain name for your site?

_____

_____

_____

_____

LAB 11.1 EXERCISE ANSWERS

11.1.1 ANSWERS

a) What would be appropriate domain names for the following businesses?

*Answer: A direct insertion of their name or a part of their name into a domain name
will most ideally represent some of these sites. Others are too long and cumbersome to
be comfortable as a domain name and will have to be represented by an acronym or
some other form of name. Some suggestions are given in the table on p. 331.*

Company	Possible Domain Names
Ace Aquatica Aquarium Products	www.ace.com, www.aquatica.com, www.aaap.com, www.fishhomes.com, www.ace-aqua.com
Dame, Underhill, Maste, and Peel	www.dame-underhill.com, www.taxprep.com, www.taxlaw.com (Note: using an acronym is not advisable with this company name; www.dump.com is not likely to lead to the kind of "presence" this firm would like to promote)
Party Time	www.partytime.com, www.party-time.com, www.party.com
Chambers School for Boys	www.chambers.edu, www.chambers-school.edu, www.csb.edu

11.1.2 ANSWERS

a) What are the steps for establishing a domain name for your site?

Answer: There are three basic steps:

1. *Create a domain name*
2. *Check on availability*
3. *Register the name and pay for it*

LAB 11.1 SELF-REVIEW QUESTIONS

In order to test your progress, you should be able to answer the following questions.

1) No one looks at URLs.

    a) _____ True
    b) _____ False

2) Your domain name should bear a close resemblance to your organization's name.

    a) _____ True
    b) _____ False

3) If your first-choice domain name is taken, you can:

    a) _____ Pick another name
    b) _____ Buy the name from whoever has already registered it
    c) _____ Complain to the registrar
    a) _____ Register the name anyway

4) A URL is the same as a domain name.

    a) _____ True
    b) _____ False

5) A company may always register the company name as the domain name.

    a) _____ True
    b) _____ False

6) Registering companyname.org means that you also own companyname.com.

    a) _____ True
    b) _____ False

7) Peter Barr owns the summer camp for boys called Andersonville Farms near Andersonville, Minnesota. Choose the best domain name for his camp:

    a) _____ andersonvillefarmscamp.com
    b) _____ peterb.camping.com
    c) _____ camping.com
    d) _____ andersonvillecamp.com

Quiz answers appear in the Appendix, Section 11.1.

L A B   1 1 . 2

LAUNCHING A WEB SITE

LAB OBJECTIVES

After this lab, you will be able to:

✔ Identify the Process Involved in Launching a Web Site
✔ Evaluate Criteria for a Web Site Host
✔ Evaluate Criteria for a Web Site Designer

So far we've looked at many of the individual elements involved in maintaining a Web site. But, what if you're charged with setting up a new Web site—from scratch. Much of what we've learned applies to this task as well, but in this section we'll organize the steps into a more cohesive checklist to get you started on the right track.

LAUNCHING A WEB SITE

Let's summarize some of the things to be considered before a Web site can be successfully launched.

PURPOSE

Think back to Chapter 7 where we provided three lab exercises to help you evaluate your organization, audience, and the purpose of the Web site. Why do you want a Web site? What purposes will it serve? The following functions can be fairly easily provided in a Web site:

- Let potential customers find you and about you 24 hours a day, 7 days a week.

- Deliver promotional and advertising information, an online version of bulk mail.

- Provide updated and detailed information about your products or services.
- Provide products, services, or information.
- Recruit employees or investors.
- Provide customer support or detailed "how-to" manuals.
- Provide knowledge and education.

AUDIENCE

Your potential customer needs to be considered during the development process. Focusing the launch on the customer will make the site more useful in the end. If your customer is the typical home user with a fairly slow connection speed and last year's browser, using bleeding-edge technology may not be the best choice. The marketing department and Web designer might want to use all the latest and greatest, but they are not the ones who will use the site.

SITE PLANNING

As is the case with any other complex undertaking in an organization, a Web site should be planned. Long before anyone begins to write a line of code or sketch a hierarchy, the planning team for a site must go to work. They must establish the goals and scope of the project, its list of deliverables, and a delivery schedule.

PREPARATION

The first task in planning a Web site is to make sure that you have all of the information that you need to produce the site. This is the preparation phase where you will gather information, listen, and find the key players from whom you can extract the information you need. Get to know the organization, its goals, its worries, and its needs. Work on developing the ideas for the site that will further their goals and solve their problems.

To be successful, your Web site must promote the organization's strategic needs such as branding and competitive edge (for more on this, see Lab 7.1, Understanding the Organization), as well as its delivery needs such as site functionality, content, and production values. In order to determine those needs, you and your clients or stakeholders need to do some serious research before you begin to build the site.

Begin to sketch out the site. This will give the designer an idea of the depth and breadth of the site and give you an idea of what kind of content development will be needed. It helps to keep a bookmark list of other sites you like or dislike, especially those of direct competitors. It is necessary to know what kind of features you will want on the site, such as database integration or e-commerce, so the appropriate hosting site and designer can be determined. Depending on funding and local talent, you may need to divide the features into "must-have" and "come later" categories.

One of the most useful tools in this process is the site profiler. This is essentially a questionnaire and "homework" assignment for the primary stakeholders, asking them to answer specific questions regarding their organization, their goals for the site, their messages, and their preferences. If the site is being developed "in house" the members of the development team may be the ones to complete the questionnaire. If the site is being developed for a client, then this will be given to the client. This is a very thorough profiler. You may choose to select portions of it, depending on the client and type of Web site.

A SAMPLE SITE PROFILER

Organizational Background

1) Who are the decision makers for this project? What are their roles?

2) What kind of personnel resources will you allocate to this project? What are their roles?

3) Please provide a brief profile of the organization, including its position in the market (primary competitors, ranking, etc.).

4) What is the mission statement for your organization?

5) What are your organization's four top concerns?

Goals for the Site

1) Give a brief description of the site you would like to develop.

2) Give us five key words to describe this site.

3) Rank the goals listed below in the order of their importance for this project (1 = most important).

____ direct sales

____ enhancing technology image

____ enhancing access to information

____ branding

____ organizational communications

____ community building

4) What are your criteria for success of this site?

5) What are the three most important pieces of information to be presented in this site?

6)   Is there a budget for this project (indicate also whether this includes internal resources)?

7)   Is there a variable budget range for this project dependent upon the complexity of the solutions designed?

8)   Describe marketing/identity resources and constraints (logos, artwork, institutional fonts, style guides, etc.).

9)   Do you use an advertising agency, public relations agency, or design firm? If so, what will be their involvement in the development of this project?

10)   Has any previous work been done regarding developing or redesigning this site?

11)   What are your scheduling needs for this project (what are your scheduling drivers)?

12)   Which of the following do you intend to use for promotion of this site:

_____ Events

_____ Prizes

_____ Direct mail

_____ Print, signage, radio, television advertising

_____ Co-branding

_____ In-store promotions or policies

13)   Rank the following in order of their importance (1 = most important)

_____ Time to market

_____ Production quality (content, graphics, flow, etc.)

_____ Enhancing organizational identity

_____ Budget

_____ Encouraging repeat visits

_____ Ease of maintenance

_____ Furthering marketing strategies

_____ Integrity of information

_____ Repurposing existing content

_____ Presenting a Web savvy presence

_____ Creating a destination value

_____ Attracting advertisers

_____ Building a community for a particular group (type of customer or business alliance)

14)   What are your long-term goals for the site?

Audience

1) Whom do you want to attract (list at least four visitor groups)?

2) Have you conducted any market research to define these groups?

3) What are the goals for your visitors?

4) What products, services, and/or information do you want to provide to visitors?

5) What would be the top three reasons that a new visitor would become a return customer?

6) How will you assess the success of these services?

7) Do you have a problematic visitor group (slow connection speed, international commerce, language, physically challenged, for example)? Describe the difficulty.

Content

1) Where will the content for the site come from?

2) Who will be responsible for the supply, validation, and licensing for this content?

3) Will the content be new (developed specifically for the site) or will it be repurposed?

4) What level of content oversight will you require (preproduction editorial work, writing, etc.)?

5) Who will maintain the site's content?

6) What are the two most important aspects of your content that you wish to communicate?

Utility

1) What kind of interactive functionality do you envision for the site (e.g., software downloads, FTP transfer, database-delivery of content, search capacity, e-commerce, bulletin boards, chat room, etc.)?

2) Who will be responsible for maintaining and updating these elements?

3) Are there existing database systems that need to be incorporated into the site?

4) What kind of reporting will you require for the site?

5) What kind of security is necessary for this site?

6) How do you plan to host and maintain the site?

7) What is the budget for the hosting and maintenance of the site?

8)   Have you made arrangements for the service/hosting of the site? Please describe.

9)   Are there any other technological considerations/constraints that should be considered?

Preferences

For this section you will need to do some "traveling" research. It is very important in determining your site's placement and presence on the Web, so be sure to investigate these topics to the best of your ability. Below are sets of categories that we can relate to your new site. Please find and cite for us the three sites that impress you most in each of these categories.

1) Size of site

2) Top competitors in your field

3) Similar content model (direct sales, corporate information, information resource, etc.)

4) Branding approach

5) Attracting new visitors to the site

6) Quality of content

7) Quality of graphic material

8) Look and feel of site (color schemes, layout, etc.)

9) Functionality/utilities (databases, chat rooms, shopping carts, etc.)

10) Targeting your defined audiences

11) Building community

12) Type of overall image projected by the site

13) Your favorite sites (please indicate the reasons that these sites appeal to you)

CONTENT

Content development is often the most difficult part of creating a new Web site. Failure to meet content delivery deadlines is one of the most common reasons for slippage in a Web site's development schedule. The content for a Web site can use materials from other media, but those materials will need to be edited and adapted, or you will end up with a site populated by "brochureware." Writing for the Web is different than other media. It is not the same as a promotional brochure, operating manual, or a commercial. People read differently on the Web—more of a scan than a word-by-word read, so using bulleted or numbered lists is much more common.

In addition to the content development, you will need to determine your content maintenance and management needs before you launch the site. This includes support for documents and other materials provided through the site, as well as schedules for updates on materials to be used.

SITE DESIGNER

Anyone can write a page of html and put it on a Web server. The tools available today make this fairly easy. However, developing a Web site with a consistent look and feel, easy-to-use navigation, and well-organized content is another story. Adding dynamic content steps up the qualifications needed. Someone with experience in organizing information (see Lab 10.1, Accommodating Growth) can improve overall site navigation. In the next section we'll look at criteria you should consider if you are hiring an outside contractor to develop the site. If you have qualified in-house staff, that is certainly a choice and does make the "iterative" process involved in site design a bit easier.

SITE DESIGN

Armed with logos, graphics, content, site sketch, site mission, completed site profiler, and audience definition, the designer is ready to create the site. This is usually an iterative process—the designer comes up with several "look and feel" ideas for top and sub level pages, the clients review what they like and dislike, the designer makes changes, the client reviews . . . This can be an infinite and expensive process if you're not careful. The more information provided to the designer up front, the better. Once the look and feel is finalized, the designer can add all the content and images to the site in an appropriately organized manner.

DOMAIN NAME

Setting up and keeping a domain name is fairly inexpensive, usually about $35 a year.

SITE HOST

If you have adequate computer support, you can host your own site. But, it is a lot more complicated today than just a few years ago. Sure, all you really need is a computer connected to the Internet and Web server software. However, you now need to consider security issues that seem to change daily, and a host of new Web features. It can be fairly inexpensive ($25 to $50 a month) to have your site hosted on a professionally managed server—well worth the cost if you choose the right host (see Lab 11.3).

The Whole Truth: So What's This Going to Cost Me?

Costs for setting up a professional Web site can range from a few thousand dollars to millions of dollars, depending on the breadth of the site's complexity, the promotional campaign, and the "names" involved in both content and infrastructure development. The table below looks at some of the costs involved in site development.

Task	Hourly Rate[1]	Comments
HTML coding	$20 – $120 per hour	College students and "dabblers" lower the bottom end dramatically in this category.
Copy writing	$30 – $125 per hour	The upper end of this category usually includes specialized knowledge in either technical fields or marketing copy.
Design	$80 – $150 per hour	
CGI Script	$60 – $175 per hour	
Software Devlopment	$60 – $140 per hour	
Quality Assurance	$15 – $120 per hour	Interns lower the low end, QA engineers raise the high end.
Strategy	$120 – $200 per hour	
Java/Shockwave programming	$140 – $250 per hour	
Database programming	$160 – $250 per hour	

[1]Rates given are compiled from sources including The Real Rate Survey 1999, the NetMarketing 1999 Web Price Index, and the Datamasters 1999 Salary Survey.

The rates in the table above represent a starting place; you may find that your experience is different, based on region, complexity of your site, resource factors, etc.

INSTALLATION, TESTING, AND VALIDATION

Once the site has been developed and the domain name obtained, the site can be moved to the host location where it should be tested, tested, and tested again. Some testing can be done during and on the development site, but final testing needs to be done on the host site. Things happen when a site is moved, no matter how carefully it is done. See Lab 10.3, Site Migration, for further discussion on the testing and staging of a site. A summary of tools that can be used to validate a Web site and maintain it after initial development can be found in Chapter 8, Site Maintenance. At this point the site can be made ready for publication and marketing—see Lab 11.3.

FIND A WEB SITE HOST

There are not quite as many Web hosts as there are Web sites, but it sure seems that way when you are shopping for one. Before shopping for a site, you need to know what you are looking for, especially any special features that might require a specific combination of server hardware and software. Let's look at what you should consider when shopping for a place to host your Web site.

If you are hosting mission critical information, look for a host that offers:

- Several T1 connections to redundant servers.
- Multiple long distance carriers, in the event that one goes down.
- 24×7 server and telephone support.
- 99.5% guaranteed "up" time.

It's a good idea to find other Web sites hosted by the same service and check the server response at several times during the day and on several days of the week. Check a time that is normally busy and see how the host responds. Most users won't tolerate a slow response for very long.

As with most things, you get what you pay for. Beware of free or discount hosting services or those with "no bandwidth limits." These hosts tend to attract very high traffic sites that slow down the server for all other hosted sites. For most average Web sites, chances are you'll never exceed the bandwidth limits.

Ask the hosting service about how it keeps up on security concerns. A good host will be familiar with the inherent risks involved in operating Web server. It is not a good idea to host your Internet Web server on the same computer that you keep your business materials. Web servers are targets for hackers, and once hacked, they can supply a path into other information on the computer. Fortunately, so far at least, most hackers are in it for the thrill and don't usually cause serious damage. They may, however, replace your homepage with something less than appropriate for your site. Web server software and the computer operating system on which they run need frequent patches to fix the security holes. The Department of Energy's Computer Incident Advisory Capability (CIAC, www.ciac.org) is a good resource. Managing Web security is an increasingly specialized field and something you may want to leave to the experts.

Finally, find out if the host offers the features that you require. Plan a bit for the future. Changing hosts isn't impossible, but is something you don't want to do frequently. Be sure that in addition to adequate current services your host has room to accommodate your plans for growth. The following is a list of features you may want available from your host site.

- Access via a Unix shell and/or Secure Shell (SSH)
- Active Server Pages
- Anonymous FTP
- CGI scripting—standard and custom
- Cold Fusion server
- Online credit card payment system
- Discussion forum
- E-commerce system (prepackaged)
- Email boxes and email system
- Extended log file format tracking
- Log file analysis tools (for traffic tracking)
- Form processing scripts
- FrontPage extensions
- Real Audio/Video server
- Search indexing and engine
- Secure Socket Layer (SSL)
- Simple password protection for a file or a subdirectory

Finally, some hosts offer browser-based administration of the Web site. That is, the administrator (Webmaster) can set up and manage site users, email accounts, password protection, and even install custom CGI scripts through a browser interface. This level of management is a convenience for an experienced administrator. But for the uninitiated it can be confusing. Some Web hosts require their own support staff manage all Web site administration. If they have 24-hour service or at least service hours that match your own, and you can live with the response time, this type of host does take some of the guesswork out of administering the site.

FIND A WEB SITE DESIGNER

Assuming you don't have in-house staff capable of designing the Web site, how should you go about hiring the right designer? The trick is finding a designer who can create a site that fits your organization's personality and attract new customers as well as draw repeat visitors. There are really four phases to consider:

1. Creating the site
2. Hosting it on a Web server
3. Publicizing the location
4. Maintaining and updating the site

A Web site is like a living, breathing organism. It is never really "done," and development is a process, not a project. You can hire a designer or design firm that can handle some or all of these phases. You may have staff that can handle the publicity or maintenance, with little or no help from the designer. As we will learn in the next lab, publicity is not a one-time event either. It takes persistence and vigilance to keep a Web site near the top of the search engines. Where do you find a good design firm? Many Web hosts offer design services. Ask others in your business who they use. Check Web sites you like to see if a designer is referenced. There are almost as many design firms as hosts, but the good ones tend to stand out. When examining designers or design firms, don't be afraid to ask lots of questions. They are the experts but should be able to explain things to you in plain language. Consider the following issues when interviewing potential firms.

ASK ABOUT COST

They should be able to give a firm cost for each phase of development. Make sure you know exactly what is covered in the price. The price range varies tremendously, so consider looking at several firms before deciding. The cost is usually dependent upon the size of the site, its complexity, and the launch deadline. Some designers base their cost on the "number of pages," maybe because this is something tangible they can offer the client. Customized features will increase the cost significantly. A good designer will let you know if there is a ready-made alternative to a custom feature that you want. One of the most vexing aspects of site design is coming up with a "look and feel" that will be approved by the client. The look is often a matter of personal taste, and if there is a committee in charge, you may never get consensus. Someone has to be the person with the final say on this issue. This process is iterative, so be sure that your agreement includes at least a couple iterations. Most design groups place a limit on the number of iterations included in their bid package. Be clear if any or all of the following items are included in the quoted price:

- Basic forms, email, and a guest book
- Digitizing photographs and other artwork (maximum number)
- Graphic design (buttons, backgrounds)
- Initial setup
- Maintenance and updating
- Monthly traffic analysis
- Number of prototypes/iterations
- Page templates
- Site promotion (registration with search engines)
- Site registration/transfer
- Customer programming
- Shopping cart/e-commerce

ASK ABOUT THE SCHEDULE

If the firm can promise the site to be up and running next week, run! Design takes time and it can't be completed until the clients provide content. It always takes longer than expected for the client to develop content. Providing designers with a sketch of the site and any artwork available from other media will assist in assigning a realistic schedule.

ASK ABOUT SERVICES

Consider some or all of the following issues. Do they do their own design work or outsource it? Can they take artwork intended for print and modify it for the Web? Are graphics handled in-house? If so, can they read the artwork you provide (considering platform and products)? Do they have experts on staff to do programming, such as database integration or scripting, or answer technical questions about servers, hardware, software, and networks? Can they offer technical editing of the content material? What are their specialties? Based on the type of site you want whom exactly will you be working with? Relaying ideas and messages through too many intermediates, such as the sales or marketing people, can slow the process down. Can they design a site that meets the World Wide Web Consortium's (www.w3C.org) Web Content Accessibility Initiative or provide the pages in text-only alternatives?

ASK FOR REFERENCES AND TO VIEW THEIR PORTFOLIO

When hiring any contractor, checking references is important for the intangibles, such as how easy they are to work with. Good Web design requires excellent communication and organizational skills. The design firm should have a list of sites you can visit.

ASK ABOUT PLATFORMS

Although the Web is intended to cross all platforms, designing and hosting a Web site is platform specific. Ask if the design firm is locked into one host that may or may not meet your needs. You may already have the site hosted and you simply want a redesign. Or you may need the server to run on a specific platform so you or someone in your firm can manage, maintain, or update the site later. Some designers are comfortable on all platforms; others will only work on one. Artwork and content must be transferred to the design firm and making sure the designer can read your files is important. This will shorten the design time and lower the cost. Designers with access to several platforms and a variety of storage devices (Zip, Jaz, FTP, and CD) can make this process easier.

LAB 11.2 EXERCISES

11.2.1 IDENTIFY THE PROCESS INVOLVED IN LAUNCHING A WEB SITE

a) There are three broad areas involved in launching a Web Site. In the following list, enter the launch phase for each.

1) Planning
2) Design
3) Hosting the site

_____ Budget

_____ Obtain domain name

_____ Assemble artwork

_____ Contract with a Web hosting service

_____ Install meta tags on top level pages

_____ Copy edit the Web pages

_____ Identify target audience

_____ Link validation

_____ HTML validation

_____ Moving the files to the Web host

_____ Assemble content

_____ Identify site purpose

_____ Test Web page for full functionality

_____ Develop site description and key words

_____ Obtain password access to host site

**LAB
11.2**

11.2.2 *EVALUATE CRITERIA FOR A WEB SITE HOST*

The FANNC Web site needs to find a permanent Web host. FANNC has, so far, been piggybacking on a local community server that will soon be going away.

a) Which of the following features should FANNC be looking for in a Web host? Which should it consider for near-future enhancements?

_____ Access via a Unix shell and/or Secure Shell (SSH)

_____ Active Server Pages

_____ Anonymous FTP uploads and downloads

_____ CGI scripting—standard and custom

_____ Cold Fusion server support

_____ Online credit card payment system

_____ Discussion forum

_____ Chat room

_____ E-commerce system (prepackaged)

_____ Email boxes and email system (10 email addresses at a minimum)

_____ Extended log format tracking

_____ Log file analysis tools (for traffic tracking)

_____ Form processing scripts

_____ FrontPage extensions

_____ Real Audio/Video server

_____ Search indexing and engine

_____ Secure Socket Layer (SSL)

_____ Simple password protection for a file or a subdirectory

b) Based on the list of criteria above, can you find two hosting services that meet their current needs and cost less than $50 per month (factoring in any set up fees) for the first year?

_____

_____

_____

11.2.3 EVALUATE CRITERIA FOR A WEB SITE DESIGNER

You want to hire someone to provide your company with an online presence. You don't have a domain name, but have a few ideas. You want ten email addresses set up, about a dozen pages of basic company information, and a "contact us for more information" form. You have a logo you like to use for marketing pieces.

a) What are five questions you would ask potential designers for this site?

_____

_____

_____

b) How would you make a decision on which design firm to use?

_____

_____

_____

LAB 11.2 EXERCISE ANSWERS

11.2.1 ANSWERS

a) There are three broad areas involved in launching a Web Site. In the following list, enter the launch phase for each.

Answer: As you can see here, some of these items span the three phases. Planning is often overlooked but is the most necessary and difficult part. Some design aspects can happen concurrent to planning, especially full content development, but having the entire package available before developing the site is a real advantage to the designer.

1, 2, 3	*Budget*
1, 2	*Obtain domain name*
1	*Assemble artwork*

1, 2	*Contract with a Web hosting service*
2	*Install meta tags on top level pages*
2	*Copy edit the Web pages*
1	*Identify target audience*
3	*Link validation*
2, 3	*HTML validation*
2	*Moving the files to the Web host*
1	*Assemble content*
1	*Identify site purpose*
2, 3	*Test Web page for full functionality*
1	*Develop site description and key words*
1, 3	*Obtain password access to host site*

11.2.2 ANSWERS

a) Which of the following features should they be looking for in a Web host? Which should they consider for near-future enhancements?

Answer: The FANNC site should look for a hosting service that currently offer at least the following features:

Discussion forum—to build community.

Email boxes and email system—for continuity of email addresses as volunteers come and go.

Extended log format tracking—to identify referring hosts and search terms.

Log file analysis tools—to help track visitors without knowing how to do the analysis or spending money on analysis tools.

Form processing scripts—to facilitate contact with site visitors.

FrontPage extensions—for ease of upkeep by volunteers.

Search indexing and engine—to provide a site-specific search tool. This is helpful with text intensive, information sites.

FANNC should consider the following services, if offered at minimal charges, for near future enhancements:

Active Server Pages or CGI scripting—FANNC may find a volunteer with some programming savvy who can add some functionality using these features.

Online credit card payment system—slick way to take donations.

b) Based on the list of criteria, can you find two hosting services that meet their current needs (N) and costs less than $50 per month (factoring in any set up fees) for the first year?

Answer: Enter "Web hosting service" or a similar search string into any search tool and you'll find a number of services. At the time of writing we found a service that offers "now" and many "future" needs at $29/month with a $35 setup fee. This service offers:

- *FrontPage 2000 Support*

- *Unlimited Telnet and FTP access*

- *POP/IMAP email with forwarding capability*

- *Custom CGI script support via your own cgi-bin directory (Cgiwrap)*

- *Unix shell account with Perl, TCL, C, C++, and access to procmail*

- *Java, Shockwave, TrueSpeech, and RealAudio (streaming http) support*

- *PHP Server-side scripting language*

- *Swish and Glimpse search engines*

- *Password protected directories*

- *Unlimited autoresponders*

- *Detailed Web usage statistics and access to raw log files provided monthly*

- *Extensive user's guide with complete instructions*

- *SSL secure Web services and MySQL database server available as an option*

- *Hewlett Packard Series 9000 Unix Servers*

- *Dual T1 Connections to the Internet*

- *Domain name registration:* www.yourdomain.com

- *Dedicated IP address*

- *10 extra email accounts*

- *50MB disk space*

- *2000MB data transfer per month*

- *Unlimited forwarding and email aliases under your domain*

- *MySQL database server and utilities available at no extra charge*

- *Weekly/daily statistics or log files upon request*

Of course, we would do more research on the hosting service before signing up. But a simple search shows just how many hosting services are available and the value of research and references before choosing a service.

11.2.3 ANSWERS

a) What are five questions you would ask potential designers for this site?

Answer: Some of the following questions could be helpful:

- *Have you done other sites this small?*
- *Can you handle the entire domain registration process and tell us how to access our new email addresses?*
- *What would you need from us before you can give us a firm bid on the project?*
- *Can you provide me with a list of the services the bid will provide?*
- *Can I get a list of references and view your online portfolio?*

b) How would you make a decision on which design firm to use?

Answer: Take a look at the online portfolio to see if the designs are ones you like and if the sites are similar in size and scope to your site. If someone is involved in large sites, this person may not want a fairly small job or may want to turn a small job into a large one. Speak with several designers or design firms before making a decision. The prices and services vary tremendously.

LAB 11.2 SELF-REVIEW QUESTIONS

In order to test your progress, you should be able to answer the following questions.

1) The site profiler does not address

    a) _____ content development processes.
    b) _____ desired site bells and whistles.
    c) _____ branding.
    d) _____ how to hire an outside design group.

2) Who should complete the site profiler?

    a) _____ The intended Web hosting service
    b) _____ The client
    c) _____ The designer
    d) _____ The client's public relations group

3) Which of the following will typically add the most expense to launching a Web site?

    a) _____ Obtaining a domain name for a two-year contract
    b) _____ Hosting the Web site at a reputable service
    c) _____ Advanced, customized, Web-database interface
    d) _____ Adapting print graphics to Web use

4) When finding a Web host, it is important to consider:

    a) _____ Redundant servers with frequent backup services
    b) _____ Whether security issues are addressed
    c) _____ If a dial-up service is also offered
    d) _____ 24 x 7 support

5) Web designers are expected to

    a) _____ offer several prototypes or design iterations.
    b) _____ explain what they do and what they need in plain language.
    c) _____ register the final site with all known search engines.
    d) _____ maintain the Web site for two years after launch.

Quiz answers appear in the Appendix, Section 11.2.

**LAB
11.2**

LAB 11.3

PUBLICIZING A WEB SITE

LAB OBJECTIVES

After this lab, you will be able to:

✔ Develop Keywords and Keyword Phrases
✔ Write Effective Meta Tag Statements
✔ Optimize for Search Engine Indexing

In June 1999 it was estimated that there were 3.7 million unique Web sites, 2.2 in public space. These numbers tripled since 1997. (Online Computer Library Center Office of Research, http://www.oclc.org/oclc/research/projects/Webstats/statistics.htm). Putting your Web site up on a public server does not guarantee anyone will find it. Having a short, memorable, and intuitive URL is certainly a good start, but is not enough. You can send email to potential customers, but where do you get the list? And, if you are like many of us, you simply ignore messages that even appear to be unsolicited mail. You can, of course, use traditional methods such as printed brochures, catalogs, and TV/radio advertisements. However, these methods can be expensive. Trade shows are also a good way to advertise a Web site, if appropriate to your business. Probably the most successful and least expensive way to drive traffic to a Web site is to have a page in the Web site appear on the first page of a search engine display after a specific keyword search. In this lab we'll look at some of the methods used by Web masters to optimize search engine indexing.

GETTING YOUR WEB SITE INDEXED

Getting your Web site indexed by search engines is pretty easy—just fill out the form offered at each site and wait. Keeping your site indexed requires persistence. Listings do go away, so checking the index and resubmitting is necessary. Getting your site near the top of the list based on a specific keyword search is more difficult, but adds the most value to the submissions. Consider, however, that less than a third of Webmasters actively use meta tags and other methods to maximize their pages in search engines. So, if you use these methods, you'll automatically be ahead of most Web sites out there.

Search engines use different methods when indexing sites. Most engines read what appears in the title tag and some also index specific meta tags. Most directory services require that you enter a description directly into their submission form. It is very difficult to design a single Web page that will be ranked equally by all search engine sites. Most search engines describe their indexing method somewhere on their site. Also, search engines go in and out of favor. So, a good place to start is to identify the search engines you like, do some research on how to maximize your pages for that set of search engines, and then prepare your site before submitting your pages.

There are many online services that summarize search engine submission strategies. For example, take a look at the Virtual Promote site at http://www.virtualpromote.com or the Web Promotion Center at http://www.westward.com/promoteit/. There are also a number of online services with information and tools to assist with the promotion process. For example, take a look at MSN LinkExchange at http://www.linkexchange.com, WebPromote at http://www.WebPromote.com, or Web Position at http://www.Webposition.com.

KEYWORDS

In terms of site promotion, keywords are the words or phrases you'd expect a potential site visitor to type into a search engine to find your site. Choosing keywords that people actually use to access your site and doing some research before choosing keywords is essential. This is not a science, but there are some tips and tools to help you in this process.

Keywords work best as phrases. Web users don't usually type a single word into a search engine because of the vast number of sites that will be returned. One way to construct phrases is to list words that apply to your site and then construct several phrases from the words. Pairing a generic keyword with one more specific to your site can be useful too. If the keywords don't truly reflect your site, the user may stop into your site only to back out. This is not the kind of traffic you want. Remember, you're not trying to get everyone to visit your site, just those who are members of your audience.

Search engines are not consistent in how they recognize plurals and capitalization. So, when developing keyword phrases, consider using singular and plural versions of keywords. Also, consider using all lowercase phrases or upper and lower case versions, if appropriate. There are some words that are almost always capitalized, such as CD (compact disc), but Web users tend to be somewhat lazy and type everything in lowercase. You may even consider entering some common misspellings of keywords—there is no spell checking in the search index form!

If you have an existing site, take a look at your referer log files. These log files often include the words entered into a search engine to reach your site. This is a great way to find actual phrases people use to find your site.

Test your potential keyword phrases in a number of search engines and see if the Web sites that are returned are similar to your site. Keep trying phrases until the sites that are returned are similar to your site.

META TAGS

Once keyword phrases are established, they need to be inserted into the Web pages so the search engine robots can index them. Again, search engines vary in what they index on a site, so it's important to incorporate the keywords into the following elements of the page.

IN THE <TITLE> TAG

Remember that the title appears in the top status bar in the browser. Most search engines index the title tag and many use it as the description that appears under your link in the returned results. To optimize the title tag, make it descriptive to the site and fairly short.

IN <H1>, <H2>, AND <H3> TAGS

Many search engines use the contents of the heading tags to outline content within Web pages.

IN <META> TAGS

Again, not all search engines index meta tags, but they are worth adding to the pages for the engines that use them. There are a number of common meta tags and the syntax is fairly simple. They should be inserted within the <head> tag on the page. A few of the most common meta tags follow.

DESCRIPTION

```
<META name="description" content="Place description here.">
```

The description meta tag will show under your link on the search results page. The description should be more than just a list of keywords. It needs to be compelling and descriptive of the site—to encourage the searcher to select your link.

KEYWORDS

```
<META name="keywords" content="keywords, keyword phrases, sepa-
rated by commas">
```

Commas should separate each keyword or phrase. In general, list keywords in lower case. Avoid repeating keywords more than ten times (this can be considered as spamming and the page may be eliminated from the index) and never list the same keyword twice in a row.

COPYRIGHT

```
<META name="copyright" content="Copyright information">
```

The owner of the copyright of material showing on the Web document.

AUTHOR

```
<META name="author" content="FirstName LastName">
```

The author of the material showing on the Web document.

REVISIT-AFTER

```
<META name="revisit-after" content="XX Days">
```

Tells search engine robots when to come back and check this site for updates.

ROBOTS

```
<META name="robots" content="INDEX">
```

Tells robots what they can do at the site—all, follow, index, noindex.

IN <IMG ALT> TEXT

If you are using a graphic as the title on your page, consider adding page specific keywords to the alternative text behind the image. Search engines can't read graphics, but they can index alternative text in the image tag.

IN THE FIRST PARAGRAPHS

Some search engines read the first 1000 characters of a Web page. So, if the keywords and keyword phrases are used within the text of the page, they are more likely to be indexed.

TIPS ON OPTIMIZING SUBMISSION

As search engines and cataloging services evolve, the methods used to optimize submission also change. However, at the time of writing, the following are some suggestions to consider.

- Do it right the first time! Don't submit until the site has been optimized. Changing a listing can be very difficult and time consuming.

- Keep records of which page was submitted and to which site. Some suggest submitting manually to the main search engines, at least the first time. You can then use a service or tool to submit to the minor search engines and other specialized category sites.

- Pick a set of search engines or catalogs to focus on. You can't get to the top in all indexes with the same set of pages. Check out their Web sites and look for tips and tricks specific to each site. Some engines have limits on the number of characters allowed in the title and meta tags. Some sites require submission based on specific categories they have set up. Make sure you know which category your site belongs in before submitting.

- Be persistent. Don't be afraid to contact the search engine administrator if you can't get your site indexed or corrected.

If you are serious about this, there are number of tools that will assist in developing keyword phrases, descriptions, write the appropriate meta tags and facilitate inserting them into the Web pages. Tools of this type include TagGen (by HISC Software) and the Page Generator in Web Position Gold (by FirstPlace Software). There are also tools that will help with the submission and continued verification of position within the search engines. Web Position Gold offers a variety of these services. Since search engines and catalog services continue to change, sometimes it is easier to let others keep track of the details.

LAB 11.3 EXERCISES

11.3.1 DEVELOP KEYWORDS AND KEYWORD PHRASES

Consider our ABC Hardware case-study site.

    a) List at least ten keywords or keyword phrases you would use to describe this site.

_____

_____

    b) Write the keyword meta tag for their top level page.

_____

_____

11.3.2 WRITE EFFECTIVE META TAG STATEMENTS

Again, consider our ABC Hardware case-study site.

    a) Write an effective description meta tag.

_____

_____

    b) In addition to keywords and description, which other meta tags would you use for this site?

_____

_____

11.3.3 OPTIMIZE FOR SEARCH ENGINE INDEXING

a) Go to three different search engine sites and find their submission tips. List the URLs and note any tips that were new to you.

_____

_____

b) Go to two different directory sites and find their submission tips. List the URLs and note any tips that were new to you.

_____

_____

LAB 11.3 EXERCISE ANSWERS

11.3.1 ANSWERS

a) List at least ten keywords or keyword phrases you would use to describe this site.

Answer: There is no single correct answer for this question. Some suggestions might be: hardware store, do-it-yourself, power tools, home improvement, home remodeling, woodworking tools, kitchen and bath, lawn and garden, painting and refinishing, fix it tips, tool tips, how do I install, interior decorating.

b) Write the keyword meta tag for their top level page.

Answer: There is no single correct answer to this question. A suggestion using the previous answer might be: <meta name="keywords" content="hardware store, power tools, home improvement, home remodeling, woodworking tools, kitchen and bath, lawn and garden, painting and refinishing, fix it tips, tool tips, how do I install, interior decorating">

11.3.2 ANSWERS

a) Write an effective description meta tag.

Answer: There is no single correct answer to this question. An example might be: <meta name="description" content="ABC Hardware home improvement center features high

quality service and products at down home prices. Visit our online store or our retail outlets in California and Oregon.">

b) In addition to keywords and description, which other meta tags would you use for this site?

Answer: There is no single correct answer to this question. The following is just one set of meta tags that could be used on the top level page.

<META name="copyright" content="2000, ABC Hardware">

<META name="author" content="Joe Webmaster">

<META name="revisit-after" content="30 Days">

<META name="classification" content="General Hardware">

<META name="robots" content="INDEX">

<META name="distribution" content="LOCAL">

<META name="rating" content="GENERAL">

11.3.3 ANSWERS

a) Go to three different search engine sites and find their submission tips. List the URLs and note any tips that were new to you.

Answer: Your answer will probably vary, but here are some suggestions for you:

*Alta Vista (http://www.altavista.com/cgi-bin/query?pg=addurl)
Contains a good summary of meta tags and the robots.txt exclusion file.*

*Excite (http://www.excite.com/info/getting_listed)
Now indexes the description meta tag.*

*MSN (http://search.msn.com/help_addurl.asp)
Provides a link to W3C notes on helping search engines index your Web site.*

b) Go to two different directory sites and find their submission "tips." List the URLs and note any tips that were new to you.

Answer: Your answer will probably vary, but here are some suggestions for you:

Yahoo (http://docs.yahoo.com/info/suggest/)

Three steps: Check to see if the site is already listed, look for the appropriate category, and submit your site from the category you choose.

SNAP (*http://www.snap.com/LMOID/resource/0,566,-516,00.html*)
Uses a check mark to indicate preferred sites. Very subjective.

LAB 11.3 SELF-REVIEW QUESTIONS

In order to test your progress, you should be able to answer the following questions.

1) Description and keyword meta tags are indexed by all search engine robots.

   a) _____ True
   b) _____ False

2) Optimizing your top-level page for submission to a search engines includes:

   a) _____ Developing and installing appropriate meta tags
   b) _____ Inserting descriptive title tag information
   c) _____ Adding alternative text to images
   d) _____ All of the above

3) Which of the following is correct syntax for a keyword meta tag?

   a) _____ <META name="keywords" content="cd repair, dvd repair">
   b) _____ <META name="keywords" words="cd repair, dvd repair">
   c) _____ <META name="keywords"=cd repair, dvd repair>
   d) _____ <META keywords="cd repair, dvd repair">

4) Once you've submitted your site to a search engine or directory service, you should never have to check on the listing again.

   a) _____ True
   b) _____ False

4) Search engines are very similar in how they obtain your site listing and display the information.

   a) _____ True
   b) _____ False

Quiz answers appear in the Appendix, Section 11.3.

CHAPTER 11

TEST YOUR THINKING

Creating a Web site from start to finish, if there is such a thing, is exciting, challenging, and fun. Walk through the process of establishing a small Web site for yourself or your company.

1) List the steps you would take, in general terms such as "obtain a domain name," in the approximate order they should be taken.
2) What research would you do before you started?
3) Who would you need to hire to complete this process?
4) How would you publicize the site?

CHAPTER 12

ADVANCED FEATURES AND ACCESSIBILITY

The power of the Web is in its universality. Access by everyone regardless of disability is an essential aspect.

—Tim Berners-Lee, W3C Director
and inventor of the World Wide Web

CHAPTER OBJECTIVES

In this chapter, you will learn about:

✔ Advanced Web Site Features, or Adding Bells
   and Whistles   Page 365
✔ Making Web Sites Accessible to All Users,
   Machines, and Browsers   Page 378

Looking at page after page of plain text is not very exciting for most Web site users. Adding animations and interactivity can make the visit more fun and informative. Multimedia, such as audio and video, is very effective for some Web sites, but these features are bandwidth-intensive. Browser plugs-ins can add "flash" and fun to a site and make legacy documents easy to access and print, but the user must be willing to add the plug-in. Newer technologies that are browser dependent, such as Cascading Style Sheets and Dynamic HTML, can make life easier for Web designers. However, uneven implementation of these features by newer browsers and the range of browsers still in use by the community at large make them more useful in a closed environment of an intranet. Knowing when and how to use these advanced features is important for the Web site manager.

Advanced features can enhance or reduce Web site accessibility. The Web Content Accessibility Initiative, developed and recommended by the World Wide Web Consortium (www.w3C.org), gives definitive guidelines to Web developers who want to provide Web access to people with disabilities, who are estimated to comprise 3 to 20 percent of Web site users. By ignoring accessibility, you could be ignoring a significant percentage of your market. By providing accessibility under these guidelines, the broad range of alternative Web delivery devices such as PalmPilots, WebTV, and cell phones, can use the Web content much more effectively. We'll look at the W3C guidelines and how to apply them to a Web site.

L A B   1 2 . 1

ADVANCED WEB SITE FEATURES, OR ADDING BELLS AND WHISTLES

LAB OBJECTIVES

After this lab, you will be able to:

✔ Evaluate Effective Use of Animations and Interactivity
✔ Evaluate Effective Use of Multimedia
✔ Evaluate Effective Use of Plug-ins
✔ Evaluate Effective Use of Style Sheets and DHTML

There can be a running battle between the Web designer and the Web manager regarding the current batch of available bells and whistles. As the manager of a Web site, part of your job is to make sure your intended audience (see Chapter 7) can get to the information you present on the Web site and keep the users coming back. Advanced features can restrict access to all or part of your site to some percentage of site users, some of these features can also distract the user from the intended message, and some can cause serious system crashes. But bells and whistles can also make your Web site look less like a page of text. Evaluating the pros and cons of these features and their implementation on your site may be assigned to you as the site manager.

ANIMATIONS AND INTERACTIVITY

Animations can be used to bring the user's attention to a particular feature on the Web page, to demonstrate how something works in time or space, or to show three-dimensional structures. When is it appropriate to use animations? Consider if the animation adds value to the page. Most appropriately, animations are used to demonstrate something rather than to just attract attention. But there is little harm in the occasional use of a small animation to draw attention to a new feature on the page. Too much animation on a page will cause many users to flee.

Although there are many ways to show movement on a Web page, the simplest and most widely recognized method is the animated gif. These images are easy to create with readily available tools, use an already recognized graphic file format so there are no special server or browser requirements, and will be displayed as a static file if the animation is not supported. For these reasons, animated gifs are very common and can be very distracting if misused. Animated gifs also give users control so that they can stop the movement. Alternatively, movement can be created using JavaScript. However, cross-browser compatibility can be an issue and the user (without disabling JavaScript) cannot easily stop this kind of movement. Therefore, it is not a recommended method. DHTML and Java can also be used to show movement on a page, but these are highly dependent on the browser version.

The most common interactivity, where something on the Web page responds to the user, is the rollover or mouseover button. This is usually just a swapping of two images when the user moves the mouse over the image. A third image can also display on the mouseover event. The JavaScript for this event is fairly easy, but since the user is now downloading two or three images in place of what could have been a simple text link, judicious use with optimized graphics is recommended.

MULTIMEDIA

Adding audio or video to a Web site ranges from simple to very complex, and the topic cannot be covered in detail here. Consider some of the following issues when making a decision about adding multimedia to your site.

Audio and video files are large and bandwidth must be considered. Users may not wait for the download unless there is true added value. Downloadable media must be provided in platform-specific versions.

Streaming technology allows the user to listen or view while the file is downloading. Serving streaming files requires additional server technology, however, and the user must first download a "player" to access the media. Even under the best conditions and an extremely fast connection speed, the video is jerky, fuzzy, and small. If something on the screen within a video needs to be read, it will probably need to be provided in an alternative format.

Technology for creating professional audio and video files for the Web can be expensive and has a fairly steep learning curve. Outsourcing is probably a good idea, but this can be expensive. Stock audio files are available, but copyright issues need to be clarified before posting files to a public location.

Providing an alternative source of the information contained in the audio or video files for those who can't see or hear should also be considered.

A great summary of audio and video on the Web is provided by Ann Navarro and Tabinda Khan in *Effective Web Design* (SYBEX Inc., ISBN 0-7821-2278-70) in Skill 19.

PLUG-INS

Plugs-ins are third party products, usually free to the user, designed to work with a browser. In the early days of the Web, finding, downloading, and installing the correct plug-in was something of a challenge. Now, when a plug-in is needed for a specific application, a link to download the plug-in is provided and the installation process is transparent. Some common plugs-ins include:

- **Acrobat Reader,** from Adobe, can be used for viewing Portable Document Format (PDF) files. PDF formats are particularly useful for making legacy documents available on the Web or for files that need to be previewed in a specific format. PDF forms now have much of the functionality of html forms: They can be filled in online and then printed for signature or the results can be submitted directly to a database. The pages within and between PDF documents can be hyperlinked for easy access. PDF files can be large, though, so bandwidth can be an issue.

- **Flash,** by Macromedia, allows for full screen animation, integrated audio, and interactive presentational materials using very small file sizes. Flash uses vector-based graphics, rather than bitmaps, to keep the file sizes small. This is fun technology to use and valuable when creating online presentations. The format is proprietary, however, and Macromedia's authoring tool is required to create Flash elements. Currently, the Flash plug-in is not available for the Unix platform. If Flash elements are used in navigational tools, nongraphical browsers will be excluded from using the elements. The latest edition of Flash uses Java technology, so a plug-in is not required.

- **Shockwave,** again by Macromedia, predated the Web as a tool for creating interactive CD-ROM–based educational materials and presentations. Shockwave files for the Web tend to be larger than Flash but can bring full CD-ROM–like interactivity to the Web. The Shockwave plug-in is fairly large and authoring is difficult, so it's not for everyone.

- **Java** applets are created using Java, Sun Microsystems's object-oriented programming language. Although widely supported by modern browsers, each version and platform can interpret the applet differently. What works perfectly on Netscape 4.06 on a Windows-based machine may not work on the Mac platform and can cause the Unix version to crash. If you are looking for something that works consistently across platforms, have a very good programmer create your applets. Applets can be used for fun things, like games and biorhythm charts, but they can also be used for performing calculations and spreadsheet functions.

Many more plug-ins are available, so check your favorite browser Web site for more information.

STYLE SHEETS AND DHTML

Style sheets and DHTML are supported by modern browsers (version 4.0 and newer), but their implementation by each browser and platform is inconsistent at best. Unless your audience is well-known and predictable in browser use, these features can be frustrating to implement. Making pages look good and consistent between platforms and browser versions limits what can be done with these tools. Cascading style sheets are described in HTML 4.0 and are used to separate format and content. Style sheets would make life much easier for Web designers *if* browsers could ever agree to apply the features consistently. Dynamic HTML, or DHTML, uses a combination of style sheets, JavaScript, and the Document Object Model (DOM) to create pages that are animated, move, or respond to the user.

LAB 12.1 EXERCISES

12.1.1 EVALUATE EFFECTIVE USE OF ANIMATIONS AND INTERACTIVITY

Consider the following examples. Discuss each situation as to the effectiveness of the animation or rollover interaction.

a) Indefinite flashing of "New," "Click Here," and "Buy me" animated .gif files on the top of a page selling electronic equipment.

_____

_____

b) There are five small .gifs that act as links to five other top-level pages in the site. When the mouse moves over the buttons, a small yellow diamond appears to the left of the text on the button.

_____

_____

c) Same situation as (b) but when the mouse moves over the buttons, a small yellow diamond appears and a large graphic appears to the left of the buttons describing what will be found if the link is chosen.

_____

_____

d) An animated graphic shows how to insert card stock into a printer for correct orientation when printing the reverse side of the card.

_____

_____

e) Consider the three case-study Web sites (ABC Hardware, Ska-Boards, FANNC). On which site would you expect to see the most animations? The fewest? Explain.

_____

_____

12.1.2 EVALUATE EFFECTIVE USE OF MULTIMEDIA

Other than those discussed above, give one good example of each of the following types of multimedia:

a) Static audio

_____

_____

b) Static video

_____

_____

c) Streaming audio

_____

_____

d) Streaming video

_____

_____

e) What are the three top considerations when making a decision about using audio or video elements on a Web site?

_____

_____

12.1.3 EVALUATE EFFECTIVE USE OF PLUG-INS

a) Match the plug-in to the Web feature.

Web Feature	Plug-in
_____ Provide online training to a closed, high-bandwidth audience	a. Flash
_____ Keep a copyright protected image from being screen captured or downloaded	b. Shockwave
_____ Show a three-dimensional view of a product for sale	c. Acrobat Reader
_____ Publish a corporate policy manual	d. Java Applet

b) Consider a Web site where essentially all information, except indexes, is provided in a source where a plug-in is required. How does this impact site users?

_____

_____

c) Consider a Web site where most information is provided in two formats, one that requires a plug-in and a second of plain html. How does this impact you as the Web site manager? How does this impact site users?

_____

_____

12.1.4 EVALUATE EFFECTIVE USE OF STYLE SHEETS AND DHTML

A few features of cascading style sheets are implemented across most modern browsers. At the very least, the pages should transform gracefully on browsers that do not yet support style sheets.

a) Is there any reason why these features should not be used on a Web site with a very wide audience?

_____

_____

b) How could style sheets be used during Web site development?

_____

_____

c) If you could picture the perfect audience/site for full implementation of style sheets and DHTML, what would it be?

_____

_____

The following are possible reasons why DHMTL is not fully implemented across the Web quite yet. Do these apply to your Web site? Explain.

    d) Uneven implementation of DHTML features across platforms and browsers.

_____

_____

    e) Dynamic HTML doesn't pay unless you are designing browser-specific showcase sites.

_____

_____

    f) Users resist upgrading their browsers to versions that support DHTML.

_____

_____

    g) Where's the beef? Flash, movement, and constantly updating data are fun, but where is the content?

_____

_____

LAB 12.1 EXERCISE ANSWERS

12.1.1 ANSWERS

Note: There are no single correct answers for these questions.

Consider the following examples. Discuss each situation as to the effectiveness of the animation or rollover interaction.

a) Indefinite flashing of "New," "Click Here," and "Buy me" animated .gif files on the top of a page selling electronic equipment.

Answer: Multiple animated or flashing items on a single page tend to be more distracting than attracting. A better choice might be to have the images flash once or at least with long pauses between animations and make sure the user can stop the animation if he or she wants to. It is generally not a good idea to place flashing items on pages where there is a lot of text to read. Of course, this is a matter of personal taste.

b) There are five small .gifs that act as links to five other top-level pages in the site. When the mouse moves over the buttons, a small yellow diamond appears to the left of the text on the button.

Answer: This seems like a reasonable use of a rollover. In fact, the small yellow diamond could be the single additional graphic added to the download to facilitate the effect. Graphics only load once, even if used many times on a page or in a Web site. This is a more prudent solution than flashing an entirely new image for each of the five graphics.

c) Same situation as (b) but when the mouse moves over the buttons, a small yellow diamond appears and a large graphic appears to the left of the buttons describing what will be found if the link is chosen.

Answer: Each of the description graphics that appears is a new graphic that will be downloaded when the mouseover event occurs. If the images are optimized and not too big, this can be a useful way to explain what the links mean. However, a better solution could be to provide a link title that is in itself descriptive enough to make the double mouseover unnecessary.

d) An animated graphic shows how to insert card stock into a printer for correct orientation when printing the reverse side of the card.

Answer: This is an excellent use of animation—showing something that can't be easily explained. To make it most useful, make it a link so it doesn't download unless the user wants that piece of information. In addition, provide a text-based description to make it accessible.

e) Consider the three case-study Web sites (ABC Hardware, SkaBoards, FANNC). Which site would you expect to see the most animations? The least? Explain.

Answer: Of the three case-study Web sites, SkaBoards is most likely to have animations and interactive content. This site will probably always be pushing the technology edge to keep its customer base. The FANNC site will be least animated. Its purpose is to provide information—it doesn't have to be fancy, just thorough and accurate. FANNC wants to have its site accessible by everyone, not those willing to upgrade to the latest and greatest technology.

LAB
12.1

Other than those discussed in the last exercise, give one good example of each of the following types of multimedia:

a) Static audio

Answer: Static audio could be used on the splash page to introduce your Web site if the clip is very small and relevant to the site. Another use would be to provide a very short "welcome" from the company president, for example, provided as a link instead of an automatic download. These files are large. The file size should be indicated so the user can decide to download that information. The file may need to be provided in multiple formats for various platforms.

b) Static video

Answer: Static video could be used to show how a product is used, as an alternative to an animation or when the procedure is too difficult to illustrate. These should also be linked, not automatically downloaded, and a file size provided. Portions of medical procedures could be illustrated this way.

c) Streaming audio

Answer: Streaming audio would be a great way to deliver music samples from a CD for sale. The user could sample the music before purchasing, a feature in many nonvirtual music stores. Streaming media is not downloaded, per se, so there wouldn't be a problem with the user distributing the music.

d) Streaming video

Answer: Streaming video is often used on news sites to show current events. Although the video portion is not always the best (due to bandwidth considerations), the combination of streaming audio and video makes a very good presentation.

e) What are the top three considerations when making a decision about using audio or video elements on a Web site?

Answer: When making a decision about incorporating audio or video three things to consider are:
   1. Does the media add value to the information?
   2. Will the intended audience have adequate bandwidth, computer speed, and browser technology to use the media?
   3. Do you have the technology to create and deliver the media? If not, do you have adequate outsource funding?

12.1.3 ANSWERS

a) Match the plug-in to the Web feature.

Answer:

Web Feature	**Plug-in**
__b.__ Provide on-line training to a closed, high-bandwidth audience	a. Flash
__d.__ Keep a copyright protected image from being screen captured or downloaded	b. Shockwave
__a.__ Show a three-dimensional view of a product for sale	c. Acrobat Reader
__c.__ Publish corporate policy manual	d. Java Applet

b) Consider a Web site where essentially all information, except indexes, are provided in a source where a plug-in is required. How does this impact site users?

Answer: A Web site where essentially all information provided is in a format where a plug-in is required restricts access to the information to those who are willing and able to download the plug-in. Those at lower connection speeds or older browsers may not want to wait for the plug-in to download.

c) Consider a Web site where most information is provided in two formats, one that requires a plug-in and a second of plain html. How does this impact you as the Web site manager? How does this impact site users?

Answer: Information on a Web site provided in multiple formats, say as PDF and html, impacts the Web site manager because maintenance of the information has now doubled, and it is easy to forget to update both formats. However, the site user has an option, which could be particularly useful in making the site accessible to more people.

12.1.4 ANSWERS

A few features cascading of style sheets are implemented across most modern browsers. At the very least, the pages should tranform gracefully on browsers that do not yet support style sheets.

a) Is there any reason why these features should not be used on a Web site with a very wide audience?

Answer: Elements of CSS that cross browsers and platforms well, or at least transform gracefully, should be used even for Web sites with a wide and diverse audience. Even minimal use of CSS can reduce file sizes and improve accessibility.

b) How could style sheets be used during Web site development?

Answer: Style sheets are very helpful when designing a Web site. Most of the formatting can be isolated to a single style sheet and global changes to the look and feel can be made quickly and easily. If the client wants the look and feel implemented with style sheets turned off, then at least the sheets can facilitate development.

c) If you could picture the perfect audience/site for full implementation of style sheets and DHTML, what would it be?

Answer: The perfect audience for full implementation of style sheets and DHTML is a closed intranet with a single computer platform, relatively similar computing styles, and control over the browser brand and version. At the very least, if a high enough minimum standard can be set for computing speed, bandwidth, and browser version, using style sheets and/or DHTML would be much easier and more cost-effective to implement.

The following are possible reasons why DHMTL is not fully implemented across the Web quite yet. Do these apply to your Web site? Explain.

d) Uneven implementation of DHTML features across platforms and browsers.

Answer: Other than the closed intranet site described above or very specialized Web sites, the problem with individual differences in DHTML implementation between platforms and browsers affects just about everyone.

e) Dynamic HTML doesn't pay unless you are designing browser-specific showcase sites.

Answer: Dynamic HTML has a steep learning curve and the tools for implementing the features are still rudimentary. Therefore, DHTML can be expensive in terms of programmer time; most of us just don't have extra programmer time that couldn't be spent better elsewhere.

f) Users resist upgrading their browsers to versions that support DHTML.

Answer: Many users think that if it isn't broke or hasn't broken their computer, then why upgrade? Until there are more reasons to upgrade than DHTML support, a large segment of Web users will choose not to upgrade. If your Web site has a wide audience, extensive use of DHTML may restrict access to some of the content.

g) Where's the beef? Flash, movement, and constantly updating data are fun, but where is the content?

Answer: DHTML and other ways to cause movement on the page may be fun, but most Web users are after information. For the right kind of site, DHTML elements on the intro page can be inviting and memorable. But having another way into the site to bypass the flash page is appreciated.

LAB 12.1 SELF-REVIEW QUESTIONS

In order to test your progress, you should be able to answer the following questions.

1) Which of the following is a very common user interaction found on a Web page?

    a) _____ Java Applet to open a new window
    b) _____ Database access to the local telephone directory
    c) _____ JavaScript that makes a graphic change when the mouse passes over it
    d) _____ Row of dancing hamsters

2) Which of the following media would be the best way to provide a "make-up" lecture for a missed class at a high technology college?

    a) _____ Static audio file and PDF versions of any overhead foils
    b) _____ Static video file and PDF versions of any overhead foils
    c) _____ Streaming audio and video
    d) _____ Streaming audio and video and PDF versions of any overhead foils

3) Browser plug-ins are platform independent.

    a) _____ True
    b) _____ False

4) Adding a flash of movement to a Web page can

    a) _____ attract attention to a new feature on the page.
    b) _____ annoy some users so much they won't come back to the site.
    c) _____ not be displayed in all browsers.
    d) _____ all of the above

Quiz answers appear in the Appendix, Section 12.1.

L A B   1 2 . 2

MAKING WEB SITES ACCESSIBLE TO ALL USERS, MACHINES, AND BROWSERS

LAB OBJECTIVES

After this lab, you will be able to:

✔ Describe Benefits to Making a Web Site Accessible
✔ Evaluate a Web Page for Conformance

In May 1999 the World Wide Web Consortium (www.w3c.org) made life easier for all of us by making "Web Content Accessibility Guidelines 1.0" a recommendation. Prior to this recommendation, making a Web site more accessible was a hit-or-miss proposition. Many thought that a text-only alternative was the only way to make a site accessible. These guidelines do not prescribe boring designs or text-only pages. In fact, text-only versions of Web sites or Web content may not be updated as frequently as the primary versions, or they may have some content excluded for easier maintenance, thus reducing accessibility to the content. We'll examine the benefits to making a Web site accessible, and then take a brief look at the guidelines, priority checkpoints, and conformance levels. In the lab, we will look at a sample Web page to determine conformance.

WHY MAKE YOUR WEB SITE ACCESSIBLE

It is estimated that people with disabilities make up from 3 to 20 percent of the population. Not all of these people want Web access and not all have disabilities that restrict Web access. Current statistics indicate that 4 to 8 percent of Internet users have some kind of disability. This number will only increase over time as the technology spreads, "baby boomers" get older, as age tends to decrease sensory function and mobility. Excluding a significant percentage of the population from your Web site is a business decision you need to consciously make. The point behind designing for accessibility is to assure that pages "transform gracefully," that is, they remain accessible, regardless of the platform, age of the machine, browser type or version, or if the user can't see, hear, use a mouse or keyboard. The second theme is to make the content understandable and navigable. This aspect of accessibility will benefit all site users, not just those who are disabled.

One added benefit to making a Web site accessible using these guidelines is that you also make your Web site more accessible to many of the new wireless Web interfaces including using Personal Digital Assistants and mobile phones. Why? Accessible Web sites provide alternatives for all nontext elements, thus the site is completely usable when graphics are turned off. Handheld devices connect at slow speed, nontext elements take time to download, and users will appreciate being able to use the site without the graphic elements. Accessibility will also make your site more likely to be used by newer technologies that haven't even been thought up yet, because they are designed to an established code. Finally, because of the text used to describe nontext elements, search engines are better able to index accessible Web sites.

GUIDELINES, CHECKPOINTS, PRIORITIES, AND CONFORMANCE LEVELS

The following is a summary of information you may obtain from the World Wide Web Consortium (W3C) Web site at <u>www.w3.org/WAI/</u>.

Fourteen guidelines are outlined in the Web Content Accessibility Guidelines. Each guideline is described by a number of specific checkpoint definitions to explain how the guideline applies to typical content or development scenarios. The checkpoints are intended to be specific enough that when reviewing a page, conformance can be verified. Each checkpoint is assigned a priority level of 1, 2, or 3.

> **Priority 1** checkpoints *must* be satisfied to meet the guideline or some groups will find it impossible to access the content.
>
> **Priority 2** checkpoints *should* be satisfied to meet the guideline or some groups will find it difficult to access the content.
>
> **Priority 3** checkpoints *may* be satisfied or some groups will find it somewhat difficult to access the content.

If all Priority 1 checkpoints are satisfied, the page is awarded Conformance Level "A." If all Priority 1 and 2 checkpoints are satisfied, the page is awarded Conformance Level "Double-A." If all Priority 1, 2, and 3 checkpoints are satisfied, the page is awarded Conformance Level "Triple-A." The conformance levels are spelled out so they render well when spoken. The guidelines are listed below.

1. Provide equivalent alternatives to auditory and visual content.

2. Don't rely on color alone.

3. Use markup and style sheets and do so properly.

4. Clarify natural language usage.

5. Create tables that transform gracefully.

6. Ensure that pages featuring new technologies transform gracefully.

7. Ensure user control of time-sensitive content changes.

8. Ensure direct accessibility of embedded user interfaces.

9. Design for device-independence.

10. Use interim solutions.

11. Use W3C technologies and guidelines.

12. Provide context and orientation information.

13. Provide clear navigation mechanisms.

14. Ensure that documents are clear and simple.

A complete list of checkpoints, sorted by priority level, is available at www.w3.org/TR/1999/WAI-WEBCONTENT-19990505/full-checklist.html. Since this lab concerns advanced technologies, let's consider Guideline 6 in some detail. The Guideline reads as follows (excerpt from the W3C recommendation, http://www.w3.org/TR/WAI-WEBCONTENT):

Guideline 6. Ensure that pages featuring new technologies transform gracefully.

Ensure that pages are accessible even when newer technologies are not supported or are turned off.

Although content developers are encouraged to use new technologies that solve problems raised by existing technologies, they should know how to make their pages still work with older browsers and people who choose to turn off features.

Checkpoints:

6.1 Organize documents so they may be read without style sheets. For example, when an HTML document is rendered without associated style sheets, it must still be possible to read the document **[Priority 1].** When content is organized logically, it will be rendered in a meaningful order when style sheets are turned off or not supported.

6.2 Ensure that equivalents for dynamic content are updated when the dynamic content changes **[Priority 1].**

6.3 Ensure that pages are usable when scripts, applets, or other programmatic objects are turned off or not supported. If this is not possible, provide equivalent information on an alternative accessible page **[Priority 1].** For example, ensure that links that trigger scripts work when scripts are turned off or not supported (e.g., do not use "JavaScript:" as the link target). If it is not possible to make the page usable without scripts, provide a text equivalent with the NOSCRIPT element, use a server-side script instead of a client-side script, or provide an alternative accessible page as per checkpoint 11.4. Refer also to guideline 1.

6.4 For scripts and applets, ensure that event handlers are input device-independent **[Priority 2].** *Device independent:* Users must be able to interact with a user agent (and the document it renders) using the supported input and output devices of their choice and according to their needs. Input devices may include pointing devices, keyboards, Braille devices, head wands, microphones, and others. Output devices may include monitors, speech synthesizers, and Braille devices. Please note that "device-independent support" does not mean that user agents must support every input or output device. User agents should offer redundant input and output mechanisms for those devices that are supported. For example, if a user agent supports keyboard and mouse input, users should be able to interact with all features using either the keyboard or the mouse.

6.5 Ensure that dynamic content is accessible or provide an alternative presentation or page **[Priority 2].** For example, in HTML, use NOFRAMES at the end of each frameset. For some applications, server-side scripts may be more accessible than client-side scripts. Refer also to checkpoint 11.4.

RESOURCES

In addition to the W3C Web site, the following resources can assist you to make your Web site accessible and in conformance with the Web Content Accessibility guidelines.

AWARE (http://aware.hwg.org/): The Accessible Web Authoring Resources and Education Web site offers a central resource for Web authors for learning about Web accessibility.

Bobby (http://www.cast.org/bobby/): This is a Web-based tool that analyzes Web pages for their accessibility to people with disabilities. While it only reviews one page at a time, you can download the product to run locally.

LAB 12.2 EXERCISES

12.2.1 DESCRIBE BENEFITS TO MAKING A WEB SITE ACCESSIBLE

Accessibility in this discussion is defined as making the Web content accessible to people or groups of people who have functional limitations related to sensory, physical, or cognitive functioning that can affect access to the Web. These conditions can be stable, progressive, or temporary.

a) How could our aging population benefit from accessible Web sites?

_____

_____

b) Give an example of how a Web site could be made more accessible for someone with these disabilities:

1) Blind or low vision

_____

_____

2) Color blind

_____

_____

3) Hearing impaired

_____

_____

4) Paralysis or limb weakness

_____

_____

5) Impaired short term memory

_____

_____

12.2.2 EVALUATE A WEB PAGE FOR CONFORMANCE

The following is a very simple Web page, as generated using a word processor using a "save as" html command.

Testing Accessible Design

This is a page of html generated from a word processor program.

- This is a link to the W3C site, just for demo purposes.

A small graphic above shows a cartoon image of a bridge. It is also a link to information about the Golden Gate Bridge.

```
<html>
  <head>
    <meta http-equiv="Content-Type" content="text/html;
    charset=windows-1252">
    <title>
      Testing Accessible design
    </title>
  </head>
  <body link="#0000ff" vlink="#800080">
    <p>
      <font face="Arial" size="4"><b>Testing Accessible
      Design</b></font>
    </p>
    <p>
      <font size="2">This is a page of html generated from
      a word processor program.</font>
    </p>
    <ul>
      <li>
        <font size="2">This is <a href="http://www.
        w3.org/">a link to the W3C site</a>, just for demo
        purposes.</font>
      </li>
    </ul>
    <p>
      <font size="2"><a href="bridge.html"><img
      src="Image1.gif"
      width="100" height="57"></a></font>
    </p>
    <p>
      <font size="2">A small graphic above shows a cartoon
      image of a bridge. It is also a link to information
      about the Golden Gate Bridge.</font>
    </p>
  </body>
</html>
```

a) Look up the Priority 1 checkpoints and determine what minimum corrections are required to assure a Competence Level A.

_____

_____

LAB 12.2 EXERCISE ANSWERS

12.2.1 ANSWERS

a) How could our aging population benefit from accessible Web sites?

Answer: With aging can come many of the same problems faced by the physically disabled. Eyesight and hearing become less acute, physical mobility and dexterity decrease, and cognition may deteriorate. An accessible Web site can meet the needs of our increasingly aging population.

b) Give an example of how a Web site could be made more accessible for someone with these disabilities:

1) Blind or low vision

   Text descriptions of non-text elements for voice or Braille output

   Relative (rather than absolute) font size for better enlargement

2) Color blind

   Good contrast between text and background

   Items identified by color only (such as links) are not named !important so they can be overridden by author style sheet.

3) Hearing impaired

   Transcription of speech and captioning of video elements

4) Paralysis or limb weakness

   Keyboard shortcuts for common links

   Larger buttons or navigation areas for alternate pointing devices

5) Impaired short term memory

   Clear and consistent page organization

   Content in redundant formats—audio and text

12.2.2 ANSWERS

Running the code through Bobby (http://www.cast.org/bobby/) yields the following results:

This page does not yet meet the requirements for Bobby Approved status. Below is a list of **Level 1**-accessibility problems that should be fixed in order to make this page accessible to people with disabilities.

1. **Provide alternative text for all images. (1 instance) Line 20:** <p><a HREF="bridge.html"><img SRC="Image1.gif" width="100" height="57"></a> </p>

    P1 - Manual check

    There are some checkpoints that an automatic program like Bobby cannot examine. These 4 item(s) are presented below. You will need to be able to respond affirmatively to these items as well to obtain Bobby Approved status.

    a. Ensure that descriptions of dynamic content are updated with changes in content.

    b. If any of the images on this page convey important information beyond what is in each image's alternative text, add a LONGDESC attribute. *(1 instance)* Line 20: <p><a HREF= "bridge.html"><img SRC="Image1.gif" width="100" height="57"> </a></p>

    c. If you can't figure out any other way to make a page accessible, construct an alternate version of the page which is accessible and has the same content.

    d. If any of the images on this page convey important information beyond what is in each image's alternative text, add descriptive (D) links. *(1 instance)* Line 20: <p><a HREF="bridge.html"><img SRC= "Image1.gif" width="100" height="57"> </a></p>

    By adding alt text to the image, a long description to show the link, and a "D" link, the page will meet Competence Level A. For example:

    <a HREF="bridge.html"><img SRC="Image1.gif" width="100" height="57" alt="Cartoon image of bridge, link to information about the Golden Gate Bridge" longdesc= "bridge.html"> D</a>

    The resulting page appears below. There is certainly more that could be done, such as replacing the font tags with a style sheet and adding the appropriate .doc type.

**LAB
12.2**

Testing Accessible Design

This is a page of html generated from a word processor program.

- This is a link to the W3C site, just for demo purposes.

A small graphic above shows a cartoon image of a bridge. It is also a link to information about the Golden Gate Bridge.

LAB 12.2 SELF-REVIEW QUESTIONS

In order to test your progress, you should be able to answer the following questions.

1) To make an accessible Web page it must be plain, boring text.

    a) _____ True
    b) _____ False

2) Accessible Web pages can be viewed in small screen Internet devices.

    a) _____ True
    b) _____ False

3) Which of the following is not one of the fourteen guidelines according to the W3C Web Content Accessibility Guidelines?

    a) _____ Use nested tables for formatting text on a page.
    b) _____ Design for device-independence.
    c) _____ Don't rely on color alone.
    d) _____ Clarify natural language usage.

4) A Web site that conforms to all Priority 1 and 2 level checkpoints according to the Web Content Accessibility Guidelines 1.0 can display the following statement:

a) _____ Conformance Level "A"

b) _____ Conformance Level "AA"

c) _____ Conformance Level "Double A"

d) _____ Conformance Level "Triple A"

Quiz answers appear in the Appendix, Section 12.2.

C H A P T E R   1 2

TEST YOUR THINKING

1) There can be a conflict between using all the latest bells and whistles and making the site accessible according to the W3C Web Content Accessibility Guidelines. Describe this conflict. How would you resolve it for your site?

2) At a recent Web conference with a ½ day devoted to the Web accessibility, all of the presentations were simulcast and archived in streaming video. One presenter noted that since we did not provide subtitles for the video, they were not accessible and we should not have presented the video at all. What do you think?

C H A P T E R   1 3

COPYRIGHT LAW BASICS

CHAPTER OBJECTIVES

In this chapter, you will learn about:

Found some great content for your Web site? Chances are that it's protected by copyright. Here's why:

- Copyright protection is available for text, art, graphics, photos, and music (both the composition and the sound recording) and is easy to obtain.

- Copyright protection lasts a long time. Under current U.S. law, the copyright term for a work created by an individual is the life of the author plus seventy years.

Copyright law is a "federal" law (known as the Copyright Act, 17 U.S.C. Sections 1 through 810), and so the law does not vary from state to state (although the interpretation of the law may be different in different courts). The entire law is available on the Web at www.loc.gov/copyright/title17.

In this part of the book, a series of scenarios are used to illustrate the legal issues associated with Web content and management. This chapter summarizes the basic principles of copyright law. Chapter 14, Steering Clear of Copyright Infringement, will explain how you can minimize your risk of being sued for copyright infringement. The basic principles discussed in this chapter are referred to in other chapters in this part of the book as well.

© 2000 by J. Dianne Brinson. Dianne Brinson is also the author of several books on Internet law, including *Internet Law and Business Handbook*, available from Ladera Press, www.ladera-press.com, tel. 800-523-3721.

L A B   1 3 . 1

HOW COPYRIGHT PROTECTION IS OBTAINED

LAB OBJECTIVES

After this lab, you will be able to:

- ✔ Understand How Copyright Protection Is Obtained
- ✔ Understand the Types of Works For Which Protection Is Available
- ✔ Understand the Standards a Work Must Meet to Get Protection
- ✔ Understand What Is Meant by "Public Domain" Works

Under current United State law, copyright protection arises automatically when an "original" work of authorship is "fixed" in a tangible medium of expression. That's right, *automatically*.

You may be familiar with the use of copyright notice (for example, "Copyright 1999 by Joe Smith") and with registering a copyright with the Copyright Office in Washington, DC. Notice and registration are now optional. An original "work of authorship" is automatically protected by copyright as soon as it has been fixed. There's no need to file anything. In the rest of this section, I'll explain the meaning of the terms *works of authorship, original,* and *fixed.*

WORKS OF AUTHORSHIP

The Copyright Act states that works of authorship include the following types of works:

- *Literary works.* Examples of works in this class are novels, nonfiction prose, screenplays, poetry, newspaper articles and newspapers, magazine articles and magazines, computer software, software documentation and manuals, training manuals, manuals, catalogs, brochures, ads (text), and compilations such as business directories.

- *Musical works.* Examples of works in this class are songs, advertising jingles, and instrumentals.

- *Dramatic works.* Examples of works in this class are plays, operas, and skits.

- *Pantomimes and choreographic works.* Examples of works in this class are ballets, modern dance, jazz dance, and mime works.

- *Pictorial, graphic, and sculptural works.* Examples of works in this class are photographs, posters, maps, paintings, drawings, graphic art, display ads, cartoon strips and cartoon characters, stuffed animals, statues, paintings, and works of fine art.

- *Motion pictures and other audiovisual works.* Examples of works in this class are movies, documentaries, travelogues, training films and videos, television shows, television ads, videogames, and interactive multimedia works.

- *Sound recordings.* Examples of works in this class are recordings of music, sounds, or words.

- *Architectural works.* This class includes building designs, whether in the form of architectural plans, drawings, or the constructed building itself.

If you're thinking that these examples encompass virtually everything you could use as content for a Web site, you're correct. Web sites themselves are also "works of authorship."

ORIGINAL

A work is "original" as long as it owes its origin to the author (as opposed to being copied from some preexisting work). A work can be original without being novel, unique, creative, or valuable. A work can incorporate preexisting material and still be original. When preexisting material is incorporated into a new work, the copyright on the new work covers only the original material contributed by the author.

■ FOR EXAMPLE

Web Developer used preexisting photographs and graphics (with the permission of the copyright owners) in a Web design project. The Web site as a whole owes its origin to Developer, but the photographs and graphics do not. The copyright on the Web site does not cover the photographs, just the material created by Developer. Even if Developer adds no new material, his "compilation" of preexisting content is protected by copyright.

FIXED

According to the Copyright Act, a work is "fixed" when it is made "sufficiently permanent or stable to permit it to be perceived, reproduced, or communicated for a period of more than transitory duration." Forms of "fixation" include writing, typing, dictating into a tape recorder, entering into a computer, and videotaping.

Under current law, registration with the Copyright Office is optional (but you have to register before you file an infringement suit). The Copyright Act provides incentives for "timely" registration, the most important of which concerns attorney's fees: If you register within three months of publication, you may be able to recover your attorney's fees if you file an infringement action and win. "Publication" is defined as distribution of copies to the public by sale, rental, lease, or lending. Information on copyright registration and copyright law is available on the Copyright Office's Web site, www.loc.gov/copyright/.

The Copyright Act states that works prepared by federal government officers and employees as part of their official duties are not protected by copyright. Consequently, federal statutes (the Copyright Act, for example) and regulations are not protected by copyright. This rule does not apply to works created by state government officers and employees.

Uncopyrightable works and works for which copyright protection has ended are referred to as *public domain* works. Some of the material on the Web is in the public domain. However, much of the material on the Web is protected by copyright. Public domain works are also discussed in Chapter 14, Steering Clear of Copyright Infringement.

Under current law, the copyright term for works created by individuals is life of the author plus seventy years. The copyright term for *works made for hire* is ninety-five years from the date of first publication or 120 years from the date of creation, whichever expires first. Works made for hire are works created by employees for employers and certain types of specially commissioned works.

U.S. authors automatically receive copyright protection in all countries that are parties to the Berne Convention for the Protection of Literary and Artistic works, or parties to the Universal Copyright Convention. Most countries belong to at least one of these conventions. Members of these two conventions have agreed to give nationals of member countries the same level of copyright protection they give their own nationals.

LAB 13.1 EXERCISES

13.1.1 UNDERSTAND HOW COPYRIGHT PROTECTION IS OBTAINED

a) Joe has just finished creating some great graphics for his Web site. He wants to obtain a copyright on his graphics before he puts them up on his Web site. What does Joe need to do in order to get copyright protection for his graphics?

_____

_____

b) If Joe puts the graphics on his Web site without a copyright notice, is he giving up his copyright rights?

_____

_____

13.1.2 UNDERSTAND THE TYPES OF WORKS FOR WHICH PROTECTION IS AVAILABLE

a) Visit one of your favorite Web sites. What "works of authorship" do you see there?

_____

_____

13.1.3 UNDERSTAND THE STANDARDS A WORK MUST MEET TO GET PROTECTION

a) There are a number of copyrighted books on the market on how to write HTML code. How can all these books meet copyright law's originality requirement?

_____

_____

b) The book *Jane Brown's New HTML Guide* is an updated version of the earlier book *Jane Brown's HTML Guide*. Is *Jane Brown's New HTML Guide* original?

_____

_____

13.1.4 UNDERSTAND WHAT IS MEANT BY "PUBLIC DOMAIN"

a) Is the Copyright Office's Web site (www.loc.gov/copyright/) protected by copyright or in the public domain?

_____

_____

b) Is the Web site of the California State Board of Equalization (www.boe.ca.gov/) protected by copyright?

_____

_____

LAB 13.1 EXERCISE ANSWERS

13.1.1 ANSWERS

a) Joe has just finished creating some great graphics for his Web site. He wants to obtain a copyright on his graphics before he puts them up on his Web site. What does Joe need to do in order to get copyright protection for his graphics?

Answer: Nothing. Under current law, copyright protection arises automatically when an original work of authorship is fixed. If Joe wants to register the copyright in his graphics with the Copyright Office (optional), he can obtain the registration form at www.loc.gov/copyright/forms. For registering the copyright in graphics, he should use Form VA (visual arts). He may also want to obtain Information Circular 40, Copyright Registration for Works of Visual Arts, from the Copyright Office Web site (www.loc.gov/copyright/). If Joe wants to register the copyright in his Web site (and not just the copyright in the graphics), he should get Circular 55, Copyright Registration for Multimedia Works, from the Copyright Office Web site.

b) If Joe puts the graphics on his Web site without a copyright notice, is he giving up his copyright rights?

Answer: No, because under current law, the use of copyright notice is optional. However, using notice informs the public—and people who want to use the copyrighted work—that the work is copyrighted.

13.1.2 ANSWER

a) Visit one of your favorite Web sites. What "works of authorship" do you see there?

Answer: The Web site's text and graphics are works of authorship. If the Web site contains photos, the photos are works of authorship. If the Web site you visited contained music, both the musical compositions and the recordings of the music are works of authorship. The Web site's program code is also a work of authorship. Finally, the Web site as a whole is a work of authorship (a compilation of the components). Any of these works of authorship may be protected by copyright—and is protected, automatically, if original and fixed, unless the copyright has expired. (Of course, material created by a federal government employee within the scope of employment is not protected by copyright).

13.1.3 ANSWERS

a) There are a number of copyrighted books on the market on how to write HTML code. How can all these books meet copyright law's originality requirement?

Answer: Each book is original as long as it owes its origin to its author (as opposed to being copied from an earlier book on how to write HTML code). Originality does not require uniqueness or novelty.

b) The book *Jane Brown's New HTML Guide* is an updated version of the earlier book *Jane Brown's HTML Guide*. Is *Jane Brown's New HTML Guide* original?

Answer: Yes, as long as Jane Brown's New HTML Guide *has additional, original material that was not included in the earlier book—for example, new chapters and revisions and updates to the earlier book's chapters.*

13.1.4 ANSWERS

a) Is the Copyright Office's Web site (www.loc.gov/copyright/) and the material on that site protected by copyright or in the public domain?

Answer: The Copyright Office is part of the federal government (a department of the Library of Congress). Any material on the site that was created by Copyright Office staff or other federal government employees within the scope of their employment is not protected by copyright. The Circulars (informational documents on copyright registration and law), for example, were probably created by Copyright Office staff members. If so, the Circulars are not protected by copyright. A federal agency or office may include material created by nonemployees on its Web site, so don't assume that everything you find on a federal site is in the public domain.

b) Is the Web site of the California State Board of Equalization (www.boe.ca.gov/) protected by copyright?

Answer: Yes, if it's original. Works created by federal government employees are not copyrightable because a provision of the Copyright Act, a federal law, states that they are not copyrightable. There is no provision in the Copyright Act making works created by state or local government employees uncopyrightable. If you looked at the BOE Web site, I hope you weren't misled by the fact that there was no copyright notice on the site. Remember, a site doesn't need a copyright notice to be protected by copyright.

LAB 13.1 SELF-REVIEW QUESTIONS

In order to test your progress, you should be able to answer the following questions.

1) How is copyright protection obtained?

a) _____ By filing a registration application with the Copyright Office
b) _____ By "fixing" an "original work of authorship"
c) _____ By filing a lawsuit in federal court
d) _____ By doing (a) and (b)

2) Which of the following are "works of authorship" that can be protected by copyright?

a) _____ Photographs
b) _____ Software
c) _____ A motion picture
d) _____ A musical composition
e) _____ All of the above

3) A work meets copyright law's "originality" requirement if which of the following is met?

a) _____ If the work is unique, "one of a kind"
b) _____ If it owes its origin to the "author" (was not copied from preexisting material)
c) _____ If it is creative
d) _____ If it meets all three of these standards

4) Which of these acts would satisfy copyright law's "fixation" requirement?

a) _____ Audio recording
b) _____ Video recording
c) _____ Writing in ink
d) _____ Entering into a computer's memory
e) _____ All of the above

5) Which categories of works are in the public domain?

a) _____ Anything that's on the Web
b) _____ Works created by state government employees as part of their official duties
c) _____ Noncreative works
d) _____ Works whose copyrights have expired and works created by federal government employees as part of their official duties

Quiz answers appear in the Appendix, Section 13.1.

L A B 1 3 . 2

THE COPYRIGHT OWNER'S RIGHTS

LAB OBJECTIVES

After this lab, you will be able to:

✔ Understand the Rights of the Copyright Owner
✔ Understand the Major Exceptions to the Copyright Owner's Rights

---

The copyright owner has five exclusive rights in the copyrighted work. These rights give the owner the legal power to control uses of the work by others (subject to a few exceptions, the most important of which are discussed later in this section). The five exclusive rights of the copyright owner are as follows:

- *Reproduction Right.* The reproduction right is the right to copy, duplicate, transcribe, or imitate the work in fixed form. Scanning a copyrighted work for use on a Web site is an exercise of the copyright owner's reproduction right.

- *Modification Right.* The modification right (also known as the derivative works right) is the right to modify the work to create a new work. A new work that is based on a preexisting work is known as a "derivative work." Altering a photograph is an exercise of the modification right, as is creating an interactive version of a novel or creating a sequel to a computer game or motion picture.

- *Distribution Right.* The distribution right is the right to distribute copies of the work to the public by sale, rental, lease, or lending. Printing copies of a copyrighted document from a Web site for distribution is an exercise of the distribution right.

- *Public Performance Right.* The public performance right is the right to recite, play, dance, act, or show the work at a public place or to transmit it to the public. In the case of a motion picture or other audiovisual work, showing the work's images in sequence is considered "performance." Showing scenes from a copyrighted motion picture on a Web site in sequence is an exercise of the public performance right, as is the use of a copyrighted musical composition on a Web site. Sound recordings—recorded versions of music or other sounds—do not have a public performance right except for a special "digital performance right," which applies when a sound recording is used on the Internet.

- *Public Display Right.* The public display right is the right to show a copy of the work directly or by means of a film, slide, or television image at a public place or to transmit it to the public. In the case of a motion picture or other audiovisual work, showing the work's images out of sequence is considered "display." Making copyrighted material available for Web users to look at on a Web site or on a bulletin board is an exercise of the public display right.

Copyright infringement is the exercise of one or more of the exclusive rights of a copyright owner.

■ FOR EXAMPLE

John scanned Photographer's copyrighted photograph, altered the image by using digital editing software, and included the altered version of the photograph in John's e-commerce Web site. If John used Photographer's photograph without permission, John infringed Photographer's copyright by violating the reproduction right (scanning the photograph), the modification right (altering the photograph), and the public display right.

A copyright owner can recover damages from an infringer. The federal district courts also have the power to issue injunctions (orders) to prevent or restrain copyright infringement, and to order the impoundment and destruction of infringing copies.

Those who use infringing material created by others can also be liable for infringement.

■ FOR EXAMPLE

Suppose John (from the previous example) was a Web site developer who used Photographer's photo in an e-commerce Web site that John created for Client. Client's use of the photo in Client's Web site makes Client an infringer, too (even if Client had no intent to infringe and didn't know that John used Photographer's photo without permission). Client, by using Photographer's photo on the Web, is exercising Photographer's public display right in the photo.

Employers are liable for infringement done by their employees within the scope of the employment. The liability of a system operator, service provider, bulletin board provider, or chat room provider for a third-party user's posting of infringing material on the system is covered in Chapter 16, System Operator Liability for Copyright Infringement by Users. Whether linking to another site without permission is infringement is covered in Chapter 18, Linking, Framing, Caching, and Meta tags.

There are two major exceptions to the copyright owner's rights: First, the copyright on a work does not extend to the work's facts or ideas. Second, "fair use" of a copyrighted work is not infringement.

The reason why copyright protection does not extend to a work's facts or ideas is that copyright protection is limited to original works of authorship. No one can claim originality or authorship for facts or ideas. Others are free to copy facts or ideas from a copyrighted work.

The "fair use" of a copyrighted work is not a violation of the copyright owner's legal rights because copyright owners are, by law, deemed to consent to the fair use of their works by others. Examples of fair use are quoting passages from a book in a book review; summarizing an article, with brief quotations, for a news report; and copying a small part of a work to give to students to illustrate a lesson.

Unfortunately, it is difficult to tell whether a particular use of a work is fair or unfair. Determinations are made on a case-by-case basis by considering four factors:

- *Factor 1: Purpose and character of use.* The courts are most likely to find fair use where the use is for noncommercial purposes, such as a book review.

- *Factor 2: Nature of the copyrighted work.* The courts are most likely to find fair use where the copied work is a factual work rather than a creative one.

- *Factor 3: Amount and substantiality of the portion used.* The courts are most likely to find fair use where what is used is a tiny amount of the protected work. If what is used is small in amount but substantial in terms of importance, a finding of fair use is unlikely.

- *Factor 4: Effect on the potential market for or value of the protected work.* The courts are most likely to find fair use where the new work is not a substitute for the copyrighted work. If the new work takes sales or licensing fees away from the copyrighted work, a finding of fair use is unlikely.

There's been some confusion about how fair use applies to the Internet. Some people think that using someone else's copyrighted material on the Internet is fair use, because the "culture" of the Internet is that it's okay to do this ("everyone does it"). And some think that copying and using material that you find on the Internet is also fair use ("the owner wouldn't have posted the material if he or she didn't want others to use it"). However, under current law, there is no absolute fair use right to post someone else's copyrighted material on the Internet or to use material you find on the Internet. If copyrighted material is used on the Internet without the owner's permission or copied from the Internet without the owner's permission, whether the use is fair use will be decided by considering the four factors discussed above.

 Here are some practical fair use guidelines for Web site developers and owners:

- *If you are creating a Web site for purely noncommercial purposes— for a nonprofit organization, for example—it is possible that you can justify copying small amounts of material as fair use.*

- *If you use copyrighted content on a Web site for a for-profit company—even an "information only" Web site—or on a Web site that serves any commercial use, it will be hard to succeed on a fair use defense. It's better to get permission.*

- *If your Web site serves traditional "fair use" purposes—criticism, comment, news reporting, teaching, scholarship, and research—you have a better chance of falling within the bounds of fair use than you do if your Web site's purpose is entertainment or business.*

LAB 13.2 EXERCISES

13.2.1 UNDERSTAND THE RIGHTS OF THE COPYRIGHT OWNER

a) Henry wants to create an interactive computer game using the
characters, setting, and plot from his favorite current television
series, *Enemies*. Does he need to worry about copyright law?

13.2.2 UNDERSTAND THE MAJOR EXCEPTIONS TO THE COPYRIGHT OWNER'S RIGHTS

a) Visit my Web site, www.laderapress.com. What sorts of things
could you do with material on that site without violating my
copyright owner's rights?

LAB 13.2 EXERCISE ANSWERS

13.2.1 ANSWER

a) Henry wants to create an interactive computer game using the characters, setting, and plot from his favorite current television series, *Enemies*. Does he need
to worry about copyright law?

*Answer: Yes. The television series is protected by copyright. Television screenplays (scripts) are
protected as literary works. Filmed episodes are protected as audiovisual works. Distinctive
fictional characters can be protected under both copyright and trademark law. The person
or company that owns the copyright in Enemies (a studio or production company, most
likely) has the exclusive right to reproduce, modify, distribute, publicly display, and publicly
perform Enemies. If Henry creates an interactive computer game using the characters, setting, and plot from the series, he will be exercising the copyright owner's reproduction and
modification rights. Henry could ask the copyright owner for permission to create a computer game based on Enemies. However, such spin-off rights are valuable, and Henry may
not be able to afford the copyright owner's fee for granting this permission (or the copyright
owner may have already granted someone else this permission on an exclusive basis).*

13.2.2 ANSWER

a) Visit my Web site, www.laderapress.com. What sorts of things could you do with material on that site without violating my copyright owner's rights?

Answer: You can use the ideas that I use in my site. Here are some examples of ideas used in my site:

Create a site giving information on copyright law

Create a site to publicize and sell books

Provide a button bar for the site

Offer sample chapters from books

Offer a free primer on intellectual property law

Offer information on copyright legislation

Offer online ordering

Provide a guest book

Provide links to other sites

You can also use facts from my site's documents—for example, the fact that copyright protection arises automatically when an original work of authorship is fixed, or the fact that Congress recently passed a new law. And you can make fair use of my site's material without violating my rights. Copyright owners are, by law, deemed to consent to fair use of their works by others. For example, including a screen shot of my site's home page in a "best and worst Web sites" article might be fair use, and printing copies of the Intellectual Property Primer to use in a high school Web design class might be fair use. (In fact, you don't have to rely on fair use to make multiple copies of the Primer for educational use, because the Web site's Conditions of Use and Disclaimer, at the bottom of the Home Page, includes a grant of permission to copy the Primer for educational use, subject to the conditions in the Primer's license notice).

LAB 13.2 SELF-REVIEW QUESTIONS

In order to test your progress, you should be able to answer the following questions.

1) Which of the following is *not* an exercise of one of the exclusive rights of a copyright owner?

a) _____ Photocopying an entire copyrighted magazine article

b) _____ Scanning the article

c) _____ Posting the article on a Web site so that others won't have to buy the magazine

d) _____ Using the facts from the article

2) Which of the following is most likely to be fair use?

   a) _____ Scanning a book and selling individual chapters from a Web site
   b) _____ Creating and selling an "updated version" of a book
   c) _____ Quoting passages from a book in a Web book review site

3) In which of these situations is the defendant most likely to be able to prove fair use?

   a) _____ The defendant used the plaintiff's copyrighted material on a fee-for-subscription Web site
   b) _____ The defendant used the plaintiff's copyrighted material to create an online version of the plaintiff's product, and people stopped buying the plaintiff's product
   c) _____ The defendant used a tiny amount of the plaintiff's copyrighted work in a Web site for a nonprofit charitable organization.

4) Client gave Web Developer a number of copyrighted photos to use in a Web site that Developer was creating for Client. Developer scanned and altered the photos for use in the Web site, which is now up on the Web. If Client did not own the copyrights in the photos or have permission to use them, who is liable for copyright infringement?

   a) _____ Client, for publicly displaying copyrighted photos on the Web without the permission of the photos' copyright owners
   b) _____ Developer, for scanning and altering the photos.
   c) _____ Both Client and Developer

5) Web Developer (from question 4) obtained and used graphics belonging to someone else in Client's Web site. If Developer did not have permission to use the graphics, who is liable for copyright infringement?

   a) _____ Client
   b) _____ Developer
   c) _____ Both Client and Developer

Quiz answers appear in the Appendix, Section 13.2.

LAB
13.2

LAB 13.3

COPYRIGHT LAW OWNERSHIP RULES

LAB OBJECTIVES

After this lab, you will be able to:

✔ Understand the Copyright Act's Three "Default"
Ownership Rules
✔ Understand What a Copyright Assignment Is

The Copyright Act has "default rules" on ownership that apply if the parties to a transaction do not reach their own agreement on ownership. They can always be varied by agreement of the parties. The basic rule is that ownership of copyright initially belongs to the author or authors of the work.

■ *FOR EXAMPLE*

Sarah, a photographer, took a photograph of the Lincoln Memorial. Sarah is the author of the photograph and the initial owner of the copyright in the photograph.

The "author" is generally the individual who created the work. However, when an employee creates work within the scope of the employment, the employer is considered the "author," and the work is a "work made for hire." Unless the parties have agreed otherwise in a signed written document, the employer owns the copyright of a work made for hire.

■ *FOR EXAMPLE*

As part of his job, John, an employee of Big Co.'s marketing department, created a Web site for Big Co. Even though John created the Web site, Big Co. is the author for copyright purposes. Big Co. owns the copyright in the Web site (unless John and Big Co. have agreed in a signed contract that John owns the copyright).

A different rule applies, however, when an independent contractor (freelancer) creates material for a client. When a hiring party and an independent contractor fail to address the issue of ownership of copyrights in works created by the independent contractor, the copyrights are owned by the independent contractor.

■ FOR EXAMPLE

Web Entrepreneur hired Freelancer on a project basis to create graphics for a Web site. If Web Entrepreneur and Freelancer did not address the issue of copyright ownership, Freelancer owns the copyright in the graphics—even though Web Entrepreneur paid Freelancer to create them.

Many people think that a hiring party who commissions and pays for material automatically owns the copyright in the material. That's wrong. There are two ways for a party who hires an independent contractor to obtain ownership of the material created by the contractor:

(1) A written, signed assignment, which is a transfer of copyright ownership
(2) A written work-for-hire agreement, which can only be used for works commissioned for use as one of these types of works:
>   Contribution to a collective work
>   Part of a motion picture or other audiovisual work
>   Translation
>   Supplementary work
>   Compilation
>   Instructional text
>   Test or answer material for a test
>   Atlas
>   Sound recording

Because a work for hire agreement can only be used for contributions to these types of works—and because these agreements have other limitations (one of which is that these agreements are not valid under the copyright laws of other countries)—it is better that an assignment be used if a hiring party wants to get copyright ownership of material created by a freelancer.

When a copyright is assigned, the assignee (individual or company to whom it is assigned) becomes the owner of the exclusive rights of copyright in the protected work.

■ *FOR EXAMPLE*

Jorge, an individual working on his own, created search engine software and then assigned the copyright in the software to Software Company. After the assignment, Software Company has the exclusive right to reproduce and distribute the software. If Jorge starts selling the software or creates a new version of the software, he will be infringing Software Company's rights as copyright owner.

An assignment is not valid unless it is in writing and is signed by the owner of the rights conveyed or the owner's authorized agent. An assignment can be recorded in the Copyright Office to give others "constructive notice" of the assignment. Constructive notice is a legal term that means you are presumed to know a fact (because it is a matter of public record) even if you have no actual knowledge of the fact.

**LAB
13.3**

A copyright owner can grant others permission to use a copyrighted work in a way that would otherwise be copyright infringement. The owner's grant of permission is known as a license. Licenses are discussed in Chapter 14, Steering Clear of Copyright Infringement.

LAB 13.3 EXERCISES

13.3.1 UNDERSTAND THE COPYRIGHT ACT'S THREE "DEFAULT" OWNERSHIP RULES

a) Maria, a freelance Web developer, created a Web site for Big Co. on a "handshake" basis (no written contract or any paperwork at all). Now Maria wants to use the "shopping cart" program that she created for the Big Co. project in a Web design project she is doing for Small Co. Is she entitled to do that?

_____

_____

b) While Sam was employed as a Web designer at Webco, he created some wonderful Web site graphics. Sam recently quit working for Webco and has gone out on his own. Is Sam entitled to use the graphics he created for Webco in the projects he does for his own clients?

_____

_____

c) Why are the Copyright Act's ownership rules referred to as "default" rules?

_____

_____

13.3.2 UNDERSTAND WHAT A COPYRIGHT ASSIGNMENT IS

a) Consider this excerpt from a publishing agreement:

Publisher agrees to file a copyright registration on the Author's book *Trashy Novel* in the Author's name. Author hereby assigns all right, title, and interest, including copyrights, in *Trashy Novel* to Publisher.

Who owns the copyright in *Trashy Novel?*

_____

_____

LAB 13.3 EXERCISE ANSWERS

13.3.1 ANSWERS

a) Maria, a freelance Web developer, created a Web site for Big Co. on a "handshake" basis (no written contract or any paperwork, no discussion of copyright ownership). Now Maria wants to use the "shopping cart" program that she created for the Big Co. project in a Web design project she is doing for Small Co. Is she entitled to do that?

Answer: Yes, because she owns the copyright in the shopping cart program. She did not assign the copyright in the Web site to Big Co., so Big Co. does not own the copyright. One who orders and pays for work created by a freelancer but does not get an assignment generally has an implied license to use the work as intended by the hiring party and the freelancer. However, an implied license to use the work is much less valuable than owning the copyright in the work. If the hiring party owns the copyright, it can exercise all of the copyright owner's exclusive rights in the work. If the hiring party merely has an implied license (permission) to use the work, it can only do those things that are within the scope of the license (and the hiring party and freelancer may disagree on the scope of the license).

b) While Sam was employed as a Web designer at Webco, he created some wonderful Web site graphics. Sam recently quit working for Webco and has gone out on his own. Is Sam entitled to use the graphics he created for Webco in the projects he does for his own clients?

Answer: No, Sam is not entitled to use the graphics, because he does not own the copyright in the graphics. Webco does. Sam is entitled to use his knowledge and skill to create new graphics, and he is entitled to use the ideas he used in Webco's graphics.

c) Why are the Copyright Act's ownership rules referred to as "default" rules?

Answer: Because these rules can be varied by agreement of the parties. For example, Maria and Big Co. (in question a) could agree that Maria would assign the copyright in the Web site design to Big Co. Sam and Webco (in question b) could agree that Sam would own the copyright in the graphics he created for Webco, his employer. These agreements need to take the form of signed writings.

13.3.2 ANSWER

a) Consider this excerpt from a publishing agreement:

Publisher agrees to file a copyright registration on the Author's book *Trashy Novel* in the Author's name. Author hereby assigns all right, title, and interest, including copyrights, in *Trashy Novel* to Publisher.

Both Publisher and Author signed the agreement. Who owns the copyright in *Trashy Novel?*

Answer: Publisher owns the copyright in Trashy Novel. *The agreement is a copyright assignment—a transfer of copyright ownership from Author to Publisher. The fact that Publisher files the copyright registration in Author's name doesn't mean that Author remains the owner of the copyright. Author is just the initial owner. Transfers of copyright ownership can be recorded in the Copyright Office. Information Circulars on recording assignments (Circular 12, Recordations of Transfers) and searching the Copyright Office's registration and assignment records (How to Investigate the Copyright Status of a Work) are available on the Copyright Office's Web site,* www.loc.gov/copyright/.

LAB 13.3 SELF-REVIEW QUESTIONS

In order to test your progress, you should be able to answer the following questions. Use the Copyright Act's "default" rules to answer the first two questions.

1) When an employee creates a copyrighted work within the scope of employment, who owns the copyright?

   a) _____ The employee
   b) _____ The employer
   c) _____ The employee and the employer jointly

2) When a freelancer creates a copyrighted work for a client and the ownership issue is not addressed in writing, who owns the copyright?

   a) _____ The freelancer
   b) _____ The client
   c) _____ The freelancer and the client jointly

3) How does a client obtain copyright ownership for material created by a freelancer?

   a) _____ By paying for the material's creation
   b) _____ By accepting delivery of the material
   c) _____ By oral or written agreement with the freelancer that the client will own the copyright
   d) _____ By getting a written, signed assignment of the copyright from the freelancer

4) Sally created a "shopping cart" program for e-commerce and assigned the copyright in the program to MegaWeb. Which statement is true?

   a) _____ Sally still has the right to create an improved version of the program.
   b) _____ Sally still has the right to make and sell copies of the program.
   c) _____ Sally still has the right to use the program in Web sites she designs for clients, but not the right to sell the program separately from her Web design projects.
   d) _____ None of these. Sally no longer has any of these rights. MegaWeb does.

5) Author assigned the copyright in her book *Trashy Novel* to Publisher. NewWay, Inc. wants to create an "electronic book" version of *Trashy Novel*. NewWay needs permission from which of the following?

   a) _____ Author
   b) _____ Publisher
   c) _____ Author and Publisher
   d) _____ None of the above

Quiz answers appear in the Appendix, Section 13.3.

CHAPTER 13

TEST YOUR THINKING

You have just been appointed director of online marketing for Z Co. Your boss, the President of Z Co., has asked you to look at Z Co.'s Web site immediately to determine if the necessary steps have been taken to get copyright protection for the Web site. The President is also worried about copyright infringement. Fast Ed, your predecessor, knew nothing about copyright. After investigating, here's what you find out:

1) Fast Ed never registered the copyright on the site, and the site does not contain a copyright notice.
2) The Web site was designed by Ann, Z Co.'s Webmaster, while she was a full-time employee of Z Co., as part of her job. She did most of the work at home on weekends. Ann quit in a huff just last week. She may claim she owns the Web site design.
3) The Web site contains several articles on Z Co.'s products written by Fast Ed. Ed is threatening to sue Z Co. if Z Co. doesn't immediately remove his articles from the Web site.
4) The Web site contains several photographs that Fast Ed scanned from a magazine travel photo article, "Best Travel Photos of 1998."

What should you tell your boss?

C H A P T E R   1 4

STEERING CLEAR OF COPYRIGHT INFRINGEMENT

CHAPTER OBJECTIVES

In this chapter, you will learn about:

Are you thinking of using pre-existing content (text, art, graphics, photos, or music) in a Web design project? Or are you planning on copying material from the Web for use in your own project? Read this chapter first. Drawing on the basic principles of copyright law explained in Chapter 13, Copyright Law Basics, this chapter will help you steer clear of copyright infringement and the costs associated with infringement.

Copyright infringement can cripple a company. For example, a few years ago, one company, Delrina, lost hundreds of thousands of dollars and had to recall all of the copies of its screen saver when it lost a copyright suit. Delrina distributed a screen saver in which one of the thirty modules showed the comic book character Opus shooting down Berkeley Systems' "flying toasters" (made famous in Berkeley's "After Dark" screen saver program). Berkeley Systems sued Delrina for copyright and trademark infringement. The court ruled for Berkeley Systems, prohibiting further distribution of Delrina's product and requiring Delrina to recall all of the product not already sold.

© 2000 by J. Dianne Brinson.

415

L A B   1 4 . 1

AN ANALYSIS FOR AVOIDING COPYRIGHT INFRINGEMENT

LAB OBJECTIVES

After this lab, you will be able to:

✔ Use an Analysis to Avoid Copyright Infringement
✔ Understand How Works Fall into the Public Domain

When you find material you want to use—whether you find it on the Web or in "old media"—use this three-step analysis in order to minimize your risk of being sued for copyright infringement:

- Is the material in the public domain or copyrighted? If it's in the public domain, you do not need permission to use it.

- If the material is copyrighted, is what you plan to do an exercise of one of the copyright owner's exclusive rights (reproduction, modification, distribution, public display, and public performance, discussed in Lab 13.2)? If what you plan to do is not an exercise of one of these exclusive rights, you do not need permission. For example, if you plan to use facts from a copyrighted work, that's not an exercise of the exclusive rights, because facts are not protected by copyright. If what you plan to do *is* an exercise of one of the exclusive rights—for example, scanning a photo to use in your Web site—generally, you need the copyright owner's permission. While using copyrighted material on the Web without permission will not necessarily get you sued, copyright owners are beginning to take legal action when they find their material used on the Web without permission.

• Is your use fair use? If so, you don't need permission to use the material, even if your use is an exercise of one of the copyright owner's exclusive rights.

There are a number of myths about the necessity of getting permission. Don't make the mistake of believing these myths:

> Myth 1: "I don't need to get permission because I'm using only a small amount of the copyrighted work."

It is true that *de minimis* copying (copying a small amount) is not copyright infringement. Unfortunately, it is rarely possible to tell where *de minimis* copying ends and copyright infringement begins. There are no "bright line" rules.

Copying a small amount of a copyrighted work is infringement if what is copied is a qualitatively substantial portion of the copied work. In one case, a magazine article that used 300 words from a 200,000-word autobiography written by President Gerald Ford was found to infringe the copyright on the autobiography. Even though the copied material was only a small part of the autobiography, the copied portions were among the most powerful passages in the autobiography. Copying any part of a copyrighted work is risky. If what you copy is truly a tiny and nonmemorable part of the work, you may get away with it (the work's owner may not be able to tell that your work incorporates an excerpt from the owner's work). However, you run the risk of having to defend your use in expensive litigation. If you are copying, it is better to get a permission or a license (unless fair use applies). You cannot escape liability for infringement by showing how much of the protected work you did not take.

> Myth 2: "Since I'm planning to give credit to all authors whose works I copy, I don't need to get permission."

If you give credit to a work's author, you are not a plagiarist (you are not pretending that you authored the copied work). However, attribution is not a defense to copyright infringement.

> Myth 3: "My Web site will be a wonderful showcase for the copyright owner's work, so I'm sure the owner will not object to my use of the work."

Don't assume that a copyright owner will be happy to have you use his or her work. The owner may be concerned that if you put the owner's work on the Web, other people will copy it from your Web site and use it without permission. Or the owner may not agree with the views expressed in your Web site, or approve of the products sold on your Web site. Even if the owner is willing to let you use the work, the owner will probably want to charge you a license fee. Content owners view the Web as a new market for licensing their material.

> Myth 4: "It's okay to use copyrighted material on my Web site without permission so long as users of my site don't have to pay anything to access the material."

Whether your site charges a fee for accessing the copied material is irrelevant. Unless fair use applies, using copyrighted material on a Web site without the permission of the copyright owner is infringement.

You don't need a license to use a public domain work. Public domain works are works not protected by copyright. No one can claim the exclusive rights of copyright in a public domain work, so such works can be used by anyone.

Works enter the public domain in several ways:

1. The term of the copyright expired.
2. The copyright owner failed to "renew" his or her copyright under the old Copyright Act.
3. The copyright owner failed to properly use copyright notice.

For works being created now, neither renewal nor copyright notice is required. Also, works created by U.S. government employees within the scope of employment are in the public domain from the moment they are created.

The rules regarding what works are in the public domain are too complex to cover here, and they vary from country to country. Material that is in the public domain in this country may be protected by copyright in other countries.

Here's a guideline to help you decide whether older works are in the public domain according to United States law: Works first published before January 1, 1923 are now in the public domain. Because Congress extended the term of copyright by twenty years in 1998, for all works that were still protected by copyright in 1998, we will have to wait until 2018 for additional works to enter the public domain through expiration of copyright.

Unfortunately, the Copyright Office does not maintain a list of public domain works. You have to find these works yourself. Some content providers sell copies of public domain works. The Library of Congress has copies of some of these works.

Don't make the mistake of thinking that a work is in the public domain because the work's author is dead. Copyrights are property. When a copyright owner dies, the owner's copyrights pass to the owner's heirs—just as tangible property such as money, real estate, and personal possessions do.

Derivative works (works based on pre-existing works) are often created from public domain works. New material in a derivative work is protected by copyright. You cannot copy the new material in a new version of a public domain work unless you obtain a license from the owner of the copyright in the derivative work, but you can use the elements that came from the public domain work.

■ *FOR EXAMPLE*

The copyrighted movie *Coast* is based on a public domain novel. If Web Developer wants to use a clip from the movie, Developer must get a license from the owner of the copyright in the movie. Developer is free to use an excerpt from the underlying novel.

If a public domain work incorporates another work, the incorporated work may still be protected by copyright. If the incorporated work is protected by copyright, you must get a license from the owner of that copyright if you want to use an excerpt of the public domain work that incorporates the protected work.

■ *FOR EXAMPLE*

The movie *Mountains* is in the public domain because the old Copyright Act's renewal requirement applies to the movie and the copyright owner did not renew the copyright. *Mountains* contains a song (sung by one of the performers) that is still protected by copyright. If Developer wants to use a clip of *Mountains* that contains the song, Developer needs a license from the owner of the song's copyright.

If you own the copyright in a work, you can, of course, use the work on your Web site. You don't need to worry about getting anyone else's permission. As the copyright owner, you own all the exclusive rights in the work and can do what you want with the work. However, copyright ownership rules are tricky. You need to be familiar with those rules (covered in Chapter 13, Copyright Law Basics).

■ *FOR EXAMPLE*

Last year, Sean, while employed full-time by Giant Co., created a fabulous "shopping cart" program for e-commerce. Now Sean is working on his own as a Web developer. Sean does not own the copyright in the shopping cart program, Giant Co. does. If Sean wants to use the shopping cart program in a project, he needs Giant Co.'s permission. (Sean, of course, is free to create a new shopping cart program).

If you are having others create new material for Web use, understanding copyright law's ownership rules and using written agreements can help you avoid future infringement risks.

LAB 14.1 EXERCISES

14.1.1 USE AN ANALYSIS TO AVOID COPYRIGHT INFRINGEMENT

a) John is thinking of using a cartoon strip from last Sunday's newspaper's comics section on his Web site. Help him decide whether that's a good idea.

_____

_____

b) Is your advice to John (in question a) any different if John found the cartoon character he wants to use in an online comics Web site?

_____

_____

c) What's wrong with this statement: "I don't need permission because I'm going to alter the work I copy."

_____

_____

14.1.2 UNDERSTAND HOW WORKS FALL INTO THE PUBLIC DOMAIN

a) Photos-To-You sells copies of photographs taken by federal government employees—Work Progress Administration photographers—during the Depression. If works created by federal government employees are not copyrightable, how can Photos-To-You sell these photographs?

_____

_____

LAB 14.1 EXERCISE ANSWERS

14.1.1 ANSWERS

a) John is thinking of using a cartoon strip from last Sunday's newspaper's comics section on his Web site. Help him decide whether that's a good idea.

Answer: The first question John should ask is whether the cartoon strip is protected by copyright or in the public domain. Most likely the cartoon strip is protected by copyright, and there's probably a copyright notice on it. If there's no copyright notice, John should still assume the comic strip is protected by copyright. Because the comic strip ran in last Sunday's paper's comics section, chances are it was not created prior to January 1, 1923, so the copyright has not expired. The second question John should ask is whether what he plans to do with the copyrighted cartoon strip is an exercise of one of the copyright owner's rights. Yes, John will be exercising the copyright owner's reproduction and public display rights if he scans the cartoon strip and uses the cartoon strip on his Web site. The third question is whether John's use of the cartoon strip could be fair use. The answer would depend on the four-factor test discussed in Lab 13.2. Even if John has a strong argument that his use is fair use, he should consider getting the copyright owner's permission to use the cartoon strip. Defending a copyright infringement on fair use grounds is expensive. Cartoon strip characters are protected by trademark law as well as by copyright law. The trademark protects the owner's right to use the character in connection with goods or services. Trademark law is discussed in Chapter 15, Other Important Laws.

b) Is your advice to John (in question a) any different if John found the cartoon character he wants to use on a comics Web site?

Answer: No, the analysis is exactly the same. While some of the material on the Web is in the public domain, much of the material that's on the Web is protected by copyright—and this comic strip is almost certainly protected. Copyright owners do not give up their copyright rights by posting their material on the Web. However, John should check the comics Web site to see if the site gives site users permission to use the site material in certain ways. For example, if the comics site grants permission to use a comic strip in a "fan" site, John could use the strip in a fan site. Web site permission grants are discussed in Lab 14.2.

c) What's wrong with this statement: "I don't need permission because I'm going to alter the work I copy."

Answer: Generally, you cannot escape liability for copyright infringement by altering or modifying the work you copy. If you copy and modify protected elements of a copyrighted work, you will be infringing the copyright owner's modification right as well as the reproduction right.

14.1.2 ANSWER

a) Photos-To-You sells copies of photos taken by federal government employees—Works Progress Administration (WPA) Photographers—during the Depression. If works created by federal government employees are not copyrightable, how can Photos-to-You sell these photographs?

Answer: Photos-To-You owns copies of the photographs, and that's what it is selling. If you want to use one of those photographs on your Web site, you don't need Photos-To-You's permission if you already have a copy of the photo. However, if you don't have a copy, one way to get one is to buy it from Photos-To-You.

LAB 14.1 SELF-REVIEW QUESTIONS

In order to test your progress, you should be able to answer the following questions.

1) In which of these situations do you need permission to copy a pre-existing work and use it in a Web design project?

   a) _____   The work is in the public domain.
   b) _____   The work is copyrighted and your use is fair use.
   c) _____   The work is copyrighted and your use is not fair use.
   d) _____   The work is copyrighted, but you plan to use only the ideas from the work.

2) Which of these works is in the public domain in the United States?

   a) _____   A work that was first published on January 5, 1920.
   b) _____   A work created in 1990 by a copyright owner who died in 1998.
   c) _____   A work first published in 1998 that was distributed without copyright notice.
   d) _____   All of these

3) If a work is in the public domain, anyone is free to use it.

   a) _____   True
   b) _____   False

4) Joe created a new arrangement of a public domain song. Which statement is true?

   a) _____   Joe should have gotten a license from the original composer of the song.
   b) _____   Joe didn't need a license from the original composer of the song.

c) _____ Joe's arrangement is protected by copyright.

d) _____ Both b and c

5) Katrina wants to use Joe's arrangement of the song (see question 4) on her Web site. Which statement is true:

a) _____ Katrina needs a license from Joe.

b) _____ Katrina needs a license from the original composer of the song.

c) _____ Both a and b

d) _____ Katrina doesn't need a license from either Joe or the original composer of the song.

6) Sue, a photographer, is a former employee of Big Co. Which statement is true concerning photos Sue took for Big Co.?

a) _____ Big Co. needs Sue's permission if Big Co. wants to use the photos on its Web site.

b) _____ Sue needs Big Co.'s permission if she wants to use the photos on her Web site.

c) _____ Both Sue and Big Co. are free to use the photos on their Web sites without the permission of the other party.

7) Five years ago, Graphic Designer, working as an independent contractor, created graphics for Client to use in a specific "print" ad. Which statement is true?

a) _____ Graphic Designer needs Client's permission if Designer wants to use the graphics now on a new client's Web project.

b) _____ Client needs Designer's permission if Client wants to use the graphics now in Client's Web site.

c) _____ Both Designer and Client are free to use the graphics on the Web without the permission of the other party.

Quiz Answers appear in the Appendix, Section 14.2.

LAB 14.2

THE LICENSING PROCESS

LAB OBJECTIVES

After this lab, you will be able to:

✔ Understand What a License Is
✔ Understand the Licensing Process

A license is a copyright owner's grant of permission to use a copyrighted work in a way that would otherwise be copyright infringement. A copyright owner who grants a license is known as a *licensor*. A party receiving a license is known as a *licensee*.

A copyright license can be exclusive or nonexclusive. An exclusive license is a license that does not overlap another grant of rights.

■ FOR EXAMPLE

Author granted Publisher the exclusive right to sell Author's novel in the United States. She granted Movie Developer the exclusive right to create and distribute a movie version of the novel. Both Publisher and Developer have exclusive licenses. There is no overlap between the two licenses.

Under copyright law, an exclusive license is considered a transfer of copyright ownership. An exclusive license, like an assignment (discussed in Lab 13.3), is not valid unless it is in writing and signed by the owner of the rights conveyed. A nonexclusive license is valid even if it is not in writing (but you should always get a license in writing so you'll have proof of the license and its terms).

There are three steps to the licensing process:

1. Locating the copyright owner
2. Determining what rights you need
3. Obtaining the license

Locating the copyright owner can be difficult. If the work you want to use contains a copyright notice (many works do, although use of copyright notice is now optional), the name on the notice is your starting point for locating the copyright owner. However, the copyright owner named in the notice may have assigned the copyright to someone else after your copy was published. You need to get permission from the current owner.

■ FOR EXAMPLE

Apexco's marketing director wants to use a chapter from a book written by Writer on the Apexco Web site. Writer assigned the copyright in his book to Publisher. Apexco must get permission from Publisher, not from Writer.

Does tracking down the copyright owner sound like a lot of trouble? One way to make licensing easier is to obtain content from photographic stock houses and music and media libraries. Stock houses and libraries frequently own the copyrights in works that they license (or they provide material that is in the public domain, such as Works Progress Administration photographs). They will, for a separate fee, do research for you to help you find suitable material.

Getting permission to use material you find on the Internet can be particularly tricky. If you want to use material posted by someone other than the copyright owner, but with the owner's permission, you need permission from the owner, not from the poster.

■ FOR EXAMPLE

Online Service Provider (OSP) got Author's permission to post a chapter from Author's new book on OSP's commercial online service. If Big Company wants to use part of the chapter on its Web site, Big needs permission from Author, the copyright owner (not from OSP).

Getting permission to use material you find on the Web is complicated by the fact that some people post copyrighted material they do *not* own, without getting permission from the copyright owner. If someone has posted copyrighted material in violation of the copyright owner's exclusive rights, getting the poster's permission to use the copyrighted material will do you no good. The poster has no right to authorize you to use the material. You need the owner's permission.

**LAB
14.2**

■ *FOR EXAMPLE*

Dewayne, a fan of the cartoon strip "Peanuts," used an image of Snoopy on his Web site without getting permission from the copyright owner. Greta saw Snoopy on Dewayne's Web site and wants to use the image on her Web site. Getting permission to copy Snoopy from Dewayne is worthless, since he does not own the copyright (and is himself probably an infringer of the owner's exclusive rights).

Do not assume that the person who posted a document on the Internet is the owner. Ask questions: Who created the document? What is its origin? If there's any doubt about whether the person who posted the document is the owner, don't use the document.

If the work you want to use incorporates several different copyrightable works, you may need more than one license.

■ *FOR EXAMPLE*

Web Publisher wants to use text and an illustration from Bookco's book in an on-line magazine. Bookco does not own the copyright on the illustration, the freelance artist who created the illustration does (Bookco just has the artist's permission to use the illustration). To use the text and the illustration, Web Publisher needs permission from Bookco and the artist.

If you want to use a photograph or video footage that prominently features a copyrighted work—particularly a work of fine art such as a sculpture or painting—you may need to obtain a license from the featured work's copyright owner. Because ownership of the copyright in a work is distinct from ownership of a copy, the owner of the copy of the work is probably not the copyright owner for the work.

■ *FOR EXAMPLE*

Mr. Rich gave Web Developer permission to photograph several copyrighted paintings from Mr. Rich's private art collection and use the photographs in Developer's Web site design projects. Unless Mr. Rich owns the copyrights in the paintings, Developer should get permission to use the images of the paintings from the copyright owners (the artists, most likely).

The second step in the licensing process is determining what rights you need to license. Think of your license as a shield from a copyright infringement lawsuit. To shield you from an infringement suit, your license must authorize every type of use that you will be making of the licensed work. Consequently, you need to determine how you will be using the work and what rights you need before you seek your license. A license is no protection for uses not authorized in the license.

■ FOR EXAMPLE

Web Publisher obtained a license to reproduce Photographer's photograph of the Golden Gate bridge in a Web site. Although the license did not authorize Publisher to alter the photograph, Publisher manipulated the image to eliminate cars and pedestrians and create an uncluttered image of the bridge. If Photographer sued Publisher for unauthorized exercise of the modification right, Publisher's license would be no defense.

Using a licensed work in ways not authorized in the license may be material breach of the license agreement. If it is, the licensor can terminate the license. In the previous example, Publisher's alteration of the photograph is probably a material breach of Publisher's license agreement with Photographer. If Photographer terminates the license, Publisher will no longer have even the right granted to Publisher in the license.

Generally, the use of text or photos on a Web site requires only a license to the reproduction, distribution, and public display rights, while the use of video footage requires a license to the reproduction, distribution, and public performance rights. However, you may need additional rights such as the right to modify the work. If you intend to use text as a voiceover in a game, you will need the public performance right. If you plan to use the licensed material on products such as toys, t-shirts, mouse pads, or coffee mugs, you need merchandising rights as well. When recognizable individuals are shown in photographs and video clips, you may need releases from the individuals as well, as discussed in Chapter 15, Other Important Laws.

If you want your site users to be able to download or copy the licensed content from your site for certain purposes, the license should give you the right to grant sublicenses to users of your Web site. For example, a license to use text on a Web site might give the licensee the right to permit users of the Web site to reproduce one copy of the licensed material for their personal, noncommercial use. User sublicenses generally appear in Web site terms of use, discussed in Chapter 19, Web Site Terms of Use and Clickwraps.

The license you obtain should address the following points:

- What is being licensed? In order to avoid later disputes, the parties should be as specific as possible. If excerpts of a work are being licensed—not the whole work—the agreement should make that clear.
- In what projects or products will you be permitted to use the licensed material? For example, are you obtaining the right to use the material in your Web site? In an online encyclopedia? In marketing material of any sort, including print media material?
- What rights are being granted?
- Is the license exclusive or nonexclusive?
- Will the licensor (owner) get a credit? If so, how will it read?
- What is the license fee? It could be a single one-time fee, an annual fee, or a royalty (percentage of your revenues or "per-unit" fee, for example). The license fee does not have to be money. It could be products or services, publicity, or just a credit.
- What is the term (duration) of the license? It can be perpetual or limited in duration.
- What warranties is the licensor giving? A warranty is a legally binding promise that certain facts are true. Try to get the licensor to warrant that (a) it owns all rights in the material and all intellectual property rights protecting them and (b) use of the material will not violate the rights of any third parties. If a licensor provides you with material that infringes a third party's copyright, the use of that material in your Web site or online products will make you liable for infringement of the third party's copyright—even if you were not aware of the infringement.
- What remedy will you have if the text is not as warranted? Try to get an indemnification provision in which the licensor agrees to defend and "hold you harmless" against any claims resulting from the breach of the warranties.

In a number of documents that are available on the Web, you'll see a statement that it's permissible to copy the document for certain purposes. Here are three examples:

1. "This article may be copied in its entirety for personal or educational use (the copy should include a License Notice at the beginning and at the end)."
2. "Permission is granted to freely copy this document in electronic form, or to print for personal use."
3. "All the text and pictures on this Web server are copyrighted. You may use the pictures for any noncommercial purpose if you attribute the source."

Authors place these "limited permission grants" on their documents because they want the documents to be shared and used for certain purposes (and they don't want to be bothered with requests for permission for such uses). Don't confuse a limited permission grant with a waiver of copyright. A limited permission grant is just a license to use the work in ways stated in the limited permission grant—and only in those ways.

If you want to use a work in a way that is not covered by the document's limited permission grant, contact the copyright owner and get permission. If you don't, you will be infringing the copyright on the work.

■ *FOR EXAMPLE*

Developer found some images she liked on the Web, at a site that said "You may use these images for any noncommercial purpose if you attribute the source." If Developer uses those images in a commercial CD-ROM product without getting permission from the owner, she will be infringing the copyrights on the images. Developer should go through the normal licensing process if she wants to use those images in her commercial product.

LAB 14.2 EXERCISES

14.2.1 UNDERSTAND WHAT A LICENSE IS

a) What's wrong with the following statement: "I paid for the photo that I'm going to use on my Web site, so I don't need a license. I already have all the permission I need."

_____

_____

b) Visit the Web site www.photodisc.com. How does this site relate to the topic of licensing?

_____

_____

14.2.2 UNDERSTAND THE LICENSING PROCESS

a) If you license a photo from www.photodisc.com for use on your Web site, can you authorize users of your Web site to download the photo for their own use?

_____

_____

b) Michelle found a short geography quiz on the Web, on a Web site that stated "Feel free to copy and use this site's material for educational purposes." Michelle wants to use the quiz in an on-line, fee-for-play children's game. Should she get permission to use the quiz?

_____

_____

LAB 14.2 EXERCISE ANSWERS

14.2.1 ANSWERS

a) What's wrong with the following statement: "I paid for the photo that I'm going to use on my Web site, so I don't need a license. I already have all the permission I need."

Answer: Copyright law distinguishes between ownership of the copyright in a work and ownership of a copy of the work. Purchasing a copy of a work (a photographic print, book, compact disc, or videotape) does not give you permission to exercise the exclusive rights of copyright. You can resell or otherwise dispose of your copy, and you can display your copy publicly to viewers "present at the place where the copy is located." That's all.

b) Visit the Web site www.photodisc.com. How does this site relate to the topic of licensing?

Answer: This site is an online photographic stock house. PhotoDisc licenses the images on its site for use on a nonexclusive, perpetual, worldwide basis. It is possible to view the license terms on the site. There are a number of other online photographic stock houses.

a) If you license a photo from www.photodisc.com for use on your Web site, can you authorize users of your Web site to download the photo for their own use?

Answer: No. The licensing information on the site states that the images are not licensed for use in a downloadable format. The license itself (PhotoDisc Image License Agreement: Online Products) states that the right granted in the license is "nonsublicensable."

If you use clip art or photographs from online or CD-ROM collections, read the license agreement and make certain that what you plan to do is covered by the license.

b) Michelle found a short geography quiz on the Web, on a Web site that stated "Feel free to copy and use this site's material for educational purposes." Michelle wants to use the quiz in an online, fee-for-play children's game. Should she get permission to use the quiz?

Answer: Yes. Michelle's use of the quiz is probably outside the scope of the limited permission grant. When you want to use Web material that comes with a limited permission grant, be cautious about concluding that your use is within the scope of the grant. If there's any doubt about whether the grant covers your use, contact the copyright owner and get permission before you use the material.

LAB 14.2 SELF-REVIEW QUESTIONS

In order to test your progress, you should be able to answer the following questions.

1) Permission to use a copyrighted work is known as:

   a) _____ A warranty
   b) _____ An assignment
   c) _____ A license
   d) _____ A licensor

2) Lee wants to use a photo he found on XYZ Co.'s Web site on his own Web site. The photo was taken by Gupta, a freelance photographer. Gupta assigned the copyright in the photo to Stock House, which licensed its use to XYZ. Lee should get a license from:

   a) _____ XYZ Co.
   b) _____ Gupta
   c) _____ Stock House
   d) _____ Any of the above
   e) _____ All of the above

3) The photo mentioned in Question 2 is a shot of a car crossing the Golden Gate Bridge. John plans to eliminate the car from the photo. Which of the following rights should his license include?

a) _____ Reproduction
b) _____ Reproduction and modification
c) _____ Reproduction and public display
d) _____ Reproduction, modification, and public display

4) Once you obtain a license, you have the right to use the licensed material forever.

a) _____ True
b) _____ False

5) George granted Sam a license to use some graphics. If the copyright in the graphics is actually owned by George's employer, which statement is true?

a) _____ Sam's license from George is worthless.
b) _____ So long as Sam uses the graphics as authorized in the license, he is not an infringer.

Quiz answers appear in the Appendix, Section 14.2.

C H A P T E R　1 4

TEST YOUR THINKING

Your company's Marketing Director is planning on using the following content in the company's new e-commerce site:

1) Product marketing text written by Marketing Department employees
2) A photo from the company's "print" marketing brochures
3) A new company logo, to be created by a freelance graphic designer (to be used on coffee mugs offered free to site visitors, as well as on the Web site)
4) Text written by a product manager for one of the company's clients

For which of these items does the company need licenses?

C H A P T E R   1 5

OTHER IMPORTANT LAWS

While copyright law is the most important intellectual property law for Web users, you need to know enough about the other intellectual property laws—patent, trademark, and trade secrets—to avoid infringing intellectual property rights owned by others and to be able to take advantage of the protection these laws provide. You also need to know about the laws of publicity, privacy, and defamation.

© 2000 by J. Dianne Brinson.

L A B   1 5 . 1

PATENTS, TRADEMARKS, AND TRADE SECRETS

LAB OBJECTIVES

After this lab, you will be able to:

✔ Understand Patent Protection
✔ Understand Trademark Protection
✔ Understand Trade Secrets Protection

Patent law protects inventions and processes ("utility" patents) and ornamental designs ("design" patents). Inventions and processes protected by utility patents can be electrical, mechanical, or chemical in nature. Examples of works protected by utility patents are a microwave oven, genetically engineered bacteria for cleaning up oil spills, a computerized method of running cash management accounts, and a method for curing rubber. Internet-related works protected by utility patents include communications protocols, data compression techniques, interfaces, networking methods, encryption techniques, online payment systems, and information processing and retrieval technologies. Examples of works protected by design patents are a design for the sole of running shoes, a design for sterling silver tableware, and a design for a water fountain.

Patent protection is obtained by demonstrating in an application filed with the U.S. Patent and Trademark Office that the invention meets the stringent standards required for the grant of a patent. The patent application process is expensive and time-consuming (it generally takes at least two years).

To qualify for a utility patent, an invention must be new, useful, and "nonobvious." To meet the novelty requirement, the invention must not have been known or used by others in this country before the applicant invented it, and it also must not have been patented or described in a printed publication in the United States or a foreign country before the applicant invented it. The policy behind the novelty requirement is that a patent is issued in exchange for the inventor's disclosure to the public of the details of the invention. If the inventor's work is not novel, the inventor is not adding to the public knowledge, so the inventor should not be granted a patent.

Meeting the usefulness requirement is easy for most inventions. An invention is useful if it can be applied to some beneficial use in society.

To meet the nonobviousness requirement, the invention must be sufficiently different from existing technology and knowledge so that, at the time the invention was made, the invention as a whole would not have been obvious to a person having ordinary skill in that field. The policy behind this requirement is that patents should only be granted for real advances, not for mere technical tinkering or modifications of existing inventions.

It is difficult to obtain a utility patent. Even if the invention or process meets the requirements of novelty, utility, and nonobviousness, a patent will not be granted if the invention was patented or described in a printed publication in the United States or a foreign country more than one year before the patent application date, or if the invention was in public use or on sale in the United States for more than one year before the patent application date. This requirement is known as "statutory bar."

If you own technology that is novel and nonobvious, you may be able to patent it. You should see a patent attorney without delay (and certainly before you publicly distribute or display that technology). By delaying, you risk losing your right to get a patent.

To qualify for a design patent, a design must be new, original, and ornamental. Design patents may be an option for protecting some elements of multimedia and online works (user interfaces, for example, which also can be protected through copyright law). However, design patents are considered rather weak intellectual property protection, and owners of design patents rarely sue to enforce their patents against infringers.

A patent owner (known as a "patentee") has the right to exclude others from making, using, or selling the patented invention or design in the United States during the term of the patent. Anyone who makes, uses, or sells a patented invention or design within the United States during the term of the patent without permission from the patent owner is an infringer—even if he or she did not copy the patented invention or design or even know about the patented invention or the grant of the patent.

■ *FOR EXAMPLE*

Developer's staff members, working on their own, developed a software program for manipulating images in Developer's multimedia works. Although Developer's staff didn't know it, Inventor has a patent on that method of image manipulation. Developer's use of the software program infringes Inventor's patent.

It is common in patent infringement suits for the defendant to challenge the validity of the patent, asserting that the Patent and Trademark Office should not have granted the patentee a patent because the invention or process did not meet one or more of the patentability requirements (novelty, usefulness, nonobviousness, statutory bar). If the court finds that the invention does not meet one or more of the patentability requirements, it will invalidate the patent, and the defendant wins the lawsuit.

■ *FOR EXAMPLE*

Big Co., which owns a patent an online payment system, sued E-commerce Co. for infringing the patent by using a very similar online payment system on its Web site. One of E-commerce's defenses was that the patent should not have been granted because the system was obvious. If the court agrees with E-commerce, E-commerce will win the lawsuit.

As of June 8, 1995, utility patents are granted for a period of twenty years from the date the application was filed. A new law, The American Inventors Protection Act of 1999, now guarantees that "diligent" applicants will receive a patent term of at least seventeen years from the date the patent is issued if certain delays on the part of the Patent and Trademark Office cause a delay in the issuance of the patent. The Patent and Trademark Office takes an average of twenty-two months to process a patent application. For inventions in the areas of electronics, computers, and software, the processing time is generally longer than twenty-two months.

For patents in force prior to June 8, 1995, the patent term is the greater of seventeen years from the date of issue (the term under prior law) or twenty years from the date of filing. Design patents are granted for a period of fourteen years. Once the patent on an invention or design has expired, anyone is free to make, use, or sell the invention or design. Patents may be viewed online at www.uspto.gov.

Patentable inventions created by employees within the scope of their employment are owned by the employee. However, the employee may have a legal obligation to transfer ownership of the patent to the employer under patent law's "hired to invent" doctrine. Also, many employers require that employees agree to assign their interests in patentable inventions to the employer.

Ownership of patents, like ownership of copyrights, can be assigned. Patent owners often grant licenses authorizing others to do things that would otherwise violate the owner's exclusive rights.

To obtain patent protection in other countries, you must comply with those countries' requirements for obtaining protection. There are no international conventions that provide automatic protection for U.S. patent owners. Some inventors file patent applications in other countries simultaneously with the U.S. filing. However, the Paris Convention and the Patent Cooperation Treaty allow an inventor who files a patent application in this country to delay filing applications in member countries, claiming priority in member countries based on the earlier U.S. application date. The European Patent Convention offers a way to file a single patent application for a patent that will be valid in seventeen European countries.

Trademarks and service marks are words, names, symbols, or devices used by manufacturers of goods and providers of services to identify their goods and services and to distinguish their goods and services from goods manufactured and sold by others.

■ *FOR EXAMPLE*

The trademark *Quicken* is used by Intuit Inc. to identify Intuit's personal finance software and distinguish that software from other vendors' software.

Trademark protection is available for words, names, symbols, or devices that are capable of distinguishing the owner's goods or services from the goods or services of others. A term that merely describes a class of goods rather than distinguishing the manufacturer's goods from goods provided by others is not protectible.

■ *FOR EXAMPLE*

The word "corn flakes" is not protectible as a trademark for cereal because that term describes a type of cereal that is sold by a number of cereal manufacturers rather than distinguishing one cereal manufacturer's goods.

A trademark that so resembles a trademark already in use in the United States as to be likely to cause confusion or mistake is not protectible. In addition, trademarks that are "descriptive" of the functions, quality, or character of the goods or services must meet special requirements before they will be protected.

For trademarks used in commerce, federal trademark protection is available under the federal trademark statute, the Lanham Act. Many states have trademark registration statutes that resemble the Lanham Act, and all states protect unregistered trademarks under the common law (nonstatutory law) of trademarks.

The most effective trademark protection is obtained by filing a trademark registration application in the Patent and Trademark Office. Federal law also protects unregistered trademarks, but such protection is limited to the geographic area in which the mark is actually being used. State trademark protection under common law is obtained simply by adopting a trademark and using it in connection with goods or services. This protection is limited to the geographic area in which the trademark is actually being used. State statutory protection is obtained by filing an application with the state trademark office.

Trademark law in general, whether federal or state, protects a trademark owner's commercial identity (goodwill, reputation, and investment in advertising) by giving the trademark owner the exclusive right to use the trademark on the type of goods or services for which the owner is using the trademark. Any person who uses a trademark in connection with goods or services in a way that is likely to cause consumer confusion as to the source of the goods is an infringer. Trademark owners can obtain injunctions against the confusing use of their trademarks by others, and they can collect damages for infringement.

■ *FOR EXAMPLE*

Small Multimedia Co. is selling a line of interactive training works under the trademark *Personal Tutor*. If Giant Multimedia Co. starts selling interactive training works under the trademark *Personal Tutor,* purchasers may think that Giant's works come from the same source as Small Multimedia's works. Giant is infringing Small's trademark.

Trademark law does not give protection against use of the trademark that is unlikely to cause confusion, mistake, or deception among consumers (but other laws, known as dilution laws, may provide such protection).

■ *FOR EXAMPLE*

Western Software has a federal trademark registration for the use of *Flash* on multimedia development tool software. If Gadget Co. starts using *Flash* on fire extinguishes, Gadget is probably not infringing Western Software's trademark. Consumers are unlikely to think that the Flash software and the Flash fire extinguishers come from the same source.

A certificate of federal trademark registration remains in effect for ten years, provided that an affidavit of continued use is filed in the sixth year. A federal registration may be renewed for any number of successive ten-year terms as long as the mark is still in use in commerce. The duration of state registrations varies from state to state. Common law rights endure so long as the use of the trademark continues.

A trademark is owned by the first party to use it in connection with goods or services or the first to apply to register it. A trademark can be owned by an individual, company, or any other legal entity. Ownership of trademarks can be assigned with the associated goodwill of the business in which they are used. Trademarks can be licensed to third parties for their use. However, the trademark owner must exercise quality control over third-party use of the trademark to ensure that the trademark indicates a consistent level of quality of goods or services. The failure to exercise quality control can result in a loss of rights.

To obtain trademark protection in other countries, you must comply with those countries' requirements for obtaining protection. There are no international conventions that provide automatic protection for U.S. trademark owners.

You should be careful to avoid using or showing other companies' trademarks on your Web site or in your online products without the owners' permission. A trademark owner may object to being associated with your business, organization, or products. For example, Nabisco objected to the use of the *Marlboro* trademark on a billboard in the background of a video game.

In naming your own products, choose trademarks that do not infringe another company's trademark or tradename. If you choose an arbitrary or fanciful term as the trademark for your product, you will receive the broadest possible trademark protection. An arbitrary term is a commonly used word that is applied to a product or service with which that term is not normally associated—for example, using *Apple* for computers. A fanciful term is a made-up word or symbol—for example, *Kodak* for film.

Using a word or name as a trademark does not automatically give you the right to use the name as your domain name. Domain name registration is discussed in Chapter 20, Domain Names.

Dilution laws give owners of strong trademarks the right to prevent a similar mark from being used on completely different products or services. The federal Trademark Dilution Act gives the owner of a famous mark the right to stop others from using a mark that causes dilution of the distinctive quality of a famous mark. Approximately half the states also have dilution laws.

A trade secret is information of any sort that is valuable to its owner, not generally known, and that has been kept secret by the owner. Trade secrets are protected only under state law. The Uniform Trade Secrets Act, in effect in a number of states, defines trade secrets as "information, including a formula, pattern, compilation, program, device, method, technique, or process that derives independent economic value from not being generally known and not being readily ascertainable and is subject to reasonable efforts to maintain secrecy."

The following types of technical and business information are examples of material that can be protected by trade secret law: customer lists, instructional methods, manufacturing processes, and methods of developing software. Inventions and processes that are not patentable can be protected under trade secret law. Patent applicants generally rely on trade secret law to protect their inventions while the patent applications are pending.

Six factors are generally used to determine whether information is a trade secret:

- The extent to which the information is known outside the claimant's business.
- The extent to which the information is known by the claimant's employees.
- The extent of measures taken by the claimant to guard the secrecy of the information.
- The value of the information to the claimant and the claimant's competitors.
- The amount of effort or money expended by the claimant in developing the information.
- The ease with which the information could be acquired by others.

Information has value if it gives rise to actual or potential commercial advantage for the owner of the information. Although a trade secret need not be unique in the patent law sense, information that is generally known is not protected under trade secrets law.

Trade secret protection attaches automatically when information of value to the owner is kept secret by the owner. A trade secret owner has the right to keep others from misappropriating and using the trade secret. Discovery of protected information through independent research or reverse engineering (taking a product apart to see how it works) is not misappropriation.

Trade secret protection endures so long as the requirements for protection—generally, value to the owner and secrecy—continue to be met.

■ FOR EXAMPLE

After Julio discovered a new method for manipulating images in multimedia works, he demonstrated his new method to a number of other developers at a conference. Julio lost his trade secret protection for the image manipulation method because he failed to keep his method secret.

The protection is lost if the owner fails to take reasonable steps to keep the information secret. Measures to maintain secrecy include such steps as marking documents as confidential; restricting employees' and outsiders' access to materials; and requiring employees and independent contractors to sign confidentiality agreements (also known as nondisclosure agreements).

An employer or hiring party generally owns trade secrets developed by employees and by independent contractors who are "hired to invent." The ownership of trade secrets can be assigned, and trade secrets can be licensed to others without losing protection if the licensees are required to maintain the confidentiality of the trade secrets.

To obtain trade secrets protection in other countries, you must comply with those countries' requirements for obtaining protection. There are no international conventions that provide automatic protection for U.S. trade secrets owners.

LAB 15.1 EXERCISES

15.1.1 UNDERSTAND PATENT PROTECTION

a) Visit www.priceline.com. Priceline has a valuable patent on something that's described on the Web site. What does the patent cover, and why is it so valuable to Priceline?

_____

_____

15.1.2 UNDERSTAND TRADEMARK PROTECTION

a) A federal court recently ruled that America Online cannot prevent other companies from using the expression "You have mail." Why not?

_____

_____

b) Toolco sells power drills in purple and yellow packaging. Toolco's competitor, Gadgetco, recently started selling its products in purple and yellow packaging, and Toolco doesn't like that. How does trademark law help Toolco?

_____

_____

15.1.3 UNDERSTAND TRADE SECRETS PROTECTION

a) Shanika used to work for Web Publishing Co. as a Web developer. Now she works for Bay Web as a Web developer. Why is it important that Shanika and her supervisors at Bay Web understand trade secrets law?

_____

_____

LAB 15.1 EXERCISE ANSWERS

15.1.1 ANSWER

a) Visit www.priceline.com. Priceline has a valuable patent on something that's described on the Web site. What does the patent cover, and why is it so valuable to Priceline?

Answer: This site collects individual customer offers to buy goods or services and communicates the offers to participating sellers. Priceline has a patent on this "name your price, reverse auction" system (known as a demand collection system). The patent is valuable because anyone who uses the same demand collection system during the term of the patent without Priceline's permission is an infringer. The Patent and Trademark Office's grant of this patent has been criticized by a number of commentators on the grounds that the Priceline system is not novel or nonobvious.

15.1.2 ANSWERS

a) A federal court recently ruled that America Online cannot prevent other companies from using the expression "You have mail." Why not?

Answer: The phrase is generic. A generic term can never function as a trademark.

If you're wondering whether America Online could protect the phrase "You have mail" under copyright, the answer is most likely "no"—because the phrase lacks originality and is probably an idea rather than the expression of an idea.

b) Toolco sells power drills throughout the United States in purple and yellow packaging. Toolco's competitor, Gadgetco, recently started selling its products in the United States in purple and yellow packaging, and Toolco doesn't like that. How does trademark law help Toolco?

Answer: Toolco's purple and yellow packaging is a device (known as "trade dress") used by Toolco to identify Toolco's goods. The distinctive packaging is entitled to trademark protection. Even if Toolco has not obtained federal or state trademark registrations on the packaging colors, Toolco has common law trademark rights under the laws of various states. If Gadgetco is selling its products in purple and yellow packaging, consumers are likely to be confused as to the source of tools sold in purple and yellow packaging. Gadgetco is an infringer. These facts are similar to the facts in a recent trademark infringement suit filed by Black & Decker against Pro-Tech Power Inc. In that case, the court found that Pro-Tech had deliberately violated Black & Decker's trademark by using Black & Decker's color combinations on Pro-Tech products. The court held that Black & Decker incurred damages as a result of consumer confusion because Pro-Tech's products suffered from serious quality problems.

15.1.3 ANSWER

a) Shanika used to work for Web Publishing Co. as a Web developer. Now she works for Bay Web as a Web developer. Why is it important that Shanika and her supervisors at Bay Web understand trade secret law?

Answer: In her new job, Shanika must avoid using trade secrets that belong to her former employer. It is likely that things that Shanika learned at Web Publishing are trade secrets—for example, Web Publishing's customer lists, methods for training new Web developers, and Web site development process could all be trade secrets. All that is required for trade secret protection is that valuable information be kept secret. Because an employer generally owns trade secrets owned by an employee, even work done by Shanika herself while at Web Publishing could be trade secrets belonging to Web Publishing. If Shanika uses trade secrets owned by Web Publishing at her new job, she and her new employer will be guilty of trade secret misappropriation. Many trade secret cases involve people who have taken their former employers' trade secrets for use in new businesses or for new employers. An employee is entitled to use his or her general knowledge and skill for the new employer, but not to use the former employer's trade secrets. Sometimes it is difficult to draw the line between knowledge/skill and trade secrets.

LAB 15.1 SELF-REVIEW QUESTIONS

In order to test your progress, you should be able to answer the following questions:

1) To qualify for a patent, an invention must be:

   a) _____ New
   b) _____ Useful
   c) _____ Nonobvious
   d) _____ All of the above

2) X Co. has sued Y Co. for infringing X's patent on an information processing and retrieval system. Y Co. will win the case if:

   a) _____ X Co.'s system is obvious.
   b) _____ Y Co. didn't know that X Co. had a patent on the system.
   c) _____ Y Co.'s employees created the system used by Y Co. on their own, without copying X Co.'s system.
   d) _____ X Co.'s system is novel.

3) Trademark protection is obtained:

   a) _____ By filing a federal trademark registration application with the Patent and Trademark Office
   b) _____ By using a mark capable of distinguishing goods from goods sold by others
   c) _____ By filing an application with a state trademark office
   d) _____ By doing any of the above

4) Y Co. is selling videogames under the trademark *Zort*. Which of the following uses of *Zort* by Q Co. is most likely to infringe Y Co.'s trademark?

   a) _____ Q's use of *Zort* on online computer games
   b) _____ Q's use of *Zort* on a flower-delivery service
   c) _____ Q's use of *Zort* on automobiles

5) A trade secret owner has the right to

   a) _____ keep others from misappropriating the trade secret.
   b) _____ keep others from discovering the trade secret through reverse engineering.
   c) _____ keep others from discovering the trade secret through independent research.
   d) _____ all of the above

6) Which of the following acts would cause a trade secret owner to lose protection?

  a) _____ Marking documents as confidential
  b) _____ Requiring contractors to sign confidentiality agreements
  c) _____ Restricting outsiders' access to the company's facilities
  d) _____ Divulging the trade secret in trade journal articles

Quiz answers appear in the Appendix, Section 15.1.

L A B   1 5 . 2

THE LAWS OF PRIVACY, PUBLICITY, AND DEFAMATION

LAB OBJECTIVES

After this lab, you will be able to:

✔ Understand the Right of Privacy
✔ Understand the Right of Publicity
✔ Understand Defamation

Most states in the United States recognize that individuals have a right of privacy. The right of privacy gives an individual a legal claim against someone who intrudes on the individual's physical solitude or seclusion and against those who publicly disclose private facts. It is the individual's right to be "let alone." Remedies for invasion of privacy include injunctions against continued intrusion and damages for mental distress. Liability exists only if the defendant's conduct was such that the defendant should have realized that it would be offensive to a person of ordinary sensibilities.

The right of privacy cannot be used to prohibit publication of a matter of public or general interest—whether as news or entertainment. Instead, this right protects the privacy of private life.

There are two special ways in which the Internet raises right of privacy questions: (1) employer monitoring of employee email and Internet use and (2) the use of personal data collected from Web site users.

Generally, employer monitoring of employees' email and Internet use does not violate the employees' right to privacy if done for legitimate business purposes. The question is whether the employer's need to monitor outweighs the employee's reasonable expectation of privacy. Employers that engage in monitoring should make it clear to their employees, in a written Internet Use Policy, that employees should not expect to be free from monitoring.

In the United States, at present there are few laws controlling the use of personal data collected from customers and Web site users. However, in the 1998 Children's Online Privacy Protection Act, Congress directed the Federal Trade Commission (FTC) to create privacy guidelines for Web sites targeting children younger than 13 years of age. The FTC Children's Online Privacy Protection Rule, which went into effect on April 21, 2000, applies to operators of commercial Web sites and online services directed to children under 13 years of age and also to operators of general audience Web sites, if the operator has actual knowledge that it collects personal information from children. "Personal information" is defined as "individually identifiable information about a child that is collected online, such as full name, home address, email address, telephone number or any other information that would allow someone to identify or contact the child." Generally, before collecting, using, or disclosing personal information from a child, operators covered by the Rule must obtain consent from the child's parent. The parent must be given the option of consenting to the child's use of the site without consenting to the disclosure of the child's information to third parties. Information on the rule is available on the FTC's Web site, www.ftc.gov, under the heading "Business Publications."

In the European Union countries, personal data may generally only be processed when the individual's consent has been obtained and may only be used for specified purposes. The European Union's Privacy Directive restricts the transfer of personal data outside the EU except where the country of transfer ensures an adequate level of protection for the data. Because the United States lacks laws regulating the use of personal data, the EU initially determined that the United States does not meet this standard. Rather than passing new laws, however, Congress has decided to rely on industry self-regulation. As this book goes to press, U.S. and European Union officials are still negotiating the details of the self-regulation approach. As a result, various industry organizations and companies are encouraging members and affiliates to post privacy policies on their Web sites to inform site users what uses the site owner will make of data provided by site users. Several templates for creating privacy policies are available online, including the Department of Commerce's "safe harbor" guidelines (www.ita.doc.gov/ecommm/shprin.html), the Better Business Bureau's template and certification program (www.bbbonline.org/businesses/privacy), and the Privacy Alliance's template (www.privacyalliance.org).

If you have a privacy policy posted on your Web site, it is important that you abide by its restrictions on the use of data.

■ *FOR EXAMPLE*

Geocities informed users of its Web site that the data it collected from membership applications would be used only to provide members with the specific advertising offers or goods and services the members requested. In fact, Geocities sold or rented this information to third parties for other purposes. The Federal Trade Commission, which regulates unfair and deceptive trade practices, charged Geocities with making false representations. Geocities is now operating under an FTC Consent Decree prohibiting Geocities from making any misrepresentation about its collection or use of personal data.

The right of publicity gives the individual the right to control his name, face, image, or voice for commercial purposes.

■ *FOR EXAMPLE*

Developer took a picture of Clint Eastwood standing on a street corner in Carmel. Developer used the picture in an e-commerce Web site. Unless Eastwood gave Developer permission to use Eastwood's image, Developer's use of the image violated Eastwood's right of publicity (even though Developer, as "author" of the photo, owned the copyright in the photo).

Almost half the states in the United States recognize that individuals have a right of publicity. You can avoid violating privacy/publicity rights by getting releases from individuals before using text, photographs, or video clips that include those individuals' names, faces, images, or voices for commercial purposes. Some writers, photographers, and video producers routinely obtain releases, but don't assume that this is the case if you are licensing content created by others.

Newspapers and news magazines have a "media use" privilege to publish names or images in connection with reporting a newsworthy event. The "media use" privilege has been held to apply to documentaries and other nonprint media, so presumably it applies to the Internet as well.

In some states, an individual's right of publicity terminates when the individual dies. In other states, the right passes to the heirs of the deceased original owner. As a guideline, don't use the name, voice, face, or image of a celebrity who has been dead less than fifty years—for example, Marilyn Monroe or Martin Luther King, Jr.—without checking applicable state law on descendability.

Defamation law (also known as libel law) protects an individual against the dissemination of falsehoods about that individual. To be actionable, the falsehood must injure his or her reputation or subject them to hatred, contempt, or ridicule. A public figure or official must prove that the publisher or broadcaster made the statement either knowing it was false or entertaining serious doubts about its truth. A private individual only has to prove that the publisher or broadcaster acted negligently in failing to ascertain that the statement was false. The higher burden for public figures and officials flows from the First Amendment.

Here are some tips for avoiding the use of defamatory material:

- *Original material:* If you plan to use any statements that could injure someone's reputation, make certain that you can prove that the statements are true. There is often a big difference between "knowing" that something is true and being able to prove that it is true. Journalists are taught to be particularly careful about statements concerning arrests and convictions and statements concerning professionals' qualifications and ethics.

- *Licensed material:* If licensed materials include potentially libelous material, don't use the material. If you use it, even though the material didn't originate with you, you could have liability for libel.

Corporations can recover damages for defamation. Many executives are zealous about protecting their corporations' reputations. If you make statements that might damage a corporation's reputation, make sure the statements are true.

An employer can be liable for defamatory statements made by employees within the scope of the employment. Many employers remind employees, in the company's Internet Use Policy, that they should not post defamatory material on the Internet or company intranet.

A truthful statement is not libel, but a truthful statement that discloses private facts about an individual in an objectionable manner may violate the individual's right to privacy.

■ FOR EXAMPLE

Web Journalist discovered that Marta was abused as a child by her uncle. Journalist reported that fact without Marta's permission in a story on child abuse. Journalist's statement about Marta is not defamation, because it was true, but Journalist may have violated Marta's right of privacy.

LAB 15.2 EXERCISES

15.2.1 UNDERSTAND THE RIGHT OF PRIVACY

a) An online magazine published a photo of a famous actress locked in a passionate embrace with her sister's husband. The actress sued the magazine for invasion of privacy. Defend the magazine.

_____

_____

15.2.2 UNDERSTAND THE RIGHT OF PUBLICITY

a) Z Co. used a photo of a famous and newsworthy individual on its "passive" Web site (which gives information about Z Co.'s products but does not offer e-commerce). Did Z Co. violate the individual's right of publicity?

_____

_____

15.2.3 UNDERSTAND DEFAMATION

a) An employee of Online Magazine merged a photo of Hillary Clinton with a photo of a notorious Mafia figure. Online Magazine published the photo, without comment, in today's edition. Was that defamation?

_____

_____

LAB 15.2 EXERCISE ANSWERS

15.2.1 ANSWER

a) An online magazine published a photo of a famous actress locked in a passionate embrace with her sister's husband. The actress sued the magazine for invasion of privacy. Defend the magazine.

Answer: Where was the passionate couple when the photo was taken? If they were in a public place or visible from a public place, there's no invasion of privacy (they exposed themselves to the public gaze). If they were in a private place and the photographer intruded on them, the best defense is that the magazine is not liable for invasion of privacy because what the two were doing is a matter of public or general interest and entertainment, given the actress's fame.

15.2.2 ANSWER

a) Z Co. used a photo of a famous and newsworthy woman on its "passive" Web site (which gives information about Z Co.'s products but does not offer e-commerce). Z Co. did not obtain a release from the woman. Did Z Co. violate the woman's right of publicity?

Answer: The question is whether this use is commercial use. Generally, you do not need a release to use a photograph of an individual for noncommercial purposes—to illustrate a point in a factual article, for example. However, if you use the same photograph to sell a product, you do need a release. Even though Z Co. is not selling products directly from this Web site, the Web site serves an advertising purpose, so I believe Z Co. did violate the woman's right of publicity. If you are uncertain about whether your use of an individual's image is commercial, you should obtain the release.

15.2.3 ANSWER

a) An employee of Online Magazine merged a photo of Hillary Clinton with a photo of a notorious Mafia figure. Online Magazine published the photo, without comment, in today's edition. Was that defamation?

Answer: Yes, if the published photo gave site users a false impression that Ms. Clinton was associating with a Mafia member and that false impression injured her reputation.

With digital editing software, it is now very easy to edit and merge photographs. Avoid using an edited image that falsely associates an individual with controversial or unsavory events, places, or people.

LAB 15.2 SELF-REVIEW QUESTIONS

In order to test your progress, you should be able to answer the following questions.

1) Which of the following violates the right of privacy?

   a) _____ Disclosing private facts about an individual
   b) _____ Monitoring employee email, after disclosing to employees that email use is subject to employer monitoring
   c) _____ Publishing a photo of an individual at a public event
   d) _____ a and c

2) Which of the following violates the right of publicity?

   a) _____ Using a photo of a celebrity on a Web site to help sell products
   b) _____ Using a photo of an individual in a Web news story about the individual
   c) _____ Using the voice of a celebrity on a Web site to help sell products
   d) _____ a and c

3) Which of these statements about an individual is defamatory?

   a) _____ A true statement that reveals details of the individual's private life
   b) _____ A harmless false statement
   c) _____ A false statement that injures the individual's reputation
   d) _____ b and c

4) Web Journalist published an article which reveals that Mary had an abortion when she was 16. If Mary really did have an abortion when she was 16, which legal theory should she use if she wants to sue Journalist?

   a) _____ Invasion of privacy
   b) _____ Defamation
   c) _____ Either a or b (she has a good case under either theory).

5) The United States currently has comprehensive laws regulating the use of personal data collected by Web site owners and merchants—far more comprehensive than the laws of European Community countries.

   a) _____ True
   b) _____ False

Quiz answers appear in the Appendix, Section 15.2.

C H A P T E R   1 5

TEST YOUR THINKING

An employee of EC Co. has figured out a way to drastically increase the security of on-line credit card transactions. In addition to using this technology on its own Web site, EC Co. would like to license this technology to other companies for use on their Web sites. EC Co. plans to start advertising the technology and showing it to potential licensees soon.

1) Explain how the laws you have studied so far can help EC Co. protect its technology from unauthorized use and make money from licensing the technology.

C H A P T E R   1 6

SYSTEM OPERATOR LIABILITY FOR COPYRIGHT INFRINGEMENT BY USERS

The topic in this chapter is whether a system operator is liable for copyright infringement when a system user posts copyrighted material belonging to someone else. Here are two examples of situations in which this question comes up:

1. Dennis Erlich, a former Scientologist, posted 154 pages of copyrighted Church of Scientology materials to a Usenet Newsgroup. Is the operator of the Bulletin Board Service (BBS) used by Erlich liable for copyright infringement? Is the BBS's Internet Service Provider (ISP) liable?

2. Giantco's Web site has copyrighted text and graphics that Giantco's marketing department used without permission. Is Giantco's ISP liable for copyright infringement?

© 2000 by J. Dianne Brinson.

As you probably know, the ISPs have taken the view they should not be liable for copyright infringement by system users. "A telephone company is not liable when a telephone subscriber transmits infringing material by phone line to someone else," they allege. "We're in the same position as a telephone company: We just provide the facilities for storing and transmitting material."

However, the authors of the Clinton Administration's 1995 White Paper concluded that ISPs are "electronic publishers"—and, like other publishers, are liable for providing infringing material. And in the case *Religious Technology Center v. Netcom Online Communication Services* (example one, above), the court held that ISP Netcom could be liable for contributory copyright infringement for postings made by a system subscriber after the copyright owner notified Netcom that the system subscriber was posting infringing material.

In October 1998 Congress clarified this situation by passing the Online Copyright Infringement Liability Limitation Act (OCILLA). The new law creates a "safe harbor" that ISPs and system operators can use to shield themselves from liability for infringing material posted by third-party system users. OCILLA also provides a new remedy for copyright owners who find their material used on the Internet without their permission.

LAB 16.1

THE ONLINE COPYRIGHT INFRINGEMENT LIABILITY LIMITATION ACT

LAB OBJECTIVES

After this lab, you will be able to:

✔ Understand the Protection from Liability the Act Provides
✔ Understand What a "Service Provider" Must Do
   to Get Protection
✔ Understand How a Copyright Owner Can Use the New Law
   to Stop Infringement

The core provision of the Online Copyright Infringement Liability Limitation Act states that a service provider is not liable for copyright infringement damages for infringing material stored on the ISP's system by a system user if the service provider, upon receiving notice of the claimed infringement, removes the material claimed to be infringing. "Service provider" is defined in the Act as "a provider of online services or network access, or the operator of facilities therefor, including an entity offering the transmission, routing, or providing of connections for digital online communications, between or among points specified by a user, of material of the user's choosing, without modification to the content of the material as sent or received."

■ *FOR EXAMPLE*

Giantco's Web site has copyrighted graphics belonging to Marcus. Giantco's marketing department used the graphics without Marcus's permission. World Internet provides the Web hosting facilities for Giantco's Web site, so the infringing material is stored on World Internet's system. World Internet will not be liable to Marcus for infringement if World, upon receiving notice from Marcus that Giantco's use of his graphics is copyright infringement, removes the graphics from Giantco's Web site.

OCILLA says nothing about the liability of Giantco, the "direct infringer," for copyright infringement. Giantco is still liable to Marcus for infringement, based on the principles discussed in Chapter 13, Copyright Law Basics, and Chapter 14, Steering Clear of Copyright Infringement. The new law only provides a safe harbor for World Internet, a service provider that has infringing material stored on its system "at the direction of a user" (Giantco). The immunity applies only to copyright infringement, not to other types of intellectual property infringement (trademark, trade secrets, and patent infringement) or to violations of other laws discussed in Chapter 15, Other Important Laws.

In order to take advantage of OCILLA's protection, a service provider must not have actual knowledge that the material is infringing and must not be aware of facts or circumstances from which infringing activity is apparent. On receiving notification of claimed infringement or obtaining knowledge of infringement or awareness of facts from which infringing activity is apparent, the service provider must expeditiously remove the material or disable access to the material. If the service provider has the right and ability to control infringing activity, the service provider cannot take advantage of the Act's safe harbor if it receives a financial benefit directly attributable to the infringing activity.

There are four threshold requirements that a service provider must meet in order to take advantage of OCILLA's safe harbor. A service provider must:

1. Designate an agent to receive notifications of claimed infringement.
2. Adopt and implement a policy of terminating the accounts of repeat infringers.
3. Inform subscribers and account holders of this policy.
4. Accommodate and not interfere with "standard technical measures" used by copyright owners to identify or protect copyrighted works.

A service provider that removes material claimed to be infringing could fear that it might have liability to its subscriber who placed that material on the system. In the example used above, World Internet might fear that if it removes the graphics that Marcus claims to own from Giantco's Web site, Giantco will sue World Internet. OCILLA deals with that issue. It states that a service provider is not liable to any person for good faith removal of material claimed to be infringing, even if the material is ultimately determined to not be infringing, if the service provider takes reasonable steps promptly to notify the subscriber that it has removed the material.

If the service provider's designated agent receives a "counter notice" from its subscriber stating that the material was removed as a result of mistake, the law's protection against liability to the subscriber applies only if the service provider replaces the removed material ten to fourteen business days after receipt of the counter notice. The service provider must send the complaining party a copy of the counter notification and inform that person that it will replace the removed material in ten business days. If, before the service provider replaces the material, the service provider receives a notice from the complaining party that it has filed a lawsuit in federal court seeking a restraining order against the subscriber, the service provider it is not required to replace the material.

Other provisions of the Online Copyright Infringement Liability Limitation Act grant service providers immunity for transmitting infringing material through the system by a system subscriber; for caching material made available online by a subscriber; and for indexing or linking to sites containing infringing material. Caching and linking are discussed in Chapter 18, Linking, Framing, Caching, and Meta Tags.

OCILLA gives copyright owners a new way of stopping infringement: Copyright owners who find their text, graphics, photos, or other copyrighted material used on the Web without their permission can contact the ISP or other service provider for the offending Web site and request that the service provider remove the material.

■ FOR EXAMPLE

One day, while Ling was surfing the Web, she found her copyrighted graphics on High Tech Co.'s marketing Web site. Ling did not give High Tech Co. permission to use her graphics. High Tech's ISP is Superb Internet. Using OCILLA, Ling sends Superb Internet a notification of claimed infringement. Superb removes Ling's graphics from High Tech Co.'s Web site (knowing that by doing so, it shields itself from liability to Ling for copyright infringement).

Ling can still recover damages for copyright infringement from High Tech Co. OCILLA gives her an additional remedy, that of having the material taken off the Web.

OCILLA states that a notification of claimed infringement must contain this information:

- A signature of a person authorized to act on behalf of the "owner of an exclusive right that is allegedly infringed"
- Identification of the copyrighted work claimed to have been infringed

- Identification of the material that is claimed to be infringing that is to be removed
- Information on how the service provider can contact the complaining party

A notification of claimed infringement must include a statement that the signing party has a good faith belief that use of the material in the manner complained of is not authorized by the copyright owner, or its agent, or the law. It must also include a statement that the information in the notification is accurate, and under penalty of perjury, that the complaining party has the authority to enforce the owner's rights that are claimed to be infringed. Any person who knowingly "materially misrepresents" that material is infringing is liable to the alleged infringer, the copyright owner, and the service provider for damages.

It's a good idea to review copyright law's ownership rules (discussed in Chapter 13, Copyright Law Basics) before filing a notification of claimed infringement. If you are not the copyright owner, you should not sign a notification of claimed infringement unless the owner has authorized you to act for it.

■ *FOR EXAMPLE*

If Ling created the graphics that High Tech "borrowed" as part of her job while working for Big Co., Big Co. owns the copyright in the text. Ling does not. Unless Ling has received permission from Big Co. to enforce Big's rights, Ling should not sign or send a notification to Superb Internet complaining about High Tech Company's use of the graphics. Big Company's rights are being infringed if High Tech used the graphics without permission, not Ling's rights (and Big Company may even have given High Tech Co. permission to use the graphics).

OCILLA is Title II of the Digital Millennium Copyright Act, available online at http://lcweb.loc.gov/copyright/title17. Other aspects of the Digital Millennium Copyright Act will become important in the future—provisions that will make it unlawful to circumvent copyright protection systems or to manufacture, import, or provide a device primarily produced for the purposes of circumventing copyright protection systems (starting in October 2000); and provisions making it unlawful to remove or alter "copyright management information" (information on a work's title, author, and copyright owner).

LAB 16.1 EXERCISES

16.1.1 UNDERSTAND THE PROTECTION FROM LIABILITY THE ACT PROVIDES

a) ABC Company's Web site has copyrighted material on it that is owned by a third party. The material was placed on the Web site by ABC's marketing director, who used it without the copyright owner's permission. Does OCILLA protect ABC Company from liability to the copyright owner?

16.1.2 UNDERSTAND WHAT A SERVICE PROVIDER MUST DO TO GET PROTECTION

a) Visit the Copyright Office's Web site and find out how a service provider designates an agent to receive notifications of claimed infringement.

16.1.3 UNDERSTAND HOW A COPYRIGHT OWNER CAN USE THE NEW LAW TO STOP INFRINGEMENT

a) Juan found his copyrighted photographs used without permission in Training Co.'s online training materials. Training Co. is a for-profit company. Site users must pay "tuition" to access the site's training materials. Training Co.'s ISP is Superb Internet. Help Juan write a notification of claimed infringement.

LAB 16.1 EXERCISE ANSWERS

16.1.1 ANSWER

a) ABC Company's Web site has copyrighted material on it that is owned by a third party. The material was placed on the Web site by ABC's marketing director, who used it without the copyright owner's permission. Does OCILLA protect ABC Company from liability to the copyright owner?

Answer: No, this material was not stored at the direction of a system user, but by an ABC employee. Employers are generally liable for copyright infringement by employees under a principle of agency law known as respondeat superior (literally, "the master must answer"). In this situation, OCILLA would protect ABC Company's ISP from liability.

OCILLA provides a limited exemption from the respondeat superior principle for public and other nonprofit institutions of higher education. When a faculty member or graduate student who is an employee of such an institution is performing a teaching or research function, the faculty member's or graduate student's knowledge or awareness of his or her infringement is not attributed to the institution under certain circumstances. However, this exemption does not apply to employers other than public and nonprofit institutions of higher education.

16.1.2 ANSWER

a) Visit the Copyright Office's Web site and find out how a service provider designates an agent to receive notifications of claimed infringement.

Answer: The Copyright Office has posted a suggested format ("Interim Designation of Agent" and "Amended Designation of Agent") for agent designation at http://lcweb.loc. gov/copyright/onlinsp. The agent designation information must be made available on the Service Provider's Web site and to the Copyright Office. The fee for filing the designation form with the Copyright Office is $20. The Copyright Office has posted a list of designated agents at www.loc.gov/copyright/onlinsp/list/index.html.

16.1.3 ANSWER

a) Jaun found his copyrighted photographs of used without his permission in Training Co.'s online training materials. Training Co. is a for-profit company. Site users pay "tuition" to access the sites training materials. Training Co's ISP is Superb

Internet. Juan did not give Training Co. permission to use the photos. Help Juan write a notification of claimed infringement.

Answer: Juan needs to identify his photos (the copyrighted works claimed to have been infringed) in such a way that Superb Internet can figure out what he is talking about—for example, "Photos of Yosemite's Half Dome taken and owned by photographer Juan Martinez." If Juan has registered the copyrights in the photos, he could also identify them by the work titles used in the copyright registrations.

He also needs to identify the material that is claimed to be infringing that is to be removed (so that Superb can locate the material). He should include the URL for Training Co.'s site and the name of the site, if there is one. He should be as specific as possible about where the photos are used in that site, including both the Web addresses for the pages where the photos are used and the titles of the documents, training courses, or topic categories where the photos are used.

He needs to include information on how Superb Internet can contact him. He should include his email address, snailmail address, telephone number, and fax number.

He needs to sign the notification. OCILLA states that the signature on the notification may be physical or electronic. Presumably "physical" means an "ink" signature (generally required on old-fashioned, hard-copy legal documents). What if Juan wants to send his notification by email? How do you "sign" an email? Including his name on the email would, I assume, count as an "electronic signature." A "digital signature" (digital code used to authenticate the origin and content of material transmitted electronically) would also be an "electronic signature," but the proposed law does not require a digital signature on the notification.

Juan must also include a statement that he has a good faith belief that use of the material in the manner complained of is not authorized by the copyright owner, or its agent, or the law. Juan has not authorized Training Co. to use his photographs. If he has a licensing agent, he should find out whether his agent granted Training Co. permission to use the photos (and drop the notification if the answer is "yes"). The only way the law would authorize Training Co. to use Juan's photographs would be as fair use (discussed in Chapter 13, Copyright Law Basics). Because Training Co. is a for-profit company that charges for access to its training courses, it is unlikely that Training Co.'s use of the photos is fair use.

The notification must also include a statement that the information in the notification is accurate, and under penalty of perjury, that the complaining party (Juan) has the authority to enforce the owner's rights that are claimed to be infringed.

LAB 16.1 SELF-REVIEW QUESTIONS

In order to test your progress, you should be able to answer the following questions.

1) XYZ Co.'s Web site has copyrighted graphics belonging to Artist. XYZ used the graphics without Artist's permission. XYZ's ISP is Bay Internet. Artist has notified Bay Internet that the use of the graphics on XYZ's Web site infringes Artist's copyright. Choose the true statement:

   a) _____ Bay Internet should not remove the graphics from the Web site, because XYZ Co.—not Artist—is Bay Internet's customer.

   b) _____ If Bay Internet removes the graphics and has met the threshold requirements for taking advantage of OCILLA, Bay will not be liable to Artist for copyright infringement.

   c) _____ If Bay Internet removes the graphics, neither Bay nor XYZ Co. will be liable to Artist for copyright infringement.

2) What must a service provider do in order to take advantage of the Act's protection from liability?

   a) _____ Designate an agent to receive notifications of claimed infringement

   b) _____ Upon receiving a notification of claimed infringement, remove material claimed to be infringing (or disable access to it)

   c) _____ Notify the Copyright Office when a notification of claimed infringement is received

   d) _____ Both a) and b)

3) Which of the following can take advantage of the Act's protection from liability?

   a) _____ Z Internet, an Internet Service Provider

   b) _____ Bay University, which provides Internet access and chat rooms for students

   c) _____ Ecommerce Co., which posts customer comments on its Web site

   d) _____ All of the above

4) If you find your copyrighted material used on a Web site without your permission, you can either get the service provider for the Web site to remove the material or sue the Web site's owner—but not both.

   a) _____ True

   b) _____ False

5) Under what circumstances must a service provider replace material it had previously removed?

    a) _____ If the complaining party files a lawsuit seeking a restraining order against the service provider's subscriber

    b) _____ If the subscriber files a lawsuit seeking a restraining order against the complaining party

    c) _____ If the service provider's designated agent receives a counter notice from its subscriber stating that the material was removed as the result of a mistake

Quiz answers appear in the Appendix, Section 16.1.

C H A P T E R   1 6

TEST YOUR THINKING

Users of ABC Company's Web site can post comments on the site. A Web site user posted copyrighted material on the site without the permission of the copyright owner. ABC Company received a complaint from the copyright owner today.

1) Does OCILLA protect ABC Company from liability for copyright infringement?

CHAPTER 17

WEB DEVELOPMENT AGREEMENTS

Do you develop Web sites for others? Or are you hiring a freelance Web developer to create a Web site for you? This chapter discusses the legal issues in Web site development agreements. It contains tips for both parties—Web site developer and client—on how to handle these issues in the agreement in order to avoid legal problems later.

© 2000 by J. Dianne Brinson.

LAB 17.1

CONTRACTS LAW

LAB OBJECTIVES

After this lab, you will be able to:

✔ Understand What Contracts Are and How They Are Formed

A contract is a legally enforceable agreement between two or more parties. The core of most contracts is a set of mutual promises. The promises made by the parties define the rights and obligations of the parties.

Contracts are enforceable in the courts. If one party meets its contractual obligations and the other party doesn't ("breaches the contract"), the nonbreaching party is entitled to receive relief through the courts.

■ *FOR EXAMPLE*

Developer promised to pay Graphic Designer $5000 for creating graphics for Developer's Web site. Graphic Designer created the materials and delivered them to Developer, as required in the contract. Developer admits that the materials meet the contract specifications. If Developer does not pay Graphic Designer, Graphic Designer can go to court and get a judgment against Developer for breach of contract.

Generally, the nonbreaching party's remedy for breach of contract is money damages that will put the nonbreaching party in the position it would have enjoyed if the contract had been performed. Under special circumstances, a court will order the breaching party to perform its contractual obligations.

Because contracts are enforceable, parties who enter into contracts can rely on contracts in structuring their business relationships.

■ *FOR EXAMPLE*

Developer entered into a contract with Composer, promising to pay Composer $4000 for composing a brief composition for Developer's interactive multimedia project. Shortly after Composer started work on the piece for Developer—before Developer paid Composer any money—Composer got an offer from a movie studio to compose all the music for a movie and abandoned Developer's project. Developer had to pay another composer $6000 to do the work that Composer had contracted to do. Developer can sue Composer and obtain a judgment against Composer for $2000 (the amount that will result in Developer's obtaining the music for a net cost of $4000, the contract price).

In this country and most others, businesses have significant flexibility in setting the terms of their contracts. Contracts are, in a sense, private law created by the agreement of the parties. The rights and obligations of the parties are determined by the contract's terms, subject to limits imposed by relevant statutes.

■ *FOR EXAMPLE*

Developer promised to pay Composer $5000 to create music for Developer's multimedia training work. Composer created the music and delivered it to Developer, as required in the contract. Developer did not pay Composer, so Composer sued Developer for breach of contract. Developer's defense was "Composer did what she promised to do, but I never should have agreed to pay her $5000 for that work. $2000 is a fair price." The court will enforce Developer's promise to pay Composer $5000.

A contract is formed when one party (the "offeror") makes an offer that is accepted by the other party (the "offeree"). An offer—a proposal to form a contract—can be as simple as the words "I'll wash your car for you for $5." An acceptance—the offeree's assent to the terms of the offer—can be as simple as, "You've got a deal." Sometimes acceptance can be shown by conduct rather than by words.

When an offer has been made, no contract is formed until the offeree accepts the offer. When you make an offer, never assume that the offeree will accept the offer. Contractual liability is based on consent.

■ *FOR EXAMPLE*

Web Developer offered to pay Photographer $500 to use Photographer's photo in Developer's Web design project. Photographer said, "Let me think about it." Developer, assuming that Photographer would accept the offer, went ahead and used the photo. Photographer then rejected Developer's offer. Developer has infringed Photographer's copyright by reproducing and using the photograph.

Developer must now either remove the photo or reach an agreement with Photographer.

Until an offer is accepted, the offeror is free—unless it has promised to hold the offer open—to revoke the offer.

■ FOR EXAMPLE

On June 1, Big Co. offered to Developer a contract to create an interactive training work for Big Co. On June 4 (before acceptance of the offer by Developer), Big Co. notified Developer that it was giving the contract to Developer's competitor. Big Co. terminated the offer to Developer. Developer has no legal recourse against Big Co.

Minors and the mentally incompetent lack the legal capacity to enter into contracts. All others are generally assumed to have full power to bind themselves by entering into contracts. In most states, the legal age for entering into contracts is 18. The test for mental capacity is whether the party understood the nature and consequences of the transaction in question.

Corporations have the power to enter into contracts. They make contracts through the acts of their agents, officers, and employees. Whether a particular employee has the power to bind the corporation to a contract is determined by an area of law called agency law or corporate law. If you doubt whether an individual with whom you are dealing has authority to enter into a contract with you, insist that the contract be reviewed and signed by the corporation's president.

A corporation has a separate legal existence from its founders, officers, and employees. Generally, the individuals associated with a corporation are not themselves responsible for the corporation's debts or liabilities, including liability for breach of contract.

Most contracts are enforceable whether they are oral or written. A deal done on a handshake—"You do X for me, and I'll pay you Y"—is a contract, because it is a legally enforceable agreement involving an exchange of promises. Nonetheless, you should always have written contracts for all your business relationships, including Web development agreements.

There are several reasons why written contracts are better than oral contracts:

- The process of writing down the contract's terms and signing the contract forces both parties to think about—and be precise about—the obligations they are undertaking. With an oral contract, it is too easy for both parties to say "yes" and then have second thoughts.

- When the terms of a contract are written down, the parties are likely to create a more complete and thorough agreement than they would by oral agreement. A hastily made oral agreement is likely to have gaps that will have to be resolved later—when the relationship may have deteriorated.

- With an oral contact, the parties may have different recollections of what they agreed on (just as two witnesses to a car accident will disagree over what happened). A written agreement eliminates disputes over who promised what.

- Some types of contracts must be in writing to be enforced. The Copyright Act requires a copyright assignment or exclusive license to be in writing (see Chapter 13, Copyright Law Basics). State law requirements vary from state to state, but in most states, a contract for the sale of goods for $500 or more must be in writing.

- If you have to go to court to enforce a contract or get damages, a written contract will mean less dispute about the contract's terms.

You do not have to hire an attorney to create a written contract. If you reach an agreement over the phone or in a meeting, write up the agreement as soon as possible and have the other party sign the written memorandum. If you are making a written offer, you may want to make your offer in the form of a letter, with a space at the end for the offeree to indicate acceptance by signing.

Your written agreement should accurately cover all aspects of your understanding with the other party. If the other party wrote the agreement based on an oral understanding reached earlier, make certain that the written terms match the terms of your oral agreement.

Don't leave points out of the written document, even if the other party says, "We don't need to put *that* in writing." In particular, you should not fail to address an issue because it is "sensitive." Deal with the sensitive issue during the negotiations and cover the issue in the written contract.

Don't try to sound like a lawyer, and don't complicate things unnecessarily. Define any ambiguous terms. There's a classic contracts case in which one party contracted to sell chickens to the other party. The seller thought "chicken" meant chicken of any age, including old and tough chickens. The buyer assumed "chicken" meant tender young chickens suitable for frying. A court had to determine which definition applied to the contract.

LAB 17.1 EXERCISES

17.1.1 UNDERSTAND WHAT CONTRACTS ARE AND HOW THEY ARE FORMED

a) Brenda, a Web developer, spent several hours working on a Web site proposal for Toy Co. Toy Co. decided to use another Web developer for the project. Can Brenda charge Toy Co. for the time she spent on the proposal?

_____

_____

b) NetResearch, Inc. has done extensive market research to determine what kinds of products middle-income consumers are interested in buying on the Web. NetResearch provided a copy of its latest report to Growing Co. for $5000. Growing Co. agreed that it would only use the report within the company. However, Growing Co. gave copies of the report to ten of its suppliers, and NetResearch is unhappy about that. How does contracts law help NetResearch?

_____

_____

c) Lisa, a Web developer, entered into a Web development agreement with Start-Up Co. Lisa fulfilled her duties under the agreement, but Start-Up Co. doesn't have the money to pay Lisa. Can she collect the money from Start-Up's president, a wealthy man?

_____

_____

LAB 17.1 EXERCISE ANSWERS

17.1.1 ANSWER

a) Brenda, a Web developer, spent many hours working on a Web site proposal for Toy Co. Toy Co. decided to use another Web developer for the project. Can Brenda charge Toy Co. for the time she spent on the proposal?

Answer: Not unless Toy Co. had agreed to pay for that time. Brenda's proposal was an offer to Toy Co. Toy Co. did not accept Brenda's offer, so no contract was formed. However, if Toy Co. agreed to pay for the proposal hours at Brenda's hourly consulting rate (a separate "consulting services" contract), Brenda can collect from Toy Co.

If you are a Web developer, don't spend a lot of time and effort on a proposal for a potential client without making sure that the client is seriously considering the project and has the ability to pay for the project. Even then, not every proposal will result in a contract. If you know you will have to spend several hours meeting with a potential client to determine what the client needs before you can even prepare your proposal, try to get the client to agree to pay you for that time at an hourly consulting rate.

b) NetResearch, Inc. has done extensive market research to determine what kinds of products middle income consumers are buying on the Web. NetResearch provided a copy of its latest report to Growing Co. for $5000. Growing Co. agreed that it would only use the report within the company. However, Growing Co. gave facts from the report to ten of its outside suppliers. NetResearch is unhappy about that. How does contracts law help NetResearch?

Answer: Growing Co. has breached its contract with NetResearch, and NetResearch can get a judgment against Growing Co. for damages. Presumably, NetResearch would have charged Growing Co. more money had Growing Co. requested the right to give the suppliers copies of the report.

You know that according to U.S. copyright law, factual material is not protected by copyright (see Chapter 13, Copyright Law Basics). NetResearch has used a contracts approach to get protection that is not available under copyright law. Many database owners do that.

c) Lisa, a Web developer, entered into a Web development agreement with Start-Up Co. Lisa fulfilled her duties under the agreement, but Start-Up Co. doesn't have the money to pay Lisa. Can she collect the money from Start-Up's president, a wealthy man?

Answer: Probably not, unless the president signed a personal guarantee that he would pay if Start-Up did not pay. A corporation has a separate legal existence from its president.

LAB 17.1 SELF-REVIEW QUESTIONS

In order to test your progress, you should be able to answer the following questions.

1) Web Developer ran into Photographer on the street and said to Photographer, "I'll pay you $200 for the nonexclusive right to use two of your photos on a Web site I'm designing." Photographer said, "Okay." Which statement is true:

   a) _____ Developer and Photographer did not form a contract, because no formal or "legal" language was used.

   b) _____ Developer and Photographer did not form a contract unless they wrote down their understanding.

   c) _____ Developer and Photographer formed a contract based on their oral exchange.

   d) _____ Developer and Photographer formed a contract based on their oral exchange, but only Developer is bound by the contract.

2) Which of the following has the legal capacity to enter into a contract?

   a) _____ A corporation
   b) _____ A 30-year-old mentally competent individual
   c) _____ A really smart 17-year-old individual
   d) _____ Both a and b
   e) _____ All three: a, b, and c

3) Ideally, a written contract should:

   a) _____ Omit sensitive, hard-to-deal with terms.
   b) _____ Cover all issues, even sensitive issues.

4) When you write up a contract, you should

   a) _____ use complicated words and make it sound like it was written by a lawyer.
   b) _____ leave all ambiguous terms undefined.
   c) _____ say as little as possible, covering only the major issues.
   d) _____ cover all issues and define ambiguous terms.

5) An offeror can revoke an offer as long as the offeree has not yet accepted it.

   a) _____ True
   b) _____ False

Quiz answers appear in the Appendix, Section 17.1.

L A B   1 7 . 2

IMPORTANT LEGAL ISSUES IN WEB DEVELOPMENT AGREEMENTS

LAB OBJECTIVES

After this lab, you will be able to:

✔ Understand the Structure of a Typical Web Development Agreement
✔ Understand What Copyright Issues Must Be Addressed in a Web Development Agreement
✔ Understand Warranties and Indemnifications

Web site development agreements are rarely simple agreements. Generally, Web site development is a multistage development process. First, the developer creates the Web site design. Next, the developer creates the beta (working) version of the Web site, tests it, and delivers it to the client for testing. Finally, the developer creates the final version and delivers it to the client for testing. Although many Web sites involve only text and graphics, more complex Web sites may include software or "scripts."

A Web development agreement will usually have the following types of provisions in it:

- *Duties and Obligations:* The duties and obligations section of the agreement is a detailed description of the duties and obligations of the parties and the deadlines for performance. Detailed specifications (discussed below) are usually included to define the developer's duties and obligations.

- *Testing and Acceptance:* A Web development agreement should include a "testing and acceptance clause" stating the number of days the client has to test and accept or reject the developer's work. Such clauses generally provide that if the client has not given notice of rejection within the stated time period, the work will be deemed to be accepted—meaning that it will then be late for the client to say, "I won't accept this. Do it again."

- *Payment:* Web development agreements often provide for several payments over the course of the development process. Typically, a first payment is due when the contract is signed. The next payment is due when the completed Web site design is accepted by the client. Additional payments are due when the client accepts the beta version of the Web site and the final version. Sometimes the agreement provides that the developer will receive a bonus for completing the entire project by a certain date.

- *Proprietary Rights:* In the proprietary rights provisions, copyright and other intellectual property ownership and licensing issues must be addressed. These issues are discussed later in this chapter.

- *Warranties:* A warranty is a legal promise that a statement or representation is true. Typical warranties for Web development agreements are discussed later in this chapter.

- *Developer's Credit:* What form will Developer's "credit" take? Credits usually consist of Developer's logo and a few lines of text, with a link to Developer's own Web site. Three possibilities are a "footer" credit, in which the credit runs at the bottom of each Web page; a "banner" credit, in which the credit is displayed on a banner on one or more pages of the site; and an "acknowledgments page" credit, in which the credit appears only on a single page.

- *Domain Name Registration:* If the client has not already registered the domain name it will be using for the Web site, who will register it? If the developer will be registering the domain name for the client, the client should make certain that it is listed as the registrant. Otherwise, the developer will be able to transfer the domain name to another individual or company. Domain name registration is covered in Chapter 20, Domain Names.

- *Termination:* Termination clauses provide that either or both parties have the right to terminate the contract under certain circumstances. Generally, termination clauses describe breach of contract events that trigger the right to terminate the contract—for example, the developer's failure to deliver an acceptable beta version or final version. Some contracts also provide that one or both parties may terminate the contract for convenience, upon notice to the other party and payment of a cancellation fee. Termination clauses also describe the methods of giving notice of exercise of the termination right and whether the breaching party must be given an opportunity to cure the breach before the other party can terminate the contract.

*   *Arbitration Clauses:* An arbitration clause states that disputes arising under the contract must be settled through arbitration rather than through court litigation. Such clauses generally include the name of the organization that will conduct the arbitration (the American Arbitration Association, for example), the city in which the arbitration will be held, and the method for selecting arbitrators.

*   *Merger Clauses:* Merger clauses state that the written document contains the entire understanding of the parties. The purpose of merger clauses is to ensure that evidence outside the written document will not be admissible in court to contradict or supplement the terms of the written agreement.

A Web site development agreement should have detailed technical and design specifications. The specifications define the scope of the developer's obligations, and they should be as specific as possible. Vagueness in the specifications can camouflage misunderstanding that will come to light when the developer delivers the material to the client for testing.

Detailed specifications serve two purposes: First, the process of creating them helps avoid misunderstandings about the responsibilities of the developer and the client. Second, if there is a dispute later about whether the developer has performed the contractual obligations, the specifications will establish the scope of those obligations.

Developer Tip: If you are dealing with a client who is a Web novice, educate the client and show the client samples of your work prior to contract signing. Make certain the client understands what you are promising to do.

Client Tip: The developer needs to understand what features you want in your Web site in order to create the specifications. If you don't know what you want, you should spend some time on the Internet reviewing existing sites; look at other sites designed by the developer; talk to Web site owners about what has worked for them; and read up on Web marketing (or hire a Web marketing consultant). If you don't understand the terminology used in the specifications, get help. Don't sign the contract without understanding what you need and what the developer is promising.

The proprietary rights section of a Web development agreement must address copyright ownership and licensing issues. The agreement must state who will own the copyright in the Web site as a whole, in individual content components created by the developer for the Web site (graphics and text, for example), and in any software created by the developer for use in the Web site.

Developer Tip: If you agree to assign the copyright in the material you create to the client, you will not be able to use that material in other projects, nor will you be able to modify it for other projects. Once you assign the copyright, the client will have the copyright owner's exclusive rights. If you are creating material to fill a client's special needs, you may not object to giving the client ownership of the copyright (particularly if the client is willing to pay a higher fee for an assignment of all rights). You may, however, want to retain copyright ownership of some components—for example, certain graphics, or a "shopping cart" program for online sales transactions—or at least reserve the right to use the components in future projects. Unless you retain copyright ownership of the components or get a license from your client to re-use them, your use of the components in future projects will infringe the client's copyright.

Client Tip: Generally, you should try to obtain ownership of copyrights in all material created for you by the developer. If you do so, you will then have all the copyright owner's exclusive rights in the material—the right to reproduce the work, distribute it, publicly perform it, publicly display it, and modify it for use in later projects and different media. However, the developer may resist giving you outright ownership. If the developer is to retain copyright ownership of all or part of the Web site material, you should make certain that the agreement gives you the right to use and modify the material owned by the developer in every way and every media that you believe will be necessary, both now and in the future.

The proprietary rights section of the agreement must state who will obtain licenses to use copyrighted content and software belonging to others (discussed in Chapter 14, Steering Clear of Infringement) and material protected under other intellectual property laws or the right of publicity (discussed in Chapter 15, Other Important Laws).

Developer Tip: If the client is expecting you to use expensive content—a clip of Madonna singing "Like a Virgin," for example, or a photo of a famous person—the contract should state who is responsible for obtaining and

paying for permission to use such rights. If it will be your responsibility to obtain these licenses, you should raise your price to cover the costs of obtaining such rights. Those costs include personnel time to negotiate the rights and the license fees. Be careful not to commit yourself to obtaining rights to use specific content, because those works may not be available.

Client Tip: If the developer uses content owned by others without permission, you will be liable for copyright infringement for using the material on your Web site. Make certain that the developer understands that using copyrighted material on a Web site without permission may be copyright infringement. You should also consider asking the developer to give you a warranty of noninfringement (discussed later in this chapter).

Often, the client will be providing some content for the Web site—for example, graphics that the client has used in the past in written marketing materials. If the client does not own this content, licenses will be required, and the agreement should state which party will get the licenses.

Developer Tip: If the client provides material for the Web site the use of which infringes the rights of others, you will be liable under copyright law for using the material. Consider asking the client for a warranty of noninfringement for material provided by the client.

Client Tip: Before you give the developer material to use in your Web site, familiarize yourself with the copyright law's ownership rules (discussed in Chapter 13, Copyright Law Basics) and review your records to determine whether you own the material. If you don't, you may need permission from the copyright owner. Don't assume that you own the copyright in material because you have used the material in the past. The past use may have been unauthorized, or it may have been authorized on a "one time use" or other restricted basis.

A warranty is a legal promise that certain statements are true. Warranty clauses typically include an indemnity provision in which the party making a warranty promises to defend, indemnify, and hold the other party harmless for the breach of any of the warranties (in other words, pay for all costs, including attorneys' fees, arising out of the breach of the warranties).

Many Web development agreements include a performance warranty from the developer—for example, a warranty that the Web site will be of high quality, will be free of defects in material and workmanship in all material respects, and will conform in all respects to the functional and other descriptions contained in the specifications.

Typically, these agreements contain noninfringement warranties from both parties—the developer warranting to the client that it has not used pre-existing materials owned by third parties, and the client warranting to the developer that material provided by the client does not infringe third party rights.

**LAB
17.2**

Developer Tip: Clients have good reason for asking for intellectual property warranties and indemnities: If you infringe any third-party intellectual property rights in creating the client's Web site, the client will become an infringer by using the Web site (even though innocent of intent to infringe). If warranty and indemnity provisions make you nervous, try to negotiate a dollar limit for your exposure on the indemnity—for example, no more than your total compensation for the development of the Web site.

Client Tip: Before you warrant that material you provide for the Web site is noninfringing, review the copyright law's rules and make certain you really own the content or have the right to use it on your Web site.

LAB 17.2 EXERCISES

17.2.1 UNDERSTAND THE STRUCTURE OF A TYPICAL WEB DEVELOPMENT AGREEMENT

    a) David created a Web site design for Harry pursuant to a written development agreement containing a merger clause. When Harry received the beta version of the Web site design, he complained that he was unhappy because the design did not include a feature for accepting email inquiries from site users. Nothing in the development agreement or specifications mentions user email inquiries, but Harry claims that he and David discussed such a feature. Does David have to add this feature?

17.2.2 UNDERSTAND WHAT COPYRIGHT ISSUES MUST BE ADDRESSED IN A WEB DEVELOPMENT AGREEMENT

a) The Web site design that Developer created for Client includes "search the site" software created by Developer. Can Developer use that software in her own Web site? In Web sites for other clients?

_____

_____

17.2.3 UNDERSTAND WARRANTIES AND INDEMNIFICATIONS

a) Web Developer promised that the e-commerce Web site he designed for Client would be free of defects in material and workmanship and would conform to the requirements stated in the Web development agreement's specifications. After six months of use, the Web site's "shopping cart" program stopped working, and Client no longer received orders from the site. Is Client entitled to a full refund from Developer?

_____

_____

LAB 17.2 EXERCISE ANSWERS

17.2.1 ANSWER

a) David created a Web site design for Harry pursuant to a written development agreement containing a merger clause. When Harry received the beta version of the Web site design, he complained that he was unhappy because the design did not include a feature for accepting email inquiries from site users. Nothing in the development agreement or specifications mentions user email inquiries, but Harry claims that he and David discussed such a feature. Does David have to add this feature?

Answer: No. The development agreement and its specifications define the scope of the developer's obligations. Because the agreement has a merger clause, contracts law provides that the written document contains the entire understanding of the parties. Even if David and Harry did discuss the additional feature, evidence of that discussion would not be admissible in court.

In complex contracts, the parties often go through several rounds of negotiations before they reach their final agreement. One purpose of merger clauses is to eliminate uncertainty about which of the previously discussed terms are part of the contract. Harry should have read the written contract before he signed it, making certain that the written contract matched his understanding of his agreement with David.

17.2.2 ANSWER

a) The Web site design that Developer created for Client includes "search the site" software created by Developer. Can Developer use that software in her own Web site? In Web sites for other clients?

Answer: Who owns the copyright in the software? If Developer has not given Client a written assignment of the copyright in the Web site (in a Web development agreement or in a separate document), Developer owns the copyright in the Web site and the software and is free to use the software on her own site and in other projects. (Ownership of works created by freelancers is discussed in Chapter 13, Copyright Law Basics). However, if Developer has assigned the entire Web site to Client, the software belongs to Client. In that case, Developer does not have the right to use the software. However, Developer is free to reuse the ideas she used in creating the software.

If Client insisted on owning the copyright in the Web site design but Developer wanted to be able to use the software in other projects, there are two ways to meet both parties' needs: (1) Developer could retain ownership just of the search software component, assigning the copyright in the Web site design to Client. (2) Developer could assign the copyright in the Web site design and the software to Client, taking back a license from Client to use the software in Developer's own site and sites for future clients.

17.2.3 ANSWER

a) Web Developer promised that the e-commerce Web site he designed for Client would be free of defects in material and workmanship and would conform to the requirements stated in the Web development agreement's specifications. After six months of use, the Web site's "shopping cart" program stopped working, and Client no longer received orders from the site. What legal action is available to Client?

Answer: Client could sue Developer for breach of warranty. Developer's promise was a warranty. Taking orders is the essence of an e-commerce site, so the Web site was not free of defects. Developer, of course, may claim that because the shopping cart program worked for six months, it is obvious that some other party (such as Client's technical staff or Client's Web hosting provider) did something that caused the shopping cart program to stop working.

LAB 17.2 SELF-REVIEW QUESTIONS

In order to test your progress, you should be able to answer the following questions.

1) Which of these types of clauses puts a deadline on a client's right to reject the developer's work?

   a) _____ Acceptance clause
   b) _____ Merger clause
   c) _____ Termination clause
   d) _____ Arbitration clause

2) Client gave Developer photographs, used in the past in Client's marketing material, to use in the Web site. Client does not own the copyrights in the photographs or have a license to use the photographs on the Web. If Client gave Developer a warranty of noninfringement covering the photographs, the warranty is not breached as long as Client honestly believed it owned the copyrights.

   a) _____ True
   b) _____ False

3) If Client in question 2 warranted to Developer that it owned the copyrights in the photographs, and the warranty included an indemnity, how does that help Developer?

   a) _____ The owner of the copyrights cannot sue Developer.
   b) _____ Developer is not an infringer.
   c) _____ Client must reimburse Developer for all costs arising out of Client's breach of the warranty, including Developer's attorney's fees for the copyright infringement suit and any damages Developer had to pay to the copyright owner.

4) If a developer is registering a domain name for a client to use, it is in the client's best interest to

   a) _____ have the developer listed as the registrant.
   b) _____ have the client listed as registrant.
   c) _____ have the developer and client listed as co-registrants.

5) A client has the right to terminate a Web development agreement without cause after the developer has begun the work.

a) _____ True

b) _____ True, if the agreement has a "termination for convenience" clause

c) _____ False

Quiz answers appear in the Appendix, Section 17.2.

CHAPTER 17

TEST YOUR THINKING

Web Developer is hiring your friend Programmer on an independent contractor basis to create a Web site search engine program for use in Web Developer's future Web design projects. Web Developer (who doesn't believe in using lawyers) has given Programmer this two-sentence development agreement to sign: "Programmer agrees to create a Web site search engine program for Web Developer. Web Developer agrees to pay Programmer $10,000 for the program."

1) What provisions should Programmer add to the agreement, for Programmer's protection?

C H A P T E R   1 8

LINKING, FRAMING, CACHING, AND META TAGS

Web site links permit Web users to click their way from one Web site to another. Framing permits a Web site user to view material from another Web site within a "frame" on the original site. Caching is the creation of a copy of a Web site by storing data on a computer. Meta tags are HTML code used to describe the contents of a Web site (and used by search engines in responding to search requests).

This chapter considers the legal questions currently raised by linking, framing, caching, and meta tag use.

© 2000 by J. Dianne Brinson.

L A B   1 8 . 1

LEGAL IMPLICATIONS OF LINKING AND FRAMING

LAB OBJECTIVES

After this lab, you will be able to:

✔ Understand When Permission Is Required for Various Types of Linking

✔ Understand that Linking May Expose You to Liability

Currently, linking can take three forms:

- A simple text hyperlink, implemented through HTML, in which a hypertext link is marked as a highlighted word or different-colored word on the linking site.

- A graphic hyperlink, in which a graphic (a logo or just a button) on the linking site alerts the user of the linking site to the existence of a link.

- "Framing," which permits a Web site user to view material from another Web site within a "frame" on the original site.

Other types of links may become possible as new technology becomes available.

Linking is so common on the Web that the idea that a Web site owner might need permission to link to another site was once considered absurd. After all, it is linking that makes the Web a "web" of interconnected sites. In the Web culture, providing a link to another site generally has been viewed as a favor to the owner of the linked site, because providing a link increases traffic to the site.

Lately, however, the increasing commercialization of the Web and the availability of new technology (such as framing technology) have caused the assumption that linking does not require permission to be reexamined, especially in light of recent lawsuits (discussed below). So far, no court has addressed the issue of whether permission is required for linking, so what follows is simply a summary of what I think about this issue.

When considering whether permission is required for linking, the three types of links—text hyperlinks, graphic hyperlinks, and framing—must be considered separately, because these three types of linking have different legal implications.

> *Text Hyperlink:* When a Web site user clicks on a link, the user is transferred to the linked site. Linking does not involve copying or displaying the linked site, so linking is not an exercise of the linked site owner's copyright rights. The current thinking is that a Web site owner who wants to provide a text hyperlink to the home page of another site does not need permission from the owner of the linked site. However, it is considered "good manners" to ask permission before linking to another site (particularly if the site says "ask permission before linking"), because some Web site owners may not want to be associated with your site or your products.

> *Graphic Hyperlink:* For graphic hyperlinks, if *you* own or have the right to use the graphic, the same rule applies: You do not need permission for a graphic link to the home page of the linked site, but it is considered good manners to ask permission. However, if you use a graphic from the linked site as the graphic hyperlink, you will be reproducing and displaying copyrighted material you do not own (the graphic). In that case, you need the copyright owner's permission, as discussed in Chapter 13, Copyright Law Basics, and Chapter 14, Steering Clear of Copyright Infringement.

> *Framing:* Framing may raise copyright infringement issues and thus should not be done without permission. Framing permits the viewer of the framing site to view the framed site while content from the framing site (such as advertising banners) is still on the viewer's computer screen. Framing changes the way the viewer experiences the framed site. One court has held that framing a site may be an exercise of the copyright owner's exclusive right to modify the site. In the case, *Futuredontics, Inc. v. Applied Anagramics, Inc.*, the defendant, a dental marketing service, framed a dental referral business's site. The frame for the framed site showed information about the defendant's services. The plaintiff maintained that the framing gave viewers the impression that the defendant was responsible for the success of the plaintiff's referral service. This suit is still pending.

> In another framing suit, *The Washington Post Co. v. Total News, Inc.*, several publishers sued Total News for copyright and trademark infringement for framing the publishers' Web sites. The Total News site's

"frame" covered up the framed site's ads (Total News filled the frame with its own ads). Viewers of the Total News site viewed content from a publisher's site but not the publisher's ads. The case was settled, with the defendant agreeing to link to—not frame—the plaintiffs' sites.

Deep linking—linking to an internal page of the linked site—may raise legal issues, even if the link is a simple text hyperlink, as Ticketmaster's 1997 lawsuit against Microsoft illustrates. Microsoft's "Sidewalk" Web city guides provided links to Ticketmaster's online ticket-ordering page (an internal page of the Ticketmaster site). Ticketmaster sued Microsoft for unfair trade practices and trademark dilution. Ticketmaster claimed that Microsoft's unauthorized links were allowing Microsoft to benefit unfairly from Ticketmaster's services and goodwill. Ticketmaster also claimed that Microsoft's links interfered with Ticketmaster's business relationship with MasterCard. Ticketmaster had agreed to give MasterCard prominence over other credit cards in any advertising. Users who came to the Ticketmaster site from a Microsoft "Sidewalk" site missed Ticketmaster's "plug" for MasterCard, which was on the home page of the Ticketmaster site. Microsoft filed a counterclaim seeking a court declaration that linking does not violate U.S. law. The parties settled the case in January 1999, so we will never know how the court would have ruled.

Linking can promote commercial objectives such as a revenue-sharing arrangement between the owners of the linking and linked sites. In a revenue-sharing linking arrangement, the linking site's owner receives—as compensation for providing a text or graphic image link to a another site—a percentage of the linked site's revenues (which come from product sales or advertising fees). The details of revenue-sharing linking arrangement should be spelled out in a written linking agreement that covers the duties and responsibilities of both parties, including such issues as link placement, exclusivity (limitations on links to competitors' sites), access to site user data, privacy policies, and site content control rights.

Linking may expose you to liability for wrongs done by the owner of the linked site under several legal theories. First, linking to another site may give viewers the impression that you are an agent or partner of the owner of the linked site, with shared responsibility for the linked site's defective products and false marketing claims—especially if you have a revenue-sharing arrangement with the owner of the linked site.

Second, if you use a graphic from the linked site as a graphic hyperlink, you may be sued for copyright infringement if the linked site's owner does not own the copyright in the graphic.

■ FOR EXAMPLE

Lucille got permission from Z Software to use a graphic from Z Software's Web site as a graphic hyperlink to Z Software's site. Z Software does not own the copyright in the graphic, Artist does. Z did not get Artist's permission to use the graphic. Both Z Software and Lucille have exercised Artist's rights of reproduction and display and are liable to Artist for copyright infringement. Z Software's grant of permission to Lucille does not protect her from liability to Artist because Z does not own the copyright in the graphic.

Finally, the possibility has been raised that a Web site owner who links to a site containing infringing material may be liable for contributory copyright infringement. Contributory copyright infringement is established when a defendant, with knowledge of another party's infringing activity, causes or materially contributes to the infringing conduct. In late 1999, a federal district court in Utah held that linking to Web sites containing infringing material coupled with messages encouraging Web site viewers to visit the linked sites to view, download, and print out the material was active encouragement of copyright infringement. However, the court in that case, *Intellectual Reserve, Inc. v. Utah Lighthouse Ministry, Inc.*, stopped short of holding that merely linking to a site containing infringing material is contributory infringement.

A provision of the Online Liability Copyright Infringement Limitation Act (OCILLA) states that a service provider is not liable for monetary relief for linking to a site containing infringing material if the service provider, upon receiving notification of the claimed infringement, removes or disables access to the material. The Act defines service provider as "a provider of online services or network access, or the operator of facilities therefor, including an entity offering the transmission, routing, or providing of connections for digital online communications, between or among points specified by a user, of material of the user's choosing, without modification to the content of the material as sent or received." In order to take advantage of this provision, a service provider must meet the OCILLA threshold requirements discussed in Chapter 16, System Operator Liability for Copyright Infringement by System Users. Also, the service provider must not receive a financial benefit directly attributable to the infringing activity, if the service provider has the right and ability to control the activity.

LAB 18.1 EXERCISES

18.1.1 UNDERSTAND WHEN PERMISSION IS REQUIRED FOR VARIOUS TYPES OF LINKING

    a) Giovanni wants to provide a link from his Web site to Z Media's Web site, using Z Media's logo as a graphic hyperlink. Does he need permission from Z Media?

_____

_____

_____

b) Medico's medical information site contains links to a number of other medical information sites. Medico's attorney is concerned that some of the linked sites may contain copyrighted material used without permission of the copyright owners. What can Medico do to protect itself from liability for contributory copyright infringement?

_____

_____

_____

18.1.2 UNDERSTAND THAT LINKING MAY EXPOSE YOU TO LIABILITY

a) The "Terms of Use" page of Giantco's Web site includes this language: "Giantco's site provides links to sites that are not under Giantco's control. Giantco does not assume any responsibility over or liability for materials available at the linked sites. Giantco does not intend for links to be interpreted as endorsements of the linked sites or the linked sites' products." What's the purpose of this language?

_____

_____

_____

LAB 18.1 EXERCISE ANSWERS

18.1.1 ANSWERS

a) Giovanni wants to provide a link from his Web site to Z Media's Web site, using Z Media's logo as a graphic hyperlink. Does he need permission from Z Media?

Answer: Yes. The graphic image of Z Media's logo is protected under copyright. If John uses the logo on his site, he will reproduce and display the logo—an exercise of Z Media's copyright owner's rights. Logos used to identify a provider's goods or services are protected by trademark law as well.

b) Medico's medical information site contains links to a number of other medical information sites. Medico's attorney is concerned that some of the linked sites may contain copyrighted material used without permission of the copyright owners. What can Medico do to protect itself from liability for contributory copyright infringement?

Answer: If Medico fits within OCILLA's definition of service provider—and it probably does, if the Medico site has interactive features—Medico should take the necessary action to meet the threshold requirements for taking advantage of OCILLA's safe harbors. The threshold requirements are discussed in Chapter 16, System Operator Liability for Copyright Infringement by System Users. Then, if Medico receives a notification that a linked site contains infringing material, it should act promptly to remove the link.

Even if Medico is not within the definition of service provider, if Medico is notified that a site to which it has linked contains infringing material, Medico should remove the link.

LAB 18.1

18.1.2 ANSWER

a) The "Terms of Use" page of Giantco's Web site includes this language: "Giantco's site provides links to sites that are not under Giantco's control. Giantco does not assume any responsiblity over or liability for materials available at the linked sites. Giantco does not intend for links to be interpreted as endorsements of the linked sites or the linked sites' products." What's the purpose of this language?

Answer: Giantco is trying to disassociate itself from linked sites—in case linked sites are selling defective products or making false advertising claims or committing other wrongs.

LAB 18.1 SELF-REVIEW QUESTIONS

In order to test your progress, you should be able to answer the following questions.

1) Copyright law requires you to get permission from the copyright owner before doing which of the following:

    a) _____ Using a simple text hyperlink to the site
    b) _____ Using a graphic from a site as a graphic hyperlink to that site
    c) _____ Framing a site
    d) _____ All of the above
    e) _____ Both b and c

2) Harold wants to provide a link from his site to a page of the Amazon.com site that features a particular book Harold likes.

a) _____ Harold should get permission from Amazon.

b) _____ Harold does not need permission from Amazon.

3) It is illegal to pay other Web site owners to link to your site.

a) _____ True

b) _____ False

4) The Online Copyright Infringement Liability Limitations Act protects a service provider from liability for:

a) _____ Linking to a site that sells defective products.

b) _____ Linking to a site that makes false marketing claims.

c) _____ Linking to a site that contains infringing material.

d) _____ All of the above.

5) Linking to a site containing infringing material is contributory copyright infringement.

a) _____ True

b) _____ False

c) _____ We don't know yet (but OCILLA provides a way for service providers to protect themselves from liability).

Quiz answers appear in the Appendix, Section 18.1.

L A B   1 8 . 2

LEGAL IMPLICATIONS OF CACHING AND META TAGS

LAB OBJECTIVES

After this lab, you will be able to:

✔ Understand When Caching Requires Permission
✔ Understand Why You Should Not Use Trademarks Owned by Others as Meta Tags

---

Caching is the creation of a copy of a Web site by storing data on a computer. Caching at the server level is done to facilitate quick linking to a popular site, to maximize site "uptime," and for security reasons, as part of a firewall. This type of caching is also called proxy caching. In copyright terms, caching a Web site is an exercise of the Web site copyright owner's reproduction and display rights. Get permission before proxy caching a site.

Temporary caching occurs within your computer's RAM when you view a Web site (your browser caches each Web page you visit in your computer's RAM). Current thinking is that by posting the document on the Web, the copyright owner has given you an implied license to make that RAM copy, since you cannot otherwise view the document. For this level type of temporary browser caching, it is not necessary to request permission. It is server level caching—for example, to create a "mirror" (copy) of an existing site—that requires permission.

Meta tags are HTML code used to describe the contents of a Web site. Search engines retrieve results for Web users by looking for keywords in domain names, actual text on Web pages, and meta tags. The more often a term appears in the meta tags for a site, the more likely it is that the Web page will be found in a search for that term. Several court decisions have held that trademark law bars a Web site owner from using a trademark belonging to someone else as a meta tag.

In *Playboy Enterprises v. AsiaFocus International, Inc.,* defendant AsiaFocus used Playboy Enterprises' federally registered trademark "Playboy" as meta tags for the AsiaFocus site. The court held that AsiaFocus had intentionally misled viewers into believing that the AsiaFocus site was connected with or sponsored by Playboy Enterprises. It enjoined the defendant from continuing to use "Playboy" as a meta tag.

Brookfield Communications, Inc. v. West Coast Entertainment Corporation went even further, holding that using a competitor's trademark as a meta tag was trademark infringement even if consumers were not misled about site sponsorship. In that case, the defendant West Coast Video was using Brookfield's federally registered trademark "moviebuff" in meta tags of West Coast's site, westcoastvideo.com. The court noted that because the westcoastvideo.com home page prominently displayed the West Coast Video name, it would be difficult to say that a consumer viewing westcoastvideo.com would think he had reached Brookfield's site (moviebuff.com). Nonetheless, the court felt that defendant West Coast Video's use of "moviebuff" in meta tags for its site was likely to result in "initial interest confusion"—meaning that westcoastvideo.com would attract the initial interest of consumers' looking for "moviebuff" because search engines would provide the URL for westcoastvideo.com in response to searches for the keyword "moviebuff." The court found that by using "moviebuff" in its site's meta tags, West Coast would improperly benefit from the goodwill that Brookfield had developed in the trademark "moviebuff." It held that federal trademark law prohibits a company from using any term confusingly similar to its competitor's trademark as a meta tag. "Using another's trademark in one's meta tags is much like posting a sign with another's trademark in front of one's store," the court said.

LAB 18.2 EXERCISES

18.2.1 UNDERSTAND WHEN CACHING REQUIRES PERMISSION

a) Web Host provides Web hosting services for a number of clients. Web Host would like to create mirror sites for all of its clients' sites. Does it need permission?

_____

_____

_____

18.2.2 UNDERSTAND WHY YOU SHOULD NOT USE TRADEMARKS OWNED BY OTHERS AS META TAGS

a) Terri Welles, 1981 Playmate of the Year, used "Playboy" and "Playmate" as meta tags for her own Web site (which is not affiliated with Playboy Enterprises). Playboy Enterprises sued her for trademark infringement and dilution. Explain Playboy Enterprises' legal theories.

_____

_____

LAB 18.2 EXERCISE ANSWERS

18.2.1 ANSWER

a) Web Host provides Web hosting services for a number of clients. Web Host would like to create mirror sites for all of its clients' sites. Does it need permission?

Answer: Yes, because a mirror site would be created by caching an existing site. If Web Host uses a written Web hosting agreement with its clients (as it should), the agreement may give Web Host the right to create mirror sites. In fact, the agreement may require Web Host to maintain mirror sites for all client sites (in order to facilitate quick user access to the clients' sites).

18.2.2 ANSWER

a) Terri Welles, 1981 Playmate of the Year, used "Playboy" and "Playmate" as meta tags for her own Web site (which is not affiliated with Playboy Enterprises). Playboy Enterprises sued her for trademark infringement and dilution. Explain Playboy Enterprises' legal theories.

Answer: Playboy Enterprises claimed that Ms. Welles' use of its trademarks as meta tags for her site might cause Web users to think that Ms. Welles' site was the official Playboy Enterprises site. Even if they weren't confused as to the site's sponsorship, they might be diverted to her site when they were looking for the official Playboy site. Playboy Enterprises actually lost this case, Playboy Enterprises, Inc. v. Welles. The court found that Ms. Welles had truthfully used the trademarks to identify herself and that she was likely to prevail in her claim that her use of the trademarks was fair use.

LAB 18.2 SELF-REVIEW QUESTIONS

In order to test your progress, you should be able to answer the following questions.

1) What is caching?

   a) _____ A synonym for linking
   b) _____ Linking without permission
   c) _____ Creating a copy of a Web site by storing data on a computer

2) Under what circumstances should you get permission to cache a Web site you do not own?

   a) _____ Every time you visit a site (because your browser is caching the site you view)
   b) _____ Before doing server-level caching (proxy caching) of a site
   c) _____ Both a and b
   d) _____ None of these situations requires permission

3) What's a meta tag?

   a) _____ Any trademark used on the Web
   b) _____ Any trademark used without the owner's permission
   c) _____ HTML code used to describe the contents of a Web site

4) Why would a Web site owner use another company's trademark as a meta tag?

   a) _____ So the owner's site will be found in a search for the trademark
   b) _____ In order to link to the trademark owner's site
   c) _____ In order to frame the trademark owner's site

5) Which statement is true?

   a) _____ It's okay to use a competitor's trademark as a meta tag in your site so long as you make it clear on your site that the trademark owner is not the site's sponsor
   b) _____ Using a competitor's trademark as a meta tag in your site may be trademark infringement even if you make it clear that your competitor is not the site sponsor
   c) _____ Trademark law does not apply to meta tag use
   d) _____ Both a and c are true

Quiz answers appear in the Appendix, Section 18.2.

CHAPTER 18

TEST YOUR THINKING

To a Web site user, there doesn't seem to be any difference between clicking on an icon that will take the user to a linked site and clicking on an icon that will bring up a cached site for the user.

1) Why is permission required for caching but not for linking?

C H A P T E R   1 9

WEB SITE TERMS OF USE AND CLICKWRAPS

Web site Terms of Use are used to remind site users that site content is protected by copyright, tell them what uses they may make of the site's content, and protect the site owner from liability.

Clickwraps—online contract terms that site users accept by clicking an acceptance button—are used in online sales and software licensing transactions to define the terms of the transaction, disclaim warranties implied under state law, and limit the site owner's liability.

© 2000 by J. Dianne Brinson.

503

L A B   1 9 . 1

TYPICAL PROVISIONS FOR WEB SITE TERMS OF USE

LAB OBJECTIVES

After this lab, you will be able to:

✔ Understand Typical Provisions for Web Site Terms of Use
✔ Understand How to Present Terms of Use

Most Web site Terms of Use pages begin with information about the copyright status of the site's material. Posting material on the Web is not an abandonment of copyright. However, some people mistakenly believe that all material on the Web is copyright-free. For that reason, a Web site Terms of Use page will usually include a statement that the contents of the Web site are protected by copyright under both United States and foreign laws. Web site owners should also use copyright notice (discussed in Chapter 13, Copyright Law Basics) on the site to remind site users that site content is copyrighted material.

Many Web site owners are willing to allow site users to print or download the site's material for certain purposes without requesting permission. These "limited permission grants" usually appear in the Terms of Use. A limited permission grant is actually a license to use the Web site's materials. (Licenses are discussed in Chapter 14, Steering Clear of Copyright Infringement).

If you want to grant users of your site permission to download or print the site's material, be careful: If your Web site contains material owned by others, which you've licensed, your license controls the extent to which you can lawfully authorize site users to use the licensed material.

■ *FOR EXAMPLE*

ABC Co.'s Web site contains graphics created and owned by Graphic Artist. If ABC's license from Graphic Artist does not give ABC the right to permit user downloading of the graphics, the ABC Co. site's Terms of Use should not authorize user downloading of the graphics.

Many licenses to use content on the Web authorize the licensee to permit site users to download the licensed material for personal, noncommercial purposes. If your current content licenses do not contain such a provision, you may want to try to obtain such a provision in future content licenses.

For material on your site that you own, the limited permission grant provision of your Terms of Use can be as broad or narrow as you wish. You may want to add a sentence telling users how to request permission if they want to use the site's material in a way not authorized in the Terms of Use.

It is not essential to state that site users are prohibited from using the site material in ways other than those expressly permitted in the Terms of Use. A copyright owner does not, by granting limited permission to others to use the copyrighted material, make the copyrighted material "fair game" for others to use as they wish. However, most Terms of Use pages include a statement of prohibited uses— for example, a prohibition against selling or modifying the content or using it on a Web site or in a networked computer environment.

Many Web sites permit users to communicate with the Web site operator. If your Web site provides this function and you want to be able to use the user submissions in the future, you will need a license from the user. Under copyright law's ownership rules (discussed in Chapter 13, Copyright Law Basics), the copyright in material created by a site user belongs to the user (or the user's employer, if the user's communication is within the scope of the user's employment).

■ *FOR EXAMPLE*

Jungle Co.'s Web site permits site users to submit product reviews for products sold on the Web site. Mehta submitted a review of a Jungle Co. product. Mehta is the copyright owner of the review. If Jungle Co. wants to post Mehta's product review on its Web site, it needs a license from Mehta.

The easy way for a Web site owner to obtain the necessary licenses from users is to state in the Terms of Use that a site user who posts a communication to the Web site automatically grants the site owner a nonexclusive license to use the material (and to sublicense others to use the material).

Of course, if a user submits copyrighted material that belongs to someone else and you post it on your site, the license in the preceding paragraph will not shield you from liability to the owner. However, the Online Copyright Infringement Liability Limitation Act (discussed in Chapter 16, System Operator Liability for Copyright Infringement by System Users) will protect you if you have met OCILLA's threshold requirements and remove the material upon receiving notice or knowledge of the infringement. A Terms of Use page should include a reminder to users that they should not post copyrighted material they do not own without the permission of the copyright owner or post material that infringes other third-party rights (such as the rights discussed in Chapter 15, Other Important Laws).

Many Terms of Use pages also include a statement that any communication posted by a user is considered to be nonconfidential. The purpose of this statement is to protect the Web site owner from claims that its use of the user communication was unauthorized disclosure of the user's trade secrets or invasion of the user's privacy. (Trade secrets and privacy law are discussed in Chapter 15, Other Important Laws.)

If information on your Web site is inaccurate and a site user detrimentally relied on the information, it is possible that you could be liable to the user for damages. Many Terms of Use pages include a provision warning site users that the Web site may contain inaccurate information. There is generally a statement that the Web site owner makes no representations about the accuracy, reliability, completeness, or timeliness of the material provided and does not warrant that the Web site will operate error-free or that it is free of computer viruses.

Make the user aware that your site has Terms of Use by placing a notice on your site's home page and make it easy for them to get to the "Terms" page. Don't just bury the "Terms" page somewhere on your Web site without mentioning it on your home page. Some Web sites include a link to the "Terms" page on every Web page.

LAB 19.1 EXERCISES

19.1.1 UNDERSTAND TYPICAL PROVISIONS FOR WEB SITE TERMS OF USE

a) Where are the Terms of Use for the Scour.Net site (www.scour.net)?

_____

_____

b) Is it okay to print materials from the Scour.Net site?

_____

_____

19.1.2 UNDERSTAND HOW TO PRESENT TERMS OF USE

a) What's the purpose of the following language on a Web site's Terms of Use page: "Please read these terms carefully. Use of this site constitutes acceptance of these terms."

_____

_____

LAB 19.1 EXERCISE ANSWERS

19.1.1 ANSWERS

a) Where are the Terms of Use for the Scour.Net site (www.scour.net)?

Answer: The Terms of Use page for that site is called "Legal Notice, Disclaimer, and Terms of Use." The page is located at www.scour.net/General/Misc/Disclaimer.phtml.

b) Is it okay to print materials from the Scour.Net site?

Answer: The "Legal Notice, Disclaimer, and Terms of Use" page states that users may print materials on the Web site for personal or educational purposes, if they include any copyright notice originally included with the materials in all copies. Printing for other purposes requires permission. By requiring that copies include copyright notice, Scour.Net ensures that those receiving the copies will be reminded that the material is protected by copyright.

19.1.2 ANSWER

a) What's the purpose of the following language on a Web site's Terms of Use page: "Please read these terms carefully. Use of this site constitutes acceptance of these terms."

Answer: A Web site's Terms of Use is the site owner's statement of the conditions under which the user may access the Web site. Technically, the Terms of Use page is an offer by the Web site owner to the potential user: "You may use my Web site, but only if you accept my conditions." For those conditions to be binding on the user, the user must accept the conditions. An offer can be accepted by conduct, and this language defines use of the page as acceptance. As an alternative, the site owner could require the user to click on an "I accept the conditions" button before accessing the site's material. Most Web site owners don't want to do that because the click-through procedure may discourage people from using the site (by slowing them down).

LAB 19.1 SELF-REVIEW QUESTIONS

In order to test your progress, you should be able to answer the following questions.

1) ABC Co. owns everything on its site other than Graphic Artist's graphics. ABC Co., can, if it wishes, authorize site users to download a copy of the material owned by ABC Co. for personal, noncommercial use.

a) _____ True
b) _____ False

2) ABC Co. (from Question 1) can authorize its site users to download a copy of the graphics owned by Graphic Artist.

a) _____ True
b) _____ True, if ABC Co.'s license from Graphic Artist gives ABC Co. the right to authorize its site's users to download the graphics
c) _____ False

3) X Co.'s Web site posts site user comments. Who owns the copyright in the user comments?

a) _____ X Co., because it owns the Web site
b) _____ The users who wrote the comments

4) X Co. (from Question 3) wants to use some of the site user comments in newspaper ads for its products. X Co. does not need to ask the comments' authors for permission.

a) _____ True

b) _____ True, if the Terms of Use for X Co.'s Web site state that a user who posts a comment automatically grants X Co. a nonexclusive license to use the comment as X Co. wishes

c) _____ False

5) Terms of Use should be hard to find.

a) _____ True

b) _____ False

Quiz answers appear in the Appendix, Section 19.1.

L A B   1 9 . 2

CLICKWRAPS

LAB OBJECTIVES

After this lab, you will be able to:

✔ Understand Why Clickwraps Are Used
✔ Understand Express and Implied Warranties

Are you licensing software or selling goods on your Web site? If so, in addition to Web site Terms of Use, you may need a "clickwrap"—online contract terms—to define the terms and conditions that apply to sales or licenses. A clickwrap can be used whether delivery of the goods or software takes place online (as it often does with software) or offline (by mail or a package delivery company, as it generally does when goods are sold online).

Usually an e-commerce Web site has a separate "order" screen that deals with terms specific to the customer's order—what the customer is buying or licensing, the price or license fee, and the payment terms and payment mechanism. General terms of sale that apply to all transactions are included in a clickwrap—delivery and return policies, support policies, product warranties and warranty disclaimers, and limitations on the seller's liability. In a "bricks and mortar" transaction, this information is often printed at the bottom of the customer's invoice or on the back of the invoice, or it's shrinkwrapped inside the packaging containing the product or software the customer buys.

Much of the language in clickwraps and shrinkwraps is designed to limit seller liability arising under state sales laws. In every state except Louisiana, a statute known as Article Two of the Uniform Commercial Code applies to all contracts for the sale of goods. According to Article Two, certain warranties automatically arise when goods are sold, unless the seller excludes the warranties. Goods are defined in Article Two as "all things (including specially manufactured goods) which are movable."

Although Article Two does not apply to software licensing and contracts for services, many courts apply Article Two's provisions by analogy in disputes involving these kinds of contracts. The National Conference of Commissioners on Uniform State Laws has recently drafted a proposed uniform law, the Uniform Computer Information Transactions Act (UCITA), for transactions involving "computer information" (software, multimedia interactive products, data and databases, and online information). However, this law has not yet been adopted by any of the states, and state legislatures may reject it (some of its provisions are controversial).

According to Article Two, a seller can create express warranties by making statements of fact or promises to the buyer, by a description of the goods, or by display of a sample or model. An express warranty can be created—in the physical world or in the online world—without using formal words such as "warranty" or "guarantee." All that is necessary is that the statements, description, or sample become part of the "basis of the bargain."

To avoid making express warranties that you don't mean to make, you must be careful about what you say in marketing your products. There are many options for express warranty provisions. For example, for software, you could warrant that the product will perform substantially in accordance with the performance specifications stated on another screen on the Web site for a limited period of time. For goods, you could warrant that the products are free of manufacturing defects. You may also choose to make no warranty as to performance, stating instead that you are providing the product on "AS IS" basis, with the user assuming the entire risk of using the product.

According to Article Two, three implied warranties are made when goods are sold.

- Implied warranty of merchantability
- Implied warranty of fitness for particular purpose
- Implied warranties of title and noninfringement

Here's an explanation of these warranties.

> *Implied warranty of merchantability*: When a merchant sells goods, a warranty that the goods are "merchantable" is implied in the contract unless that warranty is excluded. To be merchantable, goods must "pass without objection in the trade" and be "fit for the ordinary purposes for which such goods are used."

> A merchant is defined in Article Two as "a person who deals in goods of the kind or otherwise by his occupation holds himself out as having knowledge or skill peculiar to the practices or goods involved in

the transaction. . . ." If you are operating an e-commerce site, you are probably a merchant as to goods sold from your site.

To avoid disputes over whether goods are merchantable, many manufacturers and sellers of goods exclude the warranty of merchantability. Article Two states that this warranty can be excluded only with language that mentions merchantability. If the exclusion is in writing (and it should be, for evidence purposes), the exclusion must be "conspicuous" (in a different typeface, type size, or color from the rest of the contract). This warranty can also be excluded by making it clear in the contract that the goods are sold "as is."

Implied warranty of fitness for particular purpose: The "implied warranty of fitness for particular purpose" is made by a seller when two factors are present: (1)The seller has reason to know of a particular purpose for which the buyer requires the goods; and (2) the buyer relies on the seller's skill or judgment to select suitable goods. The implied warranty of fitness for particular purpose can be excluded through contract language that explicitly excludes this warranty or by selling products "as is."

Implied warranties of title and noninfringement: Unless excluded, each contract for the sale of goods includes a warranty by the seller that the seller has the right to transfer title (legal right of ownership) in the goods and that the buyer will get good title. The warranty of title can be excluded only by specific language or by circumstances that give the buyer reason to know that the person selling does not claim full title. Unless otherwise agreed, a "merchant" warrants that the goods sold do not infringe third parties' intellectual property rights.

Many manufacturers and sellers of consumer products disclaim all of Article Two's implied warranties. Instead, they warrant only that the product will, for a limited period of time, be free from defects in materials and craftsmanship under normal use and service. This disclaimer language may not be valid in other countries. It is not valid even in the United States for certain warranties on "consumer products" (defined as "any tangible personal property that is distributed in commerce and that is normally used for personal, family, or household purposes).

According to Article Two, a buyer can obtain actual damages along with "incidental damages" and "consequential damages" from a seller who breaches a contract. Incidental damages are those resulting from the seller's breach of contract, such as expenses incurred in inspecting and transporting rejected goods and obtaining substitute goods. Consequential damages include any loss that could not reasonably be prevented by the buyer that resulted from the buyer's needs, if the seller knew about those needs or had reason to know about them.

■ *FOR EXAMPLE*

Buyer, a mail-order catalog seller, bought from Seller a telephone system for use in Buyer's mail order business. Seller promised that the system would be operational on January 2. Buyer, relying on that promise, dismantled its old phone system on January 1. The new phone system was not actually operational until January 31. As a result of the delay, Buyer lost $100,000 worth of orders. If Buyer could not reasonably have prevented the loss of the orders (for example, by arranging for an answering service to handle calls), Buyer has consequential damages of $100,000.

Consequential damages also include damages for injury to person or property resulting from a breach of warranty.

Most manufacturers and sellers try to exclude consequential damages because such liability exposes a seller to a risk of having to pay damages far in excess of the product's price. Consequential damages may be limited or excluded unless the limitation or exclusion is "unconscionable." The term "unconscionable" is not defined in Article Two, but many courts have used the definition created by one of the federal appellate courts: "Unconscionability has generally been recognized to include an absence of meaningful choice on the part of one of the parties together with contract terms which are unreasonably favorable to the other party." In the case of consumer goods, limitation of consequential damages for personal injury is assumed to be unconscionable.

If a seller excludes consequential damages or otherwise contractually limits remedies and then circumstances cause the limited remedy to "fail of its essential purpose" (leave the buyer with no real remedy), a court may determine that all of Article Two's normal remedies should be available to the buyer, even consequential damages. In one case involving a contractual limitation on damages, the buyer, a hospital, had paid the seller, the software supplier Electronic Data Systems Corporation, over two million dollars for software systems. The software systems were so defective the hospital could not use them. The contract provision limited the hospital's damages to $4000, the amount of the average monthly invoice for the transaction. The court found that because the hospital had paid over two million dollars for unusable software systems, the $4000 limit on damages failed to provide the hospital with an adequate remedy and thus "failed of its essential purpose."

To avoid such an outcome, generally manufacturers and sellers who limit the customer's remedy to repair or replacement also promise that they will refund the purchase price if the product cannot be repaired or replaced. The refund promise is a "backup" remedy.

LAB 19.2 EXERCISES

19.2.1 UNDERSTAND WHY CLICKWRAPS ARE USED

a) What's the purpose of the following language on a Web site "Terms of Sale" page: "Please read this agreement carefully. To complete your order for the product you've requested, you must first accept the terms and conditions of this agreement by electronically checking the box marked 'I accept these terms and conditions.'"

_____

_____

19.2.2 UNDERSTAND EXPRESS AND IMPLIED WARRANTIES

a) What's the purpose of the following language in a clickwrap: "All services and information made available at this Web site are made available AS IS, without any warranties of any kind."

_____

_____

LAB 19.2 EXERCISE ANSWERS

19.2.1 ANSWER

a) What's the purpose of the following language on a Web site "Terms of Sale" page: "Please read this agreement carefully. To complete your order for the product you've requested, you must first accept the terms and conditions of this agreement by electronically checking the box marked 'I accept these terms and conditions.'"

Answer: The owner of the Web site, by putting this agreement in front of an online customer before the order is completed, is ensuring that the customer had an opportunity to review the terms of sale. Requiring the customer to check the "I accept" box is this site owner's way of getting the customer to take affirmative action to show acceptance of the terms.

Legal experts have questioned whether a purchaser is bound by terms that the purchaser did not have an opportunity to review prior to completing the transaction. This is often the case with shrinkwrapped software (the card containing the warranty disclaimers and other use restrictions is shrinkwrapped inside the box containing the product). For online transactions, take advantage of the fact that the Web makes it possible for you to disclose the terms before the transaction is final. Make certain that your customers have an opportunity to review the terms before completing a transaction. Your e-commerce Web site should be set up so that a buyer or licensor is required to take affirmative action to show acceptance of the terms (such as clicking an "Accept" button or typing in words "I accept.")

19.2.2 ANSWER

a) What's the purpose of the following language in a clickwrap: "All services and information made available at this Web site are made available AS IS, without any warranties of any kind."

Answer: This language excludes the Article Two warranties of merchantability and implied warranty of fitness for a particular purpose.

You'll see this language in Web site Terms of Use as well as in clickwraps and shrinkwraps—even for Web sites that do not sell goods or license software.

LAB 19.2 SELF-REVIEW QUESTIONS

In order to test your progress, you should be able to answer the following questions.

1) Clickwraps are used to do which of the following?

a) _____ Determine which products an e-commerce customer is buying
b) _____ State general terms and warranty disclaimers that apply to all online transactions
c) _____ State the conditions under which a Web site may be used

2) Software Co. sold a spreadsheet program that does not add correctly. Is the program merchantable?

a) _____ Yes
b) _____ No
c) _____ It depends on whether the Software Co. excluded the warranty of merchantability

3) Software Co.'s Web site states, "All of our products are Y2K compliant." In fact, they are not. Which type of Article Two warranty did Software Co. breach?

a) _____ Merchantability
b) _____ Fitness for particular purpose
c) _____ Noninfringement
d) _____ Express warranty

4) Consequential damages are available to a buyer only if the contract expressly says so.

a) _____ True
b) _____ False

5) It is illegal for a merchant to exclude consequential damages.

a) _____ True
b) _____ False

Quiz answers appear in the Appendix, Section 19.2.

CHAPTER 19

TEST YOUR THINKING

ABC Software licenses and delivers software online. The company owns most of the material on its e-commerce site. However, the site contains two reports owned by third parties (used with permission). ABC Software is happy to have site users download and print material from its site for any purpose. However, ABC does not want those who license its software to make copies of the software for use on multiple computers.

1) Explain how using a Web site Terms of Use page and a clickwrap can help ABC.

C H A P T E R   2 0

DOMAIN NAMES

A domain name is the way that people can identify and find you and your company on the Internet. You don't have to get a domain name—people can reach you on the Web by using your "Internet Protocol" address (a string of eight numbers). However, domain names are easier for people to remember than a string of numbers. To have an effective online presence and use the Web for marketing, you must choose and register a domain name.

© 2000 by J. Dianne Brinson.

L A B   2 0 . 1

REGISTERING DOMAIN NAMES

LAB OBJECTIVES

After this lab, you will be able to:

✔ Understand Domain Name Registration
✔ Identify Conflicts Between Domain Names and Trademarks

A domain name is a "street address" on the Internet. Here are two examples:

> aol.com (the domain name for America Online)
>
> prenhall.com (the domain name for the publisher of this book)

The suffix .com is a global top-level domain. The other "global" top-level domains are .net, .org, and .int. The suffix .com was originally intended to be used by commercial entities, .net by network providers, and .int by organizations established by international treaties and databases. However, this plan has not been enforced. An applicant for a domain name with a .com, .net, or .org suffix is not required to prove that it belongs to the class for which the suffix was intended. In the United States, three additional top-level domains are available for certain types of organizations—.gov for federal government offices, .edu for educational institutions, and .mil for military organizations. Geographic suffixes are also available. These correspond to the internationally recognized country abbreviations—for example, .uk and .fr for the United Kingdom and France.

In a domain name, the name or initials to the left of the suffix identify the host computer (America Online in the first example, Prentice Hall in the second one). For email address purposes, a third name can be added to the domain name to identify an individual—for example, smith@abcxyz.com.

From 1993 until June 1999, Network Solutions, Inc. (NSI) handled all domain name registrations in the United States in the .com, .net, and .org top-level domains, pursuant to a Cooperative Agreement with the U.S. government. Now, however, a number of additional companies are offering domain name registration services. New registrars are being accredited by the new Internet Corporation for Assigned Names and Numbers (ICANN). ICANN (www.icann.org) is a global nonprofit corporation created to oversee the Internet's core technical management functions, including Internet Protocol address space allocation, protocol parameter assignment, domain name system management, and root server system management.

Any company that meets ICANN's standards for accreditation and has signed an accreditation agreement with ICANN will be able to offer domain name registration services. The ICANN site has an up-to-date list of accredited and operational registrars.

In the past, many businesses had their Internet Service Providers (ISPs) handle registration for them. If your ISP is registering your name for you, make certain that you—not the ISP—are listed as the owner.

If you want to handle the registration yourself, you can now do so online. Each operational registrar has set up a registration Web site. The ICANN site has links to the registrars' sites. Before you register a domain name, you must obtain an Internet Protocol address from your ISP. A searchable list of ISPs is available on-line at http://thelist.iworld.com.

The basic domain name registration rule is "first come, first served"—if you apply to register a name and it has not been registered as a domain name, you'll generally get the name. However, you can lose the right to the name—even after you have started using it in your business—to someone with superior trademark rights in the name.

That's exactly what happened in the case *Brookfield Communications, Inc. v. West Coast Entertainment Corporation*. In 1993, Brookfield started using the trademark "MovieBuff." West Coast registered moviebuff.com as a domain name in 1996. Both companies provided searchable databases containing entertainment industry information. When Brookfield learned that West Coast intended to launch a Web site at moviebuff.com, Brookfield sued West Coast, claiming that West Coast's use of the domain name was likely to cause consumer confusion and therefore violated the federal trademark statute. The federal Court of Appeals for the Ninth Circuit granted Brookfield a preliminary injunction prohibiting West Coast from using the domain name moviebuff.com. The court stated that "[r]egistration of a domain name for a Web site does not trump long-established principles of trademark law. When a firm uses a competitor's trademark in the domain name of its web site, users are likely to be confused as to its source or sponsorship." (Trademark law is discussed in Chapter 15, Other Important Laws. Another aspect of this case, West Coast's metatag use of "moviebuff," is discussed in Chapter 18, Linking, Framing, Caching, and Meta Tags).

Most companies choose a domain name that is readily associated with the company's name—an acronym or shortened version of the name, for example, "aol" for America Online. However, the fact that you have incorporated under a name does not automatically give you the right to get a domain name registration for that name—nor does the fact that you have been using the name. Someone else may already have registered the name as a domain name or may be using the name as a trademark.

■ *FOR EXAMPLE*

Delta Airlines uses the name "Delta" for airline services. Delta Faucet Company uses "Delta" for faucets. Delta Financial Corporation uses "Delta" for financial services. However, there can only be one Delta.com. If you know that you and another company have the same name or are using the same word as a trademark (legitimately, in different areas of business), consider using a variation of the word as your domain name.

LAB 20.1 EXERCISES

20.1.1 UNDERSTAND DOMAIN NAME REGISTRATION

a) Is laderapress.com available for registration as a domain name?

_____

_____

20.1.2 IDENTIFY CONFLICTS BETWEEN DOMAIN NAMES AND TRADEMARKS

a) What can you do to avoid claims that your domain name interferes with someone else's trademark rights?

_____

_____

LAB 20.1 EXERCISE ANSWERS

20.1.1 ANSWER

a) Is laderapress.com available for registration as a domain name?

Answer: To answer this question, you should have gone to one of the registration sites listed on the ICANN sites (register.com, for example) and done a search to see if the name is available. It is not, it has already been registered. However, laderapress.net and laderapress.org are both available.

20.1.2 ANSWER

a) What can you do to avoid claims that your domain name interferes with someone else's trademark rights?

Answer: Avoid registering a name as a domain name if you know that someone else is using the name as a trademark (even if the name is available for domain name registration).

Ideally, you should have a trademark attorney conduct a full trademark search on the name to determine whether the name is in use as a trademark. If the name is in use as a trademark, the trademark owner may object to your use of the name as a domain name, even if the trademark is being used in a very different business from your business. For example, Hasbro, Inc., the owner of the federally registered trademark "Clue" for a mystery board name, sued Clue Computing for registering and using clue.com as a domain name. Hasbro claimed that Clue Computing's use of the domain name diluted its trademark (dilution law is discussed in Chapter 15, "Other Important Laws"). Hasbro ultimately lost the case because the court found that Hasbro had not proved the Clue mark to be famous, a requirement for federal antidilution protection.

LAB 20.1 SELF-REVIEW QUESTIONS

In order to test your progress, you should be able to answer the following questions:

1) All domain name registrations for the .com suffix now are handled by one company, Network Solutions, Inc.

a) _____ True
b) _____ False

2) All of the following top-level global domain name suffixes are currently available: .com, .org, .net, .arts, .firm, and .web.

a) _____ True
b) _____ False

3) The United States Department of Commerce accredits new domain name registrars.

a) _____ True
b) _____ False

4) If you want to register a domain name, you must have your ISP do it for you.

    a) _____ True
    b) _____ False

5) ICANN is a U.S. government agency.

    a) _____ True
    b) _____ False

Quiz answers appear in the Appendix, Section 20.1.

L A B   2 0 . 2

CYBERSQUATTING LAW

LAB OBJECTIVES

After this lab, you will be able to:

✔ Understand ICANN's Dispute Resolution Policy
✔ Understand U.S. Anticybersquatting Law

In the past few years, there have been many reports of people registering well-known trademarks and company names in hopes of forcing the trademark owner to buy the domain name, or to prevent the trademark owner from getting the domain name. These practices are known as "cybersquatting." Standardized test preparation company Princeton Review registered Kaplan.com in order to block its competitor, Kaplan Educational Centers, from getting that domain name.

Recently, both ICANN and the United States government took action to try to stop cybersquatting—ICANN by adopting policy containing a procedure for cancellation of "bad faith" domain name registrations, and the U.S. government by passing the Anticybersquatting Consumer Protection Act. Both measures apply to common law and state-registered trademarks as well as to federally registered trademarks.

ICANN's new Uniform Domain Name Dispute Resolution Policy states that any domain name registrant must submit to a "mandatory administrative proceeding" if a third party complains that:

1. The registrant's domain name is identical to or confusingly similar to a trademark or service mark in which the complainant has rights;
2. The registrant has no rights or legitimate interest in the domain name;
3. The domain name has been registered and is being used in bad faith.

Registering a domain name primarily for the purpose of selling it, preventing the trademark owner from getting it, or disrupting a competitor's business is considered evidence of bad faith registration and use. Using a domain name in an intentional attempt to attract users to a Web site, for commercial gain, by creating a likelihood of confusion with the complaining party's mark as to source, sponsorship, or endorsement, is also evidence of bad faith registration and use.

These administrative proceedings are conducted by Administrative Panels chosen by the complainant from a list of alternative dispute resolution provider organizations approved by ICANN. ICANN itself does not participate in the conduct of these proceedings. ICANN will cancel or transfer a domain name registration if the Administrative Panel for the proceeding decides that such action is appropriate. No other remedy is available to the trademark owner. The ICANN policy is available online on the ICANN site (www.icann.org).

The Anticybersquatting Consumer Protection Act makes it illegal for someone to register, sell, or use a domain name that is identical to or confusingly similar to a trademark if the registrant has a "bad faith intent" to profit from that mark. In determining whether a domain name registrant has bad faith intent, courts may consider such factors are whether the registrant intended to divert the trademark owner's customers or offered to sell the domain name to the trademark owner for financial gain without having used the mark. The law also protects personal names, making it illegal to register the name of any living person, without that person's consent, intending to profit from that person's name by selling the domain name to that person or anyone else.

The new law is a civil law (an amendment to the Trademark Act), not a criminal law. The law gives courts the power to order cancellation or transfer of the domain name registration and award actual money damages and profits or statutory damages up to $100,000 to a successful plaintiff.

LAB 20.2 EXERCISES

20.2.1 UNDERSTAND ICANN'S DISPUTE RESOLUTION POLICY

a) Internet Entertainment Group ("IEG") registered papalvisit.com for an adult Web site. The Archdiocese of St. Louis—owner of the common law trademark "Papal Visit 1999"—sued IEG to stop IEG from using the domain name. If the ICANN anti-cybersquatting policy had been in effect in 1999, could the Archdiocese have gotten ICANN to cancel papalvisit.com?

_____

_____

20.2.2 UNDERSTAND U.S. ANTICYBERSQUATTING LAW

a) K. Alzarooni and N. Abu-Robb own the domain name bradpitt.com, which they tried to sell to actor Brad Pitt for $50,000. How does the Anticybersquatting Consumer Protection Act help Mr. Pitt?

LAB 20.2 EXERCISE ANSWERS

20.2.1 ANSWER

a) Internet Entertainment Group ("IEG") registered papalvisit.com for an adult Web site. The Archdiocese of St. Louis—owner of the common law trademark "Papal Visit 1999" —sued IEG to stop IEG from using the domain name. If the ICANN policy had been in effect in 1999, could the Archdiocese have gotten ICANN to cancel papalvisit.com?

Answer: Yes, if the Archdiocese initiated an administrative proceeding and the Administrative Panel found IEG's registration and use of papalvisit.com to be in bad faith. Certainly papalvisit.com is confusingly similar to "Papal Visit 1999." It seems unlikely that IEG could have any right or legitimate interest in papalvisit.com. To establish bad faith, the Archdiocese would have to prove that IEG used the domain name to confuse Web users into thinking that the papalvisit.com Web site was the Archdiocese's Web site for the 1999 Papal Visit. The Archdiocese would also have to show that IEG was attempting to attract Web users to its site for commercial gain.

20.2.2 ANSWER

a) K. Alzarooni and N. Abu-Robb own the domain name bradpitt.com, which they tried to sell to actor Brad Pitt for $50,000. How does the Anticybersquatting Protection Act help Mr. Pitt?

Answer: He can sue them under the Act to get the domain name cancelled or transferred to him. His evidence of bad faith intent is that they are trying to profit off the use of his name. In fact, Mr. Pitt has already filed suit under the Act.

LAB 20.2 SELF-REVIEW QUESTIONS

In order to test your progress, you should be able to answer the following questions.

1) ICANN has the power to require a cybersquatter to pay money damages to a trademark owner.

   a) _____ True
   b) _____ False

2) An ICANN administrative proceeding must be conducted by a U.S. federal court.

   a) _____ True
   b) _____ False

3) The ICANN Policy and the Anticybersquatting Consumer Protection Act apply to federally registered trademarks, state-registered marks, and marks protected under common law.

   a) _____ True
   b) _____ False

4) The Anticybersquatting Consumer Protection Act does not give courts the power to cancel domain name registrations, only to award damages.

   a) _____ True
   b) _____ False

5) The Anticybersquatting Consumer Protection Act is a criminal law.

   a) _____ True
   b) _____ False

Quiz answers appear in the Appendix, Section 20.2.

CHAPTER 20

TEST YOUR THINKING

Major Co. has a federal trademark registration for "Juto." It uses "Juto" on children's clothing and has spent a lot of advertising dollars creating the "Juto" brand. Juliette wants to use juto.com as the domain name for her toy e-commerce site. The name is available for domain name registration.

1) Should Juliette choose "Juto" as her domain name?

A P P E N D I X

ANSWERS
TO SELF-REVIEW
QUESTIONS

CHAPTER 1

Lab 1.1 ■ Self-Review Answers

Question	Answer
1)	b
2)	d
3)	a
4)	b

Lab 1.2 ■ Self-Review Answers

Question	Answer
1)	a
2)	a
3)	b

Lab 1.3 ■ Self-Review Answers

Question	Answer
1)	b
2)	a
3)	a

Lab 1.4 ■ Self-Review Answers

Question	Answer
1)	b
2)	b
3)	a
4)	d

Lab 1.5 ■ Self-Review Answers

Question	Answer
1)	a
2)	a
3)	a
4)	a

Lab 1.6 ■ Self-Review Answers

Question	Answer
1)	a, b
2)	a
3)	a

Lab 1.7 ■ Self-Review Answers

Question	Answer
1)	b
2)	b, c, d, e
3)	b
4)	a

Lab 1.8 ■ Self-Review Answers

Question	Answer
1)	a
2)	b
3)	b

CHAPTER 2

Lab 2.1 ■ Self-Review Answers

Question	Answer
1)	b
2)	a
3)	a

Lab 2.2 ■ Self-Review Answers

Question	Answer
1)	d
2)	b
3)	a

Lab 2.3 ■ Self-Review Answers

Question	Answer
1)	a
2)	b

Lab 2.4 ■ Self-Review Answers

Question	Answer
1)	a
2)	b

Lab 2.5 ■ Self-Review Answers

Question	Answer
1)	a, b, c
2)	a, c

Lab 2.6 ■ Self-Review Answers

Question	Answer
1)	a
2)	b

Lab 2.7 ■ Self-Review Answers

Question	Answer
1)	a
2)	b

CHAPTER 3

Lab 3.1 ■ Self-Review Answers

Question	Answer
1)	a
2)	b
3)	a
4)	a

Lab 3.2 ■ Self-Review Answers

Question	Answer
1)	b
2)	a
3)	b
4)	b
5)	a

Lab 3.3 ■ Self-Review Answers

Question	Answer
1)	b
2)	c, a, b
3)	c

Lab 3.4 ■ Self-Review Answers

Question	Answer
1)	a
2)	a

CHAPTER 4

Lab 4.1 ■ Self-Review Answers

Question	Answer
1)	a
2)	a
3)	b

Lab 4.2 ■ Self-Review Answers

Question	Answer
1)	a
2)	c
3)	b, d

Lab 4.3 ■ Self-Review Answers

Question	Answer
1)	a
2)	b
3)	a
4)	b

Lab 4.4 ■ Self-Review Answers

Question	Answer
1)	a
2)	b
3)	a
4)	a

Lab 4.5 ■ Self-Review Answers

Question	Answer
1)	a
2)	a, c

CHAPTER 5

Lab 5.1 ■ Self-Review Answers

Question	Answer
1)	d
2)	b
3)	a
4)	a
5)	b

Lab 5.2 ■ Self-Review Answers

Question	Answer
1)	b
2)	a
3)	a
4)	a

Lab 5.3 ■ Self-Review Answers

Question	Answer
1)	a
2)	a, b, c
3)	a
4)	b
5)	a, b, d

Lab 5.4 ■ Self-Review Answers

Question	Answer
1)	d
2)	a
3)	a
4)	a
5)	a

CHAPTER 6

Lab 6.1 ■ Self-Review Answers

Question	Answer
1)	b

2)   a

3)   a

4)   b

5)   a

6)   4, 2, 1, 3

Lab 6.2 ■ Self-Review Answers

Question   Answer

1)   a

2)   a

3)   a

4)   b

Lab 6.3 ■ Self-Review Answers

Question   Answer

1)   a

2)   a

3)   a

Lab 6.4 ■ Self-Review Answers

Question   Answer

1)   a

2)   a

3)   a

4)   a

CHAPTER 7

Lab 7.1 ■ Self-Review Answers

Question   Answer

1)   b

2)   b

3)   c

4)   b

Lab 7.2 ■ Self-Review Answers

Question   Answer

1)   c

2)   d

3)   e

4)   b

Lab 7.3 ■ Self-Review Answers

Question   Answer

1)   c

2)   c

3)   b

CHAPTER 8

Lab 8.1 ■ Self-Review Answers

Question   Answer

1)   b

2)   a

3)   c

4)   d

Lab 8.2 ■ Self-Review Answers

Question   Answer

1)   b

2)   a

3)   c

Lab 8.3 ■ Self-Review Answers

Question   Answer

1)   b

2)   a, c, d

3)   a

4)   a, b

5)   b

6)   a, b

7)   a

CHAPTER 9
Lab 9.1 ■ Self-Review Answers

Question	Answer
1)	c
2)	a
3)	c
4)	b
5)	a
6)	c

Lab 9.2 ■ Self-Review Answers

Question	Answer
1)	b
2)	a
3)	c
4)	b
5)	b
6)	d
7)	a
8)	b

CHAPTER 10
Lab 10.1 ■ Self-Review Answers

Question	Answer
1)	b
2)	a
3)	c
4)	c

Lab 10.2 ■ Self-Review Answers

Question	Answer
1)	c
2)	b
3)	a, c, d
4)	a, b

Lab 10.3 ■ Self-Review Answers

Question	Answer
1)	b
2)	b, c, d
3)	a, c
4)	c
5)	a
6)	b
7)	a
8)	a, b, d

CHAPTER 11
Lab 11.1 ■ Self-Review Answers

Question	Answer
1)	b
2)	b
3)	a, b
4)	b
5)	b
6)	b
7)	c

Lab 11.2 ■ Self-Review Answers

Question	Answer
1)	d
2)	b
3)	b
4)	a, b, d
5)	a, b

Lab 11.3 ■ Self-Review Answers

Question	Answer
1)	b
2)	d
3)	a
4)	b
5)	b

CHAPTER 12
Lab 12.1 ■ Self-Review Answers
Question Answer
1) c
2) d
3) b
4) d

Lab 12.2 ■ Self-Review Answers
Question Answer
1) b
2) a
3) a
4) c

CHAPTER 13
Lab 13.1 ■ Self-Review Answers
Question Answer
1) b
2) e
3) b
4) e
5) d

Lab 13.2 ■ Self-Review Answers
Question Answer
1) d
2) c
3) c
4) c
5) c

Lab 13.3 ■ Self-Review Answers
Question Answer
1) b
2) a
3) d

4) d
5) b

CHAPTER 14
Lab 14.1 ■ Self-Review Answers
Question Answer
1) c
2) a
3) a
4) d
5) a
6) b
7) b

Lab 14.2 ■ Self-Review Answers
Question Answer
1) c
2) c
3) d
4) b
5) a

CHAPTER 15
Lab 15.1 ■ Self-Review Answers
Question Answer
1) d
2) a
3) d
4) a
5) a
6) d

Lab 15.2 ■ Self-Review Answers
Question Answer
1) a
2) d

3)   c
4)   a
5)   b

CHAPTER 16
Lab 16.1 ■ Self-Review Answers
Question   Answer
1)   b
2)   d
3)   d
4)   b
5)   c

CHAPTER 17
Lab 17.1 ■ Self-Review Answers
Question   Answer
1)   c
2)   d
3)   b
4)   d
5)   a

Lab 17.2 ■ Self-Review Answers
Question   Answer
1)   a
2)   b
3)   c
4)   b
5)   b

CHAPTER 18
Lab 18.1 ■ Self-Review Answers
Question   Answer
1)   e
2)   b
3)   b
4)   c
5)   c

Lab 18.2 ■ Self-Review Answers
Question   Answer
1)   c
2)   b
3)   c
4)   a
5)   b

CHAPTER 19
Lab 19.1 ■ Self-Review Answers
Question   Answer
1)   a
2)   b
3)   b
4)   b
5)   b

Lab 19.2 ■ Self-Review Answers
Question   Answer
1)   b
2)   b
3)   d
4)   b
5)   b

CHAPTER 20

Lab 20.1 ■ Self-Review Answers

Question	Answer
1)	b
2)	b
3)	b
4)	b
5)	b

Lab 20.2 ■ Self-Review Answers

Question	Answer
1)	b
2)	b
3)	a
4)	b
5)	b

INDEX

See It!
Hear It!
Do It!

GET ON THE ROAD TO BECOMING A PROFESSIONAL WEBMASTER WITH PTG INTERACTIVE'S HANDS-ON TOTAL LEARNING SOLUTIONS!

These interactive multimedia Training Courses on CD-ROM feature easy-to-use browser-based interfaces and fully integrated print books and searchable e-books.

- *Listen* to hours of expert audio describing key administration tasks
- *Watch* the digital videos showing a pro administrating a system and creating Web interfaces
- *Practice* your knowledge with hundreds of interactive questions and practice exercises

There's simply no better way to learn!

WOW WEB SERVER TRAINING COURSE
LARSON AND STEPHENS
©2001, Boxed Set, 0-13-089437-0

WOW WEB DESIGN TRAINING COURSE
HUBBELL, WHITE, WHITE, AND REES
©2001, Boxed Set, 0-13-040760-7

www.phptr.com/phpinteractive

ORDERING INFORMATION:

SINGLE COPY SALES
Visa, Master Card, American Express,
Checks, or Money Orders only
Tel: 515-284-6761 / Fax: 515-284-2607
Toll-Free: 800-811-0912

GOVERNMENT AGENCIES
Pearson Education Customer Service (#GS-02F-8023)
Toll-Free: 800-922-0579

COLLEGE PROFESSORS
Desk or Review Copies
Toll-Free: 800-526-0485

CORPORATE ACCOUNTS
Quantity, Bulk Orders totaling 10 or more books.
Purchase orders only — No credit cards.
Tel: 201-236-7156 / Fax: 201-236-7141
Toll-Free: 800-382-3419

INTERNATIONAL ORDERING:

CANADA
Pearson Education Canada, Inc.
Phone: 416-447-5101
Toll Free Tel: 1-800-567-3800
Toll Free Fax: 1-800-263-7733
Corporate and Gov Tel: 416-386-3633

PEARSON EDUCTION LATIN AMERICA
Attn: Lynnette Kew
815 Northwest 57th Avenue
Suite 484
Miami, FL 33126
Tel: 305-264-8344 / Fax: 305-264-7933

UNITED KINGDOM, EUROPE, AFRICA & MIDDLE EAST
Pearson Education
128 Long Acre
London WC2E9AN
United Kingdom
Tel: 01-44-0171-447-2000 / Fax: 01-44-0171-240-
Email: ibd_orders@prenhall.co.uk

JAPAN
Pearson Education
Nishi-Shinjuku, KF Building
8-14-24 Nishi-Shinjuku, Shinjuku-ku
Tokyo, Japan 160-0023
Tel: 81-3-3365-9224 / Fax: 81-3-3365-9225

ASIA Singapore, Malaysia, Brunei, Indonesia, Thailand, Myanmar, Laos, Cambodia, Vietnam, Philippines, China, Hong Kong, Macau, Taiwan, Korea, India, Sri Lanka
Pearson Education (Singapore) Pte Ltd
317 Alexandra Road #04-01,
IKEA Building, Singapore 159965
Tel: 65-476-4688 / Fax: 65-378-0370
Cust Serv: 65-476-4788 / Fax: 65-378-0373
Email: prenhall@singnet.com.sg

AUSTRALIA & NEW ZEALAND
Pearson Education Australia
Unit 4, Level 2, 14 Aquatic Drive
(Locked Bag 507)
Frenchs Forest NSW 2086 Australia
Tel: 02-9454-2200 / Fax: 02-9453-0117

SOUTH AFRICA
Pearson Education South Africa Pty Ltd
P. O. Box 12122, Mill Street
8010 Cape Town, South Africa
Tel: 021-686-6356 / Fax: 021-686-4590
Email: prenhall@iafrica.com

PEARSON PTR
interactive
We make it click.

Prentice Hall
PTR

 **Solutions from experts you know and trust.**

| Articles | Free Library | eBooks | Expert Q & A | Training | Career Center | Downloads | MyInformIT |

Login   Register   About InformIT

Topics
Operating Systems
Web Development
Programming
Networking
Certification
and more...

Expert Access

Free Content

www.informit.com

✔ Free, in-depth articles and supplements

✔ Master the skills you need, when you need them

✔ Choose from industry leading books, ebooks, and training products

✔ Get answers when you need them - from live experts or InformIT's comprehensive library

✔ Achieve industry certification and advance your career

Visit *InformIT* today and get great content from PH PTR

Prentice Hall and InformIT are trademarks of Pearson plc /
Copyright © 2000 Pearson

Prentice Hall: Professional Technical Reference

http://www.phptr.com/

PRENTICE HALL

Professional Technical Reference
Tomorrow's Solutions for Today's Professionals.

Keep Up-to-Date with
PH PTR Online!

We strive to stay on the cutting edge of what's happening in professional computer science and engineering. Here's a bit of what you'll find when you stop by **www.phptr.com**:

Special interest areas offering our latest books, book series, software, features of the month, related links and other useful information to help you get the job done.

Deals, deals, deals! Come to our promotions section for the latest bargains offered to you exclusively from our retailers.

Need to find a bookstore? Chances are, there's a bookseller near you that carries a broad selection of PTR titles. Locate a Magnet bookstore near you at www.phptr.com.

What's new at PH PTR? We don't just publish books for the professional community, we're a part of it. Check out our convention schedule, join an author chat, get the latest reviews and press releases on topics of interest to you.

Subscribe today! Join PH PTR's monthly email newsletter!

Want to be kept up-to-date on your area of interest? Choose a targeted category on our website, and we'll keep you informed of the latest PH PTR products, author events, reviews and conferences in your interest area.

Visit our mailroom to subscribe today! **http://www.phptr.com/mail_lists**

www.phptr.com